17 CARNATIONS

17 CARNATIONS

The Royals, the Nazis, and the Biggest Cover-Up in History

ANDREW MORTON

GRAND CENTRAL
PUBLISHING

NEW YORK   BOSTON

Grand Central Publishing
Hachette Book Group
1290 Avenue of the Americas
New York, NY 10104

HachetteBookGroup.com

Printed in the United States of America

RRD-C

Originally published in hardcover by Grand Central Publishing.
First Trade Paperback Edition: February 2016
10 9 8 7 6 5 4 3 2 1

Grand Central Publishing is a division of Hachette Book Group, Inc.
The Grand Central Publishing name and logo is a trademark of Hachette Book
Group, Inc.

The Hachette Speakers Bureau provides a wide range of authors for speaking
events. To find out more, go to www.hachettespeakersbureau.com or call
(866) 376-6591.

The publisher is not responsible for websites (or their content) that are
not owned by the publisher.

Library of Congress Control Number: 2014957815
ISBN 978-1-4555-2711-3 (hardcover); ISBN 978-1-4555-8397-3
(international trade paperback); ISBN 978-1-4555-2710-6 (paperback)

To Carolyn

Contents

Acknowledgments

A few years ago a passage in historian Sarah Bradford's penetrating and occasionally acerbic biography of King George VI caught my eye. It concerned the flight, just weeks after the end of World War Two, to a German castle by two royal courtiers, one later revealed as a Soviet spy. They were tasked by George VI to pick up a bundle of correspondence, ostensibly relating to Queen Victoria and her eldest daughter. It soon became clear that there may have been other, more self-serving motives behind the flight.

Bradford explained how a buried battered metal canister, protected by a tatty raincoat, had been dug up by advancing Allied troops. It contained vital documents relating to German foreign policy, including a volume on the Duke and Duchess of Windsor, whose pro-Nazi views before and during the war had made them targets for suspicion and distrust among the Allies. Once the cache of papers was secretly analyzed, powerful political "documents men" decided that this material was so incendiary it required Anglo-American co-operation at the highest level to prevent it from leaking. This was an intriguing story ripe for further investigation.

There was one problem. Most of the action took place in Europe, and I had recently married an American interior designer and was living for part of the year in Los Angeles, California. Sometimes, though, things are destined. Professor Jonathan Petropoulos, whose book *Royals and the Reich* is an absorbing and comprehensive study of the links between European royalty and Hitler's Third Reich, lived just thirty minutes down the road at Claremont McKenna College. He has been hugely generous with his time, academic contacts, and advice, a constant source of encouragement, insight, and inspiration who has also become a good friend. In the land of soccer, we even speak the same language: football.

He put me in touch with Astrid Eckert, a specialist in modern German history. Her fascinating and meticulously researched book *The Struggle for the Files* reveals the diplomatic machinations behind the capture and subsequent return of Germany's "soul"—the nation's official archives. Not only has she kindly given me hitherto unseen official documents, she also suggested many fresh lines of inquiry.

Destiny played a part too in tracking down sources. It soon became clear that some largely unseen archives in the United States were as important as, if not more so than, the more familiar dossiers in Britain and Europe. At the Hoover Institution at Stanford University in California were papers relating to, among others, David Harris and Paul Sweet, two of the feisty academics who traded blows with those who wanted to destroy or conceal the damning files about the Duke and Duchess of Windsor. The library also held documents for others involved in the story, notably Princess Stephanie von Hohenlohe, dubbed Hitler's "spy princess" and a neighbor in London of Wallis Simpson.

When the research moved on to Moscow it seemed that Lady Luck was also smiling. There were two elusive lines of inquiry: the role of Soviet spy and king's courtier Anthony Blunt in this royal detective story and the possible existence in Russian archival custody of hidden correspondence between the Duke of Windsor, Hitler, and the Nazi hierarchy. My thanks, then, to journalist Will Stewart for tracking down and having translated an obscure Russian biography of Blunt written by former ambassador to London Vicktor Popov, who had been given special access to KGB files.

Even more tantalizing was the work of researcher Dr. Sebastian Panwitz, who agreed to take a sweep through the Special Archive (Sonder Archiv) in Moscow on the last day of August, just before they closed for the winter. He emerged with a battered file with the barely legible words "Ribbentrop" and "Herzog von Windsor" handwritten on the outside. Was this the smoking gun, the documentary connection between Hitler, Ribbentrop, and the Duke of Windsor that proved his treason? Unfortunately the majority of the contents were in shorthand, and German shorthand at that. In the 1930s they used a system called Stolze-Schrey, but thanks to the good offices of Manfred Duerhammer, the Lucerne-based stenography expert Erich Werner agreed to take on the job of translation. My heartfelt appreciation for his strenuous efforts in teasing out the language from the hieroglyphics.

Less convoluted was the uncorking of a bottle of chardonnay in a Chelsea wine bar and reflecting on the dissonance between George VI and his older brother, the Duke of Windsor, with Sarah Bradford, the historian who inspired this whole journey. As ever, her insights and observations were telling.

Wallis Simpson's biographer Anne Sebba, who triumphantly transformed an ogre into a human being, was especially helpful and thoughtful, generously giving me the opportunity to take my investigation in a different and original direction.

My grateful thanks too to Barbara Mason, a descendant of Herman Rogers, who was a great friend and counsellor to both the Duke and Duchess of Windsor. As the unofficial family archivist, she kindly gave permission to use previously unpublished correspondence between Herman, the Duke of Windsor, President Roosevelt, and others in the book. She also granted access to the photographs and movie footage taken by Herman during some of the most historic events of King Edward VIII's short reign. They are seen on these pages for the first time. Barbara has been a great supporter of this project, her encouragement and enthusiasm unstinting and much appreciated.

That said, no one can journey far into Windsor territory without acknowledging a debt to Philip Ziegler, whose official biography of Edward VIII remains a restrained masterpiece, and Michael Bloch, whose prodigious research, especially into Operation Willi, and unparalleled access to the correspondence of the Duke and Duchess of Windsor, have made his scholarship, like Ziegler's, the benchmark for others to follow.

Many others have contributed to my understanding of these complex times as well as the personalities involved. I would like to express my appreciation and thanks to John Bell, Christopher and Katharine Blair, Miranda Carter, Ben Fenton, Dr. Eberhard Fritz, Delissa Needham, Professor Scott Newton, Lynne Olson, Professor Paul Preston, Associate Professor Donal O'Sullivan, Pendleton Rogers, Professor Jean Edward Smith, Gennady Sokolov, Roger Weil, Professor Gerhard Weinberg, Professor Douglas Wheeler, and Sacha Zala.

On the journey my hard-working researchers Nikki Thean, Zoya Lozoya, and Kristen Lee have produced some unexpected nuggets, Nathan Ernst has undertaken careful translations, while picture researcher Laura Hanifin and restorer Jennie Flowers at Alive Studios in Devon have worked wonders under tight deadlines. Thanks too to my agent at Folio Literary Management, Steve Troha, for getting the show on the road, Deb Futter for pointing me in the right direction, Rick Ball for skillfully editing the manuscript, and assistant editor Dianne Choie for keeping the whole caravan moving along.

Finally, thanks to my darling wife Carolyn for her constant love and support. Some things are just fated.

Andrew Morton
London
November 2014

17 CARNATIONS

CHAPTER ONE

———— ✦ ————

The Peter Pan Prince

He was the first royal sex symbol of the modern age, the wistful features of the Prince of Wales adorning the bedside tables and dormitory walls of thousands of schoolgirls and young women across Britain and the empire. He may have been the despair of his austere father, King George V, but Prince Edward—David to his family—was the undisputed darling of the empire.

Even republican America fell for the winsome charms of a bona fide war hero with matinee idol good looks. Hard-nosed celebrity journalist Adela Rogers St. Johns was such a fan that she had a picture of the Prince of Wales in a silver frame on her dressing table. "The dream of every American girl was to dance with him," she recalled. Over the next few years he tried to oblige.

During the twenties, only silent screen star Rudolph Valentino, whose seductive performances in *The Sheik* and *Blood and Sand* transformed the one-time busboy into an international heartthrob, could possibly compare with the compelling charm of the future king-emperor.

His face was everywhere, on cigarette cards, in gossip magazines and daily newspapers, his every public appearance slavishly chronicled by Pathé News and shown at the local Roxy. An appearance by the Prince of Wales set female hearts fluttering and mothers wringing their hands in the hope that their daughter would be the chosen one. Men copied his natty dress sense, the Prince of Wales popularizing and adapting the eponymous check first worn by his grandfather, King Edward VII. He had only to appear in a particular Fair Isle pullover and factories would be working overtime to keep up with demand.

His appeal, though, lay in something more than his ubiquitous presence in the popular prints. Unlike his forebears, the unsmiling Queen Victoria, the haughty Edward VII, and his stern father, King George V, there was something pliable, friendly even, about the Prince of Wales. He looked more human than the others, almost vulnerable. Perhaps it was his clean, boyish good looks—he shaved infrequently throughout his life—or the slim wiry stature that earned him the nickname, not to his face, of "little man." Most likely it was the seeming sadness that lay behind his haunted spaniel eyes which intrigued many. If eyes were truly a window into the soul, here was a young man in torment. He had what Lord Esher described as an expression of weltschmerz, the gloomy acknowledgment of the world as it is as opposed to the world as it should be. It was the look of a man who had seen more than his ration of sorrow and suffering, a quality he shared with those returning soldiers who survived the horrors of the trenches. He was the symbol, the human bridge between the war-weary millions still clinging to the fast-dimming certainties of a world before the horrors of 1914 and a fractious future where nationalism was on the rise, labour on the march, and aristocracy in retreat.

Wartime prime minister Lloyd George instinctively recognized that the prince was the most glittering jewel in the royal crown. It was, he argued, a jewel that should be on display. At the end of the war in 1918 the prince was asked to tour the colonies and Dominions to thank the people for their support of and sacrifice for the mother country. The Welsh politician wanted the Prince of Wales to play a "gay, many sided natural role." If the empire's star salesman could drum up trade for Britain's exhausted manufacturers, so much the better.

With five emperors, eight kings, and four imperial dynasties rendered obsolete by the conflict, there was never a better time to emphasize that the newly minted House of Windsor—George V changed the family name from Saxe-Coburg and Gotha in 1917 to deflect anti-German sentiment—remained the unchanging keystone in the edifice of an empire upon which the sun never set. The slaughter of Czar Nicholas II of Russia and his family at Ekaterinburg in July 1918 by Bolshevik rebels reinforced this imperial imperative, especially as George V bore an uncanny likeness to the murdered czar. Not only did the barbaric incident shake the king's "confidence in the innate decency of mankind," it inspired his son's lifetime loathing of the Bolsheviks, the murder of his godfather, Nicholas II, setting his heart against the Soviets and all their works.

Thus his seemingly endless and arduous imperial tours— during the 1920s he visited some forty-five countries and travelled an estimated 150,000 miles by sea and train—were a golden opportunity to reinforce the relevance of the monarchy and to introduce the man who one day would rule. It was a daunting assignment for a somewhat naïve young man, still only twenty-five, who was frequently overwhelmed by the straining sea of strange faces, the nervous demands of public speaking—a skill that did not come naturally—and of course the endless handshaking. The tone was set on his first tour, to Canada in September 1919, where he crisscrossed the country by train, laying wreaths and foundation stones, watching parades and pageants. His arrival was greeted with such hysteria that his right hand was so badly bruised and swollen after shaking so many eager hands that he had to resort to using his left.

At times this worship of the royal personage bordered on the messianic, the prince hearing people cry "I've touched him, I've touched him" as he walked through the press of flesh. As he laconically observed: When they were unable to pat him in person, hitting or prodding him with a rolled-up newspaper sufficed. It was a remarkable step change from the days of his grandfather, Edward VII: He would arrive at an engagement in his horse-drawn carriage, receive a loyal address, cut a ribbon, and declare something or other open without ever leaving his carriage.

This quasi-religious royal adulation was not confined to the colonies. In November 1919, when he completed his marathon three-month visit to Canada, he headed for a brief tour of Washington and New York, meeting with war wounded and rubbing shoulders with senators and congressmen. He also paid a private visit to the White House, where President Wilson was recovering from a stroke.

America was an unknown quantity and he was initially apprehensive about his reception. His only previous contact with Americans was during the war, when he reviewed a parade of some 25,000 troops at Coblenz and found himself impressed by their discipline. At the time, the military review received scant publicity, but the story of him dancing with American nurses at a later function sure did.

It was no exception: During his East Coast visit, dances laid on in his honour left many a debutante in a swoon. As one of his aides observed: "The prince holds very strongly that he can influence American feeling even better by dancing with Senators' daughters than by talking to Senators." As the world's most eligible bachelor, he was linked to so many young women that he started a "My Brides" book where he glued in all the erroneous newspaper stories about when and whom he was to marry.

His first visit culminated in a ticker-tape parade through the streets of Manhattan, which was "thrilling beyond description." As the prince later recalled: "Half asphyxiated by the smell of gasoline, I found myself sitting up on the back of the motor, bowing and waving like an actor who had been summoned by a tremendous curtain call."

Such was the excitement generated by the brief royal progress that playwright Albert E. Thomas was inspired to pen a romantic comedy, strangely prophetic, called *Just Suppose*, about a prince who falls in love with an American beauty and offers to give up the throne for her hand in marriage.

Enthusiasm on the East Coast was matched by wild adulation on the West. The following April, when he stopped in San Diego on his way to Australia and New Zealand onboard HMS *Renown*, the princely presence excited considerable civic interest. Politically his arrival on American soil suggested that all was well with the "special relationship," even if the Senate had rejected the Treaty of Versailles and membership in the League of Nations. As the first truly international royal celebrity, the prince was seen as a man of the New World, his youthful good looks, endless courtesy, and informal manner singling him out as a regular guy, modern, approachable, and democratic, not some feudal anachronism.

"That he is human is the pleasing point about him," opined a local reporter, while another observer declared that the prince was as "American" as any boy in our public schools. At a reception onboard USS *New Mexico*, the flagship of the Pacific fleet, the prince and his travelling companion and friend Lord Mountbatten met a snaking line of local dignitaries. In the reception line were Lieutenant Winfield Spencer and his wife, Wallis. They shook hands and moved on. Years later, Wallis would complain to Mountbatten and her husband, now the Duke of Windsor, that they did not recall the brief encounter. Naturally Wallis, who remembered that she was "dressed to kill" for her first royal meeting, did.

Unaware of the momentous nature of this encounter, the royal party sailed on for the antipodes, the prince once again experiencing the spontaneous adulation and adoring affection that characterized his North America trip. "They murdered him with kindness," recalled Mountbatten. It was a similar story in India, Nigeria, South Africa, and many other nations that made up the empire, or trading partners like Argentina and Japan where he was Britain's super salesman. During his tour of Australia, Prime Minister Billy Hughes told him: "The people see in you the things they most believe."

They were worshipping a false god. It was all a grotesque illusion, a monstrous charade played out before an innocent public. The mute, immovable reality was that the prince did not believe either in himself or in his future position as sovereign. In his reflective moments of melancholy and self-doubt, which were frequent, he felt he was living a lie, trying to match an image that bore no relation to the real man. He baulked at the very thought of becoming king and being revered by these adoring millions and hated a daily existence of what he derisively called "princing."

"If only the British public really knew what a weak, powerless misery their press-made national hero was," he told his girlfriend, Freda Dudley Ward.

His despondency manifested itself in frequent denunciations of his future role as king. It was such a recurring theme of his life that friends and advisors feared for the future of the Crown. A life of service was not high on his royal agenda. "Princing," as he endlessly complained to Freda Dudley Ward, "was much easier abroad. I guess it's because one isn't hit up with a lot of old-fashioned and boring people and conventions."

Prone to bouts of brooding depression, at the heart of his darkness the gloomy prince considered suicide as the only sure way out of his lifelong prison sentence. Upon his return from his wildly successful tour of North America in 1919, his morbid temperament was in full spate. He told his private secretary, Sir Godfrey Thomas, that he felt "hopelessly lost," as if he were going mad.

"I loathe my job now....I feel I am through with it and long and long to die." As an indication of his yearning to escape, he bought a 1,600-acre ranch in Alberta, the prince beguiled by a romantic vision of living the simple life, away from the cares of his position. It was, though, a bolt-hole he visited only four times in the forty years that he owned the property.

His depressions were frequent and prolonged, especially on long sea voyages during his interminable imperial tours. Lord Mountbatten recalled that the miserable prince often said how he longed to change places with his travelling companion. Before he left for his tour of Australia and New Zealand he was in floods of tears, ostensibly because he was leaving his lover, Freda Dudley Ward. As Mountbatten recalled: "He was moody—had fits of downright gloom. He made a fine appearance...but then one of his fits would come over him—and they came like a flash—and he'd shut himself in his cabin for days, alone, face drawn, eyes brooding. He was basically a lonely person, lonely and sad."

When he finally got his way and walked away from the throne in 1936, his childhood nanny Charlotte "Lalla" Bill wrote a plaintive note to Queen Mary: "Do you remember, Your Majesty, when he was quite young, how he didn't wish to live, and he never wanted to become King?" In his mind the abdication was the final renunciation of a lie that had begun in childhood. As far as the prince was concerned, the perception of the royal family in the popular imagination as the ideal family was a grotesque myth. "I had a wretched childhood," he told American writer Charles Murphy. "Of course there were short periods of happiness but I remember it chiefly for the miserableness I had to keep to myself." Beaten by sadistic nannies and tutors, bleakly observed with stiff disapproval by his remote mother and father, King George V and Queen Mary, and bullied by his peers, this sensitive, intelligent, and lonely boy realized early on that personal happiness played no part in the royal equation of existence.

The diarist Sir Henry "Chips" Channon described talking to Queen Mary as like "having a conversation with St. Paul's Cathedral," and letters the prince received from his parents during his imperial tours were "stiff and unnatural," as if from the head of a company to a line manager. In his rather pathetic attempt to find some common ground between himself and his parents, the young prince learned to crochet to please his mother. A dreaded summons to his father's library was invariably the prelude to a royal admonition to work and try harder. "Remember your position and who you are" was his father's constant refrain.

He was expected to sacrifice his life on the altar of monarchy, exchanging his privileges and status for a lifetime yoked to duty and service. It was not a contract he wanted to sign, his inner turmoil expressed in his nervy behaviour—he was continually fiddling with his cufflinks, tugging at the knot in his tie, and never without a cigarette in his hand or pipe in his mouth. Heavy bouts of drinking helped him forget, the prince arriving late for official engagements still hungover.

To the modern eye, his distorted self-image, his belief that he was fat even though he was painfully thin, his bouts of violent exercise and frugal diets—he never ate lunch—indicate that he may well have suffered from the pernicious eating disorder anorexia nervosa. At the time, his private secretary, not knowing about eating disorders, contented himself with describing the prince's eccentric lifestyle and eating habits as "idiotic" and "utterly insane and unreasonable."

More than anything else he wanted to be treated like anyone else, to blend in. He was continually reminded of his apartness, often cruelly. From the time he was enrolled into Osborne naval college at age thirteen—the prince later went to Dartmouth naval college—he had what he termed "a desperate desire to be treated like any other boy of my age." Instead he was regarded as a curiosity by the other cadets, who bullied and teased him, on one occasion dying his hair with red ink, on another staging a mock execution when they forced his head out of a sash window and brought it down on his neck like a guillotine.

Later he attended Magdalen College, Oxford, at the same time as his regal contemporary, Prince Paul of Yugoslavia. Unlike his royal friend, he was, according to Prince Paul, "reserved and shy and unable to enter into undergraduate life, or indeed make real friendships." "A lost lamb" was how one of his tutors described him, the prince leaving the college after two years without graduating.

The outbreak of World War One in August 1914 brought home the acute realization that however hard he tried, whatever he did, the Prince of Wales was different from his friends and compatriots. Even though, after much lobbying, he was granted a commission in the Grenadier Guards, he was forced to stay behind in England when his unit was ordered to the fighting in France. He asked the army commander, Lord Kitchener: "What does it matter if I am killed? I have four brothers." In the face of this fatalistic hyperbole, Kitchener explained that he could not permit the future king to be placed in harm's way, especially if he were likely to be captured and held hostage.

It was, the prince would recall, the biggest disappointment of his life; to be in war and not to see battle was utterly devastating. He went through a prolonged period of self-loathing and despair, his sense of inadequacy manifest in his meagre eating habits. At his most troubled his situation provoked thoughts of suicide, a recurring theme in his life. Eventually he was allowed to join military headquarters in France, where he was occasionally permitted near to the front lines. The experience had a sobering effect, shaping his world view profoundly, the prince blaming the malign behaviour of politicians for creating conflict between ordinary Germans and Englishmen who, he believed, had much in common.

On September 29, 1915, he joined Major General (later Field Marshal) Lord Cavan on a tour of the front line at Loos. As the party were making their way forward, a shell burst forty yards away, forcing them towards no-man's-land.

He later recorded: "Of course the dead lie out unburied and in the postures and on the spots as they fell and one got some idea of the horror and ghastliness of it all. Those dead bodies offered a pathetic and gruesome sight, so cruel to be killed within a few yards of your objective after a 300-yard sprint of death. This was my first real sight of war and it moved and impressed me most enormously."

When they returned to Vermelles church, where he had left his car and driver, they discovered that the prince's chauffeur had been killed by a burst of shrapnel. It was a tragic event that underlined the casual, random nature of death in wartime.

Prince Edward came from a generation haunted by the First World War, the industrial scale of the killing leaving a permanent scar. Years later he recalled: "I have only to close my eyes to see once more those awful charred battlefields, miles and miles of duck board winding across a sea of mud, columns of heavily laden men trudging up to the front, columns of men trudging back, their vitality gone, their eyes dead. I remember the blood-stained shreds of khaki and tartan; the ground gray with corpses, mired horses struggling as they drowned in shell holes."

When Prince Edward returned home it was as though the war to end all wars had never taken place. His father's life continued at the same imperturbable pace; at Sandringham, his Norfolk country estate, the clocks were set half an hour fast to give more daylight hours for shooting. When the guns were silent, the king busied himself with ordering his extensive royal stamp collection. For the sovereign it was a soothing pleasure, for the Prince of Wales it represented a royal court that was not just dull but stuck in the previous century. A man who considered himself a leading member of the so-called Jazz Age, he recoiled from a future mapped out in an unappealing vista of ceremonial tree plantings, laying cornerstones, meeting local worthies, and patronizing worthy charities.

As he later explained: "Being a monarch…can surely be one of the most frustrating and over the duller stretches the least stimulating jobs open to an educated independent-minded person. Even a saint would find himself driven to exasperation."

That the king never dreamed of giving his sons any sort of responsibility, treating them like small boys, merely added to the prince's frustrations. Only reluctantly did George V ever allow the future king to see State papers and then only after a near-fatal illness in late 1928. As Australian diplomat R. G. Casey told his prime minister, Stanley Bruce: "It is history repeating itself, as King Edward would never let the present King have access to such papers or indeed, I believe, have any responsibility for as long as he could keep him out of it."

The rigidity of court life, the dulling formality of the annual round, and the heavy burden of duty hung like a great bell around the neck of the Prince of Wales, sonorously summoning him onwards into a life as predictable as it was pointless. Of course, he was not the first—nor will he be the last—prince to feel that the restrictions of his birth vastly outweighed the privileges, Wordsworth's "shades of the prison-house begin to close upon the growing Boy."

Everything about his father's court, from the heavy, dark Victorian furniture and furnishings to the stilted formality of his advisors, spoke of another age, a world that had now passed. Even the king was forced, occasionally, to acknowledge the new order. In January 1924, George V received the first-ever Labour prime minister, James Ramsay MacDonald, the illegitimate son of a Highland ploughman. "What would Queen Victoria have thought?" mused King George V in his diary. Such was MacDonald's reputation as a firebrand that during the war MI5 considered prosecuting him for making seditious speeches. The Establishment—including the Prince of Wales—became even more nervous when MacDonald's government were the first in the West to give the new Russian regime de jure recognition.

The fork in the road for father and son, both philosophically and physically, was the New World. In the same year that saw Mac-Donald elected into office, the prince sailed for what he came to consider as his safe haven, the United States, a land free from the pomp and protocol that dominated the court. Here he could enjoy the semblance of a life unanchored from the restraints and restrictions imposed by his father.

His experiences in America encouraged him to believe that he could pick a pathway between his private life and his public duties. It was not a distinction that the king and queen, their advisors, or the mass media would allow him to make. The reality was that his increasingly hedonistic private life intruded into the public duty pressed on him by his family, politicians, and his people.

Ostensibly billing the trip as a holiday, the prince spent three glorious weeks during the summer of 1924 carousing, dancing, drinking, and playing polo on Long Island with a flashy set of Americans whom the British ambassador, Esme Howard, dismissed as "oily magnates."

A headline in the Pittsburgh *Gazette Times* of September 8, 1924, summarized the prince's behaviour. "Prince Likes America; Doesn't Want to Leave. Spends Another Night Out—Vanishes from Party. Later Seen in All-Night Stand Eating 'Hot Dogs.' Dances with Duchess."

While the prince resented what he called the "damned spying" of the American press, his actions served only to encourage society matrons in thinking that their daughter might be the one for the bachelor prince. When he first arrived in New York onboard the *Berengaria*, he made himself a hostage to fortune by agreeing with a leading question from a female reporter who asked if he would marry an American "gal" if he ever fell in love with one.

The chase was now on. "Never before in the history of

metropolitan society has any visitor to these shores been so persistently and so extravagantly feted," wrote one New York columnist. Little wonder that when the prince attended yet another late-night dance in his honour, his favourite tune was "Leave Me Alone."

Neither the public nor the press would extend him that courtesy. When the wallet of the prince's equerry, Fruity Metcalfe— described variously as "weak and hopelessly irresponsible" by the prince's chief of staff and "disastrous" by the British ambassador— was discovered behind the radiator in the West 72nd Street apartment of a known prostitute, New York society and the media reveled in the scandal. At court, Fruity Metcalfe was accused of being the habitual *bon viveur* who was leading the future king astray. From then on, strenuous efforts were made to keep the two apart—without much success.

In a letter to the king's private secretary, Ambassador Howard observed drily that the next time the prince came to America "he should avoid dances on Saturday nights and go to church on Sunday mornings."

There was a price to be paid. Once the king, who felt the prince's holidaymaking was of a "somewhat strenuous character," was fully apprised of his eldest son's behaviour—and that of his entourage— visits to America were no longer on the agenda. As the king's private secretary Lord Stamfordham observed to Esme Howard: "There is unquestionably a feeling of considerable uneasiness in the minds of thinking people that the whole visit has been too much characterized as one continuous form of recreation and amusement, not altogether devoid of frivolity and with a certain lack of dignity."

The prince was "bitterly disappointed," the sovereign's decision further marking the divergence between father and son, the fusty old guard and the fashionable Prince of Wales. For the future king, America represented freedom of a kind, at least time away from the restrictions of court. For George V, America was a foreign republic where the unwary royal could easily be led astray.

It was not only his behaviour in New York that caused consternation at court. The charge sheet against him seemed to grow by the day. He was often late for official engagements, and when he did turn up he seemed bored and distracted, eager to get away. During a visit to Chile he was described by one onlooker as "boredom personified, restless, impatient to be away," while in Argentina he was so exhausted by being, yet again, top of the bill in a travelling freak show that officials considered calling off the visit at the midway point. Even social functions such as balls bored him, at the last minute the prince crying off his attendance at dances held in his honour.

His racy dress sense, his heavy drinking, his improper dalliances, and his late-night revels at nightclubs infuriated the king. "You dress like a cad. You act like a cad. You *are* a cad. Get out!" he roared, his aggressively pernickety attitude towards his eldest son, who was after all a bona fide war hero with medals to boot, seeming to many overly censorious, as he had performed his duty manfully during war and peace. His reaction to fatherly rebuke is instructive, the prince, in tears, vowing to renounce his titles and go and live in the colonies. In the face of parental admonishment, or hostility of any kind, his first thought was flight. It was his default position, one he employed to catastrophic effect during the abdication crisis.

His love of point-to-point hunting with his boon companion Fruity Metcalfe further exposed the character of a man with only a tenuous acquaintance with the notions of caution and self-preservation. He was notoriously reckless and foolhardy in the saddle, the prince taking risks that would make many other riders shudder.

It was as if he was defying fate by his behaviour, challenging himself at the outer edge of life's envelope because his entire life was entirely devoid of jeopardy. This characteristic is not unique to Prince Edward—his descendant Prince Charles has cheated death on several occasions, notably by skiing and playing polo, not to mention diving under the Arctic Circle and low-level parachute jumps.

Such was the concern about Edward's behaviour that, following a fall in 1924 at Arborfield Cross, which left the prince unconscious for several hours, both Prime Minister Stanley Baldwin and George V insisted that he give up point-to-point races and steeplechasing. His stable was duly sold at auction—but not for another five years.

The prince's careless obstinacy and airy dismissal of the consequences of his actions seemed all of a piece with a man who was looking for a way out, any way out, of fulfilling his dread destiny. Ironically his reckless horsemanship merely added to his romantic appeal in the popular imagination. His close circle of advisors and confidants had an entirely different perspective. In April 1927 the prince's private secretary, Alan "Tommy" Lascelles, complained to Stanley Baldwin about the heir apparent, stating that he was "rapidly going to the devil" in his unbridled pursuit of wine and women. He famously added that the best thing that could happen to him—and the country—would be for him to break his neck in a point-to-point race.

Baldwin responded: "God forgive me, I have often thought the same."

While his halo of boyish glamour invested the prince with an undeniable appeal and popularity, up close and personal the vista was not so inviting. His advisors and courtiers were, like the prince, living a lie, covering up the stark fact that he was looking for any excuse to escape from his destiny. At some point in 1928 all his senior advisors—Admiral Sir Lionel Halsey, Sir Godfrey Thomas, and Alan Lascelles—seriously considered their positions, the trio believing that the Prince of Wales was made up of entirely the wrong stuff for a future sovereign.

The strain of juggling the growing chasm between the breezy

public image and the despondent private reality eventually became too much. Lascelles snapped, the final straw coming during a tour of Africa in 1928 when the royal party were on a train in Tanganyika, now Tanzania. He received an urgent cable from Prime Minister Baldwin saying that the king was gravely ill and that the prince should return home at once. Prince Edward thought that Baldwin was bluffing and returned to his seduction, which was ultimately successful, of a certain Mrs. Barnes, the wife of the local district officer. The prince's selfish behaviour prompted Lascelles to hand in his resignation. In their final interview the future king returned to a familiar refrain, candidly admitting: "I'm quite the wrong sort of person to be Prince of Wales."

The strains and stresses facing courtiers trying to reconcile the unsuitable reality with the radiant image of the Prince of Wales is reminiscent of the turmoil inside Buckingham Palace several decades later when it was clear that the present Prince of Wales, Prince Charles, was desperately unhappy in his marriage to Lady Diana Spencer and had returned to the arms of his lover, Camilla Parker Bowles. The difference was that during the 1930s the mass media was much more compliant, a handful of proprietors such as Lords Beaverbrook and Rothermere controlling the distribution of information.

Even so, disaster beckoned. Lord Strathmore, the father of the new Duchess of York, was one of a widening circle who reluctantly believed that the bachelor prince would never succeed to the throne of England. As the years ticked by, it was not just the prince's courtiers who were gripped by a grim sense of foreboding but the entire British ruling class.

—⟨◦⟩—

CHAPTER TWO

Adolf Hitler, Royal Matchmaker

In the royal houses of Europe marriage was a serious business. There was certainly little room for love, passion, or romance. Royal marriages were arranged, the vagaries of the heart no match for the inexorable demands of duty and dynasty. Those feckless royals who had the temerity to fall in love and marry beneath their station were abruptly cast into the outer social darkness.

The parents of the Prince of Wales, King George V and Queen Mary, were typical results of a caste system where royalty married only royalty, English royals traditionally matched with their German counterparts. Queen Victoria's writ ran large during her long reign, her decisions about and choices of marital partners for her growing family absolute and final. When her grandson and heir to the throne, Albert Victor, Duke of Clarence, died unexpectedly in 1892 shortly before he was due to marry a German princess, Victoria Mary of Teck, the old queen hardly missed a beat. She summoned his younger brother George, then an aspiring naval officer, and ordered him to quit the navy, marry Princess Mary, and prepare for kingship. Any personal ambition or feelings

George had for himself were snuffed out beneath the smothering blanket of monarchy, though fortuitously he did become very fond of Mary. He duly did his duty, married Princess Mary in July 1893, and a year later produced an heir, Edward Albert Christian George Andrew Patrick David, known in the family as David.

As procreation is the principal function of royalty, the mating game for this new arrival began pretty much from the moment Edward Albert was born. All over Europe royal parents reviewed their own broods with an eye to one day claiming the glittering prize, consort to the future king-emperor, ruler of the greatest empire the world had ever seen. It was an innocent parlour game that everyone, rich and poor, could join in. The unveiling of a statue to Queen Victoria outside Buckingham Palace provided the first public forum to discuss an issue that would come to convulse the country. Accompanying German emperor Wilhelm II to the service was his eighteen-year-old daughter, the pretty if imperious Princess Viktoria Luise. She was immediately singled out as a future bride for the sixteen-year-old prince, the *Daily Express* describing how she had taken "London by storm." The princess, who enjoyed the attention, was not so enamoured of her possible paramour, dismissing Prince Edward with faint praise. "Very nice but terribly young."

There was no hurry. The prince was still a teenager and, following the death of Edward VII in 1910, the new king, George V, had only just ascended the throne. Then forty-six, he was in robust good health. Nonetheless there was no harm in testing the waters, his son and heir visiting his German cousins in the spring and summer of 1913. Ostensibly the trip was to improve his language skills and general knowledge, but it was also for his German cousins to run the romantic rule over the young prince.

He progressed, as he noted in his memoirs, "sumptuously" from one palace to another: visiting "Onkel Willie and Tante Charlotte," the gluttonous king and queen of Württemberg; meeting with

Count Zeppelin and seeing his eponymous airship; and enjoying a curious encounter with the Kaiser, who somewhat presciently described the prince as a "young eagle, likely to play a big part in European affairs because he is far from being a pacifist."

While he danced until the early hours in the nightclubs of Berlin, the romantic highlight was his meeting at her family schloss in Gotha with Princess Caroline "May" Mathilde of Schleswig-Holstein, who is from the same branch of the royal family as the present Duke of Edinburgh, husband of Queen Elizabeth II. She was slim, elegant, and fashionable, and the prince found her easy to talk to, with a pleasing personality. Such was their rapport that the Kaiser's son August Wilhelm subsequently wrote to the prince suggesting that a matrimonial match be made. While it seems he hesitated, Edward was sufficiently enthusiastic to plan another visit the following summer. So far so conventional, the future king conforming to royal tradition by fishing for a mate in the approved gene pool of German royalty. The outbreak of war in August 1914 changed all that, Edward remarking a year later to his private secretary Godfrey Thomas about what might have been. Thomas later recalled: "HRH [His Royal Highness] was very much attracted to her and I am perfectly certain that if the War hadn't come, it would have been brought off."

As it was, the First World War harvested the royal families of Europe, drastically diminishing the prospects of the prince finding a royal mate. Initially he made it clear that he was not interested in marrying a commoner, a sentiment that precluded the chance of elevating an English subject, however high-born, into the ranks of royalty.

In this regard he was even more conservative than his father, who issued a royal proclamation in July 1917 which not only formally changed the family name from Saxe-Coburg and Gotha to Windsor but, as significantly, specifically changed the rules of marital engagement. From that date on, his children and heirs could marry into English families, royalty for the first time allowed to marry its subjects.

That the Prince of Wales preferred the former tradition greatly limited his options, perhaps deliberately so, indicating his hesitation about ever marrying.

As he told Mountbatten: "I suppose I'll have to take the fatal plunge one of these days, though I'll put if off as long as I can, 'cos it'll destroy me." This reticence did not stop him playing the field.

Like many men of his generation, he was generally bashful about the female form—"filthy and revolting" was his description of naked prostitutes posing in a Calais brothel—and both ignorant of and timid about the act of coition itself. Stories about his ambiguous, not to say confused, sexuality dogged him throughout his life. His one-time private secretary Anne Seagrim believed that his sexual ambivalence went to the heart of who he was. The cornerstone of his character was his "fundamental uncertainty about his sexuality and his ability to be a heterosexual man. He was fundamentally afraid of women."

In July 1917, thanks to the efforts of his equerries, a French prostitute called Paulette helped him overcome his fears. A subsequent six-month affair with a Parisian courtesan named Marguerite Alibert gave the prince a healthy appetite for sex that belied his boyish, almost effeminate countenance. As society belle Lady Diana Cooper crudely observed, from then on the prince was "never out of a woman's legs." Often those legs were married.

His first amour on home soil was in 1917 with Marion Coke, the wife of Viscount "Tommy" Coke, heir to the Earl of Leicester. The prince spent so much time in her company that eventually her husband warned him to stay clear. That didn't stop Edward encouraging her to visit him in Paris. Twelve years older than Edward, who was young for his age, she sensibly declined his harebrained invitation which, apart from ending her marriage, would have brought social disgrace.

More conventionally, he romanced his sister's best friend, Lady Sybil "Portia" Cadogan, one of five daughters of the Earl of Cadogan. His courtship with Portia, which coincided with his infatuation with Marion Coke, was thought by many, not least his sister, to be heading for the altar. In June 1917, when Portia telegrammed her parents and told them "Engaged to Edward," they presumed they had a future queen in the family. Actually she had ended her association with the prince and accepted the hand of the prince's university friend Lord Edward Stanley, who enjoyed a double celebration that month by winning a by-election as a Conservative candidate. He went on to become minister for the Dominions.

Spurned by one potential bride, there were plenty of other ambitious young English aristocratic ladies encouraged by the king's decree widening the marital choices for his family. So when the prince arrived in the capital in March 1918 while on leave, there was, according to writer Cynthia Asquith, "wild excitement." She observed: "No girl is allowed to leave London...and every mother's heart beats high."

Various names were in the frame as possible suitors but it was Lady Rosemary Leveson-Gower who had tongues wagging. A recognized beauty who was sketched by society artist John Singer Sargent, Lady Rosemary, the daughter of the Duke of Sutherland, first met the prince in the summer of 1917 in Calais, where she was billeted as a Red Cross nurse at the hospital run by her mother, Millicent, Duchess of Sutherland. The prince accompanied the king and queen during an official visit and was photographed, head down, chatting to the aristocratic nurse. Described by the *Illustrated London News* as "generous, cheery and kind, ready for any excitement, especially outdoor expeditions," Lady Rosemary, it seems, was the rebound girl for the prince, who fell for her shortly after being so abruptly ditched by Lady Portia Cadogan.

After a whirlwind wartime courtship the prince, according to

Lady Victor Paget, one of Rosemary's closest friends, asked her to marry him. Both his parents were against the match, Queen Mary explaining that there was "bad blood—a touch of madness—in one line of the Leveson-Gower family."

At this time mental stability was uppermost in the minds of the king and queen. The mental health of Prince Edward's younger brother John, who suffered from autism and was prone to violent epilepsy, severely deteriorated around this time. Kept in seclusion at Sandringham, he died a few months later in January 1919 from a seizure.

The prince, who felt "bitter and furious" towards his parents, was entirely unsympathetic with regard to their cautious point of view, incensed that they were preventing him from following his heart. As Lady Paget told writer Michael Thornton: "I don't think he ever forgave his father. I also felt that from that time on, he had made up his mind that he would never make what might be called a suitable marriage to please his family."

Even after she married William Ward, Viscount Ednam and later the 3rd Earl of Dudley, in March 1919 at St. Margaret's Church, Westminster, the prince continued to stay close, privately visiting his one-time paramour at her home, Himley Hall on the outskirts of Dudley in the Midlands. He was godfather to her eldest son, Billy, who became the 4th Earl. Throughout his life Billy was amused by the possibility that the prince might have been his father.

The prince's latest spat with his parents seemed to end his conventional search for a bride. From now on he yo-yoed between grand passions and casual pursuits, invariably with compliant married women. The extremes of his romantic heart matched his erratic mood swings, which rapidly fluctuated from elation to despair.

In many ways his next lover and long-time mistress Freda Dudley Ward, the half-American wife of a member of Parliament and vice chamberlain of the Royal Household, was, marital status apart, an eminently suitable choice. His family and friends pragmatically acknowledged that Freda—the daughter of a Nottingham lace manufacturer—whom he met by chance during an air raid at the end of the war, was a "good thing" in his life. She was much more than his lover, becoming his confidante, sounding board, and surrogate mother, a safe haven where he could pour out his frustrations.

His devotion to his paramour was obvious even to the casual observer. When Winston Churchill, who treated the prince like a surrogate son, travelled to Nottingham with the couple, Edward's adoration was transparent. "It was quite pathetic to see the Prince and Freda. His love is so obvious and undisguisable."

Freda, described as an "angelic waif" by Churchill's cousin Shane Leslie, was the voice of calm in the storm of emotions that swept over him, soothing and steadying his tormented soul. Not just beautiful and charming but "cosy and warm," observed Mountbatten. "She's absolutely been a mother to him, comforted and advised him and all along he has been blind in his love to what the world is saying."

At times their relationship degenerated into a mother with her baby rather than the cliché of an immature man seeking a mother figure. "I'm just DIPPY to die with YOU even if we can't live together," was just one example of a burble of baby talk that issued from the princely pen. Edward fully acknowledged the truth of Max Beerbohm's observation about King George IV: "He was indeed still a child, for Royalties, not being ever brought into contact with the realities of life, remain young far longer than other people." What was true for his ancestor, he averred, applied equally to himself. As he wrote to Freda Dudley Ward: "No one realizes how desperately true that is in my case more than I do."

While his behaviour worried the king and queen, he was not the only one of their children with an eye for married women.

His younger brother Prince Albert was infatuated with Freda's friend Lady Sheila Loughborough, a striking Australian whose marriage to Lord Loughborough was on the rocks because of his drinking and gambling. She and Freda often danced with the two princes at balls, which, as Lady Loughborough confided in her memoirs, "annoyed some of the dowagers. However, we didn't care. We knew no party was complete without us—and them."

The king used what leverage he had, warning his son that he would confer the title Duke of York only if he gave up his Sheila. He duly fell in line and, following the king's declaration that allowed his children to marry subjects, in 1923 married Elizabeth Bowes-Lyon, the daughter of the prominent Scottish noble, Lord Strathmore. While this match and the marriage the previous year of their daughter, Princess Mary, gave the king and queen much satisfaction, the behaviour of Prince Edward's younger brother Prince George was of pressing concern.

The king and queen had lost one son to congenital illness; now they were in danger of losing another to drug addiction. Prince George embraced the Roaring Twenties full on, enjoying a party life of drink, drugs, and wild sex. His string of lovers—men and women—were said to have included the singer Jessie Matthews; playwright Noël Coward; Princess Diana's step-grandmother, novelist Barbara Cartland; and Soviet spy Anthony Blunt.

However, it was his long-time association with society drug addict Kiki Preston, known as "the girl with the silver syringe," that really set alarm bells ringing. While his parents were seized with a despairing paralysis about how to handle this unthinkable situation, Prince Edward—and his mistress—took control, helping to wean his brother off cocaine and heroin.

Part of his cure was to ensure that Kiki Preston could no longer influence George, the prince "exiling" her for a time to Switzerland. It is widely believed that Prince George and his addict lover had a child together, Michael Canfield, who went on to become a New York publisher. He died in 1969. (It is hardly surprising, in view of Prince George's colourful past, that historians frequently complain about the paucity of correspondence and any other records relating to Prince George, Duke of Kent, which are held at the Royal Archives inside Windsor Castle.)

Whatever the vicissitudes facing Prince George, the fact remained that the future of the crown rested on the shoulders of the firstborn. While the king took a dim view of his eldest son's skittish but obstinate character, his louche friends, and his late-night lifestyle, he would have forgiven him anything just as long as he married and produced an heir. The public, though, saw nothing of the dramas that went on behind the royal curtain, but as the years ticked by and Edward showed no sign of weaning himself away from Freda Dudley Ward or seriously searching for a bride, concerns were being whispered beyond the tight-lipped boundaries of the royal court. The king's bouts of ill health—he never fully recovered from a fall from his horse during a review of the troops in 1915—made matrimonial matters a subject of pressing concern. In the summer of 1925 he was urged by his doctors to take a restorative Mediterranean cruise, and in November 1928 a severe bout of septicaemia left him so weakened that, as a precaution, the Prince of Wales was summoned home from an African tour by Prime Minister Baldwin. The king spent three months recuperating at the seaside resort of Bognor, his eldest son, together with Queen Mary, undertaking many of his engagements.

Such was the sense of apprehension that the prince would one day rule as a bachelor that there were plans for the Australian prime minister, Stanley Bruce, to speak to him man to man and impress on him that the "certainty of the succession ... is not less than essential for the maintenance of the Empire." As the London-based Australian diplomat R. G. Casey informed Bruce:

I hear that pressure is steadily being kept on the Prince of Wales with regard to his marriage. There is some little anxiety, I believe, with regard to the amount of heart that he would find himself able to put into it—as it would, of course, be a marriage *de convénience*. A subsequent scandal would be almost as bad as if he had never married.

At some point Louis Mountbatten drew up a list of seventeen eligible young royals. The daughters of Prince Andrew of Greece—Princesses Margarita and Theodora—were possible candidates, but for a time the front runner was eighteen-year-old Princess Ingrid of Sweden. Her family was eminently suitable, as her mother, Princess Margaret of Connaught, and King George V were first cousins, both being grandchildren of Queen Victoria.

In the summer of 1928 Princess Ingrid arrived in London, accompanied by the country's minister in London, Baron Erik Palmstierna, in the hope of snagging the Prince of Wales. Ingrid, a well-read if somewhat naïve young girl, had previously expressed the hope of one day becoming a queen. Of course the English throne would do very nicely. Palmstierna, though hopeful of a match, did not share her confidence. He admitted that the whole enterprise was somewhat "chancy," his assessment proving correct. There was little chemistry between the thirty-four-year-old prince and the teenage princess. In July, Princess Ingrid returned to Stockholm, her hopes dashed—for the moment.

During the twenties and thirties a variety of candidates, promoted by family or government, paraded before the future king. Even though, under the 1701 Act of Settlement, a Roman Catholic was barred from ascending the throne, that did not prevent King Vittorio Emanuele of Savoy making serious overtures regarding his eldest daughter, Princess Jolanda. To the king's disappointment they came to nothing, and she went on to marry an Italian nobleman.

In many ways the most serious contender was promoted by the newly elected German chancellor, Adolf Hitler. What the ambitious German Führer had in mind was a dynastic union that harked back to the days of the Hapsburgs and the Hanoverians, namely an arranged marriage between a high-born German noblewoman and the heir to the British throne.

As part of his grand diplomatic strategy after he became chancellor in 1933, Hitler encouraged marriage between German aristocrats and their European counterparts in order to improve the international position of the Fatherland. For example, he viewed the 1937 union of Prince Bernhard zur Lippe-Biesterfeld to Princess Juliana, the daughter of Queen Wilhelmina of the Netherlands, with much approval, seeing it as a chance to build closer ties between the two countries.

Before this successful union, the Führer's restless eye fell upon the Prince of Wales and Princess Friederike, the seventeen-year-old daughter of Duke Ernst August III of Brunswick and his wife, Duchess Viktoria Luise, the only daughter of German emperor Wilhelm II and Empress Augusta Viktoria.

Princess Friederike's pedigree was impeccable. As daughter of the head of the House of Hanover, she theoretically enjoyed the titles Princess Friederike of Hanover, Great Britain, and Ireland, and also Duchess Friederike of Brunswick-Lüneburg. Moreover, as a descendant of King George III, she was nominally thirty-fourth in line to the British throne, although these titles were now in abeyance following the 1917 Titles Deprivation Act, which stripped Britain's enemies of rank and honours during World War One.

Not only were her royal credentials immaculate, but her family's allegiance to the Nazi Party was impressive. Her father, Duke Ernst August, often appeared in an honorary brown SA stormtroopers uniform and regularly donated funds to the party. He never formally joined the Nazi Party but his son, also Ernst August, did sign on and became a member of the paramilitary SS, wearing its sinister black-and-silver uniform with the death's head emblem. As for Princess Friederike, she belonged to the *Bund Deutscher Mädel* (League of German Girls), the branch of the Hitler Youth movement exclusively for young women. At her private boarding school in Italy she was remembered for her defence of Nazi policies. In later life she was dubbed the "Prussian sergeant."

Her parents had met with Hitler on a number of occasions, their discussions focusing on constructing an enduring rapprochement between England and Germany. What Hitler had in mind, though, was more than just words: He wanted a union between the royal houses of Britain and Germany. His demand that Princess Friederike be offered as a possible bride for the Prince of Wales was made sometime in 1934 and conveyed to the royal couple by Joachim von Ribbentrop, the former champagne salesman turned confidant of the Führer. Ribbentrop had at that time been appointed Special Commissioner of Disarmament, his task being to convince the world of a benign Germany's desire for peace.

When he informed them about Hitler's designs for their daughter, the duke and duchess, who had only recently returned from a visit to England, where they had been received by King George V and Queen Mary, were "astounded." Friederike's mother, Princess Viktoria Luise, was particularly nonplussed, as a decade before she, too, had been considered a potential bride for the future English king.

Even these enthusiastic Nazi aristocrats were unable to countenance a match between their teenage daughter and a man twenty-two years her senior. The duchess later recalled:

> My husband and I were shattered. Something like this had never entered our minds, not even for a reconciliation with England. Before the First World War it had been suggested that I should marry my cousin [the Prince of Wales], who was two years younger, and it was now being indicated that

my daughter should marry him. We told Hitler that in our opinion the great difference in age between the Prince of Wales and Friederike alone precluded such a project, and that we were not prepared to put pressure on our daughter.

Her protestations, made in a memoir written after the war, seem somewhat disingenuous, like those of many other German aristocrats trying to distance themselves from their tainted Nazi affiliations. Only a year or so later, Friederike met Prince Paul, the crown prince of Greece, who proposed to her while he was attending the now notorious 1936 summer Olympics in Berlin. Their sixteen-year age difference did not seem to trouble her parents unduly, the couple marrying in January 1938 and Friederike ascending the Greek throne in 1947. As keen as Hitler was on seeing this royal match take place, the Duchess of Windsor's biographer Charles Higham is perhaps stretching a point when he argues that if Edward and Friederike had married and Wallis Simpson had remained a "back street mistress" it is "doubtful whether World War II could have occurred."

While Hitler's first attempt to bring the Prince of Wales into the formal orbit of the Nazi regime foundered, it was but the prelude to future ploys to woo the king who was never crowned, entreaties that lasted almost as long as the Third Reich itself—and with consequences for the duke that endured for much longer.

Unknown to Hitler—and the rest of Europe—the Prince of Wales's heart beat a little faster when he was facing west towards America rather than east to Germany. If they were married and seemingly unattainable so much the better. For practical men of the world like Hitler, to fall in love with one's mistress was simply baffling. Yet this became the prince's settled romantic routine.

In the summer of 1929 he met Viscountess Thelma Furness in the incongruous setting of an agricultural show in Leicestershire, where he had the job of handing out rosettes to prize cattle. The daughter of American diplomat Harry Hays Morgan Sr., she had been briefly introduced to the prince at a ball three years earlier. On this occasion sparks flew, the prince attracted by her beauty and her American accent. By now Thelma, who had an identical twin Gloria, was on her second marriage, to Viscount Marmaduke Furness, the head of the Furness Shipping Line. That did not stop the prince, who was beguiled by what Cecil Beaton described as her "hothouse elegance and lacy femininity." He asked Thelma for dinner at York House, his London home, and later, after seducing her, invited her and her husband to join him on a safari to Kenya. Although they were chaperoned, the lovers managed to spend time alone. "This was our Eden," she later wrote of their magical nights under canvas. "I felt content to let the prince chart the course, heedless of where the voyage would end."

When the prince returned to Britain in April 1930, his frequent weekend companion at Fort Belvedere, the prince's country home near Windsor, was the married viscountess. She was his hostess, companion, and lover—though he still remained in contact with court favourite Freda Dudley Ward, who helped redecorate his hideaway. At the Fort the prince could be himself, working on his beloved garden, playing his bagpipes or ukulele, or simply sitting quietly with Thelma doing a little needlepoint. Hardly the vision of Sodom and Gomorrah that caused his father to exclaim "Those damned weekends." Independent of Balmoral and Sandringham, it was a place he could call his own, where he could put down roots.

The prince genuinely believed that he could perform a little light "princing" during the week and then retire to the informality—a word he loved—of his weekend retreat in the Surrey countryside. Here he was free from those twin scourges of his life who watched his every move—his Scotland Yard bodyguard and what he called "the damned press." Free, too, from the constrictions of court and the strictures of courtiers concerned that he understand the true nature of his calling as sovereign-in-waiting, the living apex of the empire. Edward saw his future position, onerous as it was, as a job rather than a sacred calling, believing that if he performed his necessary quota of public duties, as he had done manfully since the end of the First World War, then his personal life would have no bearing on his role as king. Obstinate as ever, he refused to listen to more conventional voices. As his private secretary Godfrey Thomas wrote: "I'm terribly sorry for him but unless someone can succeed in disabusing him of this *idée fixe* I can see nothing but disaster ahead."

It is not that he had an awful lot to grumble about. While his imperial tours had, by any measure, tested his reserves of charm and endurance, his life at home was not especially onerous. He would typically rise not much before eleven and have a light breakfast before a game of golf—he became captain of Walton Heath Golf Club in 1935. The prince was immensely proud of the fact that during his golfing career he had managed three holes in one, whereas his golfing hero, Ben Hogan, managed only one.

After cocktails at seven o'clock on the dot, followed by dinner, he would take in a nightclub—most Thursdays he was at the Embassy Club on Bond Street—until the early hours. By his own admission he would often pull rank and ask his younger brothers to undertake official engagements he had previously agreed to perform.

Even though he had, at the request of Baldwin and the king, agreed to give up steeplechasing and point-to-point, he still played polo and went fox hunting, often staying at Burrough Court, the Furnesses' country home near Melton Mowbray, Leicestershire. It was here where the prince and his younger brother Prince George spent the weekend fox hunting in January 1931 shortly before both princes embarked on a grueling four-month, 16,000-mile tour of South America.

During his visit to Burrough Court he met a woman nursing a

heavy cold. In between sniffles, Wallis Warfield Simpson managed to drop a half-decent curtsey, which she had hastily practiced on the railway journey from London.

She and her husband, Ernest, were very last-minute additions to the house party. They had been invited only because Thelma's friends had been forced to drop out. As Edward would later recount in his memoirs, his opening conversational gambit about Americans missing central heating in the chilly English countryside cut little ice with the lady from Baltimore. "I had hoped for something more original from the Prince of Wales," she countered.

In the circumstances it was a somewhat challenging response but typical of a woman who had gone through life aware that her smart mouth rather than her angular, rather mannish looks garnered attention. Wallis remembers their first encounter somewhat differently, striking up a conversation when she was seated next to him at lunch. Although "petrified," by the time dessert arrived she found him "truly one of the most attractive personalities I have ever met." So began an acquaintance that within five years would set the throne tottering.

CHAPTER THREE

———— ⬥ ————

Sex, Drugs, and Royal Blackmail

Though born in the northern American state of Pennsylvania on June 19, 1896, two years after the prince, Bessie Wallis Warfield was a product of two proud, warring, and very different southern families, the Montagues and the Warfields. The Warfields, from Maryland, had the reputation as a staid, patrician, and religious family, whereas the Virginian Montagues, who boasted a general, a governor, and judges among their ranks, were considered reckless and irresponsible.

Alice Montague and Teackle Warfield first met in 1895 in Blue Ridge Summit, Pennsylvania, having travelled there in the hope that the pure mountain air would cure their tuberculosis. It was perhaps no surprise that when they married after an impetuous courtship, their families promptly disowned them, not just because of family differences but on medical grounds. The wiseacres on both sides of the family were proved unhappily accurate in their gloomy prognosis. Just five months after Wallis's birth her father, Teackle, died of his illness, forcing her penniless mother to rely on the grudging charity of her relatives, particularly her uncle

Sol Warfield and her sister, Bessie Merryman. While Aunt Bessie would come to have a pivotal role in Wallis's life as both a companion and a counsellor, in the early years it was her generosity that was crucial in keeping her irresponsible sister and niece financially afloat, Alice and Wallis settling in Baltimore, where Bessie paid for Wallis's private education.

For long periods, though, they led a hand-to-mouth existence, which bred in Wallis a toughness, a boldness, and a greed paired with a gnawing sense of insecurity, a fear that at any moment the trapdoor may swing open. Fear of poverty was just one of the many torments that crowded her nervy, superstitious psyche; she was terrified of thunder, flying, and the dark, quirks of character that, paired with a ready wit, made her an intriguing if challenging proposition. Nicknamed "Skinny" by her school friends, she was chic, well groomed, but not conventionally pretty. Photographs, even by society favourite Cecil Beaton, never truly did her justice—Wallis's frequent refrain: "Please don't make me look like a horse." Moving images capture her best, her face alight with easy, intelligent laughter, her manner confident and animated, her carriage graceful and self-possessed, some would say imperious. Wallis was always much more than the sum of her parts.

Like most girls, she was eager to escape the restrictions of home and took the opportunity to stay with a cousin in Pensacola, Florida, where she met a naval officer from Chicago called Lieutenant Earl Winfield Spencer Jr. or, as she wrote to her mother, "the world's most fascinating aviator." Dazzled by his military uniform and persona, she ignored the brooding violence that lurked inside a character described by his fellow naval graduates as a "merry devil." Soon after they married in November 1916 she discovered that while he was jovial in public, in private he was the very devil to live with. Spencer, eight years her senior, was a moody, violently jealous alcoholic with a sadistic streak.

By her own account, when he was away he would hog-tie her

to the bed or lock her in the bathroom to prevent her going out. Other times he would play cruel practical jokes that made her realize he couldn't possibly love her. Her own heart grew cold to him, Wallis contemplating separation and divorce. In spite of the opposition of her family—there had never been a divorce in the Warfield family—Spencer and Wallis separated in 1921, Wallis moving to Washington. That year she began an affair with Felipe Espil, first secretary at the Argentinian embassy, falling madly in love with the charming, intelligent career diplomat who was the living embodiment of a "Latin smoothie." Their affair lasted for more than a year until Espil said goodbye in the fall of 1923, leaving her in tatters and tears. As one of his friends, who watched him climb the diplomatic career ladder until he became ambassador to the United States in 1931, later observed: "Felipe had a higher regard for his career than Edward VIII had."

After a period of travel, during which she spent time in Paris with her cousin, she agreed to try again with her husband, sailing in July 1924 to Hong Kong, where he was now stationed. The reunion was not a success, the couple separating almost immediately. During what she would call her "lotus year," Wallis travelled to various Chinese cities in the company of other navy wives, before meeting up with her old friend Katherine Bigelow, a war widow who had married Herman Rogers, a wealthy and well-connected socialite who dreamed of writing the great American novel but contented himself with travelling to the world's most exotic places. His family's estate on the Hudson River, called Crumwold, adjoined Roosevelt's Hyde Park, and the president's mother, Sara Delano Roosevelt, was his godmother. Katherine and Herman were generous hosts, Wallis living with them for nearly a year at their home in Tartar City, the couple becoming her lifelong friends and supporters.

Her Far East adventures led to lurid speculation about her various liaisons, including her time learning curious sexual techniques in the brothels of Shanghai, as well as a botched abortion during an affair with the Italian diplomat Count Gian Galeazzo Ciano, who later became foreign minister and Mussolini's son-in-law. A chronicle of these sexual adventures is apparently contained in the infamous "China dossier," which was prepared for Prime Minister Baldwin and King George V years later. Even though eighty years have passed since that report was purportedly compiled, not a trace of it has been found in any official or unofficial record. The document retains a mythical status, like so much surrounding the girl from Baltimore.

Perhaps the worst that can be said of her during this time is that she harboured a crush, if not an infatuation, for her host, Herman Rogers. Tall, athletic, well read, and above all decent, Herman became her most reliable and closest male confidant until his premature death from cancer. Movies of Wallis and Herman together, parading in matching kimonos at his home in Peking, show the undoubted affection that existed between them. Certainly she was always very proprietorial towards her Herman.

She returned to America somewhat abruptly, further fuelling speculation that the ménage had run its course—at least for the moment. More likely it was to sort out the details of her divorce, which was finalized in 1927 in Virginia. Wallis was still separated when, in December 1926, she met Ernest Simpson at a Christmas party hosted by her friend Mary Kirk Raffray in New York's Washington Square, the setting for the famous Henry James novel. Ernest was also married—though unhappily—to judge's daughter Dorothea "Dodie" Parsons Dechert, with whom he had a daughter, Audrey, then aged two.

Frail and frequently hospitalized, Dodie was not the companion he had married, Ernest beginning divorce proceedings shortly after embarking on an affair with Wallis. Dodie would later tell writer Cleveland Amory, "Wallis was very smart. She stole my husband while I was ill."

At first glance Ernest was a substitute for the cosmopolitan and sophisticated but happily married Herman Rogers. He was a man of polish, intelligence, and humour, able to declaim Greek classics in the original, fluent in both French and the foxtrot. Safe, solid, and dependable, he was a quiet Renaissance man who was the polar opposite of her braggadocio first husband. Above all he was financially secure, a partner in the ship brokers Simpson Spence and Young, which his father, Ernest, co-founded.

Though his mother was the daughter of a New York lawyer, his father was British of Jewish descent. Ever since he was young he had been an Anglophile to his fingertips, brought up on the claustrophobic metropolitan tales of Charles Dickens, Rudyard Kipling's yarns of empire, and A. A. Milne's children's favourite, *Winnie-the-Pooh*. During World War One Ernest, who studied at Harvard, renounced his American citizenship and became a naturalized Briton, serving briefly as a captain in the Coldstream Guards at the end of the war. When he was demobbed, Ernest, in his pin-striped suit, bowler hat, rolled umbrella, neatly trimmed moustache, and Guards tie, was the very model of an English City gent.

Shortly after Wallis's divorce was finalized in December 1927, Ernest proposed. Even though she was now thirty-one, with no job and all but destitute, she hesitated. After all, the happiest times of her life had been when she was single or separated in Washington, Paris, and Peking. What if, she mused, she had misread Ernest just as she had Spencer? It would be too awful to make the same mistake again. As she pondered his offer, she travelled to what was to become her safe haven, the villa of Lou Viei in Cannes in the South of France, the European home of her friends and counsellors, Herman and Katherine Rogers. After a period of reflection she agreed to Ernest's suit, the couple marrying at Chelsea register office on July 21, 1928, and moving to London permanently after Ernest had taken over the running of the shipping company.

Wallis's hesitation had almost cost her dear. Most of her savings were wiped out in the Wall Street Crash of 1929, leaving her utterly financially dependent on Ernest. Fortunately the shipping business escaped the worst of the financial tsunami, enabling him to stay solvent—at least for a while. After a year leasing a Mayfair apartment, they moved into 5 Bryanston Court, a smart if anonymous mansion block just north of Marble Arch in central London.

With a dining table that seated fourteen, an elegant drawing room, which Wallis decorated, and a staff of four, including a cook, they were able to entertain in some style. Regular visitors included Javier "Tiger" Bermejillo, the second secretary at the Spanish embassy, and Ernest's friend from his time in the Guards, Reuters chief editor Bernard Rickatson-Hatt. Ernest's sister, Maud Kerr-Smiley, who was married to a member of Parliament, introduced them to Connie and Ben Thaw, who was first secretary at the American embassy. In turn, Connie—or Consuelo—one of the glamorous and rich Morgan sisters, introduced them to her sister Viscountess Thelma Furness, possibly the most gossiped-about woman in London both for her beauty and for her affair with the Prince of Wales. It was at her country estate in Melton Mowbray that Edward and Wallis had their first social encounter, and it was through Thelma that the Simpsons again met with the prince at a cocktail party in April 1931 to mark his return from his South America visit.

It was hardly as if the prince had been pining for any of the women in his life—during his visit to Buenos Aires he had relentlessly pursued "the very charming and very beautiful" Consuelo Morgan, the sister of his erstwhile mistress Thelma Furness and the wife of diplomat Ben Thaw. As American diplomat George Messersmith observed: "During his stay he had shown a great deal of attention to Consuelo and this did not please many of the young Argentinian beauties who had replenished their wardrobes in Paris for the visit." When her sister reported on his caddish behavior it may have given the royal mistress pause. Thelma may have accepted that her days as the prince's sole object of affection were now numbered.

Gradually the Simpsons began moving from the fringes to the centre of the prince's life. In June 1931 Ernest, in his full dress uniform of a Coldstream Guard, almost burst with pride and excitement as he watched Wallis drop a full curtsey to the king and queen when she was presented at court during a ceremony at Buckingham Palace. As she passed the royal party she heard the Prince of Wales mutter that all the women looked "ghastly" because of the lighting. Later, when the prince attended a party held at Thelma's apartment, he complimented Wallis on her gown, only for the sassy American to snap back: "But sir, I thought you said we all looked ghastly."

Clearly her breezy conversational style attracted him, as he accepted an invitation to Bryanston Court for dinner in early 1932, enjoying the evening so much that he did not leave until four in the morning. He became a regular visitor to the Simpsons' apartment, afternoon tea turning into cocktails ending up with long, lingering dinners. As he later recalled of Wallis's skills as a hostess, "The talk was witty and crackled with new ideas that were bubbling up furiously in the world of Hitler, Mussolini, Stalin and the New Deal. Wallis was extraordinarily well informed, her conversation deft and amusing."

He was not the only admirer, Spanish diplomat Tiger Bermejillo acknowledging the breadth of her general knowledge and her ability to draw guests into the conversation.

In turn, the Simpsons became regular visitors to Fort Belvedere, helping with the gardening, walking the prince's dogs, Cora and Jaggs, and, in time, arranging menus. During one weekend in January 1933 Wallis, Thelma, and the prince's brother and sister-in-law, the Duke and Duchess of York, went skating on a nearby frozen lake, to great hilarity. It would prove to be a significant date.

The Simpsons were there twice in February and once in March, and such was her growing proximity to the Prince of Wales that when Wallis travelled to America in March she received a bon voyage radiogram signed "Edward P." That same month she wrote: "If the Prince was in any way drawn to me I was unaware of his interest."

If she was, somewhat disingenuously, unaware of his interest, George V was alerted to her presence at the Fort—much to the embarrassment of the king's daughter-in-law, the Duchess of York. She found herself in social difficulties when she wrote to her mother-in-law, Queen Mary, denying that she had ever met "the lady." Her agitated letter, which she penned on August 1, 1933, was written five months after she and her husband had been skating with Wallis and Thelma.

Her missive to the queen was a result of a previous encounter with the king during the Cowes regatta. He had quizzed her about the fact that a "certain lady" had been at the Fort when she and the duke were present. At the time he had a good mind to discuss this matter with his eldest son, the implication being that he should not parade his mistress in front of his family.

She wrote that she hoped that the king had avoided a quarrel, continuing: "Relations are already a little difficult when naughty ladies are brought in, and up to now we have not met and I would like to remain quite outside the whole affair."

Queen Mary soothed her agitated daughter-in-law, writing that the king had not mentioned the guest list at Belvedere and so avoided a quarrel. She continued: "I confess I hope it will not occur again for you ought not to meet [David's] lady in his own house, that is too much of a <u>bad</u> thing!!!"

The exchange is noteworthy as it suggests that the intimate royal circle were fully aware that Wallis Simpson, rather than Thelma Furness, was regarded as the Prince of Wales's main object of affection.

The accepted version of events is that Thelma met with Wallis at the Ritz hotel in January 1934—nearly a year later. Over lunch Thelma, who was about to sail to New York to see friends, asked her American friend to look after "her little man" as he would be lonely. When she returned some two months later Wallis had, as Thelma acidly remarked in her memoirs, "looked after him exceedingly well." Another interpretation is that she was simply giving Wallis her seal of approval. During her New York stay she enjoyed a very public liaison with the legendary lothario Prince Aly Khan, the sexually precocious twenty-three-year-old son of the Aga Khan. Hardly the behaviour of a woman in the throes of passion for the Prince of Wales. After all, she had heard about the advances the prince had made towards her sister Consuelo when he was in Buenos Aires. It seems that episode had probably marked the beginning of the long goodbye.

Certainly, if the king was aware of his son's illicit romance with a married American, then it seems unlikely that Thelma Furness was in the dark. While Thelma was away, Edward telephoned Wallis frequently, called at the Simpsons' apartment a couple of times a week, and singled her out for dancing at the Fort, where the Simpsons were regular weekend guests.

The traditional interpretation pinpoints Wallis's ascendancy to May 1934—rather than a year earlier—when Edward invited Thelma to dinner at the Fort after she returned from New York. Her one-time lover was polite but distant, and at dinner she noticed that the prince and Wallis seemed to have developed little private jokes. When she saw Wallis playfully slapping the prince's hand when he picked up a piece of salad with his fingers, she realized she was surplus to requirements. All the while, Ernest looked on silently, prompting the diarist Chips Channon to describe them as "Menage Simpson," implying a consenting three-way relationship.

The ousting of Lady Furness by the American was the talk of London society. "Our little Prince is not so nice," one titled

Chelsea lady said. "His treatment of Thelma and Freda [Dudley Ward] is appalling. Just overnight—bang! No letter, no nothing. Just silence." It was particularly galling for Freda who, during their sixteen-year relationship, had been worshipped by the prince in a way that was, according to Mountbatten, "religious, almost holy." Now the royal iconoclast was prostrating himself at the shrine of Mrs. Simpson. At least one royal castoff enjoyed revenge of sorts, Lady Furness describing exactly why, when she was in bed with her royal lover, she had called him "my little man."

It was not just the king who was baffled by his son's behaviour. The smart set were equally perplexed. Wallis was neither gorgeous nor glamorous, had no title, standing, or lineage, nor any money or land to speak of. She was certainly not PLU—people like us.

When George V declared that his family could marry their English subjects he never for a moment considered his son would be consorting with a twice-married American of the second rank. Of course, Americans had been infiltrating the British aristocracy for well over a century, but for the most part they were wealthy, swapping weighty dowries for lofty titles. Gladys, the Duchess of Marlborough, a fellow American and a renowned beauty who had dazzled European society at the turn of the century, was dismissive. "She was just a common little American making her way in the world. She was amusing and had a good sense of fashion. Nothing more." Society photographer Cecil Beaton, himself the son of a wealthy London timber merchant, was equally scornful. "[Wallis's] voice was raucous and appalling. I thought her awful, common, vulgar, strident, a second-rate American with no charm." The prince's equerry, John Aird, considered the Simpsons to be the worst sort of Americans, pushy social climbers without breeding or money. "They seem terrible at first and this feeling does not decrease as one sees them more often."

As Wallis's relationship with Edward intensified, so did her money worries. The trapdoor was yawning open. "Business foul," recorded Wallis. "The money question is serious and we have to give up the car and pull our horns in in every way." The tidal wave from the financial crash had now swamped Ernest's shipping business, forcing stringent economies. Out went the chauffeur-driven car, holidays abroad, lavish entertaining at home, and social outings. They even tried renting out their £600-a-year apartment.

Ironically Ernest's business difficulties merely served to draw the prince and Wallis closer together, as he had to cry off numerous social outings to attend to his company. When it got to the point that he could not afford Wallis's train fare and outfits to attend Royal Ascot, the prince promptly paid and invited her to join the racing party at the Fort for the week. Similarly, Ernest was on a business trip to America during the summer of 1934 when the prince invited the Simpsons to join him for a sailing holiday setting out from Biarritz, his favourite French resort. Her aunt Bessie, Mrs. Merryman, came as her chaperone and could see "in his every glance" that Edward was in love with her. "I can see no happy outcome to such a situation," she warned. As Wallis later admitted of that holiday: "We crossed the line that marks the indefinable boundary between friendship and love."

It didn't hurt that he quietly gave her a diamond-and-emerald charm at the end of the voyage, the first of many gifts of jewels, clothes, and other treasures. As much as she began to find his puppy-dog attentions "exhausting," it was difficult for a woman who had had nothing to refuse such princely largesse. She had clawed herself out of the dark hole of penury before. Wallis did not want to go through that exercise again. As her biographer Anne Sebba observes: "Insecurity at the thought of losing everything, the deepest of all her many fears, was now corrosive; she was becoming mean and grasping in preparation for the day the clocks stopped."

As the king and his court looked on aghast, they realized that a line had been crossed, and they thought and feared the worst—of the prince but particularly the Simpsons. The king did what he could to limit their proximity to the heir—at least on official and family occasions. Several months after that fateful cruise, in November 1934, the king made his views perfectly apparent at an evening reception to celebrate the wedding of Edward's younger brother Prince George, Duke of Kent, to Princess Marina of Greece. Even though the Simpsons had met Prince George at the Fort on numerous occasions and always enjoyed his company, the king scratched their names from the invitation list. It was only after Edward's personal intervention that they were admitted. Adorned with jewels from her royal lover and a borrowed tiara, she was duly presented to the queen. Afterwards the king, furious at "that woman" invading his kingdom, gave orders that the Simpsons were barred from all functions commemorating the 1935 Silver Jubilee as well as the Royal Enclosure at Ascot. Biographer Kenneth Rose's ringing phrase encapsulated the opinion of the king and his courtiers: "George V thought her unsuitable as a friend, disreputable as a mistress and unthinkable as a queen." His private secretary went further, describing "that woman" as a witch and a vampire.

A greedy vampire who was working as a double act with her social-climbing husband, trying to suck every cent from the naïve, feckless prince who really at his age—he was now forty—should have known better. It was easy to assume that Wallis was a gold-digger with a brazen eye for the main chance and an "unattractive and common" husband who was prepared to turn a blind eye to his wife's behaviour.

When Lady Diana Cooper was a guest at the Fort in October 1934, she described Wallis as "glittering and dripping in new jewels and clothes," jewels from the prince that the unfortunate Ernest had to pay to insure. That Christmas and New Year, Edward was said to have given her £110,000 (£7 million or $11 million today) worth of jewels. A few months later the king was told that his son was giving Wallis an allowance of £6,000 a year (£370,000 or

$600,000 today). This was alarmingly different from his previous liaisons. He may have given Lady Furness and Freda Ward gifts, but nothing on this scale. At this rate the House of Windsor would very quickly become the House of Simpson.

Ernest was not left out either, the prince using his influence to ensure his smooth entry into Edward's own Masonic lodge. When other members complained that it would break the rule about Masons sleeping with other members' wives, the Prince of Wales gave a solemn pledge that nothing was going on. The king and many others thought otherwise, and he sent his private secretary, Lord Wigram, to confront the prince about his choice of companion. It was a dusty interview, the prince professing astonishment that anyone could take offence at his friends, describing Wallis as a "charming, cultivated woman." The word "blackmail" was now being uttered, though Queen Mary subscribed to the theory, which she discussed with psychologist Dr. William Brown, that Edward had been hypnotized by the American adventuress.

Such was the mounting concern about the prince's irresponsible behaviour that the king, in consultation with Prime Minister Baldwin, secretly agreed to take the extraordinary step of calling in Scotland Yard to monitor the Simpsons' movements.

It was a desperate throw of the dice with potentially dire consequences. Relations between the king and his eldest son, already strained and distant, would have been utterly severed had the prince caught wind of this covert surveillance of his paramour. During June and July 1935, as Britain celebrated the King's Silver Jubilee, the Simpsons were watched and followed every day by a team of undercover agents led by the Yard's ace detective, Superintendent Albert Canning. A Special Branch veteran of operations against the Irish Republican Army and the suffragettes, Canning had the reputation of having a phenomenal memory for faces.

Superintendent Canning's report, which was delivered to Metropolitan Police commissioner Sir Philip Game on July 3, 1935, made alarming reading, his allegations as pungent as they were shocking. Not only was it clear that the Prince of Wales was having an affair with Wallis Simpson, but the American was two-timing him and her husband with a third man, Ford car salesman Guy Marcus Trundle.

During his investigation Canning discovered that Trundle, then thirty-six, was a vicar's son born in York who was also married. Moreover, he had a reputation as a well-known rake and he lived just a short walk from the Simpsons' apartment, at 18 Bruton Street in Mayfair, next door to where the Duke of York's eldest daughter, Princess Elizabeth, later Queen Elizabeth II, was born.

He was a classic gigolo, described as a "very charming adventurer, very good looking, well bred and an excellent dancer." Not only did Trundle meet Mrs. Simpson "quite openly" at informal social gatherings; Canning noted that "secret meetings are made by appointment when intimate relations take place." As both parties were married, Canning did not describe how and where they found suitable accommodation for the unlikely lovers to consummate their illicit affair.

There was more. A grateful Mrs. Simpson had given her London lover money and expensive presents, a charge that perplexes her biographers, who characterize Wallis as a "mean and acquisitive" woman, more used to receiving than giving presents.

Now juggling two lovers, a nervous Wallis, reported Canning, had admitted she was concerned that her husband was suspicious of her relationships with other men and feared that it may "cause trouble" with the Prince of Wales. The prince was also watched and followed, seen accompanying Mrs. Simpson on shopping expeditions to antique stores in South Kensington. The resourceful Canning came so close to the couple that he was able to state with certainty that they were on "very affectionate terms" and called one another "darling."

As for the cuckold in this marital nest, Ernest Simpson was

described as a man of the "bounder type" who was given to boasting to acquaintances that he expected "high honours" once Edward became king. For this naturalized Englishman, it would be the summit of his ambition if he was made a baron, a rather curious choice of title as it was an honour with little rank or standing.

Standing outside Bryanston Court watching the comings and goings, Canning took a dim view of the Simpsons' social circle. Among their visitors, he noted Sir Oswald Mosley, the former Labour politician and now leader of the Fascist Party in Britain; drug addict and the Duke of Kent's one-time lover Alice "Kiki" Preston; and society hostess Lady Emerald Cunard, whose daughter "the notorious Nancy," Canning pointed out, was "very partial to coloured men and who created a sensation some years ago by taking up residence in the Negro quarter of New York." (In fact she was a poet, publisher, journalist, and tireless supporter of the disenfranchised, who compiled an anthology of African American culture.)

Whatever the subsequent caveats about Canning's report—particularly the veracity of Wallis's affair with Trundle—when it landed on Commissioner Game's desk it was taken at face value. Such was the Special Branch detective's reputation that he was subsequently placed in charge of the security arrangements for the crucial visit by King George VI and Queen Elizabeth to Canada and the United States in 1939. He eventually became head of the Special Branch and was awarded the MBE (Member of the British Empire) for his diligent service to Crown and country.

Sex, money, drugs, and Fascist politics—what was the Prince of Wales getting himself into? It had long been accepted by his family and courtiers that Edward was an irresponsible Peter Pan figure, prone to childish whims, stubborn in his misplaced affections, and heedless of the consequences to himself or the Crown, but his embrace of this seedy milieu was of a different order, with wide-reaching consequences for the reputation of the monarchy.

The prince's treasurer, Admiral Sir Lionel Halsey, suspected that the future king was being taken for a ride by both Mr. and Mrs. Simpson. "I also told HM [His Majesty] that in my opinion Mrs Simpson and her husband were hand in glove in getting all they could out of HRH," he noted in July 1935, shortly after Canning's report was written. In short order, senior advisors in both Buckingham Palace and Downing Street would be using the same phrase about Ernest and Wallis Simpson: "high-class blackmailers." Even the prince's own lawyer, the normally phlegmatic Walter Monckton, was moved to exclaim that this affair "smacked of blackmail upon an extravagant basis."

The case against Mr. and Mrs. Simpson was building to the point where senior Downing Street advisors considered deporting the couple. They were already suspected of blackmailing the prince, and it was but a short leap to wonder if they were members of a Nazi spy nest based at Bryanston Court. It transpired that the Simpsons were not the only occupants of the apartment block being watched by Britain's undercover police.

Since 1928 secret watchers employed by MI5, the internal security service, as well as the Foreign Office, had been monitoring the movements and the mail of the Simpsons' neighbour Princess Stephanie von Hohenlohe-Waldenburg-Schillingsfürst, the Jewish daughter of a middle-class Viennese family who married into the royal echelons of the Austro-Hungarian empire.

They were concerned that she was a political intriguer, probably a Nazi spy with direct access to Hitler himself. "She is perhaps the only woman who can exercise any influence on him," noted one secret service report. In the febrile nationalist atmosphere in postwar Europe, where spies were believed to be lurking behind every corner, the much-travelled and well-connected princess, who numbered the Kaiser's eldest son, Crown Prince Wilhelm, among her friends, was a natural target, described in newspaper headlines as a "vamp," a "German spy," and a "political adventuress"—language remarkably similar to that used for Wallis Simpson.

With her linguistic skills, relentless charm, and social connections, the princess was much more than a vapid member of the international demi-monde. In the fractured, volatile atmosphere of 1930s Europe, where talk of war hugged the horizon, she quickly became the queen of the exclusive group of well-heeled go-betweens, those royals, aristocrats, and influential businessmen who were the first line of discreet contact between wary, war-weary nations.

It was the task of "my dear princess"—Hitler's affectionate term for Princess Stephanie—to court the well born, the high, and the mighty and convince them of Germany's peaceful intentions, pointing out the injustice of the Treaty of Versailles, Germany's need to revert to its natural borders and to have the freedom to redevelop its armed forces, free of treaty restrictions. She was one of the Führer's voices in London salons, making the seductive and compelling argument that a powerful, properly armed Germany was a bulwark against the Soviet menace. Hitler, needless to say, did not know she was Jewish until much later.

Hitler and his henchmen were prepared to use every means possible to bend international opinion to favour Nazi demands. He convinced German royals and industrialists to go forth and multiply his word. A key target was the Prince of Wales, the German leadership conflating, wrongly, the prince's position at the apex of society with equal political influence. When Hitler stumbled in his plan for Edward to marry a young German princess, he came to depend on Princess Stephanie to deliver a pro-German sovereign to the throne of England. She was his secret weapon in the battle for the political heart and mind of the future king. Her title gave her access, while her vivacious personality and flirtatious charm provided an effective means of persuasion.

The *New York Mirror* described how she exerted her influence in London:

> Her apartment has become the focus for those British aristocrats who have a friendly stance towards Nazi Germany. Her soirees are the talk of the town. Prominently displayed in her drawing room is a huge portrait of Hitler.

Besides her neighbours Wallis and Ernest Simpson, the Prince of Wales, his brother George, Duke of Kent, Lord and Lady Londonderry, the Duke of Westminster, Lady Oxford, and Lady Emerald Cunard were on the first page of Princess Stephanie's little black book. She was described in newspaper reports as "Europe's number one secret diplomat" and "Hitler's mysterious courier," but Britain's secret service saw her differently, viewing her as "a very active and dangerous agent for the Nazis." It was a role that resulted in Hitler presenting her with the Gold Badge of the Nazi Party for her services to the cause.

It was not long before Establishment minds wondered if Princess Stephanie and Wallis Simpson were working hand in glove, Bryanston Court a nest of intrigue and plotting. A witch, a vampire, and a high-class blackmailer. As tensions mounted throughout Europe, Wallis was soon being spoken of openly as a Nazi spy.

CHAPTER FOUR

Seduced by von Ribbentrop's Dimple

To the victor the spoils. Wallis Simpson may have been looked upon with disdain by the king, his courtiers, and his circle of landowning friends, men of ancient lineage and impeccable deportment like Lord Curzon, Lord Derby, and the Duke of Devonshire. No matter, once it became clear to London society that she was the latest squeeze of the Prince of Wales, it was not long before the girl from Baltimore, who had learned to curtsey only a short time before, had many of the great and the good bowing and scraping at her feet.

The Simpsons' arrival in London society coincided with a new generation of transatlantic hostesses who vied with one another to preside over the most glittering balls and dinners where conversation sparkled along with the diamond tiaras. Social leaders like Laura Corrigan, Nancy Astor, Emerald Cunard, Henry Channon, and Elsa Maxwell were the hedonistic arrivistes who dominated the world of gossip, spiky chatter, and rumour that passed for polite society. While the Prince of Wales enjoyed these gatherings, the king and his men retreated from the social fray and looked down from their broad acres at this metropolitan mélange of waspish, well-heeled sophisticates. Grandees doubtless shared Lord Crawford's view: "Personally I try to keep aloof from the rich Jews and Americans and I don't want to be mixed up with Asiatics."

As an American with a Jewish husband, Wallis was never going to win over the traditional English aristocracy—even if she ever wanted to. Very soon she found herself reigning over her own court, where the principal aim was to keep the Prince of Wales entertained and amused. Her partner in this merry but demanding venture was the most provocative, exciting, and lavish hostess in London, Lady Emerald Cunard.

Twittering, sniping, and extravagantly dressed, Maud "Emerald" Cunard was married to Sir Bache Cunard, heir to the eponymous shipping line, and was for a decade the mistress of conductor Sir Thomas Beecham, consistently championing his musical projects. Cutting, occasionally cruel, and always controversial—"Christmas is only for servants" was one of her *mots*—Emerald brought excitement and challenge to the lavish parties at her London home, 7 Grosvenor Square. A native Californian who admired Hitler, adored opera, and loved poetry, Lady Cunard encouraged the diplomats and politicians at her table into embarrassing indiscretions. It was such a feature of her evenings that it prompted war leader David Lloyd George to describe her as "the most dangerous woman in London." Others considered her brilliance and vivacity as intoxicating as the champagne that always flowed freely. It kept her ahead of the social pack, the notorious and those of note always pleased to accept an invitation to her salon.

She was relentless and enthusiastic in the promotion into London society of her New Best Friend, fellow American Wallis Simpson. It got to the point where playwright Noel Coward pronounced himself "sick" of invitations to her home for so-called "quiet" suppers with the Prince of Wales and Wallis Simpson. While Emerald hoped that by championing Wallis's cause she would, in the next reign, be appointed Mistress of the Robes, the senior lady-in-waiting at court, others considered her behaviour irresponsible. Queen Mary, deaf to talk that her eldest son was the master of his own misfortunes, considered Lady Cunard to have played a very mischievous and damaging role in convincing Mrs. Simpson that she had any standing with or was held in any regard by the ruling class. That assumption encouraged the Prince of Wales to think that Mrs. Simpson would one day be accepted by the English aristocracy and the wider public. "I fear she has done David a great deal of harm as there is no doubt she was great friends with Mrs Simpson and gave parties for her," noted the queen sadly.

Emerald's rival American hostess Nancy Astor, the first woman member of Parliament, was more trenchant in her criticism, not only taking a dim view of the lady from Baltimore but also blaming Lady Cunard for encouraging the romance. The mistress of Cliveden, the impressive stately home in Berkshire that was the setting for expansive weekend parties and dinners involving the most famous literary and political figures of the day, became "terribly indignant" when she first learned that Emerald had invited the prince and his mistress to her home for dinner. Not only did she consider her social rival "bad company" and a "disintegrating influence," she believed strongly that she encouraged the pro-Nazi leanings of the Prince of Wales.

It also counted against Lady Cunard that she actively promoted Hitler's favourite, Princess Stephanie, into high society, or as an MI5 report stated: "She has . . . succeeded in worming her way into certain society circles where she speaks favourably of the present regime in Germany."

Ironically it was the "Cliveden Set" that was seen by contemporaries as a "shadow Foreign Office" where pro-German politicians and diplomats met in secret conclave.

Among the political classes, Lady Astor was viewed as a woman "fighting bravely for Hitler and Mussolini," although in her defence, she used these social occasions to tackle guests like Hitler's Special Commissioner for Disarmament, Joachim von Ribbentrop, about the failings of National Socialism. At their first meeting she asked the German politician how people could take Hitler seriously while he persisted in wearing Charlie Chaplin's moustache.

When von Ribbentrop was guest of honour at Grosvenor Square in June 1935, Emerald Cunard was no less provocative, cooing: "Tell us, dearest Excellency, why does Herr Hitler dislike the Jews?" As far as she was political, Emerald, unlike her actively left-wing daughter Nancy, whom she loathed, was conservative and subscribed to the mainstream view that Hitler was a "good thing" for Germany. Such was her enthusiasm for the Nazi cause that the American ambassador to London, Robert Worth Bingham, described the Cunard set as the "pro-German cabal."

In her attitude Lady Cunard was little different from a significant proportion of the ruling elite. During what historian John Wheeler-Bennett called the "respectable years" of the Nazi regime, most observers preferred to believe that Hitler adhered to the principles of peace and respect for national borders and the sovereignty of other nations. His was seen as an orderly, modern government with the emphasis on youth and creating jobs for the hungry working man. While there were warning signs, especially lurid stories of Nazi savagery told by fleeing Jewish Germans, few imagined the horrors to come.

Moreover, Lady Cunard was more than a little infatuated with the well-tailored, impeccably mannered, and mechanically charming von Ribbentrop. That he was notoriously pompous, humourless, and self-important merely added to his comedic fascination, Emerald's barbs bouncing off this German Zeppelin. Society diarist and fellow American Chips Channon captured the social by-play between von Ribbentrop, Emerald, and Wallis over dinner, noting in his diary: "Much gossip about the Prince of Wales' alleged Nazi leanings; he is alleged to have been influenced by

Emerald Cunard who is rather *eprise* [in love with] Herr Ribbentrop through Mrs Simpson."

"Emerald had been intriguing on behalf of the German cause,"
he noted, "inspired by Herr Ribbentrop's dimple."

However, it was not Lady Cunard's idle flirtation that had
tongues wagging in Berlin, Washington, and London, but the
attention Herr von Ribbentrop paid that evening to Mrs. Simpson
and his subsequent chivalrous, somewhat overly solicitous behaviour, sending seventeen carnations—some say roses—every day to
her apartment at Bryanston Court.

It was an association that was to haunt her at the time and
dog her for the rest of her life. She had met von Ribbentrop on
a previous occasion when the German ambassador to London,
Leopold von Hoesch, had organized a dinner to introduce Hitler's
representative to the future king. Even von Ribbentrop, normally
at daggers drawn with the urbane and sophisticated von Hoesch,
was impressed. The ambassador had gone to great lengths to make
the prince feel at home. Knowing that, like him, he loved gypsy
music, he hired a famous gypsy band from a Hungarian restaurant
on Regent Street in central London to entertain the intimate party.
Wallis always enjoyed these dinners with the German ambassador,
finding him witty, amusing, and cultured. In turn, von Ribbentrop
was suitably charmed and engaged by the American. At some point
he asked Constance Spry, the famed florist and friend of Wallis,
to make up a spray of flowers every day which were to be delivered
to her central London apartment. A former assistant, known only
as Sheila, told reporter John Edwards that it was her job to deliver
bouquets of long-stemmed roses or carnations.

This secret soon leaked out and first became the talk of the
German embassy in London and then of the German chancel-
lery in Berlin. Ambassador von Hoesch was unable to discover the
significance of the number seventeen and thought it was "the way
of the businessman."

The Prince of Wales's cousin the Duke of Württemberg, who was on good terms with his aunt Queen Mary, other royals, and senior British politicians had quite another explanation. The duke, who became a Benedictine monk known as Father Odo and an opponent of the Nazis, would later tell FBI agents that von Ribbentrop was Wallis's lover and that the number seventeen represented the occasions they had slept together. He further related a scurrilous story suggesting that the prince was impotent and only the skills of Mrs. Simpson could "satisfactorily gratify the duke's sexual desires."

It was not just in London that stories about Wallis and von Ribbentrop gained traction. In Berlin, too, the rumours went right to the top, Hitler questioning his foreign affairs advisor about the nature of his relationship with the prince's mistress. The Führer's evident curiosity regarding von Ribbentrop's love life delighted his many enemies inside the Nazi hierarchy and within the diplomatic corps, where von Hoesch was not the only one to refer to him, sotto voce, as "the fool."

Unlike Ambassador von Hoesch, who was independently wealthy, von Ribbentrop had purchased his "von" nomenclature—signifying his aristocratic background—following his marriage to Anna Henkell, the wealthy daughter of Germany's leading producer of sparkling white wine. As Propaganda Minister Joseph Goebbels remarked, von Ribbentrop had bought his name and married his money.

Born to an officer-class family, von Ribbentrop proved himself proficient at foreign languages, a gifted violinist, and a first-class tennis player. Though he was undoubtedly vain and pretentious he was, unlike the other leaders of the Third Reich, well travelled, an urbane cosmopolitan politician among a party of rabid nationalists. His sophistication, though, was only on the surface. While he spoke perfect English and dressed like a country squire, he had little understanding or appreciation of the English psyche. Princess Stephanie, who mixed with all the Nazi leaders, believed that von Ribbentrop's notions of Britain were "puerile, ignorant of all deeper issues, and often tragically misleading."

Yet it was in this snob and social climber that Hitler placed his faith, tasking him to discover "what influential Englishmen thought about National Socialism." So began frequent excursions to Britain, where von Ribbentrop, as self-important as he was overbearing, mixed in high society, making friends who would support the Führer. It was his belief that by insinuating himself into British high society, seeking out influential support for Germany, he could circumvent the Foreign Office, who were sceptical of any entente with Germany, especially as it would anger their French allies.

In November 1934, for example, von Ribbentrop spent three weeks in London, meeting the movers and shakers. He briefed Princess Stephanie, met with press baron and Nazi supporter Lord Rothermere, and dined with many others, including former foreign secretary Sir Austen Chamberlain, playwright George Bernard Shaw, and the Archbishop of Canterbury, Cosmo Gordon Lang, whom von Ribbentrop described as "a kind of English National Socialist." The cleric found him "most genial and friendly."

His most critical meeting came months later when, courtesy of Ambassador von Hoesch, he first encountered the Prince of Wales and Mrs. Simpson. Whatever the subsequent sexual shenanigans between von Ribbentrop and Mrs. Simpson, von Ribbentrop's primary task was to encourage Edward to take the hand of friendship proffered by the new German regime. He proved to be a willing acolyte.

As von Ribbentrop helpfully pointed out in a telegram to Hitler: "After all he is half German." In spite of the First World War, the prince, who spoke German fluently, retained an abiding affection for the country where so many of his family lived.

"Every drop of blood in my veins is German," he once told Diana Mitford, an adoring friend of Hitler. He looked back on the trips he made to Germany as a student with evident pleasure, describing the Fatherland as a "prosperous, industrious and agree-able country. It echoes with work and song."

He shuddered at the very idea of another European war, had little faith in France, a country he believed to be feeble and degenerate, despised the Soviet Communists for what they did to his godfather Czar Nicholas and his family, and had a wide-eyed admiration for Hitler's efforts, particularly the vigor the National Socialists had shown in providing work and housing for the working man—a cause close to his heart.

Months before he met with von Ribbentrop, Edward was confiding to Count Albert Mensdorff, the former Austrian ambassador, that he had much sympathy with the Nazi regime, a position the ambassador found "interesting and significant."

As he and his father's good friend commemorated Armistice Day on November 11, 1933, the prince told him: "Of course it is the only thing to do, we will have to come to it, as we are in great danger from the communists here. I hope and believe we shall never fight a war again, but if so we must be on the winning side, and that will be German, not the French."

He consistently saw the bigger menace to peace and security to emanate from Russia rather than Germany and strongly believed that the winner of any conflict between Britain and Germany would be the Soviets. It was his settled view, expressed in writing to his friend Herman Rogers when war broke out: "God knows how it's all going to end and a lot depends on how long it lasts. I only hope I shall eventually prove to be wrong in my contention that the victors of the contest will be the Soviets."

As for his own role in this unfolding political drama, the prince took his cue from his grandfather, Edward VII, who had a taste for fine women, splendid cigars, and political interference. The prince wrote about his reign in favourable terms, describing Edward VII as a king "who enjoyed the society of witty men and beautiful women, who relished foreign travel and the savour of high diplomacy." While Edward's constitutional position was to stay above the political fray, in his mind's eye he saw himself shaping and massaging foreign policy, using his position and influence to make a difference. He had every expectation that his views would be taken seriously. He was more widely travelled than any politician alive, had met more leaders and spoken to more people. He considered himself popular and in touch with the man in the street. His was a voice that should be heard.

Lurking at the back of his emerging ideology was an authoritarian streak, a flirtation with the idea of a dictator king. It is difficult to assess how seriously he took the concept but others, independently, duly noted the prince's predilections. The influential Rothermere journalist and editor Colin Brooks jotted in his diary: "The suggestion has been made in many quarters that he could, if he wished, make himself the Dictator of the Empire." Interestingly, Chips Channon used similar language to describe the prince's shifting political stance, observing that Edward was going "the dictator way and is pro-German. I shouldn't be surprised if he aimed at making himself a mild dictator—a difficult enough task for an English King."

For a while he thought Britain's Fascist Blackshirt movement "a good thing" and, as Superintendent Canning observed as he watched the activity at Bryanston Court, Sir Oswald Mosley, the leader of the British Union of Fascists and a fanatical monarchist, was a visitor to the Simpsons' home.

Mosley himself used the prince's name in an attempt to drum up funds, telling supporters that the Prince of Wales was sympathetic to the Fascist cause and on one occasion saying that his name might be used to get money out of Lady Houston, the snobbish, eccentric right-wing millionairess. There was even a suggestion that Mrs. Simpson's society friend, decorator and hostess Sybil Colefax, who joined Lady Cunard in launching Wallis into society, might obtain subscriptions to the Fascist cause on a commission basis.

If the prince wanted to learn more about Mosley's gang he did not have to look far. His colourful equerry, Fruity Metcalfe, was married to Lady Alexandra Curzon, who was known as Baba Blackshirt as her sister Lady Cynthia was married to Oswald Mosley and Lady Alexandra and her courtier husband were active members of the January Club, an upper-class society set up by Mosley in 1934 to encourage members of the Establishment to join his fledgling party. They also attended at least one Fascist Party dinner, held at the Savoy in May 1934. Interestingly, in March 1935 the January Club changed its name to the Windsor Club.

As for the so-called Jewish question, the prince was, like many of his class, instinctively anti-Semitic—Buckingham Palace did not employ Jews or Catholics in positions of any prominence in the Royal Household until well into Queen Elizabeth II's reign. There is, though, no evidence to suggest he ever came close to agreeing with the policy of genocide—unlike some active British Fascists. As early as 1935 Midlands councillor Arnold Leese, founder of the Imperial Fascist League, advocated gas chambers as an efficient solution to the Jewish problem. It earned him a jail term.

As far as the prince was concerned, the so-called Jewish question was Hitler's problem and had nothing to do with Anglo-German relations. He outlined his thoughts to the Kaiser's grandson, Prince Louis Ferdinand, a strong-willed young man who had chosen to work as a mechanic for Henry Ford in Detroit to really see how the other half lived. Even though the young prince, who spent the summer of 1933 in England as a guest of diplomat Sir Robert Bruce Lockhart, had little sympathy for Hitler, when they met at Edward's London home, St. James's Palace, to discuss current affairs, the future king was disarmingly unguarded in his comments. In his diary entry the following day Bruce Lockhart recorded:

> The Prince of Wales was quite pro-Hitler and said it was no business of ours to interfere in Germany's internal affairs

either re Jews or re anything else and added that dictators are very popular these days and that we might want one in England before long.

When the exiled Kaiser wrote to Bruce Lockhart thanking him for arranging the meeting, he expressed the hope that it would further German-English relations:

> *The remark of the Prince of Wales that we have a right to deal with our affairs as we deem it right, shows sound judgement. Prince Louis Ferdinand would no doubt have agreed with him on this point.*

It was no surprise then that the furtherance of Anglo-German relations was prominent on the menu at the dinner meeting between the Prince of Wales and Herr von Ribbentrop, the German diplomat instantly grasping that Edward was instinctively sympathetic towards the Fatherland and open to new ideas to encourage friendship and peace between these two former adversaries.

With the gypsy music playing in the background, von Ribbentrop had the perfect opening, discussing Anglo-German friendship in the context of reuniting the soldiers from both sides in exchange visits. He even had a name for his hobby horse—"bridge between the war veterans"—a phrase he had used consistently in conversations with European diplomats and politicians. His argument was simple and seductive: Organize war veterans to visit their German counterparts and thus help heal the wounds caused by the conflict. He left unstated the underlying aim of this policy, which was to give the impression of an equal partnership between the victor and the vanquished and thus weaken the shackles, both financial and military, imposed by the Treaty of Versailles.

The prince took up the idea with gusto. In June 1935 he made a speech to the ex-servicemen of the British Legion at London's

Albert Hall, where he articulated ideas that bore remarkable similarities to those of the German diplomat. Proposing that a group of Legion members should visit Germany in a show of friendship, he told the audience: "I feel there would be no more suitable body of men to stretch forth the hand of friendship to the Germans than we ex-Servicemen."

Naturally it was an approach taken up with enthusiasm by the Nazi hierarchy. At a rally of 200,000 in Nuremberg, Hermann Göring hailed the prince: "He can be sure the German front soldier and the German people grasp most eagerly the hand offered them."

The first delegation was received with open arms, the ex-servicemen treated like homecoming heroes. They were, according to one witness, even taken to a concentration camp at Dachau, during which time the well-fed guards took the place of the inmates, who were herded below ground. It was a prelude to many other visits, one headed by the prince's German cousin and ardent Nazi, Carl Eduard, Duke of Saxe-Coburg and Gotha. The scheme, according to von Ribbentrop's biographer Dr. Paul Schwarz, proved to be "one of the cleverest and cheapest ways to make friends for Nazi Germany in peace-loving conciliatory Britain."

Prince Henry of Reuss reflected Hitler's appreciation in a letter of thanks to the Prince of Wales. "All of us know perfectly well that You in Your exposed position would never have taken a step which would not have been felt deeply by yourself—and that's a good sport."

For his pains the prince was summoned to Buckingham Palace for a dressing-down by the king. "How often have I told you, my dear boy?" the king asked him. "Never mix in politics, especially where foreign affairs are concerned." Not only had he handed the Nazi regime a propaganda coup but he had irritated the French and affected sensitive negotiations regarding the Anglo-German naval treaty. Even those with no skin in the game could see that the prince had been cleverly outmanoeuvred, Ambassador Bingham now describing him as "the German protagonist."

For his part, Edward was angry that a non-political goodwill gesture—he later claimed that the friendship speech was the brainchild of the British Legion chairman—had been grievously misinterpreted. "It seemed to settle nothing; British foreign policy seemed paralyzed," he concluded, the episode reinforcing his growing belief that what he said and what he did could transform official thinking.

A further response to his father's admonition revealed the inner child. Shortly after Edward returned from Buckingham Palace, Wallis's cousin, who was staying at Bryanston Court, reported that the prince was "wearing a German helmet and goose stepping around the living room, for what reason I cannot imagine."

His exhibition probably says more about his personal relations with his father, by now at a very low ebb, than their political differences. More united than divided them, the king and his son both firmly of the opinion that another war was simply unimaginable. During the summer of 1935, when the prince made his notorious British Legion speech, it was Italy, not Germany, that was creating waves inside the League of Nations over its invasion of Abyssinia. The king was not prepared to confront Mussolini over his aggression, declaring: "I will not have another war. *I will not.* The last one was none of my doing and if there is another one and we are threatened with being brought into it I will go to Trafalgar Square and wave a red flag myself sooner than this country to be brought in." His son went even further, favouring a martial injection of Fascist efficiency to shake up the medieval economy of Abyssinia, later Ethiopia.

With regard to Germany they had much in common, though the king was more considered in his view than his impulsive son. George Messersmith, the American ambassador to Austria who got to know Edward well, was certain that his pro-German sentiments were inherited from his father rather than his American mistress or others in his circle. He cited the fact that when Anthony Eden was appointed foreign secretary in December 1935, King George emphasized that the new man should not disturb "good relations with Germany." The king's attitude to Germany was rather more nuanced than his son's, making clear to the German ambassador von Hoesch his concerns about what he called "Jew baiting" and the pace of German rearmament. Historian Alan Palmer is perhaps overstating the divide when he wrote: "Over the Nazi phenomenon, as over so many questions, he was at loggerheads with his eldest son."

Visits to London by members of the German nobility, as well as the Silver Jubilee celebrations in 1935, gave the king an opportunity to hear first-hand about the atmosphere inside the Nazi Fatherland. It was not all sugarcoated. In the summer of 1934 Crown Prince Rupprecht von Bayern, head of the House of Wittelsbach, had lunch with King George V at Buckingham Palace. During their conversation, in which they talked about "reasonable rearmament" for Germany, the crown prince let it be known that he remained convinced that the Führer was insane. The Kaiser's grandson, Prince Louis Ferdinand, was another unbeliever.

Nazis or not, the war was still a barrier between the royal cousins, King George not writing to his cousin Grand Duke Ernst Ludwig of Hesse until 1935. His tone was placatory. "That horrible and unnecessary war had made no differences to my feelings for you." Fence mending between the House of Windsor and the royal houses of Germany was a feature of the time; Crown Prince Wilhelm, writing secretly to Lord Rothermere in June 1934, indicates the placatory mood: "I have always regretted it that until now all contacts between our family and the English Royal Family have remained entirely disrupted...My sympathies for your people have always been great."

While the King's Silver Jubilee was the perfect opportunity to draw a line concerning the past, it was still too soon for the Kaiser, ailing in exile at Doorn in the Netherlands, to come to London. His daughter-in-law Crown Princess Cecilie, her daughter Viktoria, and Hitler's favourite royal, Carl Eduard, Duke of Saxe-Coburg and Gotha, did attend the celebrations, while Ambassador von Hoesch hosted an elaborate party at the Carlton House Terrace embassy for his friends the Prince of Wales and Mrs. Simpson.

This quiet invasion by German nobility onto English shores was no coincidence. It was all part of the Führer's master plan. At home Hitler skillfully used the German aristocracy to give a patina of respectability to his radical regime and signal to the man in the street that the traditional ruling class had faith in the new order; so abroad the German royals, by the very fact that so many joined the Nazi Party, reassured sceptical European rulers—and royals—that it was largely business as usual in the Fatherland.

Soon after Hitler took power he encouraged wave after wave of German aristocrats to spread the word. In early 1934, for example, Reichsleiter Alfred Rosenberg, head of a Nazi Party foreign policy office, contacted Prince Gottfried zu Hohenlohe-Langenburg, whose mother was a cousin of George V, "in order to discuss drawing closer to the English royal house." While nothing came of the suggestion, the prince expressed his willingness to put his shoulder to the Nazi weal.

More officially, the Prince of Wales's cousin and friend Otto Christian von Bismarck was chargé d'affaires at the German embassy in London from 1928 until 1936. He later went on to Rome, where he was deputy to the ambassador. His place was taken by Prince Ludwig von Hessen-Darmstadt—known by his family as Prince Lu and a great-grandson of Queen Victoria—who was appointed honorary cultural attaché at the embassy.

The prince, who was a good friend and cousin of the Prince of Wales, the Duke of Kent, and the Mountbatten clan, was already working for the Büro Ribbentrop, the Nazi Party agency for foreign policy which shadowed and second-guessed the established diplomatic corps. According to von Ribbentrop's biographer John Weitz: "The prince was told by the ambassador to stay as close as possible to Buckingham Palace and to report any rumours about the durability and future of the king." Not just the king but his family, Prince Lu sending an assessment of the Prince of Wales's brother the Duke of Kent back to Berlin. It was not entirely flattering: "Duke of Kent. Very German friendly. Clearly against France. Not especially clever but well-informed. Entirely for strengthening German-English ties. His wife is equally anti-French."

Among other members of the German high nobility who worked to further the Nazi cause were Prince Adolf Friedrich von Mecklenburg—a member of the German delegation that met foreign secretary Lord Halifax in London in June 1939—and Princess Marie Elisabeth zu Wied and her younger sister Princess Benigna Victoria, who accompanied von Ribbentrop, Hitler's personal foreign emissary, on the now infamous "Swastika over Ulster" visit to Lord and Lady Londonderry at Mount Stewart in Northern Ireland in May 1936.

As historian John Costello pithily observed: "Not since the balmy days before World War One had so many of the leading names in the *Almanach de Gotha* appeared together at the London dinner tables. The Duchess of Brunswick, the daughter of the exiled Kaiser, the Prince and Princess von Bismarck, and a slew of counts and barons sipped champagne with emissaries from Berlin. The Nazi leaders were quick to seize the initiative and exploit the fascination of London society for aristocratic Fascism."

The Prince of Wales—and his younger brother Prince George— were amenable and amiable recipients of Nazi hospitality and largesse, enjoying the dinners and the conversation at the German embassy and elsewhere. Edward's brother the Duke of York was more cynical about the motivation behind this Nazi courtship. He would later tell Canadian premier Mackenzie King: "My own family relations in Germany have been used to spy and get particulars from other members of my family."

CHAPTER FIVE

——— ⚬❦⚬ ———

Courting the New King

He was terrified of Alois, his violent, alcoholic father, who would regularly beat him and his gentle mother, Klara, when he arrived home, fists swinging, from the *Biergarten*. A troubled adolescent, Adolf Hitler found refuge from his father's rages in the world of fantasy, dreaming of becoming a great artist. Later he would lose himself for a time in the make-believe constructed by Hollywood. Even as Führer he was fanatical about film, delaying meetings in order to watch new movies, which were usually procured by his propaganda minister Joseph Goebbels.

Disney cartoons were his favourite; he endlessly watched the antics of Mickey Mouse and *Snow White and the Seven Dwarfs*, which was based on a German fairy story. He was delighted when one Christmas Goebbels gave him a dozen Mickey Mouse films. As his henchman recorded: "He is very pleased and extremely happy for this treasure that will hopefully bring him much joy and relaxation."

Both men were quick to recognize the persuasive power of film, using the medium to promote nationalist pride and Nazi success. Hitler commissioned the brilliant female director Leni Riefenstahl to make the classic propaganda movie *Triumph of the Will*, which turned the 1934 Nazi Party rally in Nuremberg into a cinematic projection of the overwhelming strength and power of the reborn Fatherland. It later inspired Charlie Chaplin's 1940 parody, *The Great Dictator*.

Sometime in January 1936, when Hitler settled into his leather chair in his private cinema, he chose not to watch his normal diet of animated cartoons. For once he focused on a living person, Goebbels having provided him with film of the new king of England, Edward VIII, overseeing arrangements for his father's funeral, which was due to be held at Westminster Abbey. On January 20, 1936, at his beloved Sandringham, the life of George V had, in the words of his physician Lord Dawson of Penn, drawn peacefully to a close. His continued ill health and the stresses of his jubilee year had been too much to bear.

A new king, a new era, and a golden opportunity for Hitler to bring the new head of state firmly into his orbit. In the darkened screening room, the Führer carefully and intently watched the Pathé newsreel showing King Edward VIII, focused on the nervy mannerisms and uneasy demeanour of the new king, rather like a cat idly watching a mouse at play and lazily wondering how and when to pounce. As intriguing was the presence of Mrs. Wallis Simpson, in the background but noticeably present at this most intimate of moments. This rather plain American had mesmerized the king and, as he was aware, enthralled his Special Commissioner for Disarmament, Herr von Ribbentrop. He may have acknowledged to himself that she seemed to be able to hypnotize men in the way that he could transfix audiences with his mesmerizing rhetoric and penetrating gaze.

After the short newsreel was finished, Hitler was left in no doubt that Edward VIII's adoration for Mrs. Simpson outshone his sorrow at the death of his father. Given his own traumatic relationship with his father, it was something Hitler could relate to. Subsequently the Führer was shown another newsreel, this time of the king and Mrs. Simpson on a yachting holiday in the Mediterranean, presumably the infamous *Nahlin* cruise. Both were in bathing suits, the Führer commenting that the American's figure was "not bad."

Here were a couple Hitler could do business with, the Führer ordering that the new king be treated like one of the family, coverage in the State-controlled German media suitably laudatory and sycophantic. Even though Edward had been on Hitler's radar since he became chancellor in 1933—his attempt to broker a marriage and the invasion of German royals to London evidence of his policy—there was a significant step change when Edward became king.

Once the king attracted the blazing blue-eyed scrutiny of the German leader, his life became inextricably if unintentionally entwined with Nazi ambitions. Whether they liked it or not, Edward and Wallis were the pivot for Anglo-German relations, the prince's every political intervention and pronouncement, real and imagined, exciting jubilation, anger, and despair on both sides of the Channel. As serious doubts began to be raised at home about Edward's fitness to reign, inside the Third Reich he was viewed as a friend and ally of the Nazi regime.

Hitler himself oversaw an elaborate memorial service in Berlin for the late king, at which he sat alongside Crown Princess Cecilie and the Nazi hierarchy, which included Hermann Göring, Joseph Goebbels, and Heinrich Himmler. Encouraged by the Führer, the royal house of Hohenzollern was in direct contact with the British ambassador in Berlin, Sir Eric Phipps, requesting that the deposed Kaiser be represented at the funeral. As with his British Legion speech, the new king believed that the funeral was an occasion to extend the hand of friendship to former adversaries and welcomed the idea.

He suggested that Crown Prince Wilhelm, at the time a keen supporter of Hitler, be invited to follow the coffin through the London streets. In what would become a familiar routine, his suggestions were rebuffed by the Foreign Office. They argued that, as the crown prince had been arraigned under the Treaty of Versailles for offences against "international morality," a more acceptable representative of the German royal family would be the son of the crown prince, Prince Frederick of Prussia.

Of greater political significance was Hitler's decision to send his most ardent Nazi royal, Edward VIII's cousin Carl Eduard, Duke of Saxe-Coburg and Gotha, to London to represent Germany. The British-born and Eton-educated royal, who was stripped of his English titles during the war, was one of the first aristocrats to join the Nazi Party, the town of Coburg, which was in his duchy, the first in Germany to elect a Nazi mayor.

At the funeral, as he marched behind the coffin through the rain-swept streets of London, he proudly though incongruously wore his Nazi uniform, complete with what looked like an outsize stormtrooper's metal helmet. He may have seemed foolish but his presence was effective. As historian Karina Urbach observes: "Carl Eduard was the ideal ice breaker. Hitler used him to talk to the Prince of Wales and encourage pro-German feeling."

For the next few months Carl Eduard, a childhood friend of the new king, was a key player, his presidency of the newly formed Anglo-German Fellowship group giving him frequent access not just to the king but to Britain's ruling class. Well-heeled members enjoyed lavish receptions at the German embassy and banquets at a Mayfair hotel, where guests sat at tables decorated with swastikas. On one occasion the Kaiser's daughter, the Duchess of Brunswick, and her husband were guests of honour. The AGF, which was founded in September 1935, was itself started as a direct result of the Prince of Wales's famous "hand of friendship" speech at the Albert Hall. Inspired by his speech, Conservative member of Parliament Sir Thomas Moore suggested the formation of a society that would engender positive relations between Germany and Britain. Members of this elite group included a former governor of the Bank of England and an admiral, and it had the backing of fifty members from both Houses of Parliament, including Lord Redesdale, father of rabidly pro-Nazi Unity and Diana Mitford. The group's secretary and merchant banker, Ernest Tennant, was a close friend of von Ribbentrop, who was naturally enthusiastic about the project. At his urgings Lord Londonderry—known variously as the "Londonderry Herr" or the "Nazi Englishman" by American ambassador to Berlin William E. Dodd—was encouraged to join.

Ribbentrop telegrammed Hitler: "If the King were to give his support to the idea of Anglo-German friendship, his great popularity might well help to bring about an understanding."

Ostensibly the group focused on improving relations between the two nations, though as the months passed, its membership became markedly more pro-Nazi and Fascist. The spies Kim Philby and Guy Burgess joined the AGF, which was widely seen as a far-right organization, in an attempt to disguise their Communist affiliations.

Certainly Carl Eduard, who visited Britain on ten different occasions during this period, enjoyed close access to the new sovereign. After his intimate conversations the Duke of Coburg was able to report that Edward felt the League of Nations was a farce, that a British-German alliance was essential for maintaining peace in Europe, and—shades of Edward VII—that the business of high policy should devolve as much on his shoulders as on those of the prime minister and foreign secretary.

When the duke broached with the new king the subject of face-to-face conversations between Hitler and Prime Minister Baldwin, he received a dusty answer. Edward told him: "Who is King here? Baldwin or I? I myself wish to talk to Hitler and will do so here or in Germany."

While the duke had a deserved reputation for exaggeration and was working in a German hierarchy that heard only what it wanted to hear, his report rang true. Even Ambassador von Hoesch, a professional diplomat who had enjoyed numerous intimate meetings with the king, was convinced that his "friendly attitude" towards Germany would influence the shaping of foreign policy.

He reported: "These sympathies are deep-rooted and strong

enough to withstand the contrary influence to which they are not seldom exposed. At any rate we should be able to rely upon having on the British throne a ruler who is not lacking in understanding for Germany and in the desire to see good relations established between Germany and Britain."

His indifference to French sensibilities and sympathy with regard to Nazi ambitions were music to German ears, the German ambassador in Washington reporting that Americans who knew the king believed he would oppose Cabinet decisions which he considered "detrimental" to British interests, implying that British interests marched in goose-step with German interests.

This political interference was in marked contrast to the previous reign. King George V was a stickler for following his constitutional obligations, namely to stay above matters of policy. The new king had no such inhibitions, his pro-German behaviour reportedly giving the Foreign Office "a great deal of trouble." Foreign Secretary Anthony Eden commented laconically that whereas King George V knew much but interfered little, the new tenant knew little and interfered much, making the job of the professional diplomat much more difficult. As the American ambassador to Austria, George Messersmith, commented: "It is probable that his personal influence did much to retard British policy."

There were other significant changes from his father's day that soon alarmed politicians, diplomats, and courtiers alike. Where his sober father was diligent, his martini-loving son was dilatory; where George V was punctual, Edward VIII had such a reputation for arriving for engagements late or not at all that one member of the House of Lords suggested that he would be blackballed from London clubs for such behaviour if he were a lesser personage.

The rhythms and routines of the old order were not for the matinee idol monarch. Nowhere was this contrast between father and son more clearly exposed than in the issue of red boxes, the interminable stream of important Cabinet and Foreign Office documents, many of which the sovereign must sign and give royal assent to before they can become law. Unlike his father, Edward VIII had no time for the nitty-gritty of political administration, the daily grind of reading and signing, signing and reading being of little interest to the new king.

Within weeks of Edward becoming king, there was considerable concern that the secret and confidential contents of the red boxes were being treated in a cavalier manner. In his study at Fort Belvedere, boxes went missing or were returned late, delaying government business; top secret papers were left lying around, some even covered in stains left by cocktail glasses.

On one occasion a startled American military attaché who was staying at the Fort was breezily asked to drop off several official boxes at Buckingham Palace. Only Mrs. Simpson seemed to take any notice of these sensitive documents. As for the king, he had eyes only for the American.

It soon became apparent that this was not a cosy internal domestic matter that could be solved with a quiet word in the new king's ear. In February 1936, only days after George V's funeral, a summit of civil service mandarins, including the head of the civil service, the Cabinet secretary, and George V's experienced private secretary Lord Wigram, assembled in Prime Minister Baldwin's room at the House of Commons to discuss the thorny issue. Foreign Office under-secretary Lord Vansittart, who boasted his own "private detective agency" of spies, informed the mandarins that secret codes used by British embassies could be compromised.

Furthermore, thanks to information from his spy network, he could confirm that both the French and Swiss governments knew that the king was discussing everything with Mrs. Simpson and showing her State papers. As Mrs. Simpson was believed to be, in Vansittart's words, "in the pocket of Ribbentrop," there was grave concern that the opportunistic German envoy may gain an inside track into secret British policy. Mrs. Simpson's "partiality for Nazi

Germans," as courtier's wife Helen Hardinge noted in her diary, was a further factor in the toxic mix.

It may already have been too late. In his biography of von Ribbentrop, Paul Schwarz described how Germans were often surprisingly well informed about the reports that Sir Eric Phipps, the British ambassador in Berlin, sent back to London. Significantly, Schwarz, a former German diplomat, penned his book in 1943, years before official British papers about the matter were released.

With uncanny accuracy he wrote:

Berlin was filled with loose talk about Edward. It was said that he neglected his duties in the handling of official documents. Secret Ambassadorial reports were especially emphasized. At Fort Belvedere the Foreign Office dispatch bags were said to have been left open and it was possible that official secrets had leaked out.

Was it not true that in Nazi Berlin one could hear stories which in London passed for State secrets. There can be no doubt that some people in official British circles were aware that these rumors cast an undesirable reflection upon their king.

Could it be possible that during dinnertime chitchat, Wallis Simpson or even the king were inadvertently leaking information gleaned from confidential documents? Though no one at the House of Commons meeting had the faintest inkling about Mrs. Simpson's political views, the finger of suspicion pointed firmly at her. She was a woman and a foreigner, but most important she was also not the king so inevitably she was the lightning rod for suspicions. When he was briefed, Baldwin decided to sit on his hands rather than confront the king. As a compromise the most sensitive documents were weeded out from the daily boxes before they were sent to Edward VIII—and the dubious American.

As Baldwin's biographers Keith Middlemas and John Barnes observe: "About Mrs. Simpson, greater suspicions existed. She was believed to have close contact with German monarchist circles. Behind the public façade, behind the king's popularity, the Government had awakened to a danger that had nothing to do with any question of marriage."

The influential and well-connected historian John Wheeler-Bennett told his friend Blanche Dugdale, who worked for British Naval Intelligence, that he was convinced that von Ribbentrop used Mrs. Simpson. He stopped short of accusing her of spying. Others were not so sure. American ambassador Robert Worth Bingham reported to Roosevelt: "Many people here suspect that Mrs. Simpson was in German pay. I think this is unlikely."

No matter, those in her circle were now under close scrutiny, particularly those on the fringes of the Cunard set. A regular and highly entertaining guest at Lady Cunard's table at Grosvenor Square was White Russian émigré Gabriel Wolkoff, who worked as the chief set designer at Covent Garden. His brother, Admiral Nikolai, ran a tearoom in Kensington which was a meeting place for rabidly right-wing white Russians. His dressmaker daughter Anna made clothes for Mrs. Simpson and Princess Marina, the Duchess of Kent.

Besides making dresses, Anna Wolkoff was an active member of the Right Club, an anti-Semitic, pro-Nazi, anti-war society which included the Duke of Wellington among its 350 members. Her membership and frequent visits to Germany, where she met among others Rudolf Hess and Hitler's lawyer Hans Frank—later executed for war crimes—brought her to the attention of MI5.

She was placed under surveillance, believed to be sending information to the Nazis via an intermediary at the Italian embassy. At the time, it was only a small step to assume that Wallis—and for that matter others—may, innocently or not, have been passing titbits of intelligence to Wolkoff that the Nazis found useful. (MI5 were right to target Wolkoff. In 1940 she was jailed for ten years for attempting to send the Nazis top secret communications between Churchill and Roosevelt. Her co-conspirator, American Tyler Kent, who gleaned the information through his work as a cipher clerk at the American embassy, received seven years.)

In early March 1936, as he paced the rooms of his mountain retreat at Berchtesgaden, Hitler needed all these titbits and scraps of information. He spent the weekend in virtual seclusion, deciding whether to invade the Rhineland. All the reports, from Ambassador von Hoesch, von Ribbentrop, the Duke of Saxe-Coburg, were assessed as he considered the possible British reaction. Could King Edward VIII be the mouse that roared and did Baldwin, Chamberlain, Eden, and company have the collective will to challenge the will of the Reich? Where he had doubts, his foreign minister, Konstantin von Neurath, was on hand to soothe his fears.

He decided to roll the dice. On March 7, 1936, just five weeks after George V's funeral, Hitler, in direct contravention of the Treaty of Versailles, ordered German troops into the demilitarized zone of the Rhineland. The German leader held his breath, awaiting the response from the British and French. It was the end of the "responsible" period of National Socialism, the moment when the wolf was revealed beneath the sheep's clothing. Historians now agree that prompt action from the French and British to repulse the incursion would have thwarted Hitler's ambitions and rallied German opposition to stage a possible coup.

The Allies hesitated and did nothing. Hitler's gamble had paid off. It was his belief that the new king had been a vital ally in forming Britain's inert response to his peaceful invasion of the Rhineland.

Four days after the invasion, on March 11, von Ribbentrop reported to Hitler that the king had issued a "directive to the British Government that no matter how the details of the affairs are dealt with, complications of a serious nature are in no circumstances to be allowed to develop." That is to say: Don't upset our German friends.

This was exactly the news for which Hitler had been waiting.

Hitler's architect Albert Speer, who happened to be with him at the time, recalled that the Führer let out a sigh of relief. " 'At last,' he declared. 'The king of England will not intervene. He is keeping his promise.' " The Führer later admitted that the forty-eight hours following the march into the Rhineland were the most "nerve-wracking" of his life.

High stakes, too, for the new king who, according to Fritz Hesse, the press attaché at the German embassy, threatened to abdicate if Baldwin went to war over this incursion. Hesse's account is based on a conversation he claimed to have overheard between Ambassador von Hoesch and Edward VIII.

"Hello," a voice said. "Is that Leo? David speaking. Do you know who's speaking?"

"Of course I do," replied von Hoesch.

The king went on: "I sent for the prime minister and gave him a piece of my mind. I told the old so-and-so that I would abdicate if he made war. There was a frightful scene. But you needn't worry. There won't be a war."

When he put down the telephone von Hoesch, according to his press secretary, danced a jig around the room and shouted, "I've done it. I've outwitted them all. There won't be a war. Herr Hesse, we've done it. It's magnificent, I must inform Berlin immediately."

While this colourful story has gained wide currency, it is doubtful that the king would have referred to himself so casually. His given name of David was used only by his immediate family and close royal relations. As his long-time friend Diana Mitford recalled: "To the end of his life he remained 'very royal.' He never allowed people to be casual or offhand with him, let alone impertinent or insolent. He wanted exactly what Wallis gave him, natural and unaffected good manners." As the military historian Gerhard Weinberg has soberly observed, while Hesse's account may have been extravagant, "there is ample evidence for a less spectacular role by Edward VIII."

In another version, the king, according to the London correspondent of the *Berliner Tageblatt*, was less than pleased with Hitler's
behaviour. He reported to his foreign editor on March 18: "The monarch has caused a number of important people in the Government to
come and see him and has said to them: 'This is a nice way to start
my reign.'" There was a ripple effect, Wallis worrying that Ernest,
who frequently travelled to Hamburg on shipping business, could be
interned if the international situation deteriorated.

The incursion into the Rhineland established the future pattern of German foreign policy: aggressively occupying regions
and countries, the invasions accompanied by fresh assurances and
promises in the hope that others would be lulled into acquiescence.
Over the next few years Hitler's imposing series of "triumphs without bloodshed" directed at "peace with honour"—tearing up the
Versailles settlement, winning back the Saar, restoring "military
sovereignty," recovering the Rhineland, uniting Austria with Germany, and bringing the Sudetenland "home into the Reich"—won
him support in all sections of the German people and unparalleled popularity, prestige, and acclaim.

In this first major German manoeuvre against the Treaty of
Versailles, the Nazis faced little diplomatic opposition in either
France or Britain. For the most part, British public opinion felt
that the reoccupation of German lands was just and certainly not
worth going to war over.

Hitler took no chances, on the day of the coup sending over his
trusted royal emissary Carl Eduard to soothe jangled British nerves
and ensure that his friend Edward VIII remained acceptant or at
the very least neutral with regard to the German intervention. Carl
Eduard stayed in London for over a week before returning to Germany. In April he wrote to his sister Alice, Countess of Athlone, asking
if her husband, the Earl of Athlone, had seen the king. He wanted to
know about his state of mind, that is to say he was fishing to discover if
there had been any change in the king's favourable view of Germany.

The duke soon had his response—business as usual. On April 20, Hitler's forty-seventh birthday, the king sent a telegram wishing him "happiness and welfare" in the future. Germany was much on Edward's mind—just a few days earlier his generous host and friend, Ambassador von Hoesch, had collapsed and died of a heart attack, leaving his cousin and chargé d'affaires Prince Otto von Bismarck in temporary command. Bismarck was subsequently transferred to Italy.

It was a sign of what little regard Hitler had for bothering to negotiate with Britain that he allowed this plum ambassadorial position to remain empty for several months. When Hitler was interested in a country—Spain was a case in point—he flooded the embassy with diplomats, spies, and other agents to assert German presence. Not so with Britain. When he finally appointed von Ribbentrop, kicking and squealing, into the job, von Ribbentrop agreed only if he could spend most of his time in Germany by the side of his beloved Führer. During his days as ambassador to the Court of St. James, von Ribbentrop was frequently absent, quietly negotiating secret pacts with Italy and Japan to secure alliances *against* Britain. Behind the bluster and bonhomie, this was the true measure of German intent.

The Führer, too, maintained the friendly façade. On July 16, 1936, a deranged Irishman, identified as Jerome Brannigan, drew a loaded revolver on the king as he was returning to Buckingham Palace on horseback after inspecting a military review in Hyde Park. Though the potential assassin was overpowered by police, the king was widely praised for his cool and composure. Hitler was one of the first European leaders to send a telegram conveying to the king his "heartiest congratulations" on his escape. That Brannigan claimed that he had been directed to kill the king by a shadowy pro-Nazi group was simply ignored, Hitler's concern cementing the cordial relations between the two leaders.

The few in Britain who had perceived the real nature of German expansionism were, like the deranged gunman, dismissed as mad or warmongers. Most were in step with the king who was sympathetic to Germany's grievances and hostile to the very idea of embarking on another war. On April 1, a few days after the march into the Rhineland, Conservative MP Ronald Tree, one of the few supporters of British rearmament and Churchill, described the political turmoil caused by the incursion. He told his American wife Nancy:

A wave of the strongest pro-Germanism has swept the country—which the government very stupidly has done little or nothing to counteract. What it is in fact is sheer pacifism and a refusal to face facts but it's terribly dangerous. People here behave as if Hitler and Co were ordinary people and could be trusted instead of realizing that these are a bunch of gangsters whose word is good only so long as it serves their purpose and a time will come in the next few years when a fresh appeal will have to be made and a new trick pulled out of the hat.

Sceptics were kept at arm's length. When Randolph Churchill, in his capacity as a journalist, visited Munich in September 1937 and tried to persuade his cousin Unity Mitford to introduce him to Hitler she refused to help him—his critical views of aggressive German rearmament were bound to antagonize the beloved Führer.

During his infrequent and reluctant visits to London, it was the role of von Ribbentrop to marginalize these warning voices, the new ambassador, together with Princess Stephanie, the Duke of Coburg, and others, on hand to emphasize the bonds that existed between the two countries in the face of a common enemy, the Soviet Union. A dinner at Nancy Astor's London home shortly after the Rhineland invasion brought home to von Ribbentrop just why he disliked the English—their idea of humour.

After dinner, Lady Astor made her august guests, who included delegates from the League of Nations, play musical chairs and other games. She instructed her English guests, sotto voce, that they were under orders to let the Germans win.

While he was nonplussed by this bizarre British behaviour, the new German ambassador, winning if loquacious, usually charmed his targets. It didn't hurt that society ladies wanted to see what all the fuss was about regarding his much talked-about affair with Mrs. Simpson. Inevitably he was very much in demand as a dinner party guest, inviting the great and the good to Berlin to enjoy the 11th Olympiad or, for the select few, to meet Hitler at his mountain retreat.

The seduction of the Canadian-born press baron Lord Beaverbrook was typical. As well as numerous members of Parliament, Beaverbrook accepted an invitation to the Berlin Olympics where, accompanied by his son Max and daughter Janet, he watched the opening ceremony. Years later Beaverbrook would say how he hated the "regimentation of opinion" he witnessed during the trip. At the time, though, von Ribbentrop's grandiose gesture worked, causing a breach between the press lord and his good friend Winston Churchill, whom Beaverbrook now described as a "war monger."

His rival press baron, Lord Rothermere, was already snugly in the pocket of the Nazis. Described bluntly by the Earl of Crawford as a "traitor," he danced attendance to the new German ambassador. During one lunch von Ribbentrop was at pains to emphasize Germany's "pacificism," reacting with horror at the very suggestion that Czechoslovakia would ever be attacked. "It has never entered our head," he told Rothermere straight-faced. In 1938 Germany marched into the Sudetenland, part of Czechoslovakia. Upon hearing the news, Rothermere, who was still enamoured of the German leader, sent Hitler a fawning telegram, describing the dictator as "Adolf the Great."

Following the German occupation of the Rhineland, von Ribbentrop presided over a veritable caravan of bankers, admirals, generals, and politicians heading to the Fatherland to see for themselves the economic and social miracle of National Socialism. Former prime minister David Lloyd George came away from a meeting with Hitler and declared the Führer "the greatest living

German" as well as "the George Washington of Germany." Nearly every British leader who personally met with Hitler—and there were many—was impressed by his sincerity, his reasonableness, and his integrity. It was all an act. Edward VIII was by no means alone in being fooled by a bravura performance by the Nazi leader, talking peace while planning for war.

Ribbentrop simply copied and amplified His Master's Voice. While he dressed as an English gentleman, he had utter contempt for the English, believing firmly in the necessity of another war. He was, apart from Hitler, the most vociferous Nazi warmonger in the High Command. Hence his "bridge between the war veterans" policy was so much hokum. As Princess Stephanie observed in her unpublished memoir, von Ribbentrop's motto was: "War with Britain at any time, at any cost and under all circumstances."

As a diplomat he showed a remarkable facility for duplicity and deceit, both qualities for the successful adulterer. Was this really the man who had seduced the king's mistress with a bouquet of carnations? Wallis's friend Mary Raffray always believed the truth of the allegation, insisting to her family that von Ribbentrop and Wallis were lovers. She "hated" Wallis for it, she wrote to her sister Anne, and recalled the huge boxes of "glorious flowers" sent by the German emissary.

Nearly eighty years since von Ribbentrop and Mrs. Simpson first met, there is still no settled consensus about the true nature of their relationship. In 2008 it was suggested that a distinctive blue English Heritage plaque, which commemorates historical landmarks, be mounted at Bryanston Court in memory of Wallis Simpson. It was turned down by English Heritage on the grounds that the allegations about her and von Ribbentrop had not been refuted. An official argued that relevant official British archives that might shed more light on them remain closed.

CHAPTER SIX

———— ✺ ————

Edward on a Knife Edge

In the fall of 1935 Ernest Simpson—steady, predictable, loyal Ernest, the patriot who laid down his wife for his king—hatched a plot that would plunge the monarchy into its greatest crisis since Charles I challenged the authority of the Houses of Parliament three hundred years before. This mustachioed figure in a double-breasted suit, always in the background, polite, deferential, dependable, was the unlikely catalyst who inadvertently started the countdown to abdication.

It began, as these things often do, with what H. G. Wells called "the urgency of sex." As the Silver Jubilee celebrations drew to a close, the most celebrated cuckold of the century sailed for New York on business, leaving his wife in the arms of the Prince of Wales. During his visit Ernest was entertained by the attractive and endlessly flirtatious Mary Raffray, who had been specifically asked by Wallis to look after her man. Mary, who had recently separated from her husband, Jacques, a New York real estate agent, took her at her word. It was not long before the couple became lovers, Ernest seen slinking out of her Madison Avenue apartment in the early hours of the morning, on one occasion leaving behind his hat, which was discovered by the maid. Their affair progressed to the point where they spent the weekend together at Atlantic City, the racy East Coast resort that liked to boast it was the "world's playground."

As Mary and Ernest had known one another for more than a decade—it was at the Raffrays' Christmas party in 1926 that he first met Wallis—and her own marriage had been disintegrating for some time, the affair may well have been going on for years.

Those frequent "business trips" made by Ernest to New York, normally interpreted as his way of avoiding the embarrassment of watching his wife dallying with the Prince of Wales, may have had an ulterior motive: to see Mary. Though the king, aided by Wallis, has been seen as the driving force behind the events leading to the abdication, the surviving evidence points to another interpretation, that Ernest Simpson and Mary Raffray, who would become his third wife, were not quite the innocent parties they have been depicted as.

Now formally separated, Mary was doubtless anxious that Ernest's honeyed words and protestations of love be matched by practical commitment. Feisty, fun, and endlessly sociable, she was not the kind of woman prepared to remain a long-distance lover forever. She was not mistress material. Marriage, though, was quite another matter.

Without a word to Wallis but doubtless with his lover's collusion, Ernest came to the inevitable conclusion that if he wanted Mary he had to divorce. As a man of business he had to be practical. His finances remained in dire straits. Business was still not good and he had existing commitments, financially obliged to his first wife, Dorothea, as well as the education and upbringing of their teenage daughter, Audrey. The cost of divorcing and maintaining Wallis who, thanks to her royal admirer, now had elevated expectations, would add a further burden. Then there was the outlay associated with a third marriage.

He knew that the Prince of Wales was besotted with Wallis but realized that his wife was more in love with the social status, the palaver of royalty, than the "little man" himself. If, he reasoned, the prince wanted his wife as his mistress, companion, hostess, whatever, he should damn well pay for her upkeep. Ernest had had enough of shelling out for his wife's designer clothes so that she could attend social events, and stumping up the insurance premiums for jewelry given to her by another man.

He would speak to the prince and offer him a deal—he would divorce his wife if Edward agreed to support her financially. As for the "high honour," which Superintendent Canning had heard him discuss that summer, well, maybe that would be conferred by a grateful Edward once he became king.

When Ernest and Mary mulled over this plan it probably never entered their heads for a moment that Edward would ever want to marry his wife, or for that matter that he would become king so soon. As a staunch monarchist Ernest would have been horrified at the idea that his decision precipitated the abdication. At the time he saw it as a business transaction pure and simple.

On the way home from New York, he doubtless spent time in his cabin rehearsing how he was going to broach the subject with the prince. Deferential and diplomatic—yes, that was it. As for breaking the news to Wallis, that would be an entirely different proposition.

While the death of George V forced him to stay his hand for a time, the opportunity to speak to the new king arose soon enough. In February 1936, shortly after Edward's accession on January 21, Wallis decided to take herself off to Paris, spending a week at the Hôtel Meurice. With Wallis out of the picture, arrangements were made for Ernest and the king to have supper at York House. Ernest took along his closest friend, Reuters editor in chief Bernard Rickatson-Hatt, for moral support or as a friendly witness. Or perhaps both.

It was Rickatson-Hatt's astonishing account, which he later told to Walter Monckton at the Guards Club on August 13, 1940, that rapidly reached the ears of the prime minister and his closest advisors. At the end of dinner, according to Rickatson-Hatt, Simpson asked the king point-blank if he intended to marry his wife. "Are you sincere? Do you intend to marry her?" Ernest blurted out, all diplomatic niceties forgotten in the bald drama of the moment. They may have been fellow Masons speaking man to man, but nonetheless it was an audacious question to a sovereign from a loyal subject who knew his place and had meekly stayed there.

The king's response was equally dramatic. He rose from his chair and declared: "Do you really think that I would be crowned without Wallis at my side?" With the cards now on the table, the two men got down to business, Ernest agreeing to end his marriage if the king agreed to look after Wallis financially. Of course the card he kept firmly in his hand was his affair with Mary Raffray, his own entanglement possibly giving him the courage to broach the matter with the king in the first place.

Whether the two men—the sovereign and his subject—shook hands after this horse-trading, Rickatson-Hatt does not record, but the one person who did not want to be treated like some equine commodity was the woman herself. Shortly after the York House meeting, Ernest travelled to Paris to break the news to Wallis. She was furious that the two men in her life had used her this way and made clear to her husband that she had no intention of divorcing him and had no wish to marry the king. "She was completely taken by surprise," a friend recalled later. "Her whole future decided by these two men and both without even discussing it with her. It left her absolutely shaken. And the terrible thing was, she hadn't any intention of divorcing Simpson and there it was." While she may have suspected the shadow of another woman in this affair, as yet she had no proof. That came soon enough.

In the meantime, news of this incredible story was relayed to Baldwin by Simpson's friend Sir Maurice Jenks, the former lord mayor of London who had, much to the concern of fellow Masons, facilitated the enrollment of Simpson into the Prince of Wales's own Masonic lodge. The imperturbable Baldwin summoned Wigram, now lord in waiting; Sir Lionel Halsey, then a council member of the Duchy of Cornwall; Sir Maurice Gwyer, first parliamentary counsel to the Treasury; and the king's lawyer, Walter Monckton, for a confidential discussion. When Wigram heard the tale he threw his head back with laughter at the very idea of the king marrying an American with two husbands still living.

It was the only moment of levity. Though Jenks insisted that Simpson was an honourable man, the prime minister's advisor Lord Davidson described the couple as "high-class blackmailers" who should be deported if possible. He was convinced that the king had lied about his so-called platonic relationship with Mrs. Simpson in order to ensure Ernest could join the Masons. As a result, this left him open to dishonour and blackmail.

In a top secret memo, he wrote: "S [Simpson] and Mrs S [Simpson], who is obviously a gold digger, have obviously got him on toast…Mrs S is very close to [the German ambassador Leopold von] Hoesch and has, if she likes to read them, access to all Secret and Cabinet papers."

Wigram sent Simpson a message suggesting that he remember his marriage vows and if possible take his wife back to America and out of harm's way. If he had known about the existence of Mary Raffray in Ernest's life, his view might not have been so sanguine.

At this juncture Wallis would have been astonished at the very idea of marriage to the king. It was as impossible as it was impractical. She was under no illusions, enjoying her role as his companion and hostess but knowing that the king would eventually tire of her, as he had of so many others, and find a younger and grander passion. As for being a gold-digger, well, that was open to interpretation. She made him happy and he needed her in a way that was frightening in its intensity was all she knew. If he wanted to give her jewels, clothes, and money, that was his prerogative. Who was she to refuse the sovereign?

Her view simply reflected the sensible consensus inside the inner circle. As Queen Mary told her lady-in-waiting Mabell, Countess of Airlie: "At present he is utterly infatuated but my great hope is that violent infatuations usually wear off." The Earl of Crawford reached the same conclusion, noting the affair would continue until Mrs. Simpson was "supplanted by some younger rival." Or as his assistant private secretary Alan Lascelles wrote: "Mrs S was no isolated phenomenon but merely the current figure in an arithmetical progression that has been robustly maintained for nearly twenty years."

All were agreed that the unfailing remedy for the king's condition was time.

Winston Churchill, who indulged the prince like his often wayward and spoiled son Randolph, consistently argued that the king's advisors should play the long game, believing that if the prince's passion was allowed to run its course then after a while the woman he and Max Beaverbrook called "Cutie" would become a creature of his past. He conceded, though, that Mrs. Simpson had been a positive influence in Edward's life, successfully encouraging him to eat properly, to cut down on his drinking and smoking—and to be more diligent with his red boxes.

Time, though, was running out. In March, at Wallis's previous invitation, Mary Raffray came to stay at Bryanston Court on her way to the South of France. Though relations were, by all accounts, somewhat strained, it seems that Ernest had not spoken with his wife about the existence of his lover. She stayed with them for a couple of weeks, even attending a weekend at the Fort where, as ever, Wallis was hostess. During her visit Ernest and his mistress managed to slip away to hotels in Dover and Devon without Wallis's knowledge.

After leaving her hosts Mary travelled to the South of France. From the Carlton Hotel in Cannes that Easter she wrote two letters, the first a bread-and-butter thankyou note to Wallis, the second a love letter to Ernest. She put the letters in the wrong envelopes, Wallis receiving and reading Mary's billet-doux to her husband. A Freudian slip or a classic attempt by the mistress to force the vacillating husband to make a decision? No matter, it did the trick, Ernest finally confessing his adultery and moving out of Bryanston Court to the Guards Club.

They kept the matter quiet, Ernest still appearing in public with his wife, though rather less frequently. In late May the Simpsons were guests when the king hosted a formal dinner party at York House in honour of Prime Minister Baldwin. "It's got to be done," Edward told Wallis. "Sooner or later my prime minister must meet my future wife." Wallis's response, which became a familiar refrain, was that marriage was out of the question. "They'd never let you," she told him.

That evening Edward was at his most charming and affable, his easy manner carefully observed by Anne Lindbergh, the writer and wife of the famous American aviator and Nazi admirer Colonel Charles Lindbergh. Living herself with a national icon, she was more conscious than most of the difficulties of teasing out the human being hiding behind the mask. She considered the king "the most human Englishman I've met," while Mrs. Simpson was "authentic," with a natural poise and ease. "She is not beautiful and yet vital and real to watch. Her vitality invests her movements with charm or a kind of beauty." It was this vivacity that Herman Rogers captured in the movies of their various holidays together.

While the accounts of these momentous events are incomplete or, as with the king and Mrs. Simpson, self-serving, it seems that the king, the Simpsons, and Mary Raffray remained on civil terms throughout the "change-over" period. During that summer the quartet spent the weekend at Himley Hall in the Midlands as guests of Edward's old friend the 3rd Earl of Dudley. Some time later, the earl was favoured with a teatime visit by Queen Mary, who was eager to find out just what was motivating her son's aberrant behaviour. "I understand that my son was here recently," Queen Mary said to Lord Dudley, who confirmed the visit. "And that so was Mrs. Simpson." Again Dudley agreed. "And Mr. Simpson and Mrs. Simpson's lady friend." The earl, now blushing, had to acknowledge that she was correct. Queen Mary then insisted on being shown the sleeping arrangements. It soon became obvious that the bedrooms of the king and Wallis Simpson shared a connecting bathroom, as did those of Mr. Simpson and his girlfriend. "I see," said the queen stiffly. "Very convenient."

Queen Mary was not the only one trying to understand the king's fascination with the married American; by now the whole of London society, not just the inner royal circle, was gossiping. On July 9, 1936, for the first time, Wallis's name was included alone on the Court Circular, the dry record of regal engagements, which listed the guests when the king hosted another dinner at York House. "The Simpson scandal is growing," noted Chips Channon, "and she, poor Wallis, looks unhappy. The world is closing in around her, the flatterers, the sycophants, and the malice." There were compensations, Wallis variously described as "dripping" or "smothered" in rubies and emeralds.

Two weeks later Wallis began the long, convoluted legal process of securing her second divorce and thus paving the way for a possible marriage to the king. Under Britain's arcane divorce laws, the husband had to be discovered in a compromising position, thus giving the wife grounds for divorce. As he and the king had agreed, Ernest Simpson went along with the bogus scheme, on July 21 checking with his lover, Mary Raffray, into a hotel at Bray in Berkshire where, to no one's surprise, a private detective made the necessary discovery, thus allowing Wallis to instruct her lawyer Theodore Goddard to embark on proceedings. Throughout the proceedings Wallis insisted, as she told Chips Channon, that the divorce was "at Ernest's instigation and at no wish of hers."

The king was determined to give the girl from Baltimore a taste of the sweet delights, the glorification, and the enchantment that went with life as the king's consort. Just maybe, that would still her doubts about one day becoming his wife and queen.

Rather than spend August in Balmoral, the traditional royal holiday retreat in the Scottish Highlands, he chartered the 1,391-ton yacht the *Nahlin* from eccentric millionairess Lady Yule. Among the party were Duff and Diana Cooper, Emerald Cunard, Herman and Katherine Rogers, as well as the king's aides. The king even invited a surprised Ernest Simpson, perhaps in gratitude for his going along with the divorce.

Wallis soon got a taste of the romance accompanying a royal cruise: On one occasion, peasants dressed in traditional costume appeared on the quayside chanting "Long live love"; on another, she was delighted as thousands of locals, carrying torches down a mountainside, lit up the evening sky. As the yacht proceeded along the Dalmatian coast and on to the Greek islands and Istanbul, Herman Rogers, a keen amateur cameraman, filmed the party: Wallis and Edward swimming from sandy coves, Wallis on a "terrifying" donkey ride on one island, al fresco picnics, visits to ruins and monuments, and even the naked king changing beneath a skimpy towel on a beach. He stopped filming at the vital moment. Wallis's behaviour impressed the sceptics, even the normally critical Alan Lascelles thinking her a good influence with good manners and the wit to make suggestions to the king about doing the "right thing at the right moment."

Tensions bubbled just below the surface, Edward's equerry John Aird telling him to his face that he liked him as a man but "despised" him as a king because of his association with the American. Edward himself was plunged into a black mood after a lunch with his cousin King George of the Hellenes and his beautiful English girlfriend, Rosemary Brittain-Jones. When they departed, Wallis innocently asked why they could not marry, as both parties were divorced. It was explained that it was not easy for a reigning monarch to marry a commoner, especially one who had been divorced. Consequently King George could not marry Rosemary Brittain-Jones. That she was a commoner and already married put her out of bounds. So, too, by implication was her opposite number, Wallis herself.

Once the momentous cruise was over, Wallis went to Paris for a few days. In the city of love she learned the hard facts of life about her situation. She was suffering from a heavy cold, and to while away the dreary hours in her suite at the Hôtel Meurice she read her mail and newspaper clippings sent by her friends and family from America.

As she glanced over the cascade of cuttings, she realized that she had been living in a bubble for the last few weeks, perhaps months. Unlike the British press, which had been silent on her relationship with the king thanks to a self-denying ordinance agreed by newspaper proprietors and broadcasters, the American media had shown no self-restraint. She was "amazed and shocked" that her friendship with the king had excited such hysterical comment and saw in her practical, down-to-earth way, that all the rose petals and all the torch-lit parades in all the world could not disguise the fact that she was not a suitable consort for the new king-emperor.

With a heavy heart, she came to the inevitable conclusion that their relationship should end and that she should return to the "calm congenial life" with Ernest—if he would take her back. He didn't. On September 16 she committed her thoughts to paper, writing to the king: "I am sure dear David that in a few months your life will run again as it did before and without my nagging. You will know I want you to be happy. I feel sure I can't make you so and I honestly don't think you can me." She also promised to contact the king's solicitor and return the money he had settled on her. So much for blackmail.

That anguished letter broke the king's heart, the sentiments devastating for a man who was now totally dependent on Wallis for emotional support and succour. As he later confessed: "Wallis's companionship had become my only solace in a job which otherwise would have been intolerably lonely." For the seven days that Wallis Simpson was out of his life, the king contemplated the unthinkable. He threatened to cut his throat with a royal razor if she did not return. He slept with a loaded revolver under his pillow at night, daring himself to blow out his brains. If she left the country, he vowed to follow her to the ends of the earth.

In the face of this tormented emotional blackmail, Wallis capitulated and agreed to join the king in Scotland, where he was hosting the annual house party at Balmoral. She arrived at Aberdeen rail station on September 23, 1936, with her friends the Rogerses, the first Americans, Herman liked to boast, ever invited to stay at the royal Highland home.

The king was so eager to be reunited with Wallis that he drove the sixty miles from Balmoral to pick them up. It was a tactless decision, as he had previously declined an invitation to open a new hospital in Aberdeen that day, citing the grounds that he was still in official mourning for his father. The Duke and Duchess of York, also in mourning, had been obliged to undertake the king's duty. "Aberdeen will never forgive him," Chips Channon wrote several weeks later, after seeing that the local newspaper had published a photograph of the Yorks opening the hospital alongside one of the king greeting his guests.

Sensitivities were already raw at Balmoral where, as with other royal properties, the new king had made draconian changes, cutting wages, sacking staff, and planning the sale of tenanted farms. Old retainers were horrified—and often out of a job. Naturally the blame for these changes was laid at the door of—in the Duchess of York's phrase—"a certain person." Downstairs staff gossip quickly spread a story about the king's first tour of the greenhouses at Windsor Castle, where he ordered the head gardener to cut all the peach blossom, which he was carefully nursing into ripe fruit. He wanted the delicate blooms sent to Mrs. Simpson's bedroom. It was interpreted by royal retainers as a thoughtless, nay heartless, act rather than the romantic gesture of a besotted monarch.

This almost equalled the consternation that greeted Wallis's unheard-of request for a triple-decker American-style sandwich when she arrived at the Highland castle. The downstairs staff were simply taking their cue from the upstairs folk. When the Duke and Duchess of York, who were staying at nearby Birkhall, arrived for dinner, the duchess swept by Wallis and ignored her hand, proffered in friendship. She stated loudly: "I came to dine with the king." It was remarkably rude and abrupt behaviour, especially as Wallis had been asked by Edward to act as his hostess. In truth the changes, resented by all and sundry, were testament to the years of tensions that existed between himself and his father, George V. The haste and the haphazard nature of the reforms were interpreted by novelist Virginia Woolf as the revenge of a man who had been "daily so insulted by the King that he was determined immediately to expunge his memory."

These swirling undercurrents found no place in Herman Rogers's homemade movie of the weekend visit. Describing his holiday as "delightful and interesting," he seemed to be filming a typical jolly house party in the Highlands rather than a piece of history—Edward VIII's first and last visit as king to Queen Victoria's former home. For once the weather was good enough for guests to be served outside by liveried footmen. Louis Mountbatten tried to outdo the king at a curious game of arrow golf, apparently an Austrian invention, while Mountbatten and the king's brother the Duke of Kent joked around with a huge black cloak that resembled a wizard's costume. In fact it was used by the king to disguise himself when he went stalking, so as not to alert the grazing deer. During excursions around the 40,000-acre estate the king looked relaxed, smoking his pipe and eating a snack, seemingly at peace with the world. This was hardly the appearance of a man who had contemplated suicide a couple of weeks before.

The nearest Herman Rogers came to piercing the bonhomie was a black-and-white picture he took of the king and Wallis by a waterfall at Gelder Shiel. Both the king and Wallis look warily, somewhat sadly, at the camera, as if pondering the difficult road ahead, the hunters about to become the prey.

That journey was not long coming. Shortly after leaving Balmoral, Wallis rented a house in Felixstowe on the Suffolk coast in October to await her divorce case, which was due to be heard in nearby Ipswich. "Do you still want me to go ahead?" she wrote to the king. "I feel it will hurt your popularity in the country." He brushed aside her concerns and on October 27 Wallis was granted a divorce from Ernest. A by-product was one of the most famous royal headlines ever. One Chicago newspaper screamed: "King's Moll Reno'd in Wolsey's Home Town" (Cardinal Wolsey was Henry VIII's most powerful advisor).

That night, as compensation, the king presented her with a fabulous emerald ring inscribed with the words "WE are ours now 27x36." It was intended as her engagement ring, and WE was their shorthand for Wallis and Edward. She moved to a rented apartment on Cumberland Terrace in Regent's Park, where she would stay for the next few weeks. From now on it was a waiting game—in six months' time her decree nisi would become absolute, allowing Wallis the opportunity to marry Edward before the Coronation in May 1937. At least that was the king's plan.

Wallis became increasingly jittery as the full implications of what the king was proposing gradually dawned on her. Shortly after her divorce petition was granted she had a frank conversation with Lady Londonderry at a party hosted by Emerald Cunard in Grosvenor Square. Lady Londonderry warned her about the damaging accounts appearing in the American media about her relationship with the king. Bluntly, Lady Londonderry told her that she would never be accepted as queen by the British people.

Mrs. Simpson acknowledged that no one had been really candid with "a certain person" about the true climate of opinion. Lady Londonderry agreed, saying that if the king's "real friends all help, much can be done to silence all this weird conspiracy."

That said, a "certain person" had not been forthcoming even to his closest friends and most trusted advisors. Herman and Katherine Rogers were kept in the dark, as was his lawyer, Walter Monckton. He had always believed, based on confidential conversations, that marriage was out of the question and that Mrs. Simpson was simply looking forward to enjoying her freedom. When Herman was finally let in on the king's thinking, he argued strongly that he should stay on the throne. As he told Endicott Peabody, his former headmaster at Groton School, the alma mater of FDR and Rogers himself:

> I should like you to know that every possible and sincere effort was made from this house to prevent the King from abdicating. I believe the King chose the wrong course. He knows what I think and we are still friends. But at least he made his choice soberly. I doubt if he will ever regret it.

As for Wallis, she felt trapped, realizing more than anyone that the king would literally follow her to the ends of the earth to be with her. She felt, though, that going abroad would help the king focus on his position and stem the growing tide of gossip. For a mad moment she even considered fleeing to China but knew that the king would follow her. Out of sight, out of mind was a remedy proffered by many. Even President Roosevelt's mother, Sara, pitched in, writing to her godson Herman urging Wallis to return to the United States:

> *I do so wish W Simpson would come back to Baltimore and stay where she belongs. The poor young king owed it to his country to settle down with his own people and if he does not marry in his own class he ought to give up these intimacies and leave the ladies alone.*

It was a forlorn hope, the king's private secretary, Major Hardinge, writing to Edward in early November stating baldly that the British press were about to break their silence and that the Cabinet were about to meet to discuss the serious situation. He strongly suggested Mrs. Simpson go abroad immediately to avoid a political crisis. While Wallis was stunned by the letter, she was in broad agreement, believing that their position was so "hopeless" it could only mean "tragedy for him and catastrophe for me."

The king was deaf to all entreaties. On November 16 he summoned Prime Minister Baldwin and told him that marriage to Wallis was "an indispensable condition of my continued existence, whether as a king or man." In response, Baldwin presented the king with three choices. He could give up the idea of marriage, as the Church, the British people, Parliament, and the Dominions would not contemplate the king marrying a woman with two husbands still living. Alternatively, if he chose to marry against the wishes of his ministers, this would cause a constitutional crisis, as the government would resign. The final choice was abdication. After listening carefully, Edward repeated that if the country opposed the marriage, he was prepared to abdicate. Later that evening he delivered the same obstinate message to Queen Mary and his three brothers. All were dumbstruck and horrified. They thought he had gone mad, the Duchess of York expressing her bewilderment in a letter to Queen Mary:

> Staying here, in a very normal English shooting party, it seems almost incredible that David contemplates such a step and every day I pray to God that he will see reason and not abandon his people. I am sure that it would be a great shock to everybody and a horrible position for us naturally.

Immediately after seeing his family, the king travelled to South Wales for a two-day visit to this depressed region where he uttered the immortal phrase "Something must be done about it" as he walked past the loyal crowds of impoverished families and hungry children. It was a populist gesture, one that worried politicians who felt he was trespassing beyond his constitutional role.

While he was with the destitute and homeless, Wallis was enjoying lunch at Claridge's with newspaper owner Esmond Harmsworth, Lord Rothermere. He floated the idea of a morganatic marriage, a device whereby Edward could marry Mrs. Simpson but on the condition that she would merely be his consort and would not take the title of Queen of England.

It was an idea first promoted by Princess Stephanie in tandem with Ambassador von Ribbentrop, who was desperate to keep Edward on the throne. He tried to send the king a personal message via the pro-German Lord Clive, stating that the "German people stood behind him in his struggle." He even summoned his diplomatic staff and told them: "King Edward must fight, and you will see, Gentlemen, that he is going to win the battle against the plotters!"

While Wallis listened intently as Harmsworth explained this unusual marital device, she was not aware of the social nuances that were associated with morganatic marriage. As their friend Diana Mosley later recalled, the king, acutely aware of the niceties of rank and position, was not enamoured. "A morganatic wife is a second-class wife, the target of every petty-minded Court official and the recipient of endless pin pricks."

Nonetheless the king agreed to place the idea before Baldwin who, at their meeting of November 25, promised to consult the prime ministers of the Dominions as well as his cabinet. The chances of success were slim. Under English law, such an innovation would have required a special Act of Parliament as well as the full support of all the countries throughout the empire. So it proved, Baldwin reporting a week later that there was no appetite in the empire or at home for such a matrimonial device.

In Parliament, blunt-spoken Communist MP William Gallacher

pointed his finger at the "sinister processes" of Ambassador von Ribbentrop in trying to impose a morganatic marriage on the country. "I want to draw your attention to the fact that Mrs. Simpson has a social set, and every member of the cabinet knows that the social set of Mrs. Simpson is closely identified with a certain foreign government and the ambassador of that foreign government." It was the most pointed public pronouncement yet about the machinations of von Ribbentrop, Princess Stephanie, and other foreign parties.

While these negotiations were under way, Wallis was under virtual siege from the media and the plain curious at her Cumberland Terrace apartment. Daily she received hate mail and death threats. It was only a matter of time, she feared, before one of these threats became real. Concerned for her welfare, the king asked his Scotland Yard bodyguard to see if patrols around the Terrace could be discreetly increased. She was now firmly of the opinion that for her own safety she should leave the country.

The so-called king's party, which had formed around Winston Churchill, Lord Beaverbrook, and war secretary Duff Cooper, had the same idea but for a different reason. They believed that if "Cutie" left the country for the winter it would focus the king on the Coronation in May. By then, his passion would have waned, Edward would do his duty, and the monarchy would be spared.

Years later, Churchill admitted that Wallis had been given added incentive to leave after Beaverbrook apparently instructed journalists at his *Daily Express* newspaper to mount a campaign of intimidation. "Then terrible things began to happen," recalled Churchill. Bricks were thrown at her dining room window to terrify her, poison pen letters arrived, and angry slogans were written on the walls of neighbouring houses.

It was the brick throwing that prompted her immediate flight; she left her London prison for Fort Belvedere before accepting an invitation from the Rogerses, who had been contacted by the king, to spend the next few weeks at their villa, Lou Viei, in the South of France.

After suffering a nightmare journey in the company of Lord in Waiting Lord Brownlow, she finally arrived at the Rogerses' villa, exhausted and strung out. Once settled, she wrote to the king, urging him not to abdicate. There was self-interest at stake. She believed that she would be blamed for the crisis and felt that it would be better to discuss his marital ambitions once he had been formally crowned king-emperor in May. Delay would give him a stronger negotiating position, advice also proffered by Beaverbrook and Harmsworth. They gave him to think that with time and patience he could have it all—remain sovereign and marry Mrs. Simpson.

It was apparent to everyone, including Wallis, that Edward was intent on abdicating, no matter what. He seemed to have given little if any thought to his future role, his wife's title and honours, whether they could remain or return to Britain, as well as their financial future. It was a fatal mistake.

Events were now moving towards a tragic conclusion. On December 3 the British media finally broke its silence, a gush of articles on the matter drowning out all other news. As the Earl of Crawford drily observed: "After months, one might almost say years, the torrent is overwhelming—a cascade of articles, pictures, headlines, one would think that the relations of the king and Mrs Simpson must exclude all other topics....The temptation to magnify the affair is irresistible—to propagate every possible rumour, however absurd."

He was right to be cynical, as every piece of gossip, hearsay, and innuendo was eagerly devoured. Bloomsbury Group hostess Lady Ottoline Morrell, whose circle included literary luminaries like D. H. Lawrence, Aldous Huxley, and T. S. Eliot, was typical, noting in her diary that the king "had injections to make himself more virile and they affected his head and have made him very violent. Poor little fellow, they also say he has been drinking all these last weeks and has signed two abdications and torn them up."

On the authority of the Home Secretary, the king's conversations with Wallis were now being intercepted by MI5, the prime minister anxious to know what the king was thinking. Isolated in her villa, Wallis was put under enormous pressure to give up the king, which she duly did, issuing a press statement on December 7 stating that she wished to "avoid any action or proposal that would hurt or damage His Majesty." Furthermore, she declared herself willing to withdraw from a situation which had become "unhappy and untenable."

It had no effect. By now the royal die was cast, Edward intent on abdication. On December 10, only a week after the crisis became general knowledge, the king made his historic radio address telling the world that he found it "impossible to do my duty as king and emperor without the help and support of the woman I love." He stressed that, until the last, Wallis had tried to persuade him to take a different course. As he mentioned her name, Wallis, who was listening to the broadcast hiding under a blanket on a sofa in the sitting room at Lou Viei, jumped to her feet and fled the room, crying: "Did you hear what he has said?"

Meanwhile, outside Buckingham Palace, five hundred Blackshirts, shouting support and giving the Fascist salute, chanted "We want Edward." They had no effect.

King no more, with the title HRH Duke of Windsor, Edward drove through the dark and dismal December night for HMS *Fury*, which took him across the Channel on the first leg of his journey to Austria, where the Rothschild family had offered him Schloss Enzesfeld, their castle near Vienna. He left behind him a nation in shock, if not in mourning. "I knew now that I was irretrievably on my own," he wrote in his memoirs. "The drawbridges were going up behind me."

He had reigned for just 325 days.

———— ◦◈◦ ————

CHAPTER SEVEN

Love in a Cold Climate

She was right of course. As she predicted, the American was blamed for the abdication, a nation's venom directed at the outsider who had dared take away their golden-haired boy. From the throne room at Buckingham Palace to the cowsheds in Caerphilly, Wallis Simpson was spoken of with derision and disdain.

The new queen could not, would not, utter her name, contemptuously referring to Wallis as "that woman." Princess Marina dismissed her as a "dangerous adventuress," while Queen Maud of Norway sincerely hoped that something nasty would happen to the "bad woman" who she believed had hypnotized him.

Yes, that was it. She had bewitched him with sex, using bizarre techniques she had learned in the singing houses of Shanghai and Peking. It was said she was an expert in the celebrated "Singapore Grip," or what the French called the "Cleopatra grip." The joke went round that while other harlots were able to pick up pennies, she picked up a sovereign.

He was her slave. Her sex slave. That was it.

Diarist Chips Channon recalled how she spoke to him as if he was a naughty schoolboy, then rapped his knuckles when he begged for cigarettes. Just like a trained poodle. He even got on his knees to buckle her shoes—and in front of the servants. The story soon went round about the butler who entered the sitting room at the Fort to find Edward on all fours, painting Wallis's toenails. He promptly resigned.

Not forgetting that she was an out-and-out gold-digger. "Really she seems to have turned out an arch adventuress of the worst type," noted her fellow American and Conservative MP, Nancy Astor, with barely disguised contempt. Downing Street advisor Sir Horace Wilson swallowed the thesaurus as he spat out his loathing. "Selfish, self-seeking, hard, calculating, ambitious, scheming and dangerous," he wrote in an official memorandum. Baldwin simply shrugged: "If she were what I call a respectable whore, I wouldn't mind." Sir Horace, though, was not done with her.

He continued: "Her line throughout seemed to be to feather her own nest and to save her own skin. She steadily 'fed' [the American Hearst press] with material which gradually brought matters to a head in a way which made the king's position untenable."

Though Wallis was virtually out for the count after this beating, she would have fought back at this canard. Both she and the duke bitterly concluded that it was the American press that engineered the crisis. The duke later told American ambassador to Austria George Messersmith during a visit to Vienna: "It is because of the American newspapers that I am here today."

Not just a gold-digger, but a spy to boot. That was it.

That Wallis was a potential spy, blackmailer, and Nazi-lover was never seriously challenged inside the Establishment. Indeed, on the day that Edward renounced his throne this mindset was reinforced, Downing Street being warned by Scotland Yard detectives watching Mrs. Simpson's movements in the South of France that she was planning to flee to Nazi Germany. In a handwritten note to the commissioner of the Metropolitan Police on December 10, 1936, a Scotland Yard official confirmed he had instructed the two personal protection officers to remain with her at Cannes. In guarded language the senior officer indicated that Mrs. Simpson "intended to 'flit'" to Germany.

Snubbed by local French society, watched by five French gendarmes and three Scotland Yard police officers and dozens of reporters and cameramen, Wallis was living in social purgatory. She wrote to Edward: "So much scandal has been whispered about me, even that I am a spy, that I am shunned by people, so until I have the protection of your name I must remain hidden."

At the time, the least likely explanation for the crisis was that the king was actually in love. It was the conclusion eventually arrived at by Winston Churchill, the man who had suffered most, at least politically, because of his loyalty to the king. Some time later, he reflected on the love affair that threatened Crown and country, telling Queen Mary's lady-in-waiting, Mabell, Countess of Airlie, that the duke's love was one of the great loves of history:

I saw him when she had gone away for a fortnight. He was miserable—haggard, dejected, not knowing what to do. Then I saw him when she had been back for a day or two, and he was a different man—gay, debonair, self-confident. Make no mistake he can't live without her.

Perhaps the most salient perspective on the royal drama has never before seen light of day. Throughout the abdication crisis, Herman Rogers was the calming voice at the heart of the storm, fending off the press from the gates of his villa, fielding frantic phone calls from the king, Walter Monckton, and others while soothing Wallis's jangled nerves. His conduct earned the lasting respect not just of the waiting media, Edward and Mrs. Simpson, but his neighbour in New York State, President Roosevelt. Unlike most commentators, he actually knew both parties extremely well but was never tempted to join the debate.

In a hitherto unpublished letter written to his godmother Sara Delano Roosevelt a month after the abdication, he stoutly defended Mrs. Simpson, arguing that nothing and no one could have stopped the king taking the action he did. He made clear that Wallis had every right to divorce Ernest Simpson, even if the king had not featured in her life. His argument suggests that Simpson's affair with Mary Raffray began much earlier than has been previously suspected. He wrote:

> I now know that Mrs. S was always anxious to step out of the King's life. Up until the very end she urged and begged him to give up all thought of her and remain on the throne. I like and admire the king enormously but I know just how obstinate he is. The decision was entirely his own, as he admitted in his radio farewell. Nothing and none could move him from the decision that was already firm in his mind—If Mrs. S had moved to Baltimore the king would have followed her there.
>
> I am sincerely convinced that there was no way to control him. As to Mrs. S Divorce I realize that many people believe it was based on collusion. I can only tell you that I <u>KNOW</u> there was no collusion—that king or no king she would have brought her action and that she had complete justice on her side. Time will undoubtedly prove the truth of this.
>
> You wrote to me frankly and I am doing the same to you because I feel that is what you want. What I say is between us—I have written to no one else in the world in defence of Mrs. S.

The settled view, though, was that the king had been beguiled in some way by the devious, calculating foreigner. As traumatic and dislocating as the duke's conduct had been, very quickly the country moved behind King George VI and Queen Elizabeth.

Lord and Lady Londonderry were typical, sending several unctuous letters to the Duke of Windsor offering their sympathy but privately, according to their daughter's recollection, condemning his dereliction of duty and accusing him of being "hopeless." They thought it a good thing that Mrs. Simpson had taken him away.

Other accusing fingers pointed to Mrs. Simpson's society friends, blaming them for the fiasco. In a reference to Emerald Cunard, Chips Channon, Lady Asquith, and others in the court of Queen Wallis, Nancy Astor said: "If she had not been accepted by them and run after, the King would have realized that he could not possibly get away with it." A number of friends were quick to disassociate themselves from the now exiled American. Notoriously, Lady Cunard denied ever having met her.

Poet and satirist Osbert Sitwell wrote the verse "Rat Week" about the disloyal, rootless, and shallow circle who deserted the ex-king and Mrs. Simpson following the abdication. Their influence, mused Sitwell, "must make even Judas queasy." Naturally, the new queen loved the poem. "Absolutely brilliant," she wrote to Sitwell, barely disguising her contempt for Lady Cunard and her set. She thought it "a pity" that the then German ambassador, von Ribbentrop, chose to associate with the Cunard crew, their behaviour giving him a false impression of the British people. "Do you suppose," she mused to Prince Paul of Yugoslavia, "that he made his calculations of the British character and reactions to events from a study of her and her friends?"

It was not just von Ribbentrop who had misjudged the king but the Fascists at home. In the fevered hours following the abdication it was rumoured that Britain's Fascist leader, Oswald Mosley, could form a king's government. There was even talk that he had drawn up a list of ministers—a Fascist government for a Fascist king. Mosley accused the Government of strongarm tactics, exercising "the most flagrant act of dictatorship in hustling Edward off his throne."

His newspaper, the *Blackshirt*, defended Edward under the banner headline "Let King Marry Woman of his Choice." It was to no avail.

"I regret," said Mosley at a meeting in east London the day after the abdication, "that the king did not see fit to stay and fight his battle, which is the battle of the people, because I knew the battle could have been won."

The Nazi hierarchy were equally nonplussed, angry and bewildered that, as Beaverbrook pithily put it, "their cock wouldn't fight." Given his position and popularity, the king did little, if anything, to garner political support. It was as if he wanted an excuse, any excuse, to escape his destiny. Hitler's friend Unity Mitford watched the abdication statement being read out from the gallery in the House of Lords and commented: "Oh dear, Hitler will be dreadfully upset about this. He wanted Edward to stay on the throne."

The Nazi leadership were not impressed. As Joseph Goebbels caustically observed: "He had made a complete fool of himself. What's more, it was lacking in dignity and taste. It was not the way to do it. Especially if one is king."

The Führer had every right to be confused. A senior civil servant close to Baldwin observed that it was obvious that von Ribbentrop was "stuffing Hitler with the idea that the Government would be defeated and Edward would remain on the throne." Ribbentrop blamed "the machinations of dark Bolshevist powers against the 'Führer will' of the young king." Once more he summoned his staff and informed them: "I shall report all further details orally to my Führer."

As far as von Ribbentrop was concerned, the abdication was the result of a conspiracy of Jews, Freemasons, and other dark forces inside the British Establishment. He told Hitler that the marriage issue was a false front used by Baldwin to oust the king because of his pro-German views. German diplomat Wolfgang von Putlitz, who was spying for the British, told his secret service controller: "We are absolutely powerless in the face of this nonsense."

As historian Gerhard L. Weinberg observes: "If von Ribbentrop's reports to Hitler on the abdication crisis border on the lunatic, this reflected not only their author's general level of intelligence but also his rather tenuous connection with his official post."

A quietly jubilant Sir Eric Phipps, the much put-upon British ambassador in Berlin, concluded that von Ribbentrop's carefully laid plans to carry out mischief and intrigue in Britain had "in certain important details miscarried." There was joy also in the Russian embassy in London, Ambassador Ivan Maisky reporting to Moscow that the abdication was a real blow to Hitler. It is a perspective shared by historian Ian Kershaw: "The abdication of King Edward VIII, whose strong pro-German inclinations and autocratic tendencies would almost certainly have caused difficulties for the government quite beyond the business of Mrs Simpson, proved to be an unalloyed gain for Britain."

Following Edward's unceremonious departure, von Ribbentrop, like a lover scorned, became increasingly anti-British, fervent in his belief that the pursuit of friendship with Britain was futile. It didn't help his mood that his son had been turned down for a place at the elite Eton College.

If he had been less dogmatic, a more objective reading of the British political scene would have drawn von Ribbentrop to a rather different conclusion. Winston Churchill, the most hostile of Germany's enemies and a vigorous supporter of British rearmament, was grievously wounded politically by Edward's abdication. A king's party had formed around him, the consensus being, in Beaverbrook's phrase, to "bugger Baldwin." He badly misjudged the political mood. When Churchill, "filled with emotion and brandy," rose in the House of Commons to speak in favour of giving the king time to resolve his position, he was met with such hostility that he left the chamber.

His political career lay in tatters, the way now open for Eden and Chamberlain to pursue a more conciliatory foreign policy with the Germans. Future prime minister Harold Macmillan observed that the abdication crisis "undermined the reputation and political stature of the greatest and most prescient statesman then living."

Hitler's other miscalculation was to assume that Edward VIII had as much influence over foreign policy as his forebear and namesake Edward VII, whose anti-German policies had contributed to the Triple Entente. While this error was understandable, what was unbelievable—even to fellow German diplomats—was von Ribbentrop's knee-jerk reaction, namely to blame the Jews and Freemasons.

Once Hitler was convinced of this conspiracy fairy tale, it developed in his mind until he believed that Edward had actually been removed by Churchill. The politician had cunningly manoeuvred the king into a dubious marriage so that it would be easier to oust him.

The final deduction Hitler made was that the British and French were implacable "hate opponents" of Germany. Naturally von Ribbentrop agreed, saying that once Edward was gone, all hope of an Anglo-German rapprochement was finished. Even though he was busily constructing alliances against Britain at the time, such was the self-delusion in the Nazi leadership that they persuaded themselves that they had once dreamed of a settled friendship with Britain.

An early sign that the Nazi wolf was baring its teeth came a few weeks after the abdication when the Mountbatten clan planned to throw a welcome party for diplomat Prince Ludwig von Hessen-Darmstadt, known as Prince Lu, after he arrived in London to take up a position at the embassy as von Ribbentrop's assistant. Guests invited to their magnificent Brook House home on Park Lane, Mayfair, included the new King George VI and his queen. Hitler, still fuming about Edward's departure, apparently forbade Prince Lu to attend.

The first few weeks following the abdication were undoubtedly the most difficult for the couple. For six months before Mrs. Simpson's divorce became final in April 1937, they had to remain apart, preferably in separate countries, so as to avoid possible accusations of fraternization or collusion. Christmas was the low point, away from each other and isolated from their friends and family. The duke described his new life as "hell," expressing his frustration in a letter to Herman Rogers sent three days before Christmas:

> *What a ghastly time have all of us been through but the worst is over now and I know how marvelous you have both of you been to HER. It really is hell having to be separated all these months and all so unnecessary really—however it seems we can't meet so that's that and we'll make it however hard and trying—There's something so utterly grand and lovely to look forward to.*

As the weeks passed, he was slowly discovering that life as a former monarch did not have quite the same perks and privileges as his previous occupation. First one equerry was summoned back to Buckingham Palace by the new king and then a second man, having little sympathy for Mrs. Simpson, decided to return to London as well. A junior member of the Foreign Office staff in Vienna, Dudley Forwood, was dragooned into service. For the next three years he became the duke's sole equerry and private secretary.

As Forwood later recalled: "I found out soon enough that the Duke was not altogether reconciled to his new status. Although he was plainly a broken man, a shell, he still expected a full service, a monarch's service."

Even his choice of Forwood was a tricky issue, giving him an insight into the brave new world he had embraced. His friend Sir Walford Selby—the British ambassador to Austria—and American ambassador Messersmith joined forces and pleaded with the duke not to appoint Forwood to such a sensitive and senior position as private secretary. Both men felt that the twenty-four-year-old honorary embassy attaché was too young and inexperienced. In the face of this opposition the duke exploded in irritation. "You are telling me I don't know people—that I'm no judge of people. How should I be a judge of people? I've never had the chance to form my own opinions about people. They were always made for me." A cipher no more, from now on he was determined to make his own choices in his own way and accept the consequences. For a man so used to being guided and advised by sober, serious men, relying on his own judgement or the conclusions of foreigners or expats who had lost touch with the pulse of English society was as thrilling as it was fraught. As Walter Monckton noted with some concern: "With someone so quick to take a point and so impressionable as the Duke this was a constant anxiety to me."

In the interminable weeks and months following the abdication, the duke went walking, shooting, or skiing, deliberately keeping a low profile. For Wallis, playing bridge or poker was her favourite way of killing time. After one bridge game, in the company of novelist Somerset Maugham, designer Sybil Colefax, and the Rogerses, there was an inquest about why she had not used her king of hearts. "My kings don't take tricks, they only abdicate," replied Wallis wryly.

As the months passed, it became abundantly clear that her husband-to-be had played his cards extraordinarily badly. He started with a strong hand but came away with virtually nothing, trumped on every trick by his younger brother George VI. The duke naïvely expected his family to accept the reshuffled deck, let him sit out a few hands and, at some future, mutually agreed date, allow him to continue playing as before. He believed that he could, as it were, stand behind the new king and instruct him on how best to play his hand. It was one of his first miscalculations.

In mid-January 1937 he wrote to the king promising to do all he could to help him but pleaded with his brother to help stop the constant attacks on himself and Mrs. Simpson. Most hurtful, apart from the swirling rumour of Mrs. Simpson's affair with the German ambassador, was the totally false story that she had made off with Queen Alexandra's fabled emeralds, which she had retrieved from Garrard, the royal jewelers.

This letter was followed up with numerous phone calls in which the ex-king fulminated against his mother, Queen Mary, and his stuttering, stammering brother. The duke, bored and lonely in his Austrian redoubt, bombarded him with requests, demands, and unwanted advice on how to rule his kingdom. Such were the length and frequency of his phone calls to London that his hostess, Baroness Rothschild, who joked that she was not a member of the "rich branch" of the family, worried about how she would pay the bills. Edward was also concerned with the financial settlement for himself, the title for his future wife, as well as the guest list and setting for his wedding which, he told the king, would take place after the Coronation in May. He wanted the marriage to be grand, dignified, and thronged with members of both families. The ex-king was to get a rude awakening.

Such was the persistence of this royal back-seat driver that George VI lost patience with his brother and instructed the phone operators at Buckingham Palace no longer to automatically put through the duke's calls. Instead he sent Sir Walter Monckton to Austria to explain the new facts of life to his brother.

As Walter Monckton tactfully recorded: "The Duke of Windsor was particularly quick in understanding decisions and good on the telephone, whereas King George VI had not the same quickness and was troubled by the impediment in his speech."

While the duke was not completely in the wilderness—his

sister, Princess Mary, paid a week-long visit and his "heavy" daily postbag bulged with family correspondence—there was no disguising the widening gulf between the two brothers. The process was accelerated by a campaign of malicious gossip, not only against the duke but against the new king, too. It was sparked by the king's decision not to attend the Accession Durbar in India in the winter of 1937–38, a refusal that was seen by many, especially supporters of the charismatic duke, as suggesting that George VI was not quite up to the job. There were whispers in society circles, now willing to believe anything after the drama of the abdication, that he was too nervy even to make it to the May Coronation. His cause had not been helped by the controversial radio broadcast made by the Archbishop of Canterbury, Cosmo Gordon Lang, days after the abdication, in which he unctuously criticized the duke and his social circle but also drew attention—unhelpful as far as George VI was concerned—to the new king's speech defect.

Over the next few months, despite Monckton's honeyed words and consoling gestures, the duke was thwarted at every turn in his menu of demands. The duke felt that, at some point, he could return to public life in Britain and the empire, albeit in a diminished role as the king's supportive older brother. In contrast, the king and his court saw him and his bride as a threat, Edward VIII's decision to place personal desires above duty to the Crown utterly antithetical to the meaning of monarchy.

While he had chosen not to make that personal sacrifice, the duke expected his younger brother, who was not as well equipped, either physically or mentally, for his unexpected elevation, to take on the onerous task of kingship.

There was, too, a fear, harking back to medieval times, that no shaft of light should illuminate the old king. Those at court, particularly the new queen, felt that, having willingly cast himself into the outer darkness, he should remain in exile. Any premature return would be deemed a threat to the new king and the new order. Over New Year, the abdication was the sole topic of conversation among the royal family.

Court librarian Owen Morshead recalled the king and queen dwelling on Edward's extraordinary personality and his ability to charm people. The queen, he noted, addressed the unspoken fear, saying that if he parted from Mrs. Simpson "it would be dangerous to have such a powerful personality, so magnetic, hanging about doing nothing." Even though in time the new prime minister, Neville Chamberlain, came around to the notion of allowing the duke to return to England albeit with a considerably diminished royal role, the queen was implacably opposed. As Walter Monckton recalled:

> She naturally thought that she must be on her guard because the Duke of Windsor, to whom the other brothers had always looked up, was an attractive, vital creature who might be the rallying point for any who might be critical of the new king, who was less superficially endowed with the arts and graces that please.

The queen's opinion prevailed: A sixty-four-page Downing Street report prepared on the proposed financial provision for the new duke focused on the potential difficulties for the king and queen should the newly minted American duchess set up a rival court funded from the public purse. Author Sir Horace Wilson warned:

> It must not be assumed that she has abandoned hope of becoming Queen of England. It is known that she has limitless ambition, including a desire to interfere in politics; she has been in touch with the Nazi movement and has definite ideas as to dictatorship.

After much back and forth about the vexed matter of the duke's finances it was finally decided that the king would give him an annual allowance of £25,000, with the strict proviso that he would lose the allowance should he decide to visit Britain without the king's express permission. This provoked a furious seven-page missive from the duke to the prime minister. The decision, he said, was "unfair and intolerable as it would be tantamount to my accepting payment for remaining in exile." He had "never intended to renounce my native land or my right to return to it—for all time."

The letter had no effect. His brother the king wrote back to say "the continuation of this voluntary allowance must depend on your not returning to this country without my approval."

For all the bitterness and rancour, the royal outcasts had to think practically and plan where they would live as exiles. For a long time the duke harboured the thought that he could return to his beloved Fort Belvedere and remain in quiet seclusion for part of the year. That ambition remained unfulfilled.

There was much talk, too, that they would move to the United States, the duke for a time discussing a property outside Baltimore. Even President Roosevelt was drawn into the guessing game. Shortly before Wallis and Edward planned to marry, a small army of workmen were drafted in to remodel Crumwold, Herman Rogers's home on the Hudson River. Everyone, including the president, thought he was about to get a royal neighbour.

The president sent an amused note on White House headed notepaper to Herman's brother Edmund: "You doubtless have heard the local rumors that there are thirty plumbers, painters and carpenters in the house getting it ready for the Duke of Windsor and his prospective bride! By the way I think Herman has handled himself extremely well in an extremely difficult situation." That plan, however, came to nought, the royal couple staying mainly at the Hôtel Meurice in Paris for a time after their marriage before eventually renting two different houses in Paris as well as the Château de la Croë on the Cap d'Antibes in the South of France.

As the duke slowly absorbed the reality of life in exile, so he and Mrs. Simpson had to accept that their dream of an officially sanctioned wedding was just that—a fanciful idea. It was made abundantly clear that the court was completely hostile; their wedding would not be announced in the Court Circular, there would be no royal guests or other members of the Household, and the Church of England would not allow a bishop—their preference—or any other member of the clergy to marry them. Even the duke's choice of best man, Louis Mountbatten, who had shared so many royal adventures, was barred from attending by the king. When their beloved dog Slipper was killed by a poisonous viper, they saw it as some kind of omen. The royal voodoo was working.

"It is all a great pity," wrote Wallis. "To set off on our journey with proper backing would mean so much." She felt, correctly, that her husband had been too trusting of his family, who would strain every sinew to deny him a dignified and correct position as befitting an ex-king of England. Just as the queen blamed "a certain person" for all the calamities that had befallen the House of Windsor, so Mrs. Simpson was at daggers drawn with Queen Elizabeth. "How she is loving it," she wrote bitterly to the duke. "There will be no support there." She returned to the same theme in another note: "I blame it all on the wife—who hates us both."

Wherever they turned they were confronted by enemies or friends who deserted or exploited them. For Wallis it was the last straw when Newbold Noyes, one of Mrs. Simpson's distant cousins, published a series of articles in America based on family conversations. Though the stories were utterly anodyne, she felt her privacy had been invaded. Ignoring Herman Rogers's sensible advice to rise above the fuss, Wallis started a libel action, hiring Parisian lawyer Armand Grégoire to represent her.

It was a disastrous mistake. At that time he was known to the

French security forces as a notorious Nazi activist who had earlier been described in a French secret service dispatch as "one of the most dangerous of Nazi spies." While she eventually dropped the suit, her association with a known Nazi supporter—after the war he was sentenced to hard labour for life for collaboration—did little to remove the pervasive suspicion in official circles that she was an enemy of the State.

It was not only Mrs. Simpson who was frustrated and embittered by her situation. For once, the duke forgot the first rule of royalty—never complain, never explain. He issued a libel suit in relation to an innocuous, somewhat oleaginous book, *Coronation Commentary*, which amidst the saccharine contained a couple of lemons, suggesting that the duke and his wife-to-be were lovers before her divorce and that in the days before the abdication he drank too much.

The idea of the duke being cross-examined in the witness box gave the palace palpitations—"So degrading," noted the queen—and royal lawyer Sir Walter Monckton was sent to soothe the duke and settle the case favourably without the need to go to court. He succeeded on both counts, the duke winning a substantial settlement from the hapless publisher.

If the duke was telling the truth, it meant he had given up the throne for a woman with whom he enjoyed a purely platonic relationship. It was a remarkable and, to modern eyes, barely believable admission. If, on the other hand, as Queen Mary, several courtiers, and at least one royal butler suspected, he was lying, it meant he was willing to commit perjury and risk jail as well as everlasting disgrace simply to protect Mrs. Simpson's honour, a potentially ruinous choice even for a reckless royal romantic.

Surrounded by foes, family and friends both, the duke and his wife-to-be were forced to rely on the comfort of complete strangers. Feeling hemmed in and imprisoned at the Rogerses' villa in Cannes, Wallis leapt at the invitation from Charles and Fern

Bedaux to spend time in the secluded and discreet surroundings of the Château de Candé, in the Loire region of France. Katherine Rogers, an old friend of Fern Bedaux, had previously written suggesting that she extend an invitation to the frazzled and terminally bored Mrs. Simpson. An invitation was duly sent and accepted, and the Rogerses and Wallis—with her personal maid and twenty-seven pieces of luggage—arrived at the opulent château in early March.

Charles Bedaux himself, who had never met either the duke or Mrs. Simpson, was a colourful self-made multimillionaire who started adult life as an apprentice pimp in the notorious Pigalle district of Paris before heading for New York, where he founded a management company which introduced the first scientifically based time-and-motion studies. The fortune he made from the worldwide implementation of these industrial methods allowed him to indulge his passion for big-game hunting and various extravagant expeditions to the less populated parts of the globe. In 1934 he was joined on a trip across northern British Columbia in Canada by Herman Rogers and his banker brother, Edmund.

There was another side to the flamboyant businessman. Ever since his companies were seized in Nazi Germany in 1934, he had worked hard to ingratiate himself with the leadership. He leased a schloss in Berchtesgaden so that he would be close to the Nazi hierarchy, and with his vast array of political and business connections he was a natural conduit to feed information to important contacts in the Nazi regime. As historian Professor Jonathan Petropoulos observes: "He was almost certainly a Nazi intelligence asset; he knew Göring personally and had many German business contacts."

His name, therefore, would not have appeared high on the list of people deemed suitable by the royal family to stage this ersatz royal wedding, though the attitude of the House of Windsor had in part engineered this course of action. As for Bedaux, he pronounced his sympathy for the plight of the two lovers, exiled from their home and isolated from their friends and family. The expansive, eloquent, if rough-hewn self-publicist told one journalist: "My wife and I believe that when two people sacrifice so much for love they are entitled to the admiration and the utmost consideration of those who still believe in this ideal."

The six-month separation had served only to heighten the anticipation felt by the royal lovebirds. As soon as Wallis's decree was made absolute on May 3, the duke boarded an Orient Express train in Austria and hurried to be by the side of his future wife, bounding up the stone stairs of the château in his eagerness to see her. As Wallis recorded in her memoirs: "Before we had been alone in the face of overwhelming trouble, now we could meet it side by side."

Days later, on May 12, the couple sat in the château's great room and listened to what might have been, the radio broadcasting the Coronation at Westminster Abbey of the new King George VI and Queen Elizabeth. Inside the abbey, Winston Churchill, the duke's doughtiest supporter, enjoyed something of a Pauline conversion as he watched Queen Elizabeth being crowned as consort after making solemn vows and receiving tokens of grace for her special task. The patrician statesman turned to his wife, Clementine, his eyes brimming with tears, and said: "You were right; I see now the 'other one' wouldn't have done."

Days after the Coronation, in one of his first acts as sovereign, George VI bleakly informed his elder brother that Letters Patent, a legal order emanating from the monarchy, had been issued stating that Mrs. Simpson would not be entitled to share his title or rank. It seemed to the duke—as well as legal experts—that this ruling was not just unfair, unconstitutional, and plain vindictive, it was also illegal. "This is a fine wedding present," he exclaimed bitterly.

In a letter to the duke, the new king guilelessly explained that this matter, which had given him "great trouble and concern," had been forced on him after taking the advice of his ministers. It was nothing of the kind. Recently released government documents reveal a much more telling story of a family on the brink of war. Initially the government was nervous about denying royal rank to Mrs. Simpson, believing that it was legally unjustified. It was the duke's own family who forced the government to find a legal and constitutional explanation for denying Mrs. Simpson the "Her Royal Highness" nomenclature.

As the king bluntly demanded of Baldwin: "Is she a fit and proper person to become a Royal Highness after what she has done to the country; and would the country understand if she became one automatically on marriage?" He and the rest of the family thought not.

Baldwin sucked on his pipe and pondered the issue anew. When the matter was first broached by Buckingham Palace in March 1937, the Home Secretary, Sir John Simon, wrote a bread-and-butter response to Lord Wigram setting out that "the settled general rule" was that the wife took the status of her husband and that any children of the duke's marriage would also take his style and title. The only way of changing this lay with the king. As the fountain of all honour, he would have to change the Letters Patent to specifically deny Mrs. Simpson her husband's title.

At a round-table conference, which included the Home Secretary, Attorney General, Lord Chamberlain, and the improbably titled Garter Principal King at Arms, it was concluded that as Edward VIII had given up any right to the throne by virtue of his abdication, it was an anomaly that he still held the rank of "His Royal Highness" in any case. Queen Victoria had ruled that only those in the line of succession could have the HRH prefix. As the duke continued to hold that title only by the king's grace, then neither Mrs. Simpson nor any children of their marriage could lay any claim to his rank and title.

In a memo to Prime Minister Stanley Baldwin, the Home Secretary confessed that, unless positive action were taken to deny Mrs. Simpson a title, the social repercussions would be "exceedingly awkward," especially at functions abroad, where the wife of an ambassador would be expected to curtsey. Furthermore, he warned that if they ever returned to Britain there would be a "good many" ladies who would refuse to curtsey to her whatever her style and title. Crucially it was agreed that the king should be seen to be advised by the prime minister rather than taking the initiative himself, which was in fact the case. In his letter of explanation to his brother, George VI wrote: "I am satisfied that what has been decided is in the best interests of everybody, not forgetting your own future happiness."

While the decision to issue new Letters Patent may have been an elegant and legally astute solution to a ticklish issue, everyone involved studiously tiptoed around the emotional fallout. Only Walter Monckton grasped the nettle, pointing out to the Home Secretary that there was a "real risk of a complete family rift" that "might not be easy to damp down or keep hidden." Ministers were so concerned, not to say embarrassed, by the issue that they took great lengths to keep the announcement low-key. Senior editors were primed beforehand so as not to make mischief, and the announcement itself was made on the day that Stanley Baldwin resigned as prime minister, meaning that public attention would be focused elsewhere.

Once again Monckton was proved to be accurate in his judgement. The decision to condemn Edward to a morganatic marriage—which the prime minister and Dominions had categorically rejected during the abdication crisis—was a wrenchingly painful issue that grieved Edward until the day he died. He never forgot or forgave his family, considering the ruling to be a terrible slur on his wife and therefore on himself. Impetuously, the duke promised to give up his own royal title, though Wallis convinced him not to take such a hasty step. Even thirty years later the decision still rankled, the duke writing in a New York newspaper that "this cold blooded act, in its uprush, represented a kind of Berlin wall alienating us from my family."

The couple's choice of wedding date, June 3, which coincided with the birthday of the late King George V, merely added to the expanding pool of bad blood. Queen Mary, still grieving, was deeply hurt. Rather than blaming her errant son, she pointed a finger at the bride-to-be, writing to the new queen: "Of course she did it, but how can he be so weak? I suppose it is out of revenge that none of the family is going to the wedding."

The absence of any member of the royal family, especially the Duke of Kent and his erstwhile best man Louis Mountbatten, was particularly hurtful. In a fit of hyperbole, Lord Wigram declared that for any member of the family to attend "would be a firm nail in the coffin of monarchy." In addition he threatened to "hound out" any of the king's chaplains should they agree to officiate. In the end the royal couple found what Wigram called a "scallywag clergyman" from Yorkshire who agreed to marry them. Shortly after officiating, the Reverend R. Anderson Jardine sailed for America, where he enjoyed a lecture tour round the country on the basis of his involvement in their nuptials.

So much for the grand and fitting ceremony the duke had imagined just a few weeks before. As the duke's equerry Dudley Forwood recalled: "Right up to the last minute the duke hoped that his brothers would come and that somehow the royal family would relent. But they did not. He was deeply, deeply hurt."

Wallis tried to put a brave face on things, attempting, before the wedding, to present a softer image of herself and to dispel some of the most virulent rumours about her. She asked Cecil Beaton to take photographs of her for *Vogue* magazine and granted an interview to a distant relative, Helena Normanton, who was the first woman to practice as a barrister in England as well as a fanatical royalist and sycophantic admirer of the American bride-to-be.

In the article, which gained worldwide attention, Mrs. Simpson was at pains to emphasize that she had no ambitions to the English throne. She also tackled the two most hurtful canards, namely that she had made off with Queen Alexandra's fabled emeralds and had had a love affair with the German ambassador Joachim von Ribbentrop.

She told her cousin: "I cannot recall ever being in Herr von Ribbentrop's company more than twice, once at a party of Lady Cunard before he became ambassador and once at another big reception. I was never alone in his company and I never had more than a few words of conversation with him—simply the usual small talk, that is all. I took no interest at all in politics."

All the denials and all the smiles could not cover up the fact that on their wedding day it was clear to the world that their family and friends had turned their collective back on the couple. Six months before, Edward VIII ruled over the greatest empire the world had ever seen. On the day the duke took his wedding vows, only seven English people were present at the ceremony; the rest were French or Americans, notably Katherine and Herman Rogers. It was the ever sagacious Herman who gave Mrs. Simpson away. All bowed or curtsied to the newly minted Duchess of Windsor.

After the ceremony Walter Monckton took the duchess to one side and told her that "most people in England disliked her very much, because the Duke had married her and given up his throne." If she kept him happy, all that would change. "Nothing would be too bad for her" if she failed in that task.

She replied: "Walter, don't you think I have thought of all that? I think I can make him happy." The story goes that the morning after their wedding, the duchess awoke to find the duke standing by their bed. With his boyish smile, he asked, "And what do we do now?" Her heart sank, the duchess now reconciled to devoting the rest of her days to amusing her impatient husband.

The dawning realization of what their future life together would hold came during their lengthy honeymoon, which they spent, in the company of equerry Dudley Forwood, two cairn terriers, a pair of Scotland Yard detectives, and 266 pieces of luggage, at Schloss Wasserleonburg, an Austrian country house placed at their disposal by Count and Countess Paul Münster. Henceforth, the amount of luggage that accompanied their every journey would become a constant source of fascination and comment for the media, their baggage excesses largely responsible for the duke's precipitous plunge from international statesman to playboy socialite.

After a few weeks' rest and relaxation, during which the couple endlessly dissected the abdication, the duke began to fret about his future—just as Wallis had predicted. Bored, frustrated, and angry at their treatment by the royal family, the duke was eager to return to England and take up some official post that would use his talents. He was supported by several newspapers, notably Beaverbrook's *Daily Express*, which started a campaign for the Windsors to return to England. As far as the royal family were concerned, this was a toxic ambition, the ducal couple viewed as a Fifth Column who would foster intrigue and discord should they ever set foot on English soil. The new king felt vulnerable and worried and told the Prime Minister so. "After all," he argued, "I did step into the breach."

The fog of suspicion that had swirled around the duchess ever since her arrival in society circles now began to envelop the duke. Until now she had been seen as the spy and Nazi-lover, the duke largely excused as the lovesick puppy bounding after his mistress, his pro-Nazi views largely forgiven by virtue of his exalted position. An incident in June 1937 in Vienna during their prolonged honeymoon set alarm bells ringing for diplomats in London and Washington.

During their stay at the Hotel Bristol in Vienna they were entertained for dinner at the Brazilian Legation by Ambassador Sam Gracie and his wife. Edward's friend, American ambassador George Messersmith, his wife, and a junior diplomat from the Italian embassy and his English-speaking wife were also invited.

At the end of dinner, Messersmith was called away by an emissary sent by Austrian chancellor Dr. Kurt von Schuschnigg. He was informed that there had been a derailment on a train travelling from Germany to Italy through Austria. Inside a ruptured sealed railcar were naval shells intended for storage at two Italian ports, so that German ships could replenish supplies when they were stationed in the Mediterranean. The clear implication was that the Germans were preparing for a sea war in the not too distant future, presumably with the French or the British.

The disclosure of this secret military build-up, long suspected but never proven, had ramifications for Britain's naval deployment, rearmament, and appeasement policy. It was important that this matter remain confidential and that the Germans and Italians, who had grown closer since 1936, were not made aware that the Americans and British knew about their secret traffic in armaments.

When Messersmith returned to the dinner party, the duke quizzed him closely on the message he had just received. Somewhat guilelessly, Messersmith let the duke in on the secret. He immediately took the Italian diplomat to one side and blabbed the story. As soon as it was polite, the diplomat made his way to the Italian embassy and sent a cable, duly intercepted by the Americans, informing Rome that the "cat was out of the bag" regarding the secret shipments of shells. Whether the duke's actions were deliberate, naïve, or simply showing off, it left Messersmith angry at himself for being so trusting, and increasingly suspicious of the duke.

His report to the State Department reflected that fact. During the months of his exile, Messersmith had come to admire and respect the duke. Now the worm of doubt entered into his assessment of the ducal character. Over the next few years his misgiving and concern about the duke's conduct and his dubious choice of friends would grow apace.

He was not alone.

CHAPTER EIGHT

———— ❧ ————

Hitler's Good Queen Wallis

I t was the improbable figure of Charles Bedaux, described in a *New Yorker* profile as having a "boldly battered face, dominated by his fine, dark eyes," who made the duke feel relevant and alive once more. During their stay at Bedaux's Loire château the two men had struck up an unlikely friendship, playing golf during the day and at night putting the world to rights over a couple of glasses of fine brandy. While Bedaux had made his considerable fortune studying work practice, the duke, too, along with his younger brother the Duke of Kent, had always had an interest, however sporadic, in factories and the welfare of the working man.

The duke was keen to know how the working man fared in Hitler's brave new world. Could Bedaux arrange a visit through his contacts? Ever the expansive salesman, Bedaux blithely suggested that the duke include other European countries and America in his itinerary. He had excellent business connections in many parts of the world. Unspoken was the fact that he believed that a royal association would do his name and companies no harm at all.

He contacted political advisor Robert Murphy at the American embassy and labour leader Dr. Robert Ley in Germany. Subsequently the duke met Hitler's adjutant Fritz Wiedemann, the long-time lover of Princess Stephanie, at the Ritz hotel in Paris to seal the deal.

The plight of the working man, though, was something of a fig leaf. Both men had other motives, Bedaux to use the duke's name and prestige to regain and expand his corporation in Germany and the duke to show his new bride the true meaning of being royal. His equerry, Dudley Forwood, always maintained that the reason behind the visit was "not to give a public statement of his approval for the Nazis. We went because he wanted his beloved wife to experience a State visit. He wanted to prove to her that he had lost nothing by abdicating. And the only way such a State visit was possible was to make the arrangements with Hitler."

While the proposed royal tour was being secretly arranged, the duke and duchess journeyed to Borsodivánka in Hungary, where Charles Bedaux had rented a hunting lodge. The duke was clearly intrigued by Bedaux, a man of vision and a constant fountain of utopian ideas. He had even developed his own political theory, equivalism, which he saw as the economic basis to develop an ideal world in which labour, management, and the wider community could live in harmony. At a stroke it would replace capitalism and communism and thereby bring about world peace. This was the unfolding vista the immensely persuasive Bedaux conjured up for the gullible duke, a movement for world peace where he would play a leading role. For a man seeking a sense of purpose and relevance, his honeyed words struck a chord. The duke's supporters believed he could still play a major public role, Herman Rogers writing to his former headmaster Dr. Peabody: "His future interests me. He is of great potential value to any universal—not political—world cause."

It was not idle talk. At Château Candé in the spring, the duke had been given a letter from Colonel Oscar Solbert, a senior executive at Eastman Kodak, who first met the duke on his 1924 tour of the US East Coast. In his letter he suggested that the duke "head up and consolidate the many and varied peace movements throughout the world....I am not a pacifist, as you know, but I do believe that the one thing the world needs more than anything else is peace."

On the duke's behalf, Bedaux sent Solbert an encouraging response, saying that he was interested in leading an international peace movement and "devoting his time to the betterment of the masses." As well as Solbert, Bedaux had already involved IBM executive Thomas J. Watson, who agreed to sponsor the Windsors for their projected tour of the United States. Watson, whose slogan was "World Peace through World Trade," had already met Hitler, attended a Nazi rally, and accepted the Order of the German Eagle. The German government was IBM's second-largest client, its punch card technology, according to controversial award-winning author Edwin Black, ultimately helping to facilitate Nazi genocide, a claim refuted by historian Peter Hayes among others.

Were Bedaux and Watson "naïve idealists" or cynical collaborators turning a blind eye to the unfolding horrors of the Nazi regime, their calls for world peace simply a cover for a pro-German accommodation? As Professor Jonathan Petropoulos argues in *Royals and the Reich*, there are "compelling reasons" to see Bedaux as a more "sinister" figure: "This rhetoric of peace and reconciliation was a front for pro-Nazi sentiment, and occasionally the correspondence between the Windsors, Bedaux, Solbert, and Watson reveals this thinking."

Certainly the surreptitious and secretive planning behind the visit to Germany and America caused outrage inside Buckingham Palace and the Foreign Office, his surprise announcement catching everyone off guard. The new king described it as a "bombshell and a bad one too."

Even the duke's supporters were concerned; Herman Rogers thought the visit "untimely," while Churchill and Beaverbrook both opposed it, the press baron even travelling to Paris to remonstrate with the duke. He warned him that he would offend all Britons by consorting with Hitler's bullies. The duke was unmoved.

It left the Foreign Office nonplussed about how to deal with an ex-king on a private though officially sponsored tour. The king's private secretary, Alex Hardinge, described the visits as "private stunts for publicity purposes" which would not benefit the workers themselves. The king felt strongly that the duke and duchess should not be acknowledged as having official status in the countries they visited, nor should they be invited to stay at any embassy or legation. If they were to be met at a railway station it should be by a junior member of staff. British representatives abroad were expressly forbidden from accepting invitations or hosting dinners for the duke. They were only allowed to give the ducal couple "a bite of luncheon."

The respective ambassadors argued that it would be bad policy to cold-shoulder the ex-king and his wife. Britain's ambassador to Washington, Sir Ronald Lindsay, though regarding the forthcoming visit with "unmitigated horror," still felt the embassy should host the ducal couple.

He was summoned to Balmoral for discussions, where he found the king, queen, and their advisors in a state of "near hysteria" when faced with the prospect of dealing with this loose royal cannon. In his account Lindsay later recalled that the royal family felt that "the Duke was behaving abominably, embarrassing the king and dropping bombshell after bombshell." They feared that he was trying to stage a comeback with the help of his "semi Nazi" friends and advisors.

Of course the Germans saw the twelve-day ducal visit, which began in Berlin, as a propaganda triumph. It was not just the Nazi hierarchy who welcomed his arrival but the general German public. They considered the duke to be modern, progressive, vigorous, and accessible. Even his mock Cockney accent with a touch of American seemed more down-to-earth and unaffected than the disdainful patrician tones of a man like Foreign Secretary Anthony Eden. He remained an intriguing international celebrity, his marital turmoil only enhancing the iconic mystery surrounding the man. As historian Gerwin Strobl argues, the duke was not seen, either privately or publicly, as a collaborator, appeaser, or traitor to his country. Far from it.

In his study of German attitudes to the British between the wars, he observes: "When the Nazis were dealing with a useful fool, they could never quite disguise an element of contempt in their language.... There is nothing of this in the descriptions of the Duke's conversations in Berlin or the later wartime recollections of his actions and opinions. Instead there is something one comes across only very rarely in Nazi utterances: genuine respect; the respect felt for an equal." In their eyes, the harsh treatment of this charismatic man of the people was an indication of the rottenness at the heart of the British Establishment, which they saw as increasingly incompetent, hidebound, snobbish, and decrepit.

Relentlessly insulting, too. At least in the duke's eyes. The most-travelled monarch-in-waiting in history discovered that his quarter century of loyal, dutiful service to his country counted for nothing. When the ducal couple arrived at Friedrichstrasse station in Berlin on the morning of October 11, 1937, they were met by the forlorn figure of the British embassy's third secretary. He handed them a letter from the duke's long-time friend, Sir George Ogilvie-Forbes, now the chargé d'affaires, politely and somewhat apologetically informing them that British ambassador Sir Nevile Henderson had left Berlin and that Ogilvie-Forbes had been directed to take no official cognizance of their visit.

It was their Nazi hosts who provided the duke and duchess with a friendly welcome. No effort had been spared to make them feel at home, the station decorated with Union Jacks neatly alternating with swastikas. As the duke and duchess alighted from the train the crowd cheered "Heil Edward," while a brass band struck up a hearty rendition of "God Save the King." They were greeted by the portly German Labour Front leader Dr. Robert Ley, heading a

large and deferential German delegation and watched by enthusiastic, cheering crowds.

They left the station in the company of their host, Dr. Ley,
with four SS officers hanging on to the running-boards for dear
life as Ley barrelled through the streets at breakneck speeds before
arriving at the Hotel Kaiserhof, where a specially invited crowd of
Nazi members greeted the ducal couple with a jaunty song com-
posed by the Propaganda Ministry of Joseph Goebbels.

Then their avuncular but quickly irritating host raced them
at high speed in their black Mercedes-Benz to Carinhall, the
country estate of Hermann and Emmy Göring where Hitler's
right-hand man, whose visitors included their friends Charles and
Anne Lindbergh, Italian dictator Benito Mussolini, and American
president Herbert Hoover, gave them a tour of the estate. The high
point was his pride and joy, a model train set valued at $265,000,
which had tunnels, bridges, stations, and even a miniature airfield and model planes. Unlike their vulgar escort, the head of
the *Luftwaffe* was interested in intelligent discussion, over tea he
and the duke touching on everything from the British parliamentary system to international relations and labour issues. This was
more like it.

After the royal guests departed, Frau Göring announced
that Wallis would have "cut a good figure on the throne of England." The duke was so respected that her husband, whom Wallis
described as "trustworthy," ordered Prince Christoph von Hessen
to have their phones tapped, a courtesy the Nazi regime extended
to most visiting politicians, important businessmen, and so-called
guests of the Third Reich.

It was not long before they began to realize that, as the duke
recalled, they were treated as little more than "trophies at an exhibition," raced from housing project to youth camp to hospital in
Stuttgart, Nuremburg, Munich, and Dresden, Nazi newsreel cam-
eras capturing their every gesture.

During one tour the party went to a concentration camp that appeared to be deserted. "We saw this enormous concrete building which I now know contained inmates," recalled his equerry, Dudley Forwood. "The duke asked: 'What is that?' Our hosts replied, 'It is where they store the cold meat.' In a horrible sense that was true."

All the while their "odious" host Dr. Ley entertained them with a stream of risqué jokes and boorish comments, his breath frequently smelling of alcohol. This was not at all what the duke had in mind when he described the nature of a royal tour to his wife.

Wallis loathed the man. "A drunkard, a fanatic, quarrelsome, a four flusher [an empty boaster]," she said. There was a point where they did not think they would survive the tour alive, Dr. Ley driving so fast between engagements, sirens blaring, that the duke threatened to travel in a separate motor if he did not slow down.

In spite of Dr. Ley, the duke enjoyed meeting the people, giving off-the-cuff speeches or chatting with well-wishers in the language of his childhood. Wallis was reunited with her erstwhile lover, von Ribbentrop—sans carnations—at a dinner he hosted at the gourmet restaurant Horcher in Berlin, where the ducal couple met with the Nazi leadership, including Heinrich Himmler, Rudolf and Ilse Hess, and Joseph and Magda Goebbels. All came away impressed by the duke's demeanour and integrity and the duchess's style and charm.

Goebbels gushed:

A charming, likeable chap; open, clear with a healthy common sense approach, an awareness of contemporary life and social issues.... There is nothing of the snob about him.... What a shame that he is no longer King! With him an alliance would have been possible.... The Duke was deposed because he had it in him to be a king in the true sense of the word. That much is clear to me....A great man. What a shame! What a terrible shame.

The Nazi leadership, who collectively had "bottomless contempt" for Britain's degenerate ruling class, made an exemption with the duke. They saw him not only as someone favouring an understanding with Hitler but as a hard-headed defender of the British empire. Goebbels later described him as "a tender seedling of reason," writing in his diary that he was "too clever, too progressive, too appreciative of the problem of the under privileged and too pro German [to have remained on the throne]. This tragic figure could have saved Europe from her doom."

The eagerness of the Nazi leadership was matched by the genuine enthusiasm of the crowds who followed their royal progress, the duke's magnetic appeal transcending national boundaries. After enduring a week of mixing with the common man, Wallis was treated to an elaborate "what might have been" when she and the duke were guests of honour at a glamorous dinner at the Grand Hotel in Nuremberg, hosted by Carl Eduard, Duke of Saxe-Coburg and Gotha, where the remnants of Germany's aristocracy came to pay obeisance. She was addressed as "Your Royal Highness" and accepted curtseys from the titled and the high-born. As the *New York Times* headline put it: "German Society to Fete Windsor." This was how it felt to be a queen, albeit Hitler's queen.

If the dinner in Nuremberg was the social highpoint, the private audience with the German leader at Berchtesgaden on October 22 was the political summit. During the trip, the duke had, according to the *New York Times*, given a modified Nazi salute. On two occasions he gave the full salute, the first time at a training school in Pomerania when a guard of honour from the Death's Head Division of Hitler's elite guards was drawn up for his inspection, the second time when he met Hitler at the Berghof, his residence in the Bavarian Alps. "I did salute Hitler," he later admitted, "but it was a soldier's salute." After being kept waiting for nearly an hour, they were ushered into a large room with a view towards the dramatic Untersberg massif. An aide collected the duke while Wallis was left to make small talk, mainly about music, with Rudolf Hess. Music to the ducal ears was the fact that everyone, including Hitler, addressed the duchess as "Royal Highness."

Meanwhile the duke and the Führer enjoyed a private fifty-minute discussion. Even though the duke's German was perfect, translator Paul Schmidt was also present. His recollections are the only independent witness to the nature of their talk. He later recalled: "There was, so far as I could see, nothing whatever to indicate whether the Duke of Windsor really sympathized with the ideology and practices of the Third Reich, as Hitler seemed to assume he did. Apart from some appreciative words for the measures taken in Germany in the field of social welfare the duke did not discuss political questions. He was frank and friendly with Hitler, and displayed the social charm for which he is known throughout the world."

When they emerged, Hitler entertained them to tea, Wallis mesmerized by the "great inner force" of the German leader. She was struck by his long, slim musician's hands, his pasty pallor and his eyes, which burned with a "peculiar fire" rather like Turkish dictator Kemal Atatürk's, whom they met during the cruise of the *Nahlin*. When she met his intent gaze she found herself confronted by a mask. She concluded that he was not a man who liked women.

As Hitler escorted the couple to their car, one of the reporters observed: "the Duchess was visibly impressed with the Führer's personality, and he apparently indicated that they had become fast friends by giving her an affectionate farewell. Hitler took both their hands in his, saying a long goodbye, after which he stiffened to a rigid Nazi salute that the Duke returned."

After they drove away, Hitler said to his interpreter: "The Duchess would have made a good queen." The next time Princess Stephanie von Hohenlohe met Hitler she asked him about the duchess. This time he was non-committal. "Well, I must say she was most ladylike," he said.

In conclusion, the *New York Times* reporter observed that the duke "demonstrated adequately that the Abdication did rob Germany of a firm friend, if not indeed a devoted admirer, on the British throne."

Back in Munich, the Windsors spent their final evening at the Harlaching home of Rudolf and Ilse Hess. While there is no extant record of what they discussed, both men were future advocates of a negotiated peace—Hess dramatically flying his private plane to Scotland in May 1941 in the delusional hope that he could meet with first the Duke of Hamilton and then King George VI and begin peace talks.

After the royal couple departed, both sides declared the visit a "triumph." Even Winston Churchill, an early opponent of the Nazi regime, was moved to congratulate the duke, writing that the visit had passed off with "distinction and success."

Back in Leipzig, Dr. Ley basked in the warm afterglow of a successful tour, telling the German Labour Front that the duke considered the achievements of the Third Reich nothing less than "a miracle." He quoted the duke as saying: "One can only begin to understand it when one realizes that behind it all is one man and one will." The man in the street took this, according to the British consul in Leipzig, as an indication of the duke's "strong pro-Fascist sympathies." It was also the conclusion drawn by Russian leader Joseph Stalin, who had kept a beady eye on the royal progress. In 1938, Count Friedrich Werner von der Schulenburg, the German ambassador to the Soviet Union, wrote to British spy Vera Atkins from Moscow saying that Stalin knew all about "British royalty's warm feelings for the Nazis."

The assessment was largely correct, the duke's equerry, Dudley Forwood, later confirming that both the Windsors had much sympathy and understanding for the Nazi regime, which had, in their eyes, brought order to a country collapsing into chaos during the years of the Weimar government. "Whereas the Duke, Duchess and I had no idea that the Germans were or would be committing mass murder on the Jews, we were none of us averse to Hitler politically. We felt that the Nazi regime was a more appropriate government than the Weimar Republic, which had been extremely socialist."

Naïve and gullible or conniving and complicit? It is the question that has haunted the Windsors ever since they stepped off the train in Berlin and began their infamous visit to Hitler's Germany. The duke would later confess that he was "taken in" by Hitler. Writing in the *New York Daily News* on December 13, 1966, he stated: "I believed him when he implied that he sought no war with England. I thought that the rest of us could be fence sitters while the Nazis and the Reds slogged it out."

Two weeks after he waved goodbye to the duke and duchess and whispered soothing words of peace, Hitler showed his true colours. At a secret conference of his top military advisors he outlined his vision for Germany's foreign expansion. In what was to become known as the Hossbach Memorandum, he saw the future as a series of small wars of plunder to shore up the German economy before a major conflict with Britain and France between 1941 and 1944. As far as he was concerned, 1939 was much too soon for a general conflagration. Moreover he saw Britain and France as implacable "hate opponents"—*Hassgegner*—of Germany. While the Hossbach Memorandum has divided historians, the very least that can be said is that Hitler had little if any interest in peace in Europe.

After Germany, next stop the United States. Bedaux's proposed five-week visit was to be followed by fact-finding missions to Mussolini's Fascist Italy and Sweden, where the Frenchman had lined up a meeting with controversial businessman and Nazi collaborator Axel Wenner-Gren.

At first the arrangements for the tour of America seemed to be going swimmingly, though it had the feel of a triumphal royal progress rather than a modest private visit to study working conditions, as billed by the duke. Bedaux, who was underwriting trips to

Atlanta, Baltimore, New York, Detroit, Seattle, and Los Angeles, hired a private Pullman train to convey the royal party from coast to coast; General Motors put a fleet of ninety Buicks at their disposal; US government departments offered every facility during their stop-overs; while a Madison Avenue public relations firm, Arthur Kudner, was on hand to deal with the media and publicize the mission.

The White House invited them to visit; the First Lady, Eleanor Roosevelt, intended to show them her pet housing projects, and NBC were lined up to broadcast the duke making a personal plea for world peace. What could possibly go wrong?

The British were incandescent. The duke was embarking on a populist movement at a time when the new king was still finding his feet. British ambassador Sir Ronald Lindsay bluntly explained to Sumner Welles, under-secretary of state, that this visit was viewed with "vehement indignation" by Buckingham Palace at a time when the new king was "trying to win the affection and confidence of his country's people, without possessing the popular appeal which the Duke of Windsor possesses."

The ambassador became increasingly suspicious of the real nature of the visit. He soon discovered that it was much more than an innocent fact-finding mission about housing and labour conditions; it was an attempt to launch the ex-king as a world ambassador for a peace movement that was effectively a front for Nazi ambitions. The ambassador saw his ploy of cosying up to organized labour as nothing more than an attempt to stage a "semi-fascist comeback in England."

When Lindsay surreptitiously obtained letters written by Bedaux, it confirmed his view that the tour had a quasi-political dimension. In the duke's proposed manifesto, Bedaux linked working conditions with the wellbeing of the common man, emphasizing that a worldwide peace movement must have as its task "to raise humanity's level of life's enjoyment." He went on to say: "No better leadership for such a movement could be found than in the Duke of Windsor."

Bedaux let his guard down further in the unlikely setting of a New York publisher's office, where he was discussing a self-penned medieval novel with editor John Hall Wheelock. During the meeting he described Hitler as "a man of genius" and foretold that the whole world was "going Fascist." As for his friend the Duke of Windsor, Wheelock recalled him saying that he would be "recalled to the throne as a dictator." Essentially he saw the duke's leadership of an apolitical worldwide peace movement as little more than a front, an arm of German foreign policy that would ultimately result in the duke regaining a powerful role in British governance.

Once the full itinerary was revealed, even the White House realized the duke had gone too far. The duke and duchess intended to start their tour in Washington on Armistice Day, November 11, attending the ceremony at Arlington National Cemetery before making a broadcast to the American nation in which the duke would announce his new international role. In order to avoid a diplomatic incident, Mrs. Roosevelt organized for the royal train, which would have taken them from New York to Washington, to be "delayed" so that at least they would miss the sombre ceremony of commemoration.

Indeed, a visit to America by the Duke and Duchess of Windsor had concerned the president virtually from the day they married. In order to avoid what he termed "diplomatic complications," he suggested to Herman Rogers that he should entertain the couple at his country house of Crumwold, so that the couple could meet the president informally at Hyde Park next door.

Alive to British sensibilities, the president now appreciated that the visit by the duke and duchess to America could have the makings of a "second abdication crisis." What no one foresaw was the eruption of grassroots hostility towards Bedaux and his guests, the duke and duchess. When Bedaux arrived in New York on November 1, 1937 he was met by a hostile media and organized labour unions eager to use the publicity of a royal visit to exact revenge on a man whose time-and-motion systems meant more work for less pay.

Communist-dominated unions in Wallis's home town of Baltimore led the charge, criticizing Bedaux's time-and-motion system and his association with Dr. Robert Ley, the man who had directed the destruction of all German free trade unions. The execution of two Communist labour leaders in Germany days after the Windsors left the country merely fuelled hostility. Labour leader Joseph McCurdy singled out the duchess for particular scorn, saying that when she was a young woman living in the city, she had "not shown the slightest concern nor sympathy for the problems of labour or the poor and needy." The *New York Times* weighed in, too, taking a pot shot at the duke. "He has lent himself, unconsciously but easily, to National Socialist propaganda. There can be no doubt that his tour [of Germany] has strengthened the regime's hold on the working classes." Many others, ranging from fellow trade union organizations to Jewish societies, weighed in, focusing on Bedaux, his methods, and his Nazi friends.

Several of his clients cancelled their contracts, a number of his engineers resigned in protest, while his fellow directors, seizing the opportunity to stage their own coup, demanded that he disassociate himself from the company. Stunned by the uproar, he agreed to relinquish control but not ownership.

The Internal Revenue Service got in on the act, issuing an income tax notice on Bedaux, while a former mistress lodged a legal suit for breach of promise. Such was the hue and cry that Bedaux slunk out of the Plaza hotel in New York through a side door to avoid the waiting press and drove to Montreal in Canada to take a boat out of the country. As far as Bedaux was concerned it was a government-inspired conspiracy, and he blamed Mrs. Roosevelt for stirring up the labour unions against him.

Meanwhile the Windsors, their trunks packed, waited in Paris for Bedaux to green-light the visit, their stateroom on the *Bremen*—Churchill chided them for choosing a German liner rather than a French vessel—ready and paid for. Instead they received increasingly hysterical telegrams from the beleaguered businessman urging them to cancel the visit. The duke contacted British ambassadors in Paris and Washington and the American ambassador in Paris, William Bullitt, for advice on how to proceed. Only Bullitt voiced his support. The duke, realizing that the paymaster for the visit was *hors de combat*, decided to postpone the planned tour, announcing that the ducal couple would at an unspecified date go on a fact-finding mission to the Soviet Union to balance the visit to Germany.

While President Roosevelt sent the duke a conciliatory note hoping that the visit would soon take place, in Britain the ducal farrago was greeted with undisguised glee by the ruling class. Even his supporter Lord Beaverbrook advised him to "quit public life." As for his many enemies, the Earl of Crawford reflected the views of many when he wrote:

> He had put himself hopelessly in the wrong by starting
> his visit with a preliminary tour in Germany where he was
> of course photographed fraternizing with the Nazi, the Anti-
> Trade Unionist and the Jewbaiter. Poor little man. He has
> no sense of his own and no friends with any sense to advise
> him. I hope this will give him a sharp and salutary lesson.

The duke duly retired from the fray, blaming the American media for spoiling what Wallis described as a "lovely innocent trip." Before he and the duchess set about restoring their rented home in the South of France, the duke left the British ruling class an unwelcome Christmas present revealing where his loyalties lay. In December 1937 he gave an interview to the left-leaning *Daily*

Herald, stating that if the Labour Party were ever in a position to offer it, he would be prepared to accept the presidency of the English Republic. The incendiary story, which for some reason was never published, was passed on to Sir Eric Phipps, now the British ambassador in Paris, who in turn informed Foreign Secretary Anthony Eden and thence the prime minister.

With that, the duke and duchess busied themselves shopping for designer clothes, jewelry, and furniture in Paris, leaving the possible impact of their proposed visits to America, Italy, Sweden, and Russia as one of the delicious "what ifs" of history. Even if his various peace missions had gone ahead, it is doubtful they would have made the slightest difference to Hitler's timetable of conquest. By March 1938 the government of Austria, the country the duke had chosen for his honeymoon, had allowed German troops to march into Vienna as part of the *Anschluss* or annexation.

Resource-rich Czechoslovakia was the next country on the German leader's shopping list, and when Prime Minister Chamberlain made clear that Britain would not risk war to defend Czechoslovakia's territorial integrity—"a faraway country of whom we know nothing"—it was only a matter of time before Hitler acted. The infamous Munich Agreement of September 1938 conceded the German-populated Sudetenland in Czechoslovakia to Germany, though it quickly became apparent that the piece of paper Chamberlain waved when he arrived back in Britain and his hollow boast that he had secured "peace in our time" had done nothing to quench Hitler's thirst for conquest. In March 1939 German troops marched into Prague and Hitler declared that Czechoslovakia no longer existed as a country. There was dismay in London, delirium in Berlin as the German people celebrated their nation's inexorable expansion without the cost of a single German life.

As the international scene darkened, the duke and duchess enjoyed the blue skies of the French Riviera, focusing purely on matters domestic. The news may have been bleak, the possibility of peace retreating by the day, but for the duke and duchess it was perhaps one of their happiest times. For months they energetically remodeled and restored Château de la Croë, the twelve-acre property beside the Mediterranean they now called home. Complete with gold-plated bath taps, twelve bedrooms, a tennis court, a swimming pool, and footmen in the red-and-gold livery of the British royal family, it was a fitting place for an ex-king to hang up his crown.

A convoy of vans brought heirlooms that were stored at Frogmore House in the grounds of Windsor Castle outside London. There were dozens of cases of fine wines and liquor, chests of silver and French linens, paintings and *objets* wrapped in canvas, some of which were laid out on the lawn for royal inspection, the duke letting out excited cries "like a small boy at Christmas" when he spotted a half-remembered treasure.

Largely out of the public eye, they celebrated their first anniversary as a married couple with a cruise along the Amalfi coastline onboard the luxury yacht *Gulzar* with their friends Herman and Katherine Rogers. The smiles and body language of the newlyweds were in complete contrast to the tension and strain of the infamous *Nahlin* cruise of 1936 when the king was wracked with torment, contemplating abdication so that he could secure the hand of the then married Mrs. Simpson. (The *Gulzar* had a more heroic future: Two years later, the 202-ton yacht would save forty-seven exhausted soldiers from the beaches of Dunkirk before being sunk by German air raids in Dover harbour in 1940.)

During that voyage he had to hide or disguise his affections even when onboard the yacht. This time the duke and duchess were relaxed and publicly affectionate with one another. Herman Rogers, his trusty cine camera at the ready, filmed the couple laughing and joking while they admired the Leaning Tower of Pisa. As they wandered through the ruins of Pompeii they were clearly at ease with one another, as was Wallis when she entertained the elegant Princess Maria of Piedmont, who came for lunch onboard. The duke, a cigarette or pipe never far away, even tried his hand at a concertina as he sat on deck. Fit, tanned, and frequently bare-chested, the duke looked like a man very much at peace with himself.

One incident filmed by Rogers during the holiday perfectly captures the ambivalence of the duke's position and his political affiliations. As the couple boarded the *Gulzar* after a day spent sightseeing on the island of Ischia, they were watched by a crowd of well-wishers. The duke turned to the throng and grabbed his wife's forearm, forcing her into a brief but reluctant salute before waving to the crowd. At first glance it seems as though the duke was encouraging his wife to acknowledge the watching throng. A second look reveals a large painted slogan on the quayside wall where the yacht was moored. It reads in Italian: "Europe will be Fascist." Was the duke forcing his wife to salute the crowd or to recognize the sentiments of the huge black sign? It remains an intriguing if unanswered question.

Whatever his private feelings, the duke's one public intervention that year in his self-proclaimed role as Edward the Peacemaker came when he accepted an invitation from American NBC radio to make a broadcast from Verdun, the First World War battle site, appealing for world peace. "I speak simply as a soldier of the last war, whose most earnest prayer is that such a cruel and destructive madness shall never again overtake mankind. The grave anxieties of the time compel me to raise my voice in expression of the universal longing to be delivered from the fears that beset us." While the emotional text, which the duke wrote himself, attracted thousands of letters of praise and support from worried citizens around the world, it did nothing to appease the royal family. As the king and queen were on their way to Canada and the United States on a crucial visit to drum up support for Britain and to introduce the new king to her most important allies, it was seen as yet another attempt by the duke to steal his brother's thunder.

The queen complained to Queen Mary: "How troublesome of him to choose such a moment."

During these critical months, while the duke fretted over the designs for the livery, linen, and stationery for his palatial home, his brothers King George VI and the Duke of Kent, and his German cousins, most notably the Hessen family and Prince Max Egon von Hohenlohe-Langenburg, were working to avert the coming storm. The Duke of Windsor may have garnered the headlines, but other royal princes were doing the heavy lifting for peace backstage. The Duke of Kent, who travelled extensively throughout Europe, ostensibly on family business, used these visits to maintain a diplomatic back channel with Germany. As one journalist noted at the time: "The private journeys of members of the British royal house in fact have been quite often equivalent to discreet political missions."

According to the memoir of Frederick Winterbotham, the head of British air intelligence, the Duke of Kent regularly met with the British agent and aircraft salesman Baron William de Ropp, a clandestine figure who became a confidant of Hitler and Rosenberg.

Though little is known about these meetings—Winterbotham even excised mention of the Ropp-Kent meetings in the second edition of his book—commentators have concluded that "the Duke of Kent obviously had a very real influence on political events. He was uniquely placed to act as an intermediary between high-ranking Nazis and the movers and shakers of British society for the betterment of Anglo-German relations."

Perhaps his most delicate and controversial meetings were with his cousin and ardent Nazi, Prince Philipp von Hessen, who, for a time, had the ear of both Hitler and Göring. As Prince Philip, the Duke of Edinburgh, has confirmed, there was a "tremendous amount" of contact between the Duke of Kent and Prince Philipp von Hessen, the two men, for example, having diplomatic talks at the funeral of Queen Maria of Romania in Bucharest in July 1938.

The most important meeting between the two royals took

place a year later in Florence on July 1, 1939, at the wedding of Princess Irene, the daughter of Constantine I, the king of Greece, and Prince Aimone Roberto di Savoia-Aosta, the Duke of Spoleto, the cousin of the Italian king.

The Duke of Kent was ostensibly sent along to represent the British royal family. Much more was going on behind the scenes. With war seemingly inevitable, Britain aimed to keep Italy out of the conflict for as long as realistically possible. The duke was to influence the Italian king in Britain's favour.

George VI and Prime Minister Chamberlain had discussed the diplomatic brief for the Duke of Kent, even down to the language he would use when he met the king in Florence. Furthermore, George VI argued that his brother should invite Prince Philipp to Britain, where he could be used as a messenger to convey to Hitler that Britain was in earnest about declaring war should he try and invade Poland, the next target on his shopping list of countries.

The prime minister and Foreign Secretary Lord Halifax disagreed with the king. They felt that the situation was too complex and unsettled for well-meaning amateurs rather than professional diplomats to be used to conduct negotiations.

While the king, according to his biographer John Wheeler-Bennett, did not press the issue, it is clear that he went "rogue," defying his prime minister and foreign secretary and instructing his younger brother to initiate delicate conversations with the Italian king as well as with his German cousin Prince Philipp. It is a sign of how strongly the king felt about the possibility of royalty influencing the course of events that he decided to go way beyond his constitutional remit, which is to "advise, encourage, and warn" the government of the day. As historian Tom MacDonnell has argued: "George VI was haunted by the memory of the Great War, and he had been an enthusiastic supporter of Chamberlain's appeasement policies. Repeatedly he had offered to make his own appeal to Hitler, sharing with his brother the Duke of Windsor the idea that kings and princes still had a meaningful part to play in diplomacy, as if nothing had happened to the map of Europe since 1914 when the Continent had been the private domain of royal cousins."

At the war's end Prince Philipp offered his own account of these unofficial royal discussions. He recalled that the Duke of Kent warned him that Britain would regard an invasion of Poland as a *casus belli* and that Germany should be under no illusions as to the possible consequences. Furthermore, the duke had pointed out that Foreign Minister von Ribbentrop was a "perpetual insult" to Britain and that conflict would always be imminent as long as the former wine salesman was in office.

As Professor Petropoulos observes: "It was bold for a British royal to circumvent established diplomatic and political procedures, and communicate to the Germans what acts would precipitate a war. According to the established practices of the British constitutional monarchy, this was not the purview of the royals."

After his discussions with the Duke of Kent during the wedding in Italy, Prince Philipp returned to Germany to report to Hitler. The Führer was not especially interested in listening to the German royal, and it was not until August that he was granted an audience.

By then, events had moved on apace. Hitler brushed aside the warning from the Duke of Kent and then showed Prince Philipp exactly why he no longer cared what the British thought. As he stood in the room, the Führer took a phone call from von Ribbentrop, who was then in Moscow. At precisely the moment Prince Philipp was relating the warning from Buckingham Palace, Germany and Russia were signing the infamous Molotov-Ribbentrop non-aggression pact. Both Hitler and von Ribbentrop believed that the British were too "decadent" to fight. They were proved wrong; Europe plunged into war a month later when Germany invaded Poland.

Just as Hitler ignored the warning from Buckingham Palace, he ignored the urgent telegram sent from the Duke of Windsor on August 29 urging restraint. At least he did him the courtesy of responding, telling him that "if war came" it would be England's fault. A similar cable, which the duke sent to King Vittorio Emanuele of Italy, evinced a more conciliatory response, the king assuring him that he would do his best to avert conflict. As his equerry, Dudley Forwood, observed: "I think he may have thought that his wise counsel might sway the Führer from confrontation with England." The same could also have been said about his brother George VI who, in the dogged pursuit of peace, was prepared to provoke a constitutional crisis by exceeding his authority and defying his ministers. In the parallel world of what might have been, if George VI and the Duke of Windsor had reached an accommodation, the king could have used his brother, now a private citizen, to influence the course of war and peace.

For even though the Duke of Windsor believed, according to Forwood, that as abdicated royalty he was of little consequence on the international stage, he had an undoubted charisma that evaded his brother. For the man in the *Strasse* he remained, whatever his diminished status, a talisman of peace, a living icon who could change events. The profound, almost visceral response he provoked among the public was shown just a few weeks after war was declared.

A wildfire rumour spread throughout the Reich in early October 1939 suggesting that George VI had abdicated and that the Duke of Windsor, once more in possession of his crown, was calling for an end to the war. Propaganda chief Joseph Goebbels recorded that work in shops, factories, and offices, including some government ministries, was suspended amidst spontaneous celebration. "Complete strangers embraced in the streets as they told each other the news."

It was a false hope but a reminder of the charismatic appeal of the ex-king. Though he was diminished, he was very relevant to the future of Europe—but not in the way he could ever have imagined.

———— ⬩⬦⬩ ————

CHAPTER NINE

The Game of Thrones

Once war was declared on September 3, 1939, the chances of peace breaking out inside the warring House of Windsor rose dramatically. The Duke of Windsor, arguably the most famous private British citizen on the world stage, was keen to sign up and help the country he once ruled in its hour of need. He contacted Walter Monckton in London and offered to assist his brother in any way he deemed appropriate.

It may have crossed his mind that, given his international appeal and high-level contacts, particularly in Germany, he could have been used as a peace emissary or at the very least a recognized broadcaster whose words would have had an impact on the listening public of Europe. Undoubtedly he was an asset who could have been used effectively and imaginatively by the ruling class when Britain needed all the help she could muster. At the very least the First World War veteran may have been forgiven for thinking that on his return to his homeland he could be used to help rally the troops.

This was so much wishful thinking. Instead of offering a truce, the royal family hunkered down in the Buckingham Palace bunker and dug in for a long war of attrition with one of their own. The duke and duchess, who were at the La Croë villa in the South of France when hostilities broke out, were informed that they could return to Britain only if the duke accepted either the post of deputy regional commissioner to Sir Wyndham Portal in Wales or liaison officer with No. 1 British Military Mission, which was based in France, under the command of Major General Howard-Vyse. They were, both in title and intent, non-jobs.

The government offered to fly them home but as the duchess had a morbid fear of flying, having watched numerous plane crashes when living with her first husband, a naval aviator, they elected to sail back, the duke suggesting to the British embassy in Paris that a destroyer should be sent to pick them up. This self-absorption at time of war was too much for the ever-loyal Fruity Metcalfe, who accused them of behaving "like two spoilt children....Women and children are being bombed and killed while YOU talk of your PRIDE."

After that spat, the ducal couple, together with a calmer Metcalfe, drove to Cherbourg, where they were picked up by the destroyer HMS *Kelly* commanded by the duke's choice for best man, Lord Louis Mountbatten. They arrived in Portsmouth in blackout conditions, met on the quayside by Lady Alexandra Metcalfe and their urbane lawyer, Walter Monckton.

On his own initiative Winston Churchill, now First Lord of the Admiralty, had organized for a Royal Marines band to play the national anthem when they stepped on British soil for the first time in three years. However, the band played only the first six bars—the full version, as the duke ruefully explained to his wife, was only for the sovereign. As for the royal family, they totally ignored their arrival, the queen sending a message to the Duchess of Windsor explaining that she could not possibly meet her. "He might not even exist," noted Lady Metcalfe in her diary.

As Buckingham Palace had made clear that they would not be organizing transport or accommodation for the Windsors, the Metcalfes placed their country home and London residence at their disposal. For the next two weeks the duke busied himself meeting ministers and military top brass as well as renewing old friendships.

During their stay they lunched with Lady Colefax, diplomat and author Harold Nicolson, and the novelist H. G. Wells. As they left the house, Nicolson said to Wells: "Admit that man has charm." "Glamour," said H. G. Wells, a telling insight into the human potential which could have been harnessed. Enthusiastic crowds spontaneously surrounded him or his car when he was spotted out and about in London, while a Gallup poll indicated that a clear majority—more than 60 percent—would welcome his return from exile with the duchess by his side. Even Prime Minister Chamberlain was in favour of that idea. Not the king and his family, who consistently viewed his personal magnetism as a threat to the newly established order.

The queen, ever protective of her husband, led the charge, telling Prince Paul of Yugoslavia in early October: "What a curse black sheep are in a family! I think he *at last* realizes that there is no niche for him here—the mass of the people do not forgive quickly the sort of thing that he did to this country, and they *HATE* her!"

She was not able to contain the utter loathing she felt towards the American adventuress. "I trust that she will soon return to France and STAY THERE," she wrote to Queen Mary. "I am sure that she hates this dear country and therefore she should not be here in war time."

Unsurprisingly, the new queen made sure she had left Buckingham Palace on September 14 when the duke arrived for a meeting with his brother to discuss his future employment. While the talk was amicable enough, the duke's first choice of the civil defence

post in Wales was later inexplicably withdrawn by the king, presumably, the duke and duchess suspected, as he did not want a
shadow king residing on home soil. Instead he was assigned to the
British Military Mission in Vincennes outside Paris.

Besides the raw antipathy of the duke's immediate family, he
was treated with mistrust by some in the military establishment
who feared that he would, inadvertently, give away secrets to the
enemy. The story of the Italian naval shells and the duke's eager
disloyalty had by now gained traction among those in the know.

After leaving his brother at Buckingham Palace, he made the
short journey to the Admiralty, where he was shown around by
Winston Churchill. Much to the consternation of watching naval
officers, Churchill took him to the Secret Room—the basement
area where the position of the British and enemy fleets was marked
hourly. The ever suspicious Earl of Crawford noted with alarm:

> He is too irresponsible a chatterbox to be entrusted with
> confidential information which will all be passed on to
> Wally at the dinner table. That is where the danger lies—
> namely that after nearly three years of complete obscurity,
> the temptation to show that he knew, that he is again at
> the centre of information will prove irresistible and that he
> will blab and babble out state secrets without realizing the
> danger.

Now he had his orders, the ducal couple returned to France,
viewing their brief sojourn in Britain with very mixed feelings.
Shortly after arriving in Paris, he described the dismal atmosphere
prevailing in Britain to Herman Rogers:

> *I had the opportunity of talking with most of the*
> *Cabinet Ministers and the senior officers of all three*
> *services, which helped me pick up the threads after three*

> *years absence. We found England definitely gloomy... But*
> *there is no enthusiasm over this war; a grim and rather*
> *sullen determination to make the best of the hopeless mess*
> *that successive bad governments have got the British people*
> *into is the atmosphere we left not unwillingly behind us!*
> *God knows how it's all going to end and a lot depends on*
> *how long it lasts.*

His worst fears about the enthusiasm for war were confirmed within days of returning to France. For a man who was so distrusted, he was given a particularly sensitive task. The French military were intensely secretive about their defences and fortifications, refusing to allow the Allies to inspect the Maginot Line, the chain of fortresses that formed the spine of their military redoubt. It was frustrating for the British.

While the mission was debating how to discover French military planning and deployments the duke was deputed to join them. As Brigadier Davy, the mission's chief of staff, recorded: "At last we were given the heaven-sent opportunity of visiting the French front."

The duke, who was as popular in France as he was in Germany and Britain, was the key to unlock the French military safe, General Gamelin, the French commander in chief at Vincennes, proud to give the ex-king tours of inspection of the front line. He proved himself to be adept at using his modest charm to tease out French secrets, Major General Howard-Vyse informing the War Office that he had produced five "valuable" reports on the inadequacies of the French defence, particularly the poor training of antitank crews. While the original thinking behind his role as liaison officer was simply to get the duke out of the way, in fact the task, which required discretion and diplomacy, was eminently suited to the duke's royal pedigree, his status opening all doors.

The duke did not see it that way, irritated at being deliberately kept from the British front lines and perfectly aware that nothing he said or reported was being acted upon by the military top brass in London. For her part the duchess, who was snubbed by all British charitable organizations, joined the French Red Cross, delivering medical supplies to field hospitals. It did not take long for them to feel bored, unappreciated, and resentful, the duke spending more time playing golf and attempting to secure the services of his French chef—who had been called up to the army—than working on military business. On several occasions the restless duke returned to London in the winter of 1940 without the knowledge of the king. He briefly saw Churchill, went to the Foreign Office to complain about his treatment by the embassy in Paris and, perhaps most significantly, to intrigue.

At a secret conclave with Walter Monckton and Lord Beaverbrook at Monckton's home in early 1940 he seriously considered a suggestion that he lead an international peace movement, as he was poised to do when Bedaux was the paymaster. Beaverbrook, at his most mischievous, egged the duke on, suggesting that the war could be ended by a peace offer to Germany. The press baron thought that the duke should return to civilian life, enlist City support, and go around the country as a "peace candidate." "Go ahead sir, I will back you," said the impish Canadian before taking his leave. For some minutes the duke took up the idea with enthusiasm, pausing only when Monckton pointed out that he would be committing "high treason." What really ended this delicious dalliance with a new important role was when Monckton indicated that if he returned to Britain he would have to pay income tax. At this the "little man" blanched and declared that the whole scheme was off; once he had to spend his own money, as with the aborted Bedaux tour of America, his enthusiasm instantly waned.

Though the duke was frustrated by the lack of appreciation for his military assessment of French defences, it was those very observations that reinforced suspicions about his loyalty to the Allied cause. Hitler's audacious advance into France and the Benelux countries on May 10, 1940, bypassing the Maginot Line and over-running the inadequate antitank defences previously identified by the duke, was the pivot for renewed concern.

That the duke's recommendations about strengthening the very defences that were breached by General Guderian's Panzers were ignored is rather lost in the shuffle. If they had been acted upon, the thrusting tank attack may have been blunted. When Hitler launched the Battle of France, the Western powers had the upper hand in terms of the number and quality of armaments, the Germans gaining an advantage thanks to superior strategy and execution. As historian Professor Petropoulos observes: "The questions that would logically follow center on whether espionage or indiscretion contributed to this superiority and whether the Windsors were the source of any intelligence."

The finger of suspicion has pointed at Charles Bedaux. During the so-called Phoney War, Bedaux was close to von Ribbentrop and his emissary in Paris, Otto Abetz, and had also been a frequent dinner guest of the duke, now "Major General Edward," and the duchess. He also made sure that he was on good terms with the ducal entourage. Over dinner at Claridge's in London he offered Forwood a "good post," implying he would do well in a new pro-German government. His conspiratorial attitude merely baffled Fruity Metcalfe. "I can't make him out. He knows too much," Metcalfe observed.

Nonetheless it was the doggedly loyal Metcalfe who organized dinners between Bedaux, now under secret service surveillance, and the duke and duchess when they first returned to Paris. After the humiliating debacle of the cancelled visit to the United States, the duke may have been more guarded with a man described by Dudley Forwood as a "clever manipulator." However, as Bedaux invariably picked up the tab for dinner, it could be that the duke felt obligated to sing for his supper, inadvertently giving away important military information to this Nazi collaborator.

The duke had always taken a dim view of the French, thinking them decadent and corrupt. His first-hand investigation into the country's defences had merely reinforced that view. It may well have been that he communicated those views more freely than he ought.

During the Phoney War, Bedaux still believed that active hostilities were not inevitable between the combatants and used his contacts to try to resolve the potential conflict. As historian Gerhard Weinberg observes: "In the critical period of May and June 1940 Bedaux was pro-Nazi and thought it best for the Western powers to make peace with the Nazis on any terms they could."

The evidence that Bedaux was a possible channel of communications between Windsor and Hitler appears in January 1940 communications from the German ambassador in The Hague in Holland, Count Julius von Zech-Burkersroda, to Germany's undersecretary for foreign affairs, Baron Ernst von Weizsäcker.

"Through personal relationships I might have the opportunity to establish certain lines leading to the Duke of Windsor," the count reported, explaining that the duke was "not entirely satisfied" with the role he had been given with the British Military Mission. "Also there seems to be something of a *Fronde* [a rebellious conspiracy among nobles] forming around Windsor which for the moment had nothing to say but which at some time under favourable circumstances might acquire a certain significance." During this time, according to historian John Costello, Bedaux made frequent trips to his offices in The Hague, and it was Zech-Burkersroda who identified the duke in his reports to Berlin as the source of military intelligence.

As Costello states: "By comparing Allied and German records it is now possible to develop a convincing case that an intelligence leak leading back to the Duke of Windsor may well have played a significant part in prompting Hitler to order his generals to change their battle plan."

In his own extensive investigations, Professor Weinberg, a former diplomat, came to believe that it was a German agent attached to the duke's office rather than the duke himself who was leaking information to the Nazis. "During the first months of the war important information passed from his blabbering through that agent to the Germans." The question is: Did the duke know what this person was doing?

Biographer Charles Higham goes further, asserting that on November 4, 1939, the duke wrote to Hitler under the name EP (Edward Prince), saying that he had information regarding his trip north to survey the British troops and that Bedaux was entrusted with that information. "I am hardly able to stress the importance of the information which is why I have gone into so much detail in explaining it to our friend," he wrote. Bedaux handed the report to Hitler in Berlin on November 9. Bedaux further claimed that during dinner parties the duchess was passing on classified military information which she had gleaned from her husband. "As a result the information made its way into German hands," wrote Higham.

This is an enduring perception of the duchess as a spy, collaborator, or plain disloyal, which was widespread in the British Establishment at the time and became an accepted fact after the war. With some justification. Her friend, journalist and playwright Clare Boothe Luce, vividly recalls one evening in May 1940 when the Windsors were playing cards at their Paris home and she was listening to the BBC news, which was describing Luftwaffe fighters strafing English coastal towns. When Luce said how sorry she felt for them, the duchess briefly looked up from her cards and replied: "After what they did to me I can't say I feel sorry for them—a whole nation against one lone woman."

The most damning assertions about the duke's behaviour

during the fall of France come from author Martin Allen, who argues in his book *Hidden Agenda* that the ex-king spied for Hitler, supplying Bedaux with crucial information about French troop deployment which he passed on to the Nazis. As a result of the duke's betrayal, Hitler was able to change his battle plans and ordered the thrust of his attack on France through the poorly defended Ardennes forest, resulting in the German army's stunning victory.

Here the plot thickens. In his book Allen cites a number of documents held at the National Archives in London, some of which were subsequently discovered to be forgeries. A police investigation during 2007 discovered that no fewer than twenty-nine documents had been placed in twelve separate files and cited in one or more of Allen's three books. As *Financial Times* journalist Ben Fenton, who spent months investigating the whodunit, states: "According to the experts at the Archives, documents now shown to be forgeries supported controversial arguments central to each of Allen's books: in *Hidden Agenda*, five documents now known to be forged helped justify his claim that the Duke of Windsor betrayed military secrets to Hitler." While the police made an arrest in the case, the Crown Prosecution Service decided that it was "not in the public interest" to pursue the matter.

Even though the forgeries at the National Archives in London muddied the waters about the wartime activities of the Duke of Windsor, the irony is that they are entirely consistent with the way Britain's ruling elite viewed the ex-king and his American wife. He was seen as a loose-lipped defeatist who could not be trusted with information of any military importance. As for the duchess, for the past several years she had been suspected of being in cahoots with her "lover" von Ribbentrop and other leading Nazis.

An FBI report which was sent by J. Edgar Hoover to President Roosevelt in September that year distilled official thinking in London and Washington about the ducal couple. "For some time the

British Government has known that the Duchess of Windsor was exceedingly pro-German in her sympathies and connections and there is strong reason to believe that this is the reason why she was considered so obnoxious to the British Government that they refused to permit Edward to marry her and maintain the throne." For good measure, the report's author, agent Edward Tamm, added that the duke was often too drunk to make sense and that the duchess was in "constant contact" with von Ribbentrop. "Because of their high official position the Duchess was obtaining a variety of information concerning the British and French government official activities that she was passing on to the Germans," stated agent Tamm.

Add to this toxic mix of royal distrust and perceived disloyalty the elderly personage of Lloyd George, the former prime minister and Liberal leader. In May 1940, at the moment of Britain's greatest peril, when the island stood alone against Hitler, he refused all entreaties to join a government of national unity now led by Winston Churchill.

Chamberlain suggested that perhaps the defeatist Lloyd George, who once lauded Hitler as Germany's "George Washington," saw himself as Britain's equivalent to France's Marshal Pétain, who was then desperately suing for an armistice with Germany. Churchill thought that speculation highly likely. Other senior politicians cast Lloyd George in the role of veteran politician Pierre Laval, Pétain's deputy, who was executed by firing squad at the war's end, with the Duke of Windsor as Marshal Pétain, a popular war hero but also guilty of collaboration.

In June 1940, when Britain's army was awaiting rescue on the beaches of Dunkirk, it was not an implausible scenario to believe that Lloyd George could engineer a coup d'état against the "Churchill clique," sue for peace with the Germans, and install the Duke of Windsor as puppet king. As the duke's official biographer Philip Ziegler has argued: "A great many people believed in June and July 1940 that Britain was likely to lose the war. The Duke's fault was that he said it out loud, and not just to his fellow countrymen."

At the time, though, the ducal couple's thoughts were focused on how to get away from the Germans rather than represent them. The duke had engineered a switch from northern France and was seconded to the Armée des Alpes on the Italian frontier and then attached to the French command in Nice. The posting was conveniently near to the Château de la Croë, their rented villa in Cap d'Antibes. It proved to be only a temporary stay, Italy declaring war on France in the second week of June. With the German army advancing southwards and the Italian army poised to invade the holiday towns along the Côte d'Azur, prudence dictated that they return to Britain immediately or head to a neutral country. While the local British consul suggested that they should go to Lisbon and from there back to England, the duke had grander plans. In a show of "incredible self-importance, which wasn't completely out of character," early in the morning of June 17 the duke telephoned Major General Edward Spears and asked him to arrange a Royal Navy warship to pick him up from Nice.

An irritated Spears tersely informed the duke that no warship could be made available and that the road to Spain was open to motor cars. So Franco's Fascist Spain, some three hundred miles south-west, it was. Though Spain was officially neutral—or "non belligerent"—Hitler was putting great pressure on the *Caudillo*, who had benefited from German military support during the vicious civil war, to join the Axis.

By heading to Spain, Major General Windsor was entering the lion's den, gambling that he would be given safe passage. This was by no means certain. As a military man entering a country that was officially neutral, he could be arrested and detained. The precarious situation was such that several days before, Britain's new ambassador to Spain, Sir Samuel Hoare, had contacted air minister Sir Archibald Sinclair in London, urgently requesting a plane be sent to Madrid in case of "a coup organized by German gunmen."

The duke and duchess decided to take their chances. They said their farewells to their American friends Herman and Katherine Rogers, who decided to stay on at Lou Viei and continue running a soup kitchen which was feeding up to sixty people a day. Herman went on to become the local head of the Red Cross, delivering essential food supplies to refugees and helping the homeless find shelter. On June 19, just as the French were contacting their putative Nazi rulers for armistice terms, the ducal couple, two consular officials, and royal staff set off in a four-car convoy—one hired van just for the royal luggage—and headed for the Spanish frontier. With the country in turmoil, barricades manned by locals had sprung up along the route. At each checkpoint the duke would announce: "*Je suis le Prince de Galles. Laissez-moi passer, s'il vous plaît.*" The magic name parted the way, the party arriving in Barcelona on June 20.

In the fevered atmosphere, the ex-king was a lightning rod for rumour and speculation. As with the wildfire story claiming that George VI had abdicated and the duke was seeking peace, which had gripped the German public the previous October, the duke was once again seen as Edward the Peacemaker. This time the story, which appeared in the Rome newspaper *Il Messaggero* and the Madrid paper *Arriba*, alleged that the Duke of Windsor had not merely been restored to his throne following a popular mutiny by British troops but had flown to Berlin to negotiate an end to hostilities. According to these excited reports, Prime Minister Churchill had even threatened to jail the duke if he returned to Britain. While the stories in Fascist newspapers could be dismissed as irritating propaganda, even Ambassador Hoare, who had advised the ex-king during the abdication crisis and was intimately aware of the concern in Downing Street and the Palace about the duke's loyalties, was uncertain of what to think. In a cipher to London he said that he planned to extend the "usual courtesies" to the duke but asked: "In view of press articles saying that it is intended to arrest him on arrival in England please confirm that I am acting correctly." As a hive of journalists buzzed around the duke's hotel in Barcelona it was left to his comptroller, Major Gray Phillips, to swat the story.

Within twenty-four hours of Sir Samuel Hoare contacting London about the duke's status, the German ambassador to Madrid, Dr. Eberhard von Stohrer, was alerting his own boss, German foreign minister von Ribbentrop, about the movements of the royal couple. In his telegram he said that the Spanish foreign minister, Colonel Juan Beigbeder y Atienza, had asked for guidance on how to handle the imminent arrival of the Duke and Duchess of Windsor in Madrid.

In his message Stohrer stated: "The Foreign Minister gathers from certain impressions which General Vigón [Head of the Spanish Supreme General Staff] received in Germany that we might perhaps be interested in detaining the Duke of Windsor here and eventually establishing contact with him."

Vigón's evidence is fascinating. On June 16 the general, who was representing Franco, met with Hitler at the Château de Lausprelle in Acoz, Belgium, two days before the Germans entered Paris. He was there for discussions concerning the role of Spain in the conflict. While his primary purpose was to deliver a message from Franco stating that Spain was in no position, after three years of debilitating civil war, to join the Axis offensive, during their conversation Hitler intimated that the Duke and Duchess of Windsor would be arriving in Spain. "He suggested that Nazi Germany would have substantial interest if the Duke and Duchess could be delayed long enough for secret contacts and peace talks."

As Hitler's conversation with Vigón had taken place three days *before* the duke and duchess had actually left their villa for Spain, it further suggests that the Germans had an agent within the duke's entourage or at least with knowledge of his proposed movements. This lends further credibility to Professor Weinberg's assertion that the military information the duke gleaned from his "spying mission" in northern France was intentionally leaked to the Germans by a member of staff or Nazi sympathizer.

When von Ribbentrop was told about the couple's arrival in Spain he was, according to his young aide, Erich Kordt, "electrified" by the idea of them staying for a time. He telegraphed Stohrer:

Is it possible to detain the Duke and Duchess in Spain for a couple of weeks to begin with before they are granted an exit visa? It would be necessary to ensure at all events that it did not appear in any way that the suggestion came from Germany.

From von Ribbentrop's point of view, here was a heaven-sent opportunity to have a pro-German head of state waiting in the wings once Britain had capitulated. With the Spanish clearly eager to act as middlemen, who could blame him for exploring the situation? While the plot, which was eventually codenamed Operation Willi, has been dismissed as "ludicrous and naïve," at the time it seemed eminently prudent to see if a major British figure could be lured into the Nazi net.

As Edward VIII's biographer Frances Donaldson observed:

The Germans believed themselves to be within an ace of conquering Britain. What more certain than that they would be on the lookout for a man who, while not the stamp of a traitor, might see his duty to his country in the light that Pétain had seen his? And what more likely prospect than the man who as King had made no bones about his admiration for the German nation and his belief that war could settle nothing in the modern world, who less than three years before had travelled through Germany with the most notorious of the Nazi leaders, reportedly giving a 'modified version' of the Nazi salute, and who had appealed directly for peace?"

In the days following the "miracle of Dunkirk," with most of the British army's modern equipment abandoned on French fields, a negotiated peace seemed a likely option. The empire would be preserved and England would live to fight another day. In a now overlooked episode in the heroic Battle of Britain, in June 1940 Foreign Secretary Lord Halifax—the king and queen's preferred candidate as prime minister—and his political aide R. A. Butler were in touch with Swedish diplomats with a view to asking them to act as intermediaries regarding possible peace talks with Germany. On June 17, just after Hitler had talks with Spanish general Juan Vigón, Butler told the Swedish minister that "no chance would be missed to reach a compromise peace if reasonable conditions could be obtained." Several weeks later, Prince Max von Hohenlohe reported a meeting between himself and the British representative in Switzerland where ill-defined and somewhat nebulous peace overtures were made.

It was entirely plausible that the Duke of Windsor would have been invited to take on the role of honest broker. The duke was seen by the Nazi hierarchy as "no enemy of Germany." According to official documents released in 2003, German diplomats considered him to be "the only Englishman with whom Hitler would negotiate any peace terms, the logical director of England's destiny after the war."

Certainly the duke and duchess's sojourn in Spain coincided with the only period during World War Two when a negotiated peace was possible and plausible.

The duke and duchess may have arrived in war-torn Madrid

unscathed, but the sniper fire from Buckingham Palace was unrelenting. From the moment they had returned to France in late September, the palace had tried to keep the duke in virtual quarantine, isolated from British troops and "kept under control" by his military minders so that he could not stage any kind of comeback. Fearing his charismatic personality, they deliberately starved him of the oxygen of publicity. So when, in November 1939, he took a salute meant for his brother the Duke of Gloucester, the ex-king was formally reprimanded. Naturally he was ordered to make himself scarce when the king toured the British positions before Christmas. As the duchess wrote in her memoirs: "We had two wars to deal with—the big and still leisurely war, in which everybody was caught up, and the little cold war with the Palace, in which no quarter was given."

Buckingham Palace had driven the duke to distraction; now the Germans, watchful and waiting, hoped that he would be driven to desertion. The secret tug-of-war between Germany and Britain for the hearts and minds of the Duke and Duchess of Windsor led to one of the most bizarre episodes of World War Two, a story that was kept under lock and key until the late 1950s.

With the Windsors now in Madrid and von Ribbentrop pondering his next move, Churchill telegraphed the duke, informing him that he and the duchess should come home as soon as possible. A Sunderland flying boat was assigned to fly to Lisbon in Portugal to pick them up. Ambassador Hoare was further instructed by the Foreign Office:

Please invite Their Royal Highnesses to proceed to Lisbon.

The palace was furious at this false appellation. At this critical moment in the war, when the royal family were debating whether to evacuate Princesses Elizabeth and Margaret to Canada, the king's private secretary, Alex Hardinge, found time to chastise the

Foreign Office for using the forbidden words "Their Royal Highnesses." He expressed the king's desire that steps be taken to ensure that such an error never occur again.

In this high-stakes game of thrones the duke and duchess were not the only royal chips on the table. On the very day Churchill became prime minister, May 10, he tried to entice the eighty-one-year-old Kaiser to cross the Channel from his exile in Doorn in the Netherlands. An RAF plane was readied and the former monarch told he would be treated with "consideration and dignity." The Kaiser was not impressed, saying that he would not become involved in what he called Churchill's game of "political chess," especially as twelve members of his family were serving in the German armed forces. Clearly Churchill's aim was to use the Kaiser as a potential rallying point for disaffected German monarchists and other opponents of Hitler in precisely the same way that von Ribbentrop envisioned using the duke and duchess.

Rumours of anti-Nazi plots had already reached the ears of the British, one secret envoy reporting that a group of generals wished to establish a new government in Berlin that would be monarchist in character. As early as December 1939, for instance, Father Odo, the former Duke of Württemberg, reported directly to Foreign Office mandarin Sir Alec Cadogan with information that two anti-Nazi generals with the support of three tank divisions were preparing for a military uprising. Nothing came of it.

Nothing may have come from the Windsors' stay in Madrid either. After receiving Churchill's telegram, the duke and duchess planned to leave the Ritz hotel, where they were staying, and drive to Lisbon the following day, thus severely constraining von Ribbentrop's options. The long-running War of the Windsors now helped von Ribbentrop in his secret schemes. As luck would have it, it was belatedly discovered that the Duke of Kent was paying an official visit to Portugal in order to cement ties with Britain's oldest European ally. It was thought prudent by the British and

Portuguese president Salazar for the ducal couple to arrive in Lisbon after the Duke of Kent departed on July 2.

Such was the antipathy between the once inseparable brothers that when the Duke of Kent was asked if he wished to meet his elder brother before his own departure from Lisbon he was reported by a Portuguese diplomat to have answered "Good God, no." With the duke and duchess forced to stay in Madrid for a further week, von Ribbentrop was given breathing space to bring them into the Nazi orbit.

The duke, too, tried to exploit the hiatus, doubtless assuming that with his great political ally Winston Churchill at the helm of government, outstanding and contentious royal issues would be settled in his favour. In a series of increasingly querulous telegrams to the new prime minister he reopened negotiations on some matters that should have been dealt with before he abdicated. Irritated by his treatment in France, he wanted a firm assurance that a proper job would be waiting for him when he returned home.

Furthermore, he wanted an undertaking that "simple courtesies" would be extended to his wife. The ducal couple had been treated as outcasts when they first returned in September 1939, and he was adamant it would not happen again, insisting that his wife be received by the king and queen.

Ever the practical politician, Ambassador Hoare boiled the matter down to the duke and duchess meeting the king and queen privately for no more than fifteen minutes and that meeting appearing in the Court Circular. He even suggested that Churchill give the duke a naval command; otherwise he feared Edward might never leave mainland Europe.

Churchill, all too aware of the unbending obduracy of the court and the fabled obstinacy of the ex-king, sent a non-committal response, saying, somewhat lamely: "It would be better for Your Royal Highness to come to England as arranged, when everything can be considered."

It was a holding position, Churchill consulting closely with the king and his advisors before firing his big guns. As his assistant private secretary John Colville noted in his diary entry of June 29, the prime minister met with Beaverbrook and the king's private secretary, Alex Hardinge, to discuss the duke's demands. "It is incredible to haggle in such a way at this time, and Winston proposes to send him a very stiff telegram pointing out that he is a soldier under orders and must obey. The King approves and says he will hear of no conditions, about the Duchess or otherwise."

Even the duke's friends agreed that at this moment of crisis it was not appropriate to raise these personal matters. It was, according to his friend, right-wing political commentator Kenneth de Courcy, an enduring character fault in the duke, namely a persistent stubbornness about trivia and a "dithering" about decisions:

> Unhappily the Duke lacked both tact and skill in arguing his case. He annoyed or neglected important persons who, had they not been snubbed, would have been his very important allies. As a shadow king he would constantly and repeatedly get himself into trouble and they concluded that he was only fitted to be a café society royal.

As his ghost writer Charles Murphy, who worked with the duke for several years, observed: "The kindest judgement in the face of the evidence is that if Windsor was only playing a game with the object of forcing his government's hand it was brinkmanship of an appalling kind."

With his as-yet unanswered ultimatum hanging in the air, the duke went sightseeing, cheering crowds watching the royal progress. His own country might not want him, but there was little doubt of his popularity elsewhere. Presumably, then, he was flattered and not a little intrigued when the Spanish foreign minister, having been given the green light by von Ribbentrop, secretly invited the duke and duchess to stay in Spain as long as they wished. He proposed to put at their disposal the palace of the Moorish kings situated in the remote hilltop town of Ronda in Andalusia.

After the bleak two weeks he spent in blacked-out England—and with the prospect of invasion imminent—it was such a tempting proposal that he telegraphed Churchill and asked if there was any need for a prompt return.

He did not mention the offer of the palace to either Churchill or Hoare. Nor did he discuss the secret contact he had made with the Axis powers during his stay in Madrid. In a display of questionable judgement he asked his good friend and boon companion, Spanish diplomat Don Javier "Tiger" Bermejillo, to contact the German and Italian embassies in Madrid and ask if they could protect, for the duration of the conflict, his two houses, on the Boulevard Suchet in Paris and La Croë in Cap d'Antibes.

Was this a straightforward if misguided request or, given the very recent Swedish initiative, a coded peace overture via diplomatic back channels to the two enemies of Great Britain? Axis diplomats mulled over the significance of the duke's entreaty, trying to divine meaning in the royal tea leaves. The Italian chargé d'affaires in Spain, Count Zoppi, reported on the duke's state of mind thus: "The Duke is not certain he will be returning to Great Britain in spite of the pressure of the British Government upon him to do so. Rather he seems to wish to keep himself outside events, following developments from afar."

On June 30 the Germans responded by letting the duke know, through Tiger Bermejillo, that they would indeed protect his properties. It was made clear that nothing was to be put in writing about this secret arrangement. In an ironic juxtaposition, the diplomatic telegram preceding the duke's matter, which was subsequently revealed in captured German Foreign Office documents, unveiled the true attitude of the Nazi regime towards Britain. A top secret message from the secretary of state at the Foreign Office, Ernst von Weizsäcker, to government heads of department stated baldly: "Germany is not considering peace. She is concerned exclusively with preparations for the destruction of England." It was these German Foreign Office telegrams that would come to haunt the duke and the British and American governments after the war.

Yet three weeks later, on July 19, Hitler was still paying lip service to peace, in his famous speech to the Reichstag suggesting that England should call off the war and shelve their plans to invade Belgium and Holland. "Herr Churchill may dismiss this declaration of mine. In that case I have freed my conscience about what is to come." Three days earlier he had ordered preparations for the invasion of England to begin.

The duke exercised a similar diplomatic duplicity. In public he was circumspect about the war: At a cocktail party for five hundred influential Spaniards held at the British embassy, the ducal couple were the souls of discretion, going out of their way, as Hoare reported, to show their belief in final victory.

In private it was a different story. Their defeatist attitude greatly concerned the British ambassador, especially as they consorted with influential pro-Fascist Spanish aristocrats and others who would have no hesitation about making mischief for the duke. As Michael Bloch, author of *Operation Willi*, says:

> He believed that Great Britain faced a catastrophic military defeat, which could only be avoided through a peace settlement with Germany. Even if successful resistance were possible for a period, there was little point in continuing a struggle which could no longer attain any of its original objectives and which could only lead to prolonged destruction and suffering.

When he and the duchess were invited by Alexander Weddell, the American ambassador in Madrid, to watch a tennis match at the residence, the ducal couple were on good form. An astute judge of character, Weddell was suitably impressed, writing to his sister Elizabeth:

Our chief excitement in the past few days was the visit to Madrid of Wally Simpson and her Boy Friend. We invited no one except two or three people that they asked for. He is immensely improved and I think that she has had a wonderfully good effect on him. Wally herself gives every suggestion of extreme acuteness and unlimited ambition; her exterior suggests heavy armour plate or some substance slightly harder than a diamond. But very pleasant, very genial, and very witty.

When conversation turned to the war, the duke, speaking with first-hand knowledge, was dismissive of the organization behind the French military. He observed, as Weddell duly reported back to Washington, that Germany had spent a decade reorganizing their society so that they could accept the sacrifices of war. France had not. The duchess was more direct, saying that France had lost because the country was "internally diseased." "A country which was not in a condition to fight a war should not have declared a war," she argued. Weddell further reported that the duke was the natural leader of any peace party that may emerge in Britain.

Similar sentiments, relayed by Tiger, reached the ears of Franco, who together with his brother-in-law, the minister of the interior Ramón Serrano Suñer, believed that the ex-king was keen to act as peacemaker. Throughout the summer of 1940 Suñer and the Caudillo were willing collaborators in German machinations to keep the duke in Spain, an ill-defined strategy linked to the overarching scheme to use the duke for future negotiations with the "Churchill clique." Their reward would be a seat at the table when the spoils of war were carved up.

As Franco's biographer Paul Preston observes: "With France on her knees and Britain with her back to the wall, Franco felt all the temptations of a cowardly and rapacious vulture."

In spite of all these plots and secret manoeuvres, on July 2, as planned, the ducal couple left Madrid and drove to Lisbon. While von Ribbentrop was furious that they had escaped the Nazi net, it was by no means certain that they were prepared to return immediately to Britain.

In his report to Berlin, Ambassador Stohrer confirmed that the duke would return to Spain after replenishing his money supply, as it was "out of the question" that the British government would agree to his demands for a position of influence either in a civilian or military capacity, or for the duchess to be recognized as a member of the royal family. He added: "Windsor has expressed himself to the Foreign Minister and other acquaintances in strong terms against Churchill and against the war." (When the duke eventually saw the telegrams, he agreed with the observation about the duchess but not Churchill.)

As Madrid was a centre for Nazi diplomatic and espionage activity and Spain was teetering on the brink of entering the war on the side of the Axis, it seemed eminently prudent to travel to Portugal. It was, as the visit by the Duke of Kent had just shown, a much safer and friendlier country. With their good friend Sir Walford Selby, the former ambassador to Austria whose wife was a guest at their wedding, in charge of the embassy, they thought it was a chance to catch up on gossip and enjoy some fine wine, courtesy of the embassy cellars. They were to be proved sadly mistaken.

—— ⚜ ——

CHAPTER TEN

Plot to Kidnap a King

I n the turmoil of the first months of the war, the duke and duchess were not the only homeless royals fearful for their personal safety. Kidnap, ransom, and abduction have been the lot of royalty in wars down the ages. It was no different in 1940. As the duke and duchess whiled away the days in Nazi-dominated Madrid, another European royal was also at the centre of a German plot. The Nazis were desperate to prevent the "playboy king," Carol II of Romania, from fleeing Europe. Anxious about his security, the ousted monarch, who was lurking in Madrid, sent a message to the Portuguese dictator António de Oliveira Salazar, pleading for sanctuary. He agreed, provided that Carol II sail for exile in Mexico at the earliest possible opportunity.

If the duke and duchess thought that Lisbon—a city of spies, refugees, and double agents—was more of a safe haven than Madrid, they enjoyed a rude awakening. The welcome they received, at least from the British government, was hardly the one they expected. When they arrived in Lisbon on July 3, there was a telegram from Churchill waiting for the duke. His hope that the prime minister was going to comply with his demands quickly evaporated.

The telegram, which had followed them from Madrid to Lisbon, read:

Your Royal Highness has taken active military rank and refusal to obey direct orders of competent military authority would create a serious situation. I hope it will not be necessary for such orders to be sent. I most strongly urge immediate compliance with wishes of the Government.

The terse tone distilled an ocean of discussion inside the palace and Downing Street, much of it uncomplimentary. It fell short of accusing him of desertion—but not by much. In the original version, Churchill asked pointedly about the circumstances in which he left Paris for the South of France, implying that he had acted without appropriate military orders.

For a man who had, in his own mind, served his country loyally for all his adult life, this came as a slap in the face, especially as it was signed by the man he saw as his ally, friend, and advisor. Impetuous as ever, the duke drafted a furious response, resigning all military rank. Wallis stayed his hand, though he later wrote bitterly to the prime minister complaining about his "dictator methods."

The episode marked a sea change in the relationship between the two men. As Churchill's biographer Roy Jenkins observed: "This exchange probably marked the end both of Churchill's romantic attachment to the duke, and of the duke's belief that he could get Churchill to go on being as totally in his favour as he had been in December 1936." Later in the war, as Churchill's physician Lord Moran recounted, every time he was informed that the Duke of Windsor had asked for an appointment, the prime minister "sighed before arranging the day and time."

Furious and feeling beleaguered, the duke abruptly decided that he would communicate with the British embassy in Lisbon only via courier, fearing that if he went into the embassy building he might be arrested. The lack of trust was mutual: The embassy held the ducal passports for their security—and to forestall flight out of the country.

Even as the duke and duchess absorbed this magisterial rebuke, Churchill, with the king's agreement, had worked out a solution to the conundrum of what to do with an ex-king in a time of war. The answer, as he gleefully told Lord Beaverbrook, was to make him the governor and commander in chief of the Bahamas. Dictating a telegram to the duke, he said to Beaverbrook: "It is a good suggestion of mine, Max. Do you think he will take it?"

"Sure he will," said Beaverbrook, "and he will find it a great relief."

"Not as much as his brother will," replied Winston.

The archipelago, which comprised seven hundred tropical islands, was one of the farthest and most insignificant outposts of the British empire, and had the advantage of keeping him out of Britain, out of mischief but with something useful to do.

In a draft telegram to the prime ministers of the Dominions, Lord Caldecote, secretary of state for Dominion affairs, writing as if he were Churchill, bluntly laid out the underlying reason for the decision—essentially, the duke was viewed as a potential Fifth Columnist.

> The activities of the Duke of Windsor on the Continent in recent months have been causing HM [His Majesty] and myself grave uneasiness as his inclinations are well known to be pro-Nazi and he may become a centre of intrigue. We regard it as a real danger that he should move freely on the Continent. Even if he were willing to return to this country his presence here would be most embarrassing both to HM and the Government.

Though the eventual message was reworked considerably by Churchill, it does demonstrate the raw hostility and suspicion felt by the governing class towards the ex-king. In spite of Churchill's evident enthusiasm, the curious appointment was a classic compromise that suited nobody. Tory grandee Leo Amery described it as "a rather absurd appointment which is likely to be pretty freely criticized."

He was proved to be correct. The queen wrote to the colonial secretary, Lord Lloyd, predicting a "difficult" situation for the "good people of the islands who were used to looking up to the king's representative." The duchess, she scornfully observed, "is looked upon as the lowest of the low." She was not alone in this attitude, the Duke of Kent seeing the appointment as an opportunity to stop the ex-king from making trouble, telling Prince Paul of Yugoslavia that "my brother has behaved disgracefully."

On July 4, the unhappy tidings were relayed to the duke and duchess, not by their friend Ambassador Selby, who was a shadow of the man he once was, but by British diplomat David Eccles. He drove to the large villa near Cascais, along the coast from Lisbon, where they were staying as guests of banker Dr. Ricardo Espírito Santo Silva. The well-connected businessman, a Salazar loyalist who had played host during the recent visit of the Duke of Kent, was also a friend of the German ambassador to Portugal, Baron von Hoyningen-Huene.

Eccles, like many in the ruling class, took a dim view of the ducal couple, considering the duke part of the "canker in public life" that had led to the dramatic collapse of France. "I distrust the Duke of Windsor," he wrote to his wife, Sybil. "I shall watch him at breakfast, lunch, and dinner with a critical eye."

Nor was his opinion improved on closer acquaintance, subsequently describing the duke as "pretty Fifth column" and seeing the duchess as "a poor creature...a battered war horse in a halo hat." Later, Eccles relented somewhat and allowed himself to be seduced by the charm of a couple he described as "the arch beachcombers of the world."

As the duke and duchess sullenly mulled over Churchill's job

offer—Eccles recommended acceptance on the ground of safety—
it meant that, whatever their decision, they would remain in Portugal for the near future until they could acquire suitable berths
on a passenger ship. As it was, the duke accepted the same day,
morosely telegraphing Churchill: "I am sure you have done your
best for me in difficult circumstances."

It was left to the wife of the new governor to express the couple's
true feelings. She considered it a "pathetic little job in a ghastly
backwater," the social equivalent of Napoleon's exile to St. Helena.

The only consolation was that the prime minister allowed them
to make their own travel arrangements. It was a fatal mistake. The
ducal couple planned to sail for New York on August 1 onboard
the liner *Excalibur* for a few days' shopping and relaxation before
heading onward to the Bahamas.

They were not about to escape the Continent so easily. For the
next few weeks they were at the centre of Nazi intrigues to frighten
and cajole them back to Spain and into the German sphere of
influence. As the Germans discovered, the Portuguese were not
such willing accomplices as Franco's Fascists. For a start the man
in charge of the security surrounding the Duke and Duchess of
Windsor was well known to the former king. Captain Agostinho
Lourenço, the head of the PVDE, the Portuguese secret police,
had fought in France on the British side during World War One
but, more important, he had been made a Commander of the
Royal Victorian Order for personal services to the then Prince of
Wales when he visited Lisbon in April 1931.

It was a matter of high professional honour that nothing happen to the royal couple. As Professor Douglas Wheeler, an authority on contemporary Portuguese history, asserts:

> Lourenço knew everything that was going on in Lisbon as
> his men took bribes from both sides. He would never have
> let anything happen to the Duke and Duchess as he would

have been held responsible. While Salazar was afraid of German designs and the possibility of being invaded, they were not going to allow a senior personality of their closest European ally to be kidnapped.

As an added precaution, which the duke and duchess were not aware of at the time, any news about the royal couple was stopped from appearing in local and international media by British officials. Ambassador Hoare's press attaché, Tom Burns, was sent from Madrid to Lisbon to beef up the propaganda effort, using political and media contacts to counter Axis misinformation about the couple. The duke's access to the local media was controlled by the Allies and heavily restricted, as it had been in Madrid, so that nothing said privately by the royal couple could be exploited by the Germans.

Besides a news blackout, the ducal couple were monitored closely by an ad hoc team of watchers. For example, British journalist Josie Shercliff, a *Times* correspondent who served as a wartime agent, was encouraged to keep an eye on their movements. She was joined by, among others, Tom Burns and a young intelligence officer called Ian Fleming who hung around the casino at Estoril waiting for the duke to make one of his regular appearances. The casino—"a haunt of spies and many shady characters"—was the inspiration for his future James Bond books.

In a true-life *Casino Royale* moment, Burns was playing roulette when a voice behind said: *"Dix mille sur le noir."* It was the unmistakable voice of the duke, who stayed at the gaming tables that night until four in the morning.

While the duke spun the gaming wheel, the Germans, aided by Franco and assorted Spanish politicians and diplomats, endeavoured to encourage the duke and duchess to cash in their chips and head back to Spain. Even the public announcement on July 9 that the duke had accepted the post of governor of the Bahamas did little to dim German enthusiasm for snaring the duke.

If anything, reports received by von Ribbentrop from his ambassadors about the duke's defeatist attitude made him more hopeful and enthusiastic about effecting a return.

On July 10, the day after the announcement of the duke's appointment, ambassador Hoyningen-Huene reported that the duke intended to postpone his journey to the Bahamas for as long as possible, at least until August.

He continued:

> He is convinced that had he remained on the throne war could have been avoided and describes himself as a firm supporter of a peaceful compromise with Germany. The Duke believes with certainty that continued heavy bombing will make England ready for peace.

If true, the duke's attitude was recklessly disloyal, if not treasonous. (When shown this document in 1953, he wrote "NO" beside it in capital letters.) There was more. Ambassador Huene later confided to a senior Portuguese politician that if the duke returned to England he faced certain arrest. Once Germany prevailed in the conflict he was, according to Huene, destined to become "our first President of the Great British Republic."

The duke's attitude was music to von Ribbentrop's ears, the foreign minister desperate for the duke and duchess to march to his tune. For one delicious moment they seemed to be playing right into his hands: The ducal couple, fretting about the security of La Croë, their home in the South of France, briefly toyed with the idea of returning to collect their important possessions. As their passports were held by the British embassy, the duke asked officials to obtain the necessary visas for France and Spain so that they could undertake this mission. When it was pointed out to the duke and duchess that it would be neither prudent nor safe to undertake a hazardous journey in these uncertain times, they abandoned the scheme.

The Prince of Wales was the matinee idol of his age, the first royal pin-up whose face adorned magazine covers and cigarette cards the world over. Here he is in Halifax, Nova Scotia, during his 1919 Canadian tour.

Behind the smiling image was a morose, often depressed young man who hated the whole palaver of what Edward called "princing." When he was at sea during his extensive tours of the British Empire after the war, he would often spend days alone in his cabin. Only his cousin Lord Louis Mountbatten could rally his spirits.

Edward enjoyed a chilly, distant relationship with his father, King George V, and mother, Queen Mary. The future king was, though, idolized by his brothers and his sister, Princess Mary. Here are the family at the wedding of Albert, Duke of York, later King George VI, to Lady Elizabeth Bowes-Lyon in 1923. From left to right: Prince Edward; Princess Mary; Henry, Duke of Gloucester; King George V; Albert, Duke of York; Queen Mary; and George, Duke of Kent.

The prince standing between Rosemary Leveson-Gower (on his left) and Diana Capel at the Duchess of Sutherland's field hospital in Calais, France, in 1917. His parents vetoed his decision to marry Lady Leveson-Gower, Queen Mary arguing that there was a touch of madness in her mother's family.

Prince Edward first met Freda Dudley Ward during an air raid on central London while he was on army leave. The wife of a Liberal Member of Parliament, Freda became his first great love and long-term mistress.

In the late 1920s Thelma, Viscountess Furness, the part-American second wife of a shipping company chairman, became Edward's companion and mistress, acting as hostess at Fort Belvedere, his country home near Windsor Great Park. She first introduced the Prince of Wales to Wallis Simpson.

Finding a bride for the Prince of Wales became an international parlor game. Even German leader Adolf Hitler played, in 1934 suggesting Princess Friederike (far right), the daughter of Prince Ernst August and Princess Viktoria Luise, as a bride.

By the time Hitler became involved, the Prince of Wales was enamored with another married American, Wallis Simpson, pictured with her second husband, Ernest.

Wallis and her great friend Herman Rogers, who took many of the photographs seen for the first time in this volume, pictured in kimonos at his home in Peking, where Wallis stayed for a time in 1924.

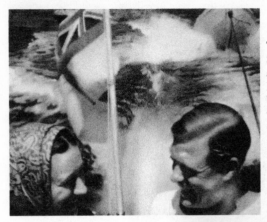

The new king and Mrs. Simpson share an affectionate look during the famous Mediterranean cruise on board the *Nahlin* yacht in 1936, which confirmed to the watching world that she was the new royal mistress. Only the British were kept in the dark, thanks to the silence of the Establishment media.

The fact that the new king allowed himself to be photographed bare-chested horrified many, who considered his behaviour undignified.

Wallis Simpson about to take a dip from the yacht *Nahlin*.

The king, pictured in snorkeling goggles, joins Mrs. Simpson on a secluded beach during the cruise.

The king had threatened suicide unless Wallis join him at Balmoral, the royal family's Highland retreat. She did her best to lighten the mood, acting as his hostess.

Guests at Balmoral included the king's younger brother the Duke of Kent and his wife, Princess Marina, as well as Louis and Edwina Mountbatten. They played arrow golf, a curious game imported from Austria.

The king takes a break to admire the scenery during a morning out stalking deer.

The king wearing a stalking cape, which provoked much mirth among the guests. From left to right: Lord Mountbatten, Edward Vlll, Katherine Rogers, Gladys Buist, Wallis Simpson, and Edwina Mountbatten.

Wallis's affair with the king made her notorious. She was also said to have had an illicit romance with Italian foreign minister Galeazzo Ciano (left) and his German counterpart Joachim von Ribbentrop (centre). Here Hitler (right) is entertained at von Ribbentrop's German home.

According to Father Odo, the Duke of Württemberg, von Ribbentrop sent Mrs. Simpson seventeen carnations to mark the number of occasions they had slept together.

Car salesman Guy Trundle was said by Scotland Yard to be yet another lover of Mrs. Simpson.

The king's German cousin Carl Eduard, the Duke of Saxe-Coburg and Gotha, who was also president of the German Red Cross, was often sent to London by Hitler to pick up the latest gossip and intrigue with his royal relations.

The popular new king championed the plight of war veterans and the unemployed, saying famously that "something must be done" during this tour of South Wales.

Protests—some spontaneous, some organized by British Fascist leader Sir Oswald Mosley—broke out after the king's abdication broadcast.

The king makes his famous abdication broadcast, which he wrote himself with help from Winston Churchill, on December 11, 1936, from Windsor Castle.

During his exile in Austria in December 1936, the Duke of Windsor wrote to Herman Rogers, saying what a "ghastly time" he had experienced.

DATE OF ARRIVAL	NAME	HOME ADDRESS	DATE OF DEPARTURE
May 22, 1937	Bessie L. Merryman	Ferm S. Bedaux	June 1st
" "	A. G. Allen	A. G. Allen	"
May 28, 37	Marcel Dupré	Randolph S. Churchill	June 2nd
" "	Ferm S. Bedaux	Walter Monckton	"
June 1st, "	E. J. Metcalfe	Chas E Bedaux	"
"	Alexandra Metcalfe	R. Anderson Jardine	"

Herman and Katherine Rogers brought the guest book from their villa in the south of France for members of the wedding party to sign in order to mark the Duke and Duchess of Windsor's marriage at the Château de Candé. Signatures include Wallis's aunt Bessie Merryman; Fruity Metcalfe and his wife, Lady Alexandra; Walter Monckton; and the officiating cleric, R. Anderson Jardine.

Wallis in gay mood after she and the duke were reunited after six months apart. Here taking tea are her future husband, her aunt Bessie Merryman, Katherine Rogers, and equerry Dudley Forwood.

The duchess poses for the camera in the days leading up to the wedding.

DATE OF ARRIVAL	NAME	HOME ADDRESS	DATE OF DEPARTURE
June 3rd	*Real Berhaud Commissaire Spécial Rhodestier*	*Edward Wallis*	June 3rd
	A. E. Mercier	*McCarter & Mrs*	
	Maurice Dupré	*Gertrude Beckford.*	
	Jean Dupré	*Dorothy Selby*	
	A. E. Allen	*Constance Spry*	
	G. D. Metcalfe	*Palmer Vine.*	

Edward and Wallis signed the wedding guest book together with members of their staff, who included the duke's private secretary Thomas Carter and the duchess's secretary Gertrude Bedford, as well as their florist Constance Spry.

A moment of reflection for the newly married couple following the short ceremony.

The duke and duchess celebrating their union with a cup of tea. Also seen are Dudley Forwood, Katherine Rogers, and the Rev. R. Anderson Jardine, who defied the church hierarchy to marry the exiled couple.

In spite of dire warnings, the duke insisted on visiting Germany in October 1937, ostensibly to review housing conditions. Here he listens with amusement to Dr. Joseph Goebbels, German propaganda minister, at a party given in honour of the duke and duchess by their host, Nazi labour minister, Dr. Robert Ley.

During the visit, the normally animated duchess seemed subdued, shooting a look of undisguised loathing at their host, the bibulous labour leader Robert Ley (left), during a tour of Berlin. She found his frequent drunkenness and off-colour jokes offensive.

The duke, in the company of Dr. Ley, inspects a Reich guard of honour. On several occasions the duke responded in kind to Nazi salutes.

The duke's fifty-minute solo meeting with Adolf Hitler at the Berghof, Obersalzberg, was the highlight of the twelve-day visit. It is hard to see what they had in common; one man wanted to rule the world, the other gave up his world for the woman he loved.

Hitler says goodbye to the duke after their one-on-one conversation, while his translator Paul Schmidt (far left) and Dr. Ley (left) look on. During their time together, the duchess was entertained by deputy Nazi leader Rudolf Hess.

A Nazi soldier salutes the duke and duchess as they drive away, following the historic meeting with Hitler.

In the summer of 1938, as Europe stood on the brink of war, the Windsors went sightseeing, visiting the Leaning Tower of Pisa with Katherine (pictured) and Herman Rogers onboard the yacht *Gulzar*. The ducal couple had planned to visit the United States but faced hostile opposition from labour unions, who were furious at their trip to Nazi Germany, a nation where unions had been crushed.

As the couple leaves the island of Ischia, it looks like the duke is forcing the duchess either to wave to the crowd gathered on the quayside or salute a slogan that reads EUROPE WILL BE FASCIST. The ambiguity of the picture reflects the duke's mixed public messages regarding his political beliefs and the true nature of his feelings about Hitler and fascism.

Controversial businessman Charles Bedaux was the focus for union hostility after he organized an extensive tour of America so that the duke and duchess could visit factories and housing projects. He aimed to promote the duke as "Edward the Peacemaker," but widespread opposition forced an abrupt cancellation. Clockwise from left: Charles Bedaux, Katherine Rogers, the Duke of Windsor, Fern Bedaux, and the Duchess of Windsor.

The Windsors at war, Wallis in her French Red Cross uniform and the duke in the uniform of a major general in the Welsh Guards. The couple's loose table talk was suspected of aiding the Nazis.

During their flight from France after the German invasion in May 1940, the duke and duchess stayed in Madrid and Lisbon, where they were the subject of a kidnap plot nicknamed Operation Willi.

As the memo from von Ribbentrop to Hitler shows, the German leader was kept up to date with every twist and turn in the plot to kidnap the duke and duchess. In the last throw of the dice, Hitler ordered them to be taken by force.

Notiz für den Führer

    Beiliegendes Telegramm ist am 9.7. in Angelegenheit Herzog von W i n d s o r hier eingegangen. Ich habe nun zunächst folgende Maßnahmen eingeleitet:
    1.) Beifolgendes Telegramm nach ......, aus dem Aktionsplan klar ersichtlich, ferner Telegramm des ..., das heute hier eingeht.
    2.) Dort Stellung von Schellenberg mit seinen Leuten mit deutscher Botschaft in Spanien und ev. Personal zur Verfügung zu stehen. Abflug Schellenberg morgen oder übermorgen. Schellenberg ist morgen zur Besprechung mit mir in .... (?)
    3.) Dort Stellung eines dem Herzogs-Paar Windsor engst befreundeten Ehepaars, das dort ist, sobald Herzog in Spanien ist, sofort Zweck dauernder Fühlungnahme und Beeinflussung desselben und seiner Frau nach Spanien abzureisen

The duke was made Governor of the Bahamas to keep him out of trouble. However, in late 1940 he seems to have become implicated in a freelance British plot to engineer a peace deal.

Also involved in the peace plot were Hitler's favourite spy Princess Stephanie von Hohenlohe and her lover, Hitler's former adjutant Fritz Wiedemann.

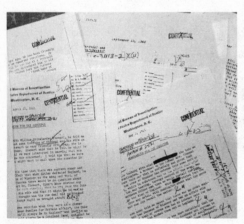

Such was the official suspicion surrounding the ducal couple that when they visited America in early 1941, President Roosevelt ordered the FBI to place them under surveillance.

The duke's friendship with Swedish businessman Axel Wenner-Gren (right), who was placed on an official blacklist, was also deemed suspect by the American government.

General Motors executive James Mooney (left), a long-time friend of the duke, was treated with suspicion because of his links with the Nazi hierarchy.

The attempt by the British first to destroy and then delay publication of the sensational Windsor file relating to the duke's wartime behaviour placed a severe strain on relations between the Allies. King George Vl was greatly agitated by the possible consequences for the monarchy should the file be published.

The duke and his loyal legal advisor Walter Monckton addressed the numerous issues raised by the existence of the Windsor file, which suggested that the duke was defeatist and did not believe Britain could survive an invasion by the Nazis.

Within weeks of the war ending, royal courtier and Soviet spy Anthony Blunt, pictured when he was a student at Cambridge University, was sent by King George Vl to a German castle to pick up historic letters from Queen Victoria. It was thought that his short trip had an ulterior motive—to bring back to Buckingham Palace any correspondence between the Duke of Windsor and the Nazi hierarchy.

Foreign Office librarian and translator Lieutenant Colonel Robert Currie Thomson, pictured here with a young family friend at Thomson's north London home, found the incriminating microfilmed royal cache buried in a wood on a German country estate.

American historian and wartime State Department official David Harris was the David who took on the government Goliath, warning his superiors that they would be breaking the law should they agree to British demands to destroy the Windsor file.

The instinctive deference of the British even towards an ex-king living in exile was the main stumbling block between the Allies regarding the vexatious Windsor file. Prime Minister Winston Churchill bows as he bids farewell to the duke in 1953 during an infrequent visit to London.

The Queen Mother's bereavement was used as a reason for delaying publication of the Windsor file. Here she is at Malvern College, watched by King George VI's biographer, stick-wielding Sir John Wheeler-Bennett. He tried to have the project to release German wartime documents scrapped in order to stop publication of material that may damage the royal family.

The duchess, agitated by the inconvenience of war, had other pressing concerns. She had left her favourite Nile-green swimsuit behind at La Croë. It was vital it be returned before she sailed for the Bahamas. To this end she enlisted the American minister in Lisbon and the American consul in Nice to repatriate the garment. Even though their rented villa was locked and shuttered and that part of the coast was occupied by the enemy, American diplomats duly did her bidding. In the midst of war the swimsuit was found and dispatched safely to the grateful duchess. The task was known privately as "Operation Cleopatra Whim."

The duchess was also worried about their possessions at their rented home in Paris, particularly their fine bed linens and the contents of a locked safe. She suggested that her trusted French maid Mademoiselle Moulichon travel to the French capital and bring them to Lisbon so they could take them to the Bahamas.

As with their previous request regarding the safekeeping of their French properties, the duke asked the Spanish authorities to act as intermediaries with the Germans. He sent word through the Spanish ambassador to Portugal, Don Nicolás, the rotund elder brother of General Franco, for a trusted Spaniard to be sent to pick up an important if mysterious message. Once more the duke did not trouble to inform his embassy, and again the eager Germans were intrigued by this latest development.

When the trivial nature of the mysterious ducal request was revealed, even the Spanish were astonished. It was one thing to ask for informal protection of a royal home, quite another to ask an enemy to be caretaker of the ducal pillows and sheets, however dense the thread count. Ambassador Don Nicolás expressed his disgust freely to Dr. Luis Teixeira de Sampaio, a senior advisor to Dr. Salazar: "A prince does not ask favours of his country's enemies. To request the handing over of things he could replace or dispense with is not correct."

Distasteful or not, the Spanish complied with the duke's

wishes, their great friend Tiger Bermejillo arriving in Lisbon to discuss the mechanics of obtaining travel visas from the Germans for their maid. During his five-day stay Tiger, who was as close to the Spanish leadership as he was to the ducal couple, once again formally invited them to sit out the war in Spain. He also passed on a warning for them not to go to the Bahamas as they would be in danger. It was the beginning of the German-inspired scare tactics to keep the duke and duchess in Europe.

Once back in Madrid, Tiger briefed the German ambassador and Spanish foreign minister about the duke's agitated state of mind. Based on his account, Ambassador Stohrer telegraphed von Ribbentrop, informing him that Churchill had threatened to court-martial the duke unless he took up the post of governor, and that his relations with the British embassy in Lisbon were very chilly. As far as von Ribbentrop was concerned, things were boiling up very nicely.

He had his own scheme for the duke and duchess. He outlined his thinking in a lengthy telegram marked "Top Secret, Confidential Handling," which he sent to Ambassador Stohrer in Madrid on July 11. In the dispatch he explained his plan to entice the Windsors back to Spain. He suggested that their Spanish friends might invite them for a brief visit or the Spanish authorities warn the duke that there was a British plot to assassinate him and that he should flee across the border for his own safety.

"After their return to Spain," continued the German foreign minister, "the Duke and Duchess must be persuaded or compelled to remain on Spanish soil." In the worst-case scenario the Spanish could detain him as a "deserting military refugee." At no point should it become known that the Nazis were behind the plot.

Once back in Spain, the duke would be told by a suitable trusted emissary that the only hindrance to Germany's ambition of peace with England was the Churchill clique. As von Ribbentrop explained to Stohrer: "Germany is determined to force England to peace by every means of power, and upon this happening would be prepared to pave the way for the granting of any wish expressed by the Duke, especially with a view to the assumption of the English throne by the Duke and Duchess." Even if he did not wish to avail himself of that opportunity, von Ribbentrop promised that he could lead a life "suitable for a king."

While it was clear that the duke and duchess were to be tricked into returning to Spain, the tone of von Ribbentrop's telegram suggested a belief that the duke might be amenable to collaborating with the Nazis. It was a belief based on the duke's current disenchantment with Churchill and the royal family, his desire for peace, and the mutual respect felt by both sides, Hitler and the duke enjoying continued cordial relations. It was a gamble but not a quixotic one. With Hitler actively preparing for the invasion of Britain, the duke was undoubtedly the preferred candidate for the job of puppet king.

Stohrer put the von Ribbentrop plot in motion, he and the Spanish interior minister, Ramón Serrano Suner, asking the duke's long-time friend, the playboy Duke Miguel Primo de Rivera, to travel to Lisbon to warn the duke about the threat to his life and to suggest a hunting expedition in the mountains by the border as his pretext for leaving Lisbon.

In the meantime Ambassador Stohrer suggested to von Ribbentrop that the duchess's maid be granted a visa from the German embassy in Madrid, which would allow her to travel to Paris to collect the cherished royal possessions. Then, he suggested, she should be deliberately held up on her way to Lisbon so as to postpone the departure of the ducal couple to the Bahamas.

While the duchess's maid waited for her visa, Don Miguel and his wife enjoyed the company of his English friend in Lisbon, returning a few days later to Madrid, where he was debriefed by ambassador Stohrer. Unsurprisingly, the Duke of Windsor felt like a prisoner in Lisbon, suspecting that he was surrounded by spies.

Stohrer duly cabled von Ribbentrop:

Politically the Duke has moved further and further away from the King and from the present English government. The Duke and Duchess do not fear the King, who is utterly stupid, as much as the clever Queen, who is said to intrigue constantly against the Duke and particularly the Duchess. The Duke is toying with the idea of disassociating himself from the present tendency of British policy by a public declaration and breaking with his brother.

He went on to outline how the ducal couple were enthusiastic about returning to Spain, though they were concerned that they would be taken prisoner. When the duke was shown this German Foreign Office telegram in 1953, he agreed with the sentiments regarding his family but disagreed that he planned a public declaration.

In a second dispatch, Stohrer added a further—rather telling— report from Don Miguel. It indicated that the English duke was not as keen on getting back his old job as von Ribbentrop might have hoped.

When he [Don Miguel] advised the Duke not to go to the Bahamas but to return to Spain as the Duke might yet be destined to play a large part in English politics and even ascend the English throne, both the Duke and Duchess seemed astonished. Both seemed completely enmeshed in conventional ways of thinking, for they replied that under the English constitution this would not be possible after the abdication. When the confidential emissary then expressed the expectation that the course of the war might produce changes even in the English constitution, the Duchess in particular became very thoughtful.

The duke may have been reluctant to reclaim the throne, but nonetheless von Ribbentrop remained excited by the mouth-watering prospect of the ex-king "doing a Pétain" and making a broadcast or issuing a public statement asking his people to lay down their arms for the sake of peace.

While von Ribbentrop and Stohrer pondered the duke's possible role in the Nazi plans to conquer Europe, the duke was fighting more important battles, insisting that his two soldier servants be withdrawn from active service and join him in the Bahamas. He felt so strongly about the fact that it would be a "serious handicap starting with a new valet" that he sent his comptroller, Gray Phillips, to see Churchill personally to plead his case. It was a telling sign of how out of touch the duke now was from his countrymen. Even his supporters described him as acting like a "petulant baby," while Churchill's secretary, Jock Colville, said he was "cantankerous and maddening."

On top of that, it was belatedly realized that a stopover in New York would present the duke with the opportunity to make mischief in the midst of a presidential election campaign. It was feared that any indiscretion by the duke would give succour to the isolationist cause. Nerves were further jangled by a story in the *New York Times* suggesting that the duke was urging his brother the king to form a peace cabinet around Chamberlain, Halifax, and Lloyd George with a view to making an "honourable" peace with the Nazis. Was this the public declaration he had discussed with Don Miguel, and would he elaborate on the subject once on American soil? That was the abiding fear.

When the duke was informed that, because of the American election, he and the duchess would have to travel to the Bahamas via Bermuda, the duke was incandescent, writing petulantly to Churchill that he had been "messed about quite long enough."

He continued his rant by cable: "Strongly urge you to support arrangements I have made as otherwise will have to reconsider my position." When the king's private secretary, Alex Hardinge, read the duke's telegram he blamed the duchess, observing, rather unfairly: "This is not the first time that the lady has come under suspicion for her anti-British activity, and as long as we never forget the power she can exert on him in her efforts to avenge herself on this country, we shall be alright."

As a result, just days before the Battle of Britain, the prime minister was spending precious hours as a royal travel agent, organizing the duke's itinerary and staff. While the ducal couple were concerned about shopping in New York, his fellow country-men were worried about their survival. With children being evacu-ated from London, workers travelling everywhere with gas masks, the queen learning how to fire a revolver, and the king hiding the Crown jewels in the bowels of Windsor Castle in case of an expected German parachute invasion, the duke's demands were grotesquely self-centred. Eventually, after much back and forth, the duke agreed to sail directly to the Bahamas and Churchill allowed him to have one soldier servant released from active service.

Hemmed in, bored, and frustrated, with every passing day the table talk of the duke and duchess grew ever wilder and more extreme, much to the delight of the Germans. The American ambassador to Portugal, Herbert Claiborne Pell, was so alarmed by their attitude that he sent a warning cable to the secretary of state, Cordell Hull, in Washington:

Duke and Duchess of Windsor are indiscreet and outspoken against British Government. Consider their presence in the United States might be disturbing and confusing. They say that they intend remaining in the United States whether Churchill likes it or not and desire apparently to make propaganda for peace.

It was not only American diplomats but British embassy staff who were getting reports of the duke's increasingly eccentric thinking. For a man schooled in the arts of discretion and prudence, he was making the most tactless and incendiary statements. Word reached junior British embassy secretary Marcus Cheke via an informant that the duke was talking about his restoration, the fall of the Churchill clique, and its replacement by a Labour government that would negotiate peace terms with the Nazis. While his utterances bore remarkable similarities to the unpublished 1937 interview with the *Daily Herald*, Cheke cautioned that these ideas seemed to have emanated from pro-German Spaniards and Frenchmen in his company.

By now the British watchers were hearing alarming news about a plot to kidnap the ducal couple or at least entice them back to Spain to sit out the war. When the duke, after all his complaints about being a prisoner in Portugal, asked to delay his departure by a week to give time for personal effects to be delivered from the South of France, alarm bells began ringing in Whitehall. It was feared the ex-king could be preparing to head for Spain.

Fortunately for the British, they had a secret weapon in the form of Spanish ambassador Don Nicolás, who was indiscreet and probably in the pay of British embassy official David Eccles, the self-confessed "apostle of bribery." Nicolás warned Eccles that Berlin was eager to see the duke and duchess return to Spain so that Hitler could use him in some way following a successful invasion of Britain. This warning was underscored by a Portuguese double agent who was passing to the British plans by the Nazis to abduct the royal couple.

The warnings came not a moment too soon. Wary of leaving the Spanish in charge of the day-to-day organization of the plot, the Germans, with Hitler's personal authority, dispatched to Lisbon one of their finest undercover operatives, Walter Schellenberg, the head of the *Sicherheitsdienst* (SD), the German foreign counter-intelligence organization. The British had every reason to fear this man. He was behind the notorious Venlo affair, in which two senior

British secret agents were kidnapped in then neutral Holland. Not only did the incident destroy Britain's espionage ring in Holland, it gave the Nazis a pretext for invading the neutral country.

This time it was not spies Schellenberg was tasked to kidnap, but the former king of England and his wife. With Hitler's blessing, Operation Willi swung fully into action. Schellenberg was instructed to bring the royal couple to Spain by fuelling their sense of insecurity. Once they had taken fright, he and his fellow agents were to ensure that their flight would not be impeded at the border.

Both von Ribbentrop and Hitler viewed the duke as a man kept virtual prisoner by the British secret service who had tried but so far failed to escape their clutches. As the Führer's personal representative, it was Schellenberg's delicate task to make exploratory contact with the ex-king. As a sweetener he was authorized to offer the duke up to 50 million Swiss francs—about $200 million today—if he agreed to break with Britain and live in a neutral country like Switzerland.

At his briefing in Berlin, von Ribbentrop explained to Schellenberg that the Führer would not object to him using force should the duke and duchess prove hesitant in co-operating with this plan. Before he left, Hitler telephoned Schellenberg and advised him to win over the duchess. "She has great influence over the duke," he observed.

Hitler placed great store by this plot, von Ribbentrop taking pains to keep him fully informed of its progress. A sheaf of yellowing papers in a tatty manila folder bearing the translated words "Material in Special Custody, 1525-1-69," found in a Moscow archival library, the Sonder Archiv, gives a snapshot of the inner workings of the Foreign Ministry and the importance attached to the mission by the Führer.

It also contains largely undated correspondence relating to the Duke of Windsor and von Ribbentrop, including abbreviated elements of the foreign minister's top-secret telegrams to German ambassador Stohrer. There is, too, a partial and undated briefing for Hitler from von Ribbentrop. A brief extract gives a flavour of how closely Hitler was involved in this escapade:

Note to the attention of the Führer

Enclosed telegram re. Duke of W. has arrived on July 9. I have at first initiated the following arrangements:

1) Enclosed telegram to Madrid, from which action plans are clearly apparent, furthermore telegram of W. which came in today.

2) Positioning there of Schellenberg with his men with German embassy in Spain and xxx xxx to be at disposition. Take off Schellenberg tomorrow or the day after tomorrow. Schnellenberg [sic] is with me tomorrow for briefing in xxx.

(The briefing took place on July 24 and xxx represents unreadable words)

Once Schellenberg arrived in Lisbon, he had little time to waste. Within a matter of hours he had eighteen Portuguese agents working for him in the vicinity of the Windsors' house and had even managed to infiltrate a Japanese agent inside the villa where the royal couple were staying.

At night, stones were thrown at the windows, a bouquet of flowers containing warnings was delivered, and the wife of an eminent Portuguese official added her own warning when she spoke to the duchess. Staff were bribed to say that all these bizarre occurrences were the work of the British secret service. All this was to encourage an atmosphere of fear, suspicion, and uncertainty—and to soften them up for the dire warnings to be uttered by the second emissary, former bullfighter and prominent Falangist Don Angel Alcazar de Velasco, who was due to meet the duke on Sunday, July 28, just days before they sailed.

He was tasked to inform the duke and duchess that their lives were in peril, that the British secret service planned to murder the couple in either Portugal or the Bahamas, and that their only chance of safety was to return to Spain using the pretext of a hunting expedition to escape detection in Lisbon. His sombre warning, made on the appropriately named promontory called Boca do Inferno—the Jaws of Hell—was amplified by the contents of a letter written by their friend Duke Miguel Primo de Rivera, which was handed over to the duke during the tense meeting.

Three times the duke read the letter, which, among other warnings, stated that the Spanish interior minister had information of such gravity that he could tell the duke its import only in a face-to-face conversation. The demeanour of the ex-king was understandably grave as he pondered the startling news. Given the ostracism he and his wife had faced, it was not beyond the bounds of possibility that he could be singled out for assassination. (At another time, another ousted royal, the late Diana, Princess of Wales, harboured similar fears.) The duke asked for forty-eight hours to think things over.

By now forewarned, the British had sent in the cavalry in the rotund shape of the duke's lawyer and confidant, the bespectacled Walter Monckton. He was a welcome friendly face who, along with the duke's comptroller Major Gray Phillips and his valet, Piper Alistair Fletcher, arrived in Lisbon just a few hours after the duke had his unnerving secret meeting with the second Spanish emissary.

The arrival of the trio changed the mood completely. Charming, gregarious, and amusing, Monckton was always a welcome visitor, full of insider gossip and risqué stories. He was often, though, the bearer of bad tidings. This occasion was no exception, Monckton undertaking a very "odd job" on behalf of the British prime minister.

Like Don Angel, he, too, was entrusted with a letter, this time from Churchill. It was a salutary warning, the prime minister venturing a "word of serious counsel" and "cautioning the new

Governor of the Bahamas about expressing any views which were out of harmony with the British government."

He wrote:

> *Many sharp and unfriendly ears will be pricked up*
> *to catch any suggestions that Your Royal Highness takes*
> *a view about the war, or about the Germans, or about*
> *Hitlerism, which is different from that adopted by the*
> *British nation and Parliament. Many malicious tongues*
> *will carry tales in every direction.*
>
> *Even while you have been staying at Lisbon,*
> *conversations have been reported by telegraph through*
> *various channels which might have been used to Your Royal*
> *Highness' disadvantage. In particular there will be danger*
> *of use being made of anything you say in the United States*
> *to do you injury and to suggest divergence between you*
> *and the British Government. I am so anxious that mischief*
> *should not be made which might mar the success which*
> *I feel sure will attend your mission. We are all passing*
> *through times of immense stress and dire peril and every*
> *step has to be watched with care.*

With the sombre mood suitably set by Churchill's letter, it was left to Britain's "confidential emissary" to inform the duke and duchess about the imminent dangers they faced and the German plot to kidnap them. When the duke asked incredulously, "But how can we be of any use to them?" Monckton explained that in the event of a German invasion of Britain, Hitler planned to put the duke back on the throne in the hope of dividing the people and weakening their resolve to resist.

Not to be outdone, the duke informed Monckton about the British plot to assassinate him and his wife either in Portugal or in the Bahamas. On this fateful Sunday, he was so spooked by the turn of events that he refused to divulge the source of this intelligence. It was only after Monckton agreed to telegraph London for a Scotland Yard detective to accompany the ducal couple on their voyage to the Bahamas that he finally agreed to sail.

Once their British bodyguard was arranged, the duke sent a one-line note to Churchill confirming the departure date of August 1. It didn't take long for the Germans to learn of the duke's decision, Schellenberg writing in his diary the pithy phrase: "*Willi will nicht*" [Willi doesn't want it]. Hitler, according to Schellenberg's memoirs, would have none of it, ordering an immediate abduction of the ducal couple. Given the beefed-up security surrounding them, that proved impractical.

The duke did meet with the second Spanish emissary, Don Angel, as promised two days later. His response was disappointing, at least for the Germans and Spanish. The gist of his remarks was that the time was not ripe for him to be involved in negotiations that were contrary to the orders of his government and would only antagonize his opponents and undercut his influence and prestige. He added that he could take action from the Bahamas if need be.

Ducal doubts remained. Just the day before his departure, "a very troubled" duke secretly visited Spanish ambassador Don Nicolás for a final discussion. The diplomat urged the duke not to leave Europe, saying that Britain should have some "force in reserve with which to confront the unknown things of tomorrow. The moment may come when England will feel the need to have you once more at her head, and therefore you should not be too far away."

It was a subtle argument, at once flattering and sensible. He made a similar case to President Salazar, his argument reflecting the duke's international standing:

> It has always been my impression that the Duke, despite his temperament, might be a trump for peace; I still feel he might have a role to play today, provided he is not too far

away. The trumps for peace are not so numerous that they may be disregarded or allowed to be destroyed.

A further last-ditch plea came from his great friend, the first confidential emissary Don Miguel, who flew to Lisbon to make his case for delay. He met stiff British resistance in the shape of Monckton, who demanded specific evidence of a British plot against the ducal couple. When Don Miguel asked for a few days' delay to assemble the evidence, Monckton would have none of it. He did, though, agree with the duke's request that when they arrived at Bermuda, Monckton would personally assure them that they were safe to travel on to the Bahamas. Such was the concern for the royal wellbeing that Churchill himself asked the Admiralty if a cruiser could be spared to convoy the passenger liner across the Atlantic. The former First Lord of the Admiralty was informed that every naval ship was needed in case the expected invasion of Britain went ahead.

In a final throw of the dice von Ribbentrop agreed to show himself, at least through the good offices of the Windsors' banker host, Dr. Santo Silva. In a telegram sent to Ambassador Huene he outlined the case that Dr. Silva should make to the duke.

When Dr. Silva discussed the matter, he should refer to an "authoritative German source" rather than von Ribbentrop himself. The duke was to be told the following by Dr. Silva:

Germany truly desires peace with the English people. The Churchill clique stands in the way of such a peace. Following the rejection of the Führer's final appeal to reason, Germany is determined to compel England to make peace by every means of power. It would be a good thing if the Duke were to hold himself in readiness for further developments. In such case Germany would be prepared to co-operate most closely with the Duke and to clear the way for any desire expressed by the Duke and Duchess.

He added that, if the duke still insisted on leaving Portugal, Dr. Silva should arrange a secret channel of communication so that the Germans could keep in contact. The duke's host duly delivered this message but the duke remained adamant that he would sail.

On the day of departure Schellenberg watched the ducal party march onboard the American Export Lines passenger ship through a pair of high-powered binoculars as he stood in the tower room of the German embassy. "It appeared so close that I seemed almost able to touch it," he recalled. Helplessly he watched the frantic preparations for departure, which, thanks to his alarums and excursions, included the scouring of the vessel several times for possible explosive devices—or "infernal machines" as Schellenberg called them. Even hand baggage was searched.

On the day they set sail, August 1, 1940, Hitler finally issued Directive 17 "for the conduct of air and naval warfare." He may have lost the first round in the War of the Windsors. The Battle of Britain was going to be a different story.

Even though the duke and duchess were now out of sight, they remained in German minds, especially after Ambassador Huene telegrammed Berlin with the duke's reaction to von Ribbentrop's offer.

In his report of August 2, he described how von Ribbentrop's words had made the "deepest impression" on the royal:

He felt very appreciative of the considerate way his personal interests were being taken into account. In his reply the Duke paid tribute to the Führer's desire for peace, which was in agreement with his own point of view. He was firmly convinced that if he had been King it would never have come to war. To the appeal made to him to co-operate at a suitable time in the establishment of peace, he gladly consented.

The duke, the ambassador reported, had, as with the second Spanish emissary, Don Miguel, emphasized that he had to obey orders from his government and that the present moment was too early for him to make a diplomatic intervention. If this changed he was prepared to return immediately, no matter what his personal sacrifice. He agreed to remain in "continuous communication" with his host Dr. Santo Silva and agreed a code word which, if triggered, would secure his immediate return.

The report concluded:

The statements of the Duke were, as the confidant stressed, supported by firmness of will and the deepest sincerity, and had included an expression of admiration and sympathy for the Führer.

While historian John H. Waller described von Ribbentrop's message as "remarkable for its effrontery," he pointed out that it "nonetheless elicited a response from the duke that was even more remarkable for its innuendos of serious indiscretion. While declining Hitler's offer lest it bring about a scandal, he expressed his appreciation for it and implied that if the state of affairs changed, he would reconsider his position. This compromising document left the door open for further German intrigues with the duke."

While the tale of Operation Willi is spicy enough, many historians have added further seasoning. A common royal condiment is the duke's cousin Prince Philipp von Hessen who, it has been claimed, met the duke in Lisbon during July 1940 for informal peace talks. It is not such a far-fetched theory; the prince was used by Hitler as a diplomatic go-between, he was linked to Göring's peace wing of the Nazi hierarchy, was part of the entourage during the ducal visit to Germany in 1937, and like the Duke of Windsor he was in favour of a peaceful settlement.

After an exhaustive investigation Prince Philipp's biographer, Professor Jonathan Petropoulos, found no evidence to support any secret royal meeting. But, as he admitted: "That there were no meetings does not mean that Philipp and his cousins did not try to work for a negotiated peace."

Further spicing the story was a 1979 article in the London *Sunday Times* in which Prince Philipp's twin, Prince Wolfgang, claimed that the Duke of Kent served as an intermediary between Prince Philipp and the Duke of Windsor. Given the icy relations that existed between the royal brothers, this is doubtful. However, the suspicious absence of and denial of access to papers relating to the Duke of Kent in the Royal Archives at Windsor Castle has only served to fuel speculation.

Most piquant is the story stirred into the mix by historian Peter Allen, who claimed that deputy Führer Rudolf Hess flew himself to Portugal for face-to-face peace discussions with the duke on July 28, the day the duke was also seeing the second Spanish emissary. He was accompanied on this mission by the notorious secret service chief Reinhard Heydrich, who acted as Hess's bodyguard. It was, claims Allen, Hess's secret visit to Portugal and his negotiations with the duke and an "important" but unnamed British minister that were the catalyst behind Hess's secret flight in May 1941 to Britain, where he hoped to organize peace talks with the Duke of Hamilton. Given the duke's discussions with the second emissary and the arrival of Monckton on the same day as Rudolf Hess, this theory seems implausible.

During their voyage, as the Windsors sunbathed on deck, chatted with their fellow passengers, and watched movies in the ship's theatre, their indefatigable maid, Mademoiselle Moulichon, endeavoured to deliver the duchess's precious possessions taken from her Paris home. After waiting for days at the Portuguese border, she found herself jailed for her trouble. "Please ask your friends to release Marguerite quickly as maid situation desperate," telegrammed the duchess to her friend Tiger Bermejillo.

When the queen later heard about the duke and duchess's obsession with their possessions—"their pink sheets" as she called them—she compared their self-absorbed behaviour with the resolute courage of "our poor people spending nights in little tin shelters, and then going to work in the morning."

Even though they were thousands of miles away from falling bombs, the Windsors were still agitated about their safety. On August 9, as the Battle of Britain began in deadly earnest, the duke, still worried about an assassination attempt, cabled Monckton as soon as they arrived in Bermuda, saying that it was impossible to continue their journey until he gave them the all-clear, which he duly did. As Churchill remarked, Monckton had done a first-class job of dissipating "strange suspicions."

Their one-time cheerleader was equally dismissive of the duke and duchess. At a dinner held at Lambeth Palace as the Windsors sailed off into the sunset, Churchill observed: "The Duke of Windsor's views on the war are such as to render his banishment a wise move." Accusations of treachery and treason aside, it seems that Churchill had concluded that, based on their recent behaviour in Madrid and Lisbon, the only cause the Duke and Duchess of Windsor truly cared about was themselves.

CHAPTER ELEVEN

—— ⬥ ——

A Shady Royal in a Sunny Place

Though they were now firmly planted in the tropics, the topic of conversation for the duke and duchess was quintessentially English—the weather. They arrived from Bermuda to the islands' capital, Nassau, in the unbearable summer heat and humidity to find all their worst nightmares come true. This was St. Helena in a sauna.

When they managed to cool down after their arrival on August 17, the duchess instantly realized that Government House, their official home, was certainly not fit for any king, even an ex. They moved out while she undertook extensive and expensive renovations, dragging local politicians, kicking and screaming, to pay for a £5,000 (£200,000 or $320,000 today) redecoration. She did not help her cause by frequently flying her hairdresser Antoine in from New York to tend her tresses. When the works were completed, pride of place in the drawing room was given to a full-length portrait of Wallis by Gerald Brockhurst. On her bedroom dressing table was said to be an autographed photograph of von Ribbentrop, deliberately displayed as a "show of loyalty to friends." With the completion of the works, the duke at last had his "treasures" around him—a rack of fifty pipes; a box made of wood from Nelson's ship, HMS *Victory*; a midshipman's dirk; and a field marshal's baton. "Don't you see I must make a home for him?" the duchess said. He thought she had succeeded.

Meanwhile, the duke fretted about their properties in France, organizing payment of the remaining staff through the good offices of his friend Herman Rogers who, with Katherine, remained at Lou Viei in Cannes. He described his new life in a letter to his American friend:

> *Although my job as Governor luckily keeps me very busy, it is a very narrow and restricted life for both Wallis and myself. The thermometer registered a steady 80 degrees Fahrenheit and upwards for the first six weeks we were here; the temperature is now in the 70s but this is mainly due to a persistent northeast wind which has the worst "mistral" beat as regards it getting on your nerves.*
>
> *There is a flat and very uninteresting golf course, very similar to Cagnes; but at least one can exercise yourself sometimes—and you would of course love the swimming.*
>
> *Government House was in such a filthy state, almost denuded of furniture and having the appearance more of an institution than an official residence, that we refused to live in it after a week until it was reconditioned. We have been living in two rented houses—and the people here work so slowly that we will be lucky if we get in before Christmas. However, Wallis has contrived to make it quite habitable; in fact the rooms and furniture are really very attractive—but it has been disheartening for her redecorating an official residence when we have just completed our two private houses in France. However... c'est la guerre.*

The duke, who had managed to send £1,000 to Rogers, discussed the detailed arrangements to enable him to pay "hungry and faithful" servants in France and have the telephone and electricity, which had been cut off by the municipality because of unpaid bills, reconnected.

He concluded:

You can well imagine how desperately faraway from
all our interests and possessions we feel but one has to be
philosophic these days and remember that there are many
others who are in a far worse plight.

At the same time, the new man in the Bahamas was constantly reminded that those he served felt barely disguised hostility towards himself and his wife. During his stopover in Bermuda he had, to his mortification, discovered a secret telegram from the secretary of state at the Foreign Office on the official etiquette to be observed for those meeting the royal couple.

Unlike the Nazi hierarchy or the aristocratic Falangists of Spain, no one in the British empire was allowed to curtsey to the duchess or address her as "Your Royal Highness." She was referred to as "Your Grace." When they finally arrived in the Bahamas, the caste system continued, the duchess sitting one step below the new governor in the council chamber but one step higher than the normal place reserved for the wife of a governor. It had taken hours of discussion to reach this diplomatic decision.

The duke was constantly on his mettle, sensitive to any perceived insults to his wife. When the wealthy Canadian Sir Frederick Williams-Taylor gave a speech of welcome to the royal couple before two hundred invited guests at a dinner-dance held at the Emerald Beach club in Nassau, the duke had to correct him publicly. During his address Williams-Taylor never once mentioned the duchess. When the duke rose to reply he explained to the audience that in the original approved version of the welcome address the ducal couple were both welcomed, but that their Canadian host had not read the text clearly in the dim light.

The numerous "petty humiliations" to which the duchess was subject, the "chronic insult" of her status, and the hostility of the court weighed heavily upon the duke. He penned but did not send a long heartfelt letter to Churchill enumerating his complaints. He had a point. However the British Establishment chose to portray him, the duke remained much more than a minor colonial governor. Powerless yet internationally influential, he and the duchess were the social equivalent of Semtex, inert on their own yet highly explosive when mixed with the electric charge of publicity. "Handle with Care" was the watchword for any British—or American— officials dealing with the ducal couple.

Even in exile the Duke of Windsor was a lightning rod, the talisman for international peace movements; the very mention of his name in conjunction with peace could set church bells ringing in Germany and elsewhere. When he told the governor of Bermuda, Lieutenant General Sir Denis Bernard, "If I had been king there would have been no war," he was speaking no more than many believed. In the first few months of his tenure as governor, the duke was at the swirling centre of several so-called "peace plots" which, like tropical tornadoes, pulled him hither and thither into a vortex of hope, conjecture, and speculation.

Some plots were more sinister than others. Almost before he had unpacked his toiletries—or rather his soldier valet had—the duke received a telegram from his Portuguese host, Dr. Silva, the chosen conduit for the Germans to send messages. The telegram, sent on or about August 15 on what became known as "Black Tuesday" during the Battle of Britain, asked if "the moment had arrived." That is to say, did the duke feel ready to return to Europe to accept the German offer?

Clearly it hadn't, or else British intelligence would have been aware of it at the time. As they suspected that Dr. Silva's bank was funding German secret agents, they were routinely monitoring correspondence sent to and from the bank.

The Nazis, orchestrated by von Ribbentrop, were also pursuing other avenues to keep alive their dream of winning over the duke. They had, according to a secret report from a Lisbon-based British intelligence agent, approached the duke's friend, Nazi collaborator Charles Bedaux, and asked him to find out if the duke would become king in the event of a German victory. His conduct, which was described in MI5 deputy director Guy Liddell's diaries, suggests that Bedaux turned down the German request, though a telegram sent by his wife, Fern, to the Duchess of Windsor reveals that the two couples had been in conversation about the duke's possible role long before he sailed for the Bahamas.

In her message Mme. Bedaux referred to a talk they had in 1937, when the duke and duchess visited Germany. The issue discussed was not mentioned but presumably was related to the duke's possible return to the throne. That same question was, hinted Fern Bedaux in her telegram, "very prominent in the minds of certain powers today," meaning the Nazis. Her cable continued:

We have been asked seriously of the possibility, and we, continuing to believe that you and ——— [presumably the Duke of Windsor] are still of the same opinion, have given absolute assurance that it is not only possible but can be counted on. Are we right?

The ambiguous nature of Fern Bedaux's telegram was later put in context by spy chief Liddell in his August 24, 1945, diary entry:

I gather that Censorship obtained during the early days of the war a telegram from Mme Bedaux to the Duchess in the Bahamas which seemed to be of a singularly

*compromising nature. There were a lot of blanks in this
telegram but the sense of it seemed to be that the question
either of the Duke's mediation or of his restoration was
discussed at some previous date and Mme Bedaux
was anxious to know whether he was now prepared to say
yes or no.*

At the time, the telegram was seen by a second pair of eyes, Alec Cadogan, permanent under-secretary at the Foreign Office, who gave the duke the benefit of the doubt: "The paragraph is certainly capable of the blackest interpretations. But it would be difficult to get a conviction on it." The Liddell diaries, released only in 2012, give a sharper perspective on this incident. In his August 24, 1945, entry he makes clear that the security forces were monitoring the telegrams sent and received by Bedaux and Dr. Silva. If the Duke of Windsor had indeed replied in the affirmative, the information would have given Churchill a dilemma: whether to charge the ex-king with treason or collaboration.

He was certainly mixing with murky company. Two years later Charles Bedaux himself was arrested in North Africa by American troops on the direct orders of General Dwight D. Eisenhower. At the time, Bedaux was preparing to build a pipeline to transport oil across the Sahara desert for the Vichy French government and the Nazis. He spent two years in detention in Miami before dramatically committing suicide in February 1944.

It was not long after the Germans tried to entice the duke into their fold that he was involved, at least tangentially, in another intriguing and complex British-inspired plot to begin peace negotiations, brokered by the Americans, between Britain and the Axis powers. The tentative talks had their genesis in the power struggle between new prime minister Winston Churchill and his foreign secretary, Lord Halifax. With the fall of France in May 1940 and the disaster of Dunkirk the following month, Halifax was broadly in favour of a negotiated settlement with Hitler. He oversaw tentative contacts with the Nazis via the papal nuncio in Berne as well as neutral missions in Portugal and Finland. There were hopes that if Washington organized a peace conference this would start a rapid military de-escalation on both sides.

Churchill set his face against any compromise with the Nazis, telling a tense War Cabinet meeting that "nations which went down fighting rose again, but those which surrendered tamely were finished." In any case, based on past behaviour, Hitler was unlikely to honour any agreement. When various peers and MPs sent Churchill a memo in July about a negotiated peace, he replied that this "dangerous" discussion was "an encouragement to a Fifth Column."

With Halifax thwarted by the prime minister, it was now too politically dangerous to attempt peace feelers via the representatives of neutral missions in London. The search for settlement went underground and moved abroad, to both Switzerland and the United States. In both countries the senior British diplomats—Ambassadors David Kelly and Lord Lothian respectively—favoured talks with Hitler.

Lothian, a tall, bespectacled Christian Scientist, had visited Germany in 1935, and his earlier sympathy for the country was well known. Roosevelt, though, was angered by his attitude of "complete despair" in the face of German aggression. "What the British need today is a good stiff grog, inducing not only the desire to save civilization but the continued belief that they can do it," he told his old Harvard professor Roger B. Merriman.

Nonetheless, in the early months of the war Roosevelt had sent emissaries to Germany to assess the mood and demands of the Reich leaders. In February 1940 Sumner Welles, under-secretary of state, sailed to Europe on a fact-finding mission while James Mooney, the European head of General Motors, was also given permission by Roosevelt to have informal talks with the Nazi

leadership, in a March meeting with Hitler and Göring. The catastrophic events of the summer made that avenue no longer worth
exploring, Roosevelt much more comfortable with Churchill's
robust response to Nazi aggression than the appeasement policies
pursued by Halifax and Chamberlain.

It seemed that the door to any peace negotiations was now
closed—on Churchill's direct orders. Others linked to the Halifax
cabal still thought there was a chance. Secretly, Lothian's close
friend Sir William Wiseman, the former head of British intelligence in America, began putting out feelers among influential
Americans. On September 2, 1940, he met with James Mooney
and admitted that he was "groping about for some means of initiating an effective peace move."

In Mooney he had chosen an odd bedfellow. Though he had
been an informal emissary for the president, his reputation was
that of a right-wing zealot eager to see the fall of Britain. George
Messersmith, now ambassador to Cuba, described Mooney, whom
he considered a friend, as "dangerous and destructive," part of an
Irish Catholic group of influential Americans "so blind in their
hatred of England that they are prepared to sell out their own
country in order to bring England down."

There was another side to the businessman who was awarded
the Order of the German Eagle in 1938—he was a good friend of
the Duke of Windsor. They first met in 1924 when, as Prince of
Wales, Edward had ordered two custom-built Buicks, their friendship blossoming on the golf course. That Christmas, Mooney
planned to join the duke on a foursome at Cat Cay, an island north
of Nassau. They were scheduled to spend several days onboard the
Rene, a sleek yacht owned by Mooney's boss, GM chairman Alfred
P. Sloan, another businessman who was pro-Nazi and a financial
supporter of the fiercely anti-Semitic Sentinels of the Republic.

This, then, was the man in whom the peace wing of the British government placed their trust. During their initial discussions,

Wiseman emphasized that, in order to be acceptable to the British, any peace moves would have to be initiated by the Nazis. The two men accepted that only the Pope could make the necessary public utterances that would prepare world opinion for a negotiated peace.

As Wiseman didn't have any contacts with the Vatican, Mooney arranged for him to meet New York archbishop Francis Spellman. While that meeting came to nothing, Wiseman suggested that Mooney travel to Germany via London under the guise of General Motors business in order to discover the minimum terms necessary for ending the war. Such was the delicacy of the task assigned to Mooney that when he informed Wiseman that he had been invited to play a foursome at golf with the duke over Christmas, Wiseman advised against it, as it would give the Germans the impression that Mooney was too pro-British.

Yet on September 26, 1940, within weeks of the first encounter between Wiseman and Mooney, Sir Joseph Ball, chairman of the Security Intelligence Centre, a secret body set up in 1940 to monitor the work of MI5 and MI6, was discussing the following agenda item: "US reports Windsor linked to Mooney separate peace." Frustratingly it gives no further details. As the duke and duchess were confined to the Bahamas and still finding their feet, it is difficult to see what useful contribution he could have made other than, in a telephone conversation with Mooney, to voice his approval. Certainly the secret peace manoeuvres chimed with his own thinking—he saw himself in the role of honest broker, cheerleading the diplomats and politicians to come to an agreement.

During this time, the Windsors came under close scrutiny from the FBI, agent Edward Tamm specifically tasked by director J. Edgar Hoover to report on their activities. In Hoover's eyes the duchess was a Fifth Columnist at best, a Nazi spy at worst. In his September 13 report the diligent agent Tamm described how the British had taken special precautions to stop her from "establishing any channel of communication with von Ribbentrop." Such was the fetid atmosphere of suspicion surrounding them that when the duchess sent her clothes to New York for dry cleaning, the FBI's second in command, Clyde Tolson, was informed that the exercise could allow the "violently pro German" duchess to transfer messages through her clothes. The dry-cleaning run was promptly halted.

As Roosevelt would read, she had, according to Father Odo, who was recounting her sexual activities to FBI agents in New York at the time, enjoyed a torrid affair with the former ambassador to Britain. In the Bahamas, reported agent Tamm, there was concern that the duplicitous duke and duchess would align themselves with the Swedish millionaire businessman Axel Wenner-Gren, a self-styled peace emissary and friend of Herman Göring who had recently settled on the islands.

As far as the authorities were concerned, Wenner-Gren, like his friend Charles Bedaux, was too wealthy, too independent, and too closely connected with the Nazi enemy. As recently as March that year he had "shadowed" Roosevelt's emissary Sumner Welles during his visit to Germany and Italy, the businessman inserting himself onto a complex, ever shifting stage he didn't fully comprehend. The president was not amused, and from then on Wenner-Gren was firmly in the sights of the Americans and the British. Such were the suspicions surrounding him that his FBI file is one of the most extensive on any private citizen in American history. He became a mythic figure. Not only was he said to be the go-between who hid Nazi gold in South America at the end of the war but he was also believed to have shared a mistress with John F. Kennedy, two decades before JFK became president.

The British, according to FBI agent Tamm, had deputed socialite Lady Jane Williams-Taylor, the queen of Bahamas society and the wife of the myopic Canadian banker, to keep the toxic Swede away from the royal governor. She was signally unsuccessful, the duke and duchess warming to Wenner-Gren and his wife,

Marguerite. They were smart, cosmopolitan, and well read, the antithesis of the insular, parochial Bay Street Boys, the corrupt cabal of petty-minded white businessmen who effectively ran the islands.

Meanwhile, Sir William Wiseman continued his freelance quest for peace, hoping that after the presidential elections in November he could manoeuvre the incumbent into the role of peacemaker without letting the Germans know in advance that the proposal originated from the British. The merest hint that this was a British-inspired proposal would undercut their bargaining position and cripple British morale and prestige.

As far as Wiseman was concerned, the White House should use their military and economic might to force the combatants to the negotiating table and then take such a prominent role that the Germans would be prevented from using their supremacy in Europe to demand harsh terms from the British. Wiseman thought Churchill would vigorously reject any peace proposal but be secretly pleased he was being compelled to accept it.

Once again Mooney used his good offices to introduce Wiseman to Roosevelt's one-time law partner and legal advisor Basil O'Connor, who was asked if he could broach this idea in confidence with the president. The prognosis was pessimistic, O'Connor reporting back that Roosevelt, elected president by a landslide in November for a third term, was hostile to the idea of a negotiated peace.

It was not just influential Americans Wiseman was sounding out but potentially friendly Germans. In November he had a preliminary meeting with the duchess's former neighbour and the duke's sometime golf partner Princess Stephanie von Hohenlohe and her lover, Captain Fritz Wiedemann, who helped broker the ducal visit to Germany in 1937. Hitler's former adjutant, based in San Francisco, was now the Nazis' West Coast consul, in charge of an extensive spy network and tasked with the vital propaganda job of stoking the cause of isolationism in a bid to keep America neutral and out of the war.

After secret consultations with ambassador Lord Lothian and secret service chief Sir William Stephenson—known by the code name "Intrepid"—Wiseman met with the lovers in the Mark Hopkins Hotel in San Francisco on November 26. The FBI, who had placed Wiedemann, Wiseman, and Princess Stephanie under round-the-clock surveillance, had the room wired and eavesdropped on the conversation. The recordings were in essence a detailed discussion of possible peace negotiations between Britain, Germany, and the United States.

Initially Wiseman unveiled his own position, stating that he was the spokesman for a British political group headed by Lord Halifax. He made clear that any agreement had to be made with a "Hitler-free" Germany, as Hitler was not a man they could trust. The two Germans were sympathetic, suggesting a monarchist restoration or an administration run by Himmler. Wiedemann warned Wiseman that Hitler was unstable and had a split personality, at times considering himself greater than Napoleon. Though the German leader was intent on conquering Britain, Princess Stephanie suggested that she travel to Berlin to place a peace proposal before Hitler and von Ribbentrop. She was confident that she could make Hitler realize that he was butting his head against a stone wall by continuing his fight with Britain.

When FBI director J. Edgar Hoover reported a summary of the meeting to the president, Roosevelt was furious and demanded that Princess Stephanie, whom he considered to be a spy, be deported forthwith. He took a personal interest in her case and took to describing her as the "girlfriend" of his attorney general, Robert Houghwout Jackson, after he failed to find suitable legal grounds to kick her out of the country.

As Jackson observed: "I could not say that her activities amounted to espionage. It was not at all certain that there were not some kinds of negotiations between Sir William Wiseman and Fritz Wiedemann, in which she was a go-between."

By now the peace train had pulled out of the station. Wiseman had to concede that neither Roosevelt nor the Halifax cabal had much enthusiasm for continuing the secret process. When Lord Lothian, effectively the ghost in this ad hoc peace machine, died from a kidney ailment on December 12, 1940, it shut out the chance of any backdoor peace initiative. Once Churchill appointed Halifax as Lothian's successor, the door was well and truly locked.

One man, though, had not heard the door slam shut on the peace process. Even after Lothian's death, the Duke of Windsor, who seems to have had merely a cheerleading role in the Wiseman imbroglio, continued to believe in Wiseman's strategy, namely a negotiated peace settlement brokered by the Americans. In pursuit of this ambition the colonial governor took enormous personal risks, which further nourished the dark suspicions with which he and his wife were regarded by the Americans and the British.

Typically, brokering a peace deal came second to their personal needs. In public the couple were the very picture of dedicated local leaders; the duchess immersed herself in the local Red Cross while the duke tried to come to grips with the odious Bay Street Boys and effect some much-needed reforms. In private, however, they were desperate to escape the dreary climate and the suffocating company.

As the torpid days rolled into unending weeks, the dulling realization slowly sank in that he had spent all his life as an exotic if protected species of caged animal. By abdicating, all the duke had done was swap one restricting cage for another. He tried to escape in drink, but the duchess reined him in, not allowing him his first cocktail until seven in the evening.

The duchess made her own frustrations known in an interview with an American journalist in which she emphasized that they wanted to do their duty but not in this tropical backwater. She complained that in Nassau there was no scope for his "great gifts, his inspiration, his long training. I'm only a woman, but I'm his wife, and I don't believe that in Nassau he's serving the Empire as importantly as he might."

Her words did little to ingratiate her with the socialites of Nassau but she was past caring. It didn't help that she was suffering from a nagging toothache that seemed to be getting worse by the day.

It was not long before the royal prisoners were plotting their great escape, dreaming of sailing to the United States or spending time on the ducal ranch in Alberta, Canada. These aspirations caused apoplexy in London and Washington, the Colonial Office feeling it was way too soon to leave their post and the White House worried that the defeatist duke would only aid the isolationists in the country, a loose-knit right-wing group, mainly Republicans and Roman Catholics, who viewed the duke as a potential mascot and cheerleader. It was felt that any meeting between the Democratic president and the ex-king before an election would be pounced on by the German propaganda machine.

While telegrams were passing back and forth between Washington and London about this matter, as if on cue German radio, broadcasting in English, announced in October that the duke might play a part in possible peace negotiations in Europe headed by President Roosevelt. British officials seized on it as an example of the harmful speculation that would be unleashed should the duke visit the White House.

A month later Roosevelt won a third term and felt that the time was right to meet the fabled couple. On a personal level he was intrigued to meet the man and woman at the beating heart of a compelling romantic story, especially as his neighbours at Hyde Park, Herman and Katherine Rogers, had been so closely involved in the drama. As an astute political operator he was acutely aware of the numerous reports that had crossed his desk, not only from

J. Edgar Hoover but various diplomats commenting on the pro-German, defeatist sentiments uttered by the indiscreet duke.

The president set the course for a meeting in December, when he was due to spend a week onboard the USS *Tuscaloosa* inspecting potential naval bases in the Caribbean as part of an agreement with the British whereby they would receive fifty destroyers in return for the right to lease air and sea bases on British colonies. He informed Lord Lothian that he would like the duke to join him when his ship entered Bahamian waters. It would be a combination of state business and the chance for the president to give the royal governor the once-over.

The British wanted to scupper this meeting at any price. When the duchess's medical condition deteriorated to the point where she needed specialist dental treatment in Miami, the Colonial Office gave them permission to travel as it coincided with the dates suggested by Roosevelt for the naval base inspection.

As luck would have it, the regular passenger ferry to Miami was out of service, so the Windsors were authorized to sail onboard the *Southern Cross*, the $2 million yacht owned by Axel Wenner-Gren, the very industrialist the British were trying to keep away from the Windsors. As the *Daily Mirror* helpfully headlined: "Goering's Pal and Windsors." When they docked at Miami the royal couple were greeted by 12,000 curious onlookers, with 8,000 lining the streets to St. Francis Hospital, where the duchess was due to have her operation. It was almost like old times.

Even the local British consul, James Marjoribanks, could find nothing for the Foreign Office to complain about, reporting: "Britain's stock soared with the advent to Miami of our former sovereign. The trip was a success from every point of view."

On December 12, as the duchess was recovering, the duke was invited by Roosevelt to join him onboard the *Tuscaloosa*, now off Eleuthera Island. By then the duke had uncovered the elaborate and mealy-mouthed British subterfuge to keep the two men apart.

He was delighted to accept, flying to the island the next day on an American seaplane to join the president, White House aide Harry Hopkins, and various ranking American naval officers for a discussion about using several Bahamian islands as American naval bases.

It was a jolly two-hour luncheon, much of the preliminary conversation focusing on a fishing trip that morning, when Hopkins had caught a three-foot grouper, the record for the trip thus far. There was, though, a serious purpose. Aboard the ship, a few days earlier, the president had received Churchill's long and eloquent letter requesting aid from America, a plea that led to the Lend-Lease Act.

During the discussions the duke, who had already talked about several potential island sites at a previous meeting with an American admiral, promised to do everything he could as governor to facilitate any American request to use Bahamian islands for navy ships. As the president later recalled, the nearest they came to discussing the war was when he praised the great courage and fighting spirit of the British people, Roosevelt eager to stave off a potential defeatist ducal diatribe.

The duke flew back to Miami with a warm glow, feeling that for once his opinions and actions mattered, that in some small way he could make a difference. He was reunited with the duchess, and their friend Wenner-Gren took them back to Nassau onboard *Southern Cross*, the party briefly visiting the Western Bahamas.

The president was suitably impressed by the former monarch—but not by his friends. At a later meeting in Britain his friend Harry Hopkins told Churchill and others about the encounter. As Churchill's private secretary, Jock Colville, recalled:

> He told us of the Duke of Windsor's recent visit to the President on his yacht when the former spoke very charmingly of the King (a fact which touched Winston) and he said that the Duke's entourage was very bad. Moreover HRH's recent yachting trip with a violently pro-Nazi Swede did

not create a good impression. It was the astounding success of the King and Queen's visit to the U.S. which had made America give up its partisanship of the Windsors.

A week later, when the duke and duchess stepped off the landing barge from the *Southern Cross* on the morning of December 19, 1940, they were watched by a sometime magician, ventriloquist, psychic investigator, undercover FBI agent, and influential writer, Fulton Oursler. Earlier, the editor of *Liberty* magazine had flown with his family from Miami to Nassau to prepare for an interview with the new governor. Oursler, a friend of politicians and presidents, had used every card, every contact to finesse his way into the duke's presence. At first even his friendship with Roosevelt had failed to open doors but finally, and somewhat mysteriously, an interview was arranged.

They met in the evening at Government House, Oursler amazed that the royal luggage brought from Europe still lined the great ballroom. He found the duke fit and invigorated after his visit to Miami, his first to America in sixteen years. In the back and forth of the conversation, the duke proved as keen to learn about Oursler's views as the journalist was to glean the duke's opinions.

When the magazine editor, a professed isolationist, told him that he did not believe America should enter into the war, it was the first of many points of agreement.

The duke, fresh from his meeting with the president, was at pains to point out that Britain must have due respect for America, a country that could implement a peace settlement. During a series of rhetorical questions he averred that there was no such thing in modern warfare as victory, reminding Oursler that the German armies were never defeated in the First World War.

When Oursler asked if Hitler could be removed by an anti-war revolution by the German people, the duke's reply left the experienced interviewer "dazed" and disbelieving. He told Oursler:

There will be no revolution in Germany and it would be a tragic thing for the world if Hitler were to be overthrown. Hitler is the right and logical leader of the German people. It is a pity you never met Hitler, just as it is a pity I never met Mussolini. Hitler is a very great man.

In the ensuing stunned silence, the duke leaned forward conspiratorially and asked: "Do you suppose that your president would consider intervening as a mediator when, as, and if the proper time arrives?" Oursler presumed that he would if he considered it in the interests of humanity so to do.

The duke went on to say that few people really understood what a perilous situation Britain faced, with U-boat submarine activity "creating havoc" with merchant shipping. The time was coming when someone would have to make a move to end this war between "two stubborn peoples." He added: "It sounds very silly to put it this way, but the time is coming when somebody has got to say, you two boys have fought long enough and now you have to kiss and make up."

He warned that if the United States entered the war it would continue for another thirty years, an opinion straight out of the isolationist playbook. The time was coming, sooner rather than later, when the president would have to step in to end the conflict—the goal Wiseman had tried and failed to achieve.

The discussion continued on other matters for two hours, a somewhat stunned Oursler leaving the royal presence in the company of his aide-de-camp, Captain Vyvyan Drury, who quietly emphasized how the duke, who had been subject to "cruel persecutions," could be of the greatest service to both Britain and America. When he arrived back at the hotel he hustled his wife, Grace, into the closet, shut the door, and then whispered the import of his interview. He confided his "uneasy suspicion" that the duke wanted him to convey his thinking to the president himself. This was confirmed the following morning when Captain Drury arrived at their hotel and asked him if he would enter into a "Machiavellian conspiracy" and tell the president the substance of their conversation.

The duke's emissary said: "Tell Mr. Roosevelt that if he will make an offer of intervention for peace, that before anyone in England can oppose it, the Duke of Windsor will instantly issue a statement supporting it and that will start a revolution in England and force peace." He asked him not to print anything immediately, otherwise "the lid would be blown off the British Empire." Oursler promised silence and agreed to speak with the president.

As Oursler's son Fulton Jr. remarked: "By sending his plea to the president he had already stepped beyond the bounds of diplomacy and trespassed on treason. Nothing less than revolution was on his mind."

Oursler, who dictated a seventeen-page memo describing this extraordinary affair, took the precaution of telling his publisher, one-time bodybuilder Bernarr Macfadden, the gist of the interview when he arrived back in Miami. Feeling himself in an isolated and dangerous predicament, he also took fellow *Liberty* contributor Walter Karig into his confidence, just in case anything untoward happened to him. Indeed, he never published the full story in his lifetime, Fulton Jr. saying that he feared for his life should he do so.

He duly arranged the appointment with the president for the morning of December 23—though no official records exist of that meeting. The president, with only his Scottie dog present, asked Oursler about his daughter April and her school. As the two men got down to business, Roosevelt interrupted the journalist as he began his story.

"Fulton," he said, "nothing can surprise me these days. Nothing will seem too fantastic. Why, do you know that I am amazed to find some of the greatest people in the British Empire, men of the so-called upper classes, men of the highest rank, secretly want to appease Hitler and stop the war? I call these people ignorant, uneducated"—a clear reference to Halifax, Lloyd George, and other appeasers.

Oursler sensed that the president was already aware of what was on the duke's mind, information probably conveyed to him by the FBI. When he recited the duke's remarks he noticed that the president became greatly agitated. "His hands trembled. His whole body shook. It was an unparalleled exhibition."

The president exploded: "When little Windsor says he doesn't think there should be a revolution in Germany, I tell you, Fulton, I would rather have April's opinion on that than his." Then he proceeded to dictate a gnomic letter to Captain Drury, whom he described as a "bad boy." It read:

> Dear Captain Drury,
>
> On my way home from Florida, I stopped off in Washington and had a talk with my friend. His answer to my conversation was that in Washington today everything is on a twenty-four-hour basis and no man has the gift of being able to read the future. If you have anything else in mind, let me know.

In short he was giving the duke the presidential brush-off. Then he gave Oursler the presidential perspective on the duke's behaviour and character, touching on many concerns expressed by Britain's ruling classes, notably the contents of red boxes left open at Fort Belvedere, Mrs. Simpson's dalliance with the von Ribbentrop set if not von Ribbentrop himself, the duke's association with his German friends after the abdication, and his dubious approach to soldiering when he was liaison officer in France, loitering in Paris for days after discussing top secret plans with field officers.

This was his most damning observation, stating: "I have nothing to prove what I am going to say, but I do know that there were

nine shortwave wireless sets in Paris constantly sending information to the German troops, and no one has ever been able to decide
how such accurate information could be sent over these wireless
stations." He was clearly implying that the duke was involved in
this betrayal of Allied secrets.

Beneath this extraordinary, almost surreal, royal encounter are
many of the familiar contours of the duke's political journey. Like
other European princes—including his brother the Duke of Kent,
cousins Prince Philipp and Prince Max von Hohenlohe—and well-
connected businessmen such as his friend Wenner-Gren, he saw
himself as an honest broker in an ongoing European peace process. The difference was that their actions took place either before
the war or with the consent of their governments. With the war
well into its second year, freelance peace overtures were unwelcome, dangerous, and possibly treasonous. Much as he detested
the folly of war and desired peace, his noble motives could also be
construed as the activity of a man, bored and isolated, who wanted
to be at the centre of events once more.

This is perhaps the most benign interpretation, the duke's curious interview taking on more sinister, conspiratorial overtones
when set in context with the pronouncements of leading American industrialists, for the most part pro-Nazi and anti-Semitic,
who wanted to continue doing business with Nazi Germany at
any price.

The duke was the poster boy for many American capitalists for
whom "negotiated peace" amounted to the chance to continue
business with Nazi Germany. Many of the companies he was due
to visit on the ill-fated Charles Bedaux tour of the United States
in 1937 were those whose owners and directors had considerable
financial interests in Nazi Germany.

As a pin-up for America's isolationist wing, the duke attracted
the favourable attention of right-wing radio star Boake Carter,
the Rush Limbaugh of his day. English-born but a naturalized

American, the radio commentator had an intense loathing of the country of his birth, railing constantly against America's decision to send economic aid to the beleaguered nation.

Believed by Messersmith to be in the pay of the Germans and the Japanese, he frequently singled out the Duke of Windsor for praise, contrasting his man-of-the-people approach with the prejudice and snobbery of the British ruling classes. It was noticeable that he lauded the duke's Christmas radio broadcast that December, telling his listeners: "Of all the messages delivered by world leaders on Christmas Day, the only one which showed any glimmer of understanding as to where the real battle lies was Edward, Duke of Windsor."

A misguided foot soldier for peace, a naïve dupe of American business, a man eager to reclaim his crown, or a disloyal, possibly treasonous servant of the Crown; in the first few months of his tenure in the Bahamas the duke could be accused of all those charges.

In spite of his minor position in the British colonial service, his undoubted charisma and magnetic appeal ringed the world. After Lord Lothian's death, his name was one of the first thrown into the ring by several excitable commentators as the replacement British ambassador in Washington. When the president received a cable mentioning the duke's name, he scrawled on the document: "There isn't a chance."

The same could be said of the peace manoeuvres he was involved with.

CHAPTER TWELVE

Tropic of Rancour

During Prohibition, shady businessmen in the Bahamas made a fortune smuggling rum, gin, and other spirits to Florida and other places on America's East Coast. The duke, who liked several stiff drinks every evening, clearly caught the bug, bringing in hundreds of bottles of spirits under the guise of "diplomatic packages" and having them stored at the British embassy in Washington before shipping them on. In this way the dodgy duke avoided paying US Customs duties.

The new ambassador, Lord Halifax, studiously ignored this shady behaviour, just as he and British intelligence turned a blind eye to the duke's illegal currency dealings through pro-Nazi connections. As with the saga of the Nile-green swimsuit and the Duchess's fine linens, the personal comfort and ease of the duke and duchess were always their primary concern.

His judgement, or rather lack thereof, came to the attention of the prime minister, who wrote to the duke warning him about the cabal of wealthy cosmopolitan businessmen who formed his circle of friends. In particular, in his cable of mid-March 1941—his first communication since the royal couple had left Lisbon in August—Churchill took it upon himself to warn the duke that his Swedish friend Wenner-Gren was a "pro-German International Financier with strong leanings towards appeasement and suspected of being in communication with the enemy." The Swede had recently set up a bank in Mexico which was suspected of funneling money to aid the Nazi war machine.

The prime minister's warning came shortly after Sumner Welles, under-secretary of state, wrote to his State Department colleague Fletcher Warren reporting that the Duke of Windsor and Axel Wenner-Gren were seeing a great deal of prominent and influential businessmen from the Midwest, where a "strictly commercial point of view would prevail in business circles with regard to relations between the United States and Germany."

In his memo of January 25, 1941, he went on to describe, as had George Messersmith and other diplomats, how the two men were "stressing the need for a negotiated peace at this time on account of the advantages which this would present to American business interests."

The duke's folly was compounded when he agreed, at the urging of "Mr. Bahamas," Harold Christie, to receive a man of "boundless corruption," Maximino Camacho, brother of the pro-Fascist president of Mexico, a country that had just broken off diplomatic relations with Britain and appropriated all its oil interests. Camacho, who owned twenty houses, dozens of cars, and a stable of Arabian horses, had a huge portrait of Mussolini dominating his bedroom in Puebla. Describing the Italian leader as "one of the great men of our age," Camacho was an enthusiastic supporter of the Axis.

In that critical month of March 1941, when Roosevelt, much to Churchill's relief, had managed to have the Lend-Lease Act signed into law by Congress, thus ending America's pretence of neutrality, the duke managed to rock the boat.

Just as Churchill began to think the tide was now turning in Britain's favour, the duke and his pessimistic talk hove into view in the shape of the good ship *Liberty* magazine article. The prime minister felt that the tone of the article was unpatriotic and defeatist, the duke seeing no hope of a British victory or a change of policy in Germany. Answering a series of rhetorical questions, he said: "You cannot kill eighty million Germans and since they want Hitler, how can you force them into a revolution they don't want?" He went on to argue that only America could impose a peace settlement, once again the New World sorting out the Old.

Oursler kept his side of the bargain and never mentioned the duke's plan to endorse Roosevelt should he decide to mediate in any peace talks.

As it was, given the duke's standing among American isolationists, his statements clearly gave ammunition to their cause. Even Goebbels was nonplussed, noting in his diary of March 1941 that the duke "frankly disclaims all chance of an English victory." He instructed the media not to use his remarks to avoid discrediting the duke.

As for Churchill, he may well have sympathized with a respectable old doctor who, somewhat the worse for drink, went up to the duke at a reception at Government House in Nassau, shook him, and shouted: "Why don't you try and grow up and behave?" Opinion was divided between shock and approval.

The article marked yet another low point in the avuncular father-and-son relationship between the duke and the prime minister. Retribution was not long coming. During the duke's visit to meet with Roosevelt, the president had invited him to return to America to see the work of the Civilian Conservation Corps, which he had set up in 1933 to alleviate unemployment.

Shortly after the article appeared, the duke duly requested permission to visit the CCC in the United States. While the new British ambassador, Lord Halifax, who was no admirer of the duke, felt on balance the visit should go ahead, Churchill had other ideas. In a telegram of March 18, 1941, hard on the heels of his note about Wenner-Gren, he wrote that "after much consideration and enquiry, I have reached the conclusion that Your Royal Highness' proposed visit to the United States would not be in the public interest or your own at the present time." The reason became clear at the end of the message, where he took "exception" to the recent interview, which "will be interpreted as defeatist and pro-Nazi and approving of the isolationist aim to keep America out of the war.... I must say it seems to me that the views attributed to Your Royal Highness have been unfortunately expressed by the journalist.... I could wish indeed that Your Royal Highness would seek advice before making public statements of this kind. I should always be ready to help as I used to in the past."

There followed an increasingly splenetic exchange of telegrams. Given the true nature of the interview, the duke was being disingenuous when he claimed that most of what he said had been put into his mouth. Impulsive as ever, he threatened to resign if Churchill felt he was a detriment rather than an asset to Britain. If Churchill had been aware of what was really discussed, he would have been within his rights to accuse him of behaving like a Fifth Columnist.

The prime minister refused to let the issue rest, pointing out that the article was not repudiated by the duke and could "indeed only bear the interpretation of contemplating a negotiated peace with Hitler." In a pointed rebuke, he continued: "This is not the policy of His Majesty's Government; nor is it the policy of the Government and vast majority of the United States, where there is a very fierce and passionate feeling rising.... Later on when the atmosphere is less electric, when the issues are more clear cut and when perhaps Your Royal Highness's public utterances... are more in harmony with the dominant tides of British and American feeling, I think that an agreeable visit for you both might be arranged. Meanwhile in this sad time of sacrifice and suffering it is not I think much to ask that deference be shown to the advice and wishes of His Majesty's Government and of Your Royal Highness's friends, among whom I have always tried to play my part."

The duke was firmly on probation until he came to heel. As a parting salvo he complained that, in an interview with the American *Time* magazine, the queen had referred to his wife as "that woman," a deliberate insult and one that must have been approved by the British censor. The spat with Churchill did not seem to have altered his views; he told New York stockbroker Frazier Jelke that spring that he firmly opposed the entry of the United States into the war. In echoes of his conversation with Oursler, he stated: "It is too late for America to save democracy in Europe. She had better save it in America for herself."

Not only was he now on probation, he was under formal surveillance, Roosevelt ordering the FBI to monitor his movements when he and the duchess were given permission to pay a brief and strictly private five-day visit in April to see his financial advisor Sir Edward Peacock in Florida. Particular emphasis was placed on recording whom they met, the authorities aware that the duke was possibly being used or manipulated by a cabal of wealthy industrialists who were, in the words of American ambassador to Germany William E. Dodd, "hell bent to bring a fascist state to supplant our democratic government."

When they arrived in Miami on the regular passenger ship, the SS *Berkshire*, among the two thousand curious onlookers was FBI agent Percy Wyly, detailed with tracking their every move and reporting every visitor. Not only did he have to evade detection by the duke and his entourage, he also had to avoid being spotted by the American secret service detail assigned to protect the royal couple. In Hoover's estimation, Wyly, a graduate of Vanderbilt University, didn't do a very good job, the director sending a scathing memorandum complaining about the "grossly unsatisfactory" report that he submitted. Hoover complained that he failed to annotate the identity of everyone with whom the ducal couple came into contact and the subject of their conversations. Even though all telephone calls to the Everglades Club in Palm Beach, where the Windsors stayed from April 18 to 23, were logged and the identity of the callers established, including local taxi companies to men's stores, Hoover still was not satisfied.

If his own men were not up to the job—Wyly was later involved with the investigation into a possible UFO landing at Roswell—Hoover enjoyed support from a willing platoon of informants. A lady from Cincinnati, Ohio, relayed a third-hand story of the Duchess of Windsor going to London's East End to pick up supplies of dope. She was equally convinced that while having lunch at the Waldorf-Astoria hotel in New York she observed Adolf Hitler at the next table. His customary black moustache was dyed blonde. A somewhat more convincing report came from one of the duke's acquaintances, New York property owner and socialite William Rhinelander Stewart, who visited him in Nassau from time to time. He repeated the familiar story about Hitler installing the duke as king once he had defeated England—though he was rather more sceptical about the veracity of this information than others among Hoover's correspondents, and probably Hoover himself.

It was clear to Stewart that the duke was acutely aware of being spied on, during one social event joining in the singing of "There'll Always Be an England" and then adding "and a Scotland Yard." Hoover encouraged Stewart to report on his impressions of the duke and duchess when he visited them again. From a hodge-podge of hearsay and unsubstantiated allegations, including information from Captain Alastair "Ali" Mackintosh, a friend of the duchess and a playboy who "spun through the Palm Beach social scene like a whirling top," in April the FBI chief sent a potentially sensational report to Roosevelt via the presidential secretary Major General "Pa" Watson.

First Hoover informed him that former ambassador to Britain Joseph Kennedy and Wall Street operator Ben Smith, who were both pro-Nazi, had met with Hermann Göring in Vichy, France, and donated a "considerable" amount of money to the Nazi cause.

He then turned his attention to the Duke of Windsor:

> This same source of information advised that the Duke of Windsor entered into an agreement which in substance was to the effect that if Germany was victorious in the war, Hermann Göring through his control of the Army would overthrow Hitler and thereafter install the Duke of Windsor as the King of England.

Hoover was not the only one questioning the duke's patriotism: Roosevelt's great friend Harry Hopkins sent him a copy of a letter he had received from Pulitzer Prize–winning journalist Herbert Bayard Swope about "your friends the Duke and Duchess of Windsor."

> *This is straight. It can be relied upon: The Duke and Duchess of Windsor are, by some who know, listed among the appeasers. When they come here they see that type . . . which properly can be called pro-Nazi.*
>
> *Personally, from inquiries I have made, I have no doubt that the Duke stands very well with the Nazis. He might be returned to the throne if the impossible of an English defeat were to be achieved.*

Swope's dyspeptic attitude towards the duke and duchess did not prevent him from entertaining the ducal couple at Land's End, his Long Island home.

The irony is that the duke, whether he knew it or not, was not only pro-Nazi and a fervent appeaser but also, probably without his knowledge, the leader of the anti-Hitler movement. He was the face of the German resistance, in the popular imagination a talisman for peace as well as a potential puppet king.

He was respected by all sides. In October 1940, for instance, after a brief meeting with Pétain in the small French town of Montoire, the Führer, accompanied by Göring and von Ribbentrop, drove the thirty-three miles to Charles Bedaux's Château de Candé, where the duke married Mrs. Simpson. The three leaders of the Third Reich walked into the library, solemnly stood before the portraits of the duke and duchess, and gave the Nazi salute.

Though the duke never did Hitler's bidding, the Führer, according to his biographer John Toland, never lost that respect for the ex-king. He wrote in his private notes: "England for the good of the world must remain unchanged in her present form. Consequently after final victory we must effect a reconciliation. Only the King must go—in his place the Duke of Windsor. With him we will make a permanent treaty of friendship instead of a peace treaty."

Respect for the ex-king was perhaps the one point of agreement between Hitler and his sworn enemies. In August 1941 Nazi opponent Ambassador Ulrich von Hassell visited like-minded friends in Hungary and asked Archduke Albrecht, who was seen as a future regent, how he thought the war would end. "He banks on the Duke of Windsor," recorded Hassell, who "he believes is holding himself in readiness."

In the second full year of war, surrounded by a sea of suspicion—and hope—the duke's ambitions were much more prosaic. He and his wife simply wanted to escape the constricting climate of the tropical islands where, to their minds, they were prisoners in all but name. Several months after his contretemps with Churchill in March 1941, he sent him a long and emollient letter in which he effectively promised not to be, in the Duchess's words, "a naughty boy" if he was allowed to visit his ranch in Alberta, Canada, and spend several weeks touring the United States in September and early November 1941.

The prime minister relented, allowing him off the island to conduct official business in Washington, visit the Duchess's relatives in Maryland, and go to his ranch, as well as spend a few days in New York. Lord Halifax drily remarked that it would be "cruelty to animals" not to allow this request.

Like a prisoner on day release, it was made clear that he was on licence and that his itinerary should be strictly vetted. For his part the duke asked for one favour: "I only wish you would do something to dispel this atmosphere of suspicion that has been created around me, for there is a good deal more I could do to help on this side of the Atlantic."

Proving that what the world loves more than a maverick romantic is a royal maverick romantic, the duke and duchess were rapturously received when they arrived in Miami before travelling to Washington in a special train supplied by their friend, railroad tycoon Robert R. Young. By all accounts the crowds that greeted them were larger than those for the king and queen during their own highly successful tour in 1939.

For once the main focus was not on the long-running royal family feud but the amount of luggage accompanying the royal couple. For the five-week visit it was estimated that they had brought between thirty-five and eighty pieces, British ambassador Lord Halifax describing it as "ridiculous" and chafing at the price the embassy paid for hiring a truck to transport their baggage to and from the station.

The perceived excess didn't stop there, the ducal couple checking into the swankiest suite on the twenty-eighth floor of the Waldorf Towers in New York and travelling around the city in a custom-built saloon supplied by their friend, General Motors' pro-Nazi chairman Alfred P. Sloan. It gave the duchess the chance to catch up with her shopping. Stung by stories that she had bought thirty-four hats, the duchess retorted that it was only five. "Since I am actually shopping for a year, I don't think anyone could consider this outrageous," she said. It didn't play well in rationed Britain, an outraged Labour member of Parliament, Alexander Sloan, asking for the recall of the governor and his wife. He complained that, with their "ostentatious display of jewelry and finery" their visit was "evidently doing a certain amount of harm and not good."

The controversy merely added to their appeal; in Baltimore an estimated 250,000 people lined the streets to catch a glimpse of the homecoming duchess. Even in the isolationist Midwest their reception bordered on the rapturous.

Crucially, carmaker Henry Ford, a fully paid-up member of the Hitler Admiration Society, was also impressed with the duke, who visited Detroit and Dearborn to meet up with his friend, General Motors chief—and now FBI suspect—James D. Mooney. Shortly after seeing the duke, Ford, the only American to make an appearance in *Mein Kampf*, announced that, contrary to his previous policy, he was now prepared to make arms for England.

The trip was seen by the *Miami Herald* as a personal triumph for the duke, who was dubbed a "super salesman" for the British empire as well as doing a "bang up job" of beating the drum for America. By contrast, when Halifax visited Detroit two weeks later he was pelted with eggs and tomatoes by anti-war protesters, and his hotel was picketed.

Even Roosevelt, who met the couple on two occasions, was charmed in spite of the warnings of Swope, Hoover, and others. He told Ambassador Halifax that the duke was "robust" on Britain's eventual victory, which was a "great improvement" on his attitude when he met him in the Bahamas.

A month after the duke and duchess returned to Nassau, everything changed when the Japanese bombed Pearl Harbor on Sunday, December 7, and the world's most powerful neutral nation joined what was now a world war. If the duke was ambivalent about the war with Germany, the conflagration with the Japanese was an entirely different matter, especially after the sinking of the *Repulse* and the *Prince of Wales*, which was named after him, several days later. He hated the Japanese with a passion he never felt for the Germans, his strikingly racist views for once out of kilter with those of Adolf Hitler, who had conferred the title "honorary Aryans" on the whole Japanese race. The duke had no such sympathies, describing the architects of Pearl Harbor as "the Nipponese hordes" and viewing them as a yellow disease contaminating the Far East.

There was no longer any secret talk about negotiated peace settlements. After what he described as Japan's "unparalleled treachery," he was fully committed to the war effort. As the duchess wrote: "I am glad we are going to be in the war which is better than being on the outside." She threw herself into her war work, organizing the local Red Cross and the Daughters of the British Empire, as well as setting up a maternity centre for all races in Nassau. At the military canteen she regularly served servicemen with their morning breakfast and loved the fact that many letters home ended or started with the fact that the airman had been handed bacon and eggs by the Duchess of Windsor.

Her husband believed that the sapping climate and the energy she expended on local charities contributed to her bouts of ill health, notably stomach ulcers and a successful operation for cancer in August 1944. The duke was now equally committed to supporting the British and the Americans in any way he could. His primary task as governor was to focus his energies on the economic crisis in the Bahamas which, with the outbreak of hostilities, faced a collapse in tourism. With widespread unemployment and subsequent destitution and starvation for the majority black population threatening to overwhelm the islands, help came in the nick of time.

After a disastrous few months, America's involvement in the

war proved a godsend to the colony, the United States and Britain deciding to build bases there to train air crews. The islands were buoyant once more—the new tourists wore uniforms and spent freely in the bars and hotels of Nassau. During this period, the duke settled a serious race riot and managed to reduce the muscle of the "overmighty" Bay Street mafia.

There was one man missing from the changing face of Nassau—his Swedish friend Axel Wenner-Gren who, much to the duke's distress, was placed on an official US economic blacklist within seven days of the attack on Pearl Harbor. He was a substantial investor in the islands, and this was a considerable financial blow. Though the duke asked Ambassador Halifax to explain why the decision was taken, the response he received was singularly opaque. The real reason was that he was too powerful. His great wealth had enabled him to become the de facto economic czar of Mexico, which meant that he had more control over precious resources than the Americans were prepared to concede. Central America and Mexico were their backyard, and Wenner-Gren was trespassing.

The American media, though, subscribed to the simplistic view that he was a friend of the Nazis, labeling the Swede an enemy agent who had built a base on Hog Island in the Bahamas in order to guide U-boats to their targets. While this was a wild story, even an official denial by the duke did little to stop the speculation; furthermore, it was undeniable that the Bahamas was a potential haven for U-boats and that Nassau was virtually unprotected. They had just two light machine-guns to defend the town. Given the antics of the Germans during the ducal stay in Spain and Portugal in 1940 and the bizarre flight of Rudolf Hess to Scotland in May 1941, the imaginations of the duke and duchess worked overtime. They feared that they could be snatched from Government House by Nazi commandos landing from a submarine and then held as hostages in exchange for the now imprisoned Hess. For once, the

British and Americans listened to the royal governor, especially after Italian submarines sank two ships off the Bahamian coast. Churchill personally ordered the deployment of two hundred Cameron Highlanders to Nassau, while the Americans promised to set up air and sea reconnaissance stations and a string of intelligence posts around the islands.

Several months later, in August 1942, the death of his younger brother the Duke of Kent in a flying accident in Scotland brought home the dreadful human cost of the war. It also reminded him, if he needed any reminding, that the family dispute meant that he had not seen his brother since a brief encounter in Vienna in 1937. The duke was devastated. At a memorial service held for the Duke of Kent in Nassau he broke down and wept throughout, mourning his brother and perhaps his own life and what he had become.

Yet this family tragedy did nothing to heal the divide between the duke and his brother George VI. Even Churchill was shocked when he asked the king if he wished to send his brother fraternal greetings, as he was due to see him during a visit to Roosevelt at his East Coast home, Hyde Park. The prime minister, who tried where possible to mend the broken royal relationship, received a "most cold message" from the king in reply. His secretary, Jock Colville, recalled: "The P.M. dictated to me rather a crushing answer [to the king], but, as often, he subsequently had it destroyed and replaced by one more conciliatory."

For the duration of the war the Windsors were treated with a mixture of scorn, suspicion, and celebration. It was at times simply bewildering for the duke and duchess, met with enthusiasm one minute, icy silence the next. In May, Churchill invited the duke and duchess to hear him address Congress. When they took their seats on May 18, 1943, they were given an ovation by the assembled dignitaries and politicians greater than that enjoyed by the prime minister. He was not amused. "As the Duke descended to his seat in the front row, he got as much clapping as Winston, or more, by which we were surprised," observed Lord Moran, who watched from the diplomatic gallery.

Yet even though they dined with Roosevelt, whose considered view of the duke became far more positive, and enjoyed cheering crowds wherever they went, they were treated like outcasts and Fifth Columnists by what the duke called "Official England" and by many in Washington.

Shortly after the ducal couple were Churchill's guests for his address to Congress, Ambassador Halifax asked the State Department if letters written by the duchess could be freed from censorship. The State Department refused the request, Adolf Berle, co-ordinator of intelligence, determined that she should be kept under watch. In a memorandum of June 18, 1943, he wrote to Cordell Hull setting out the reasons why:

> I believe that the Duchess of Windsor should emphatically be denied exemption from censorship. Quite aside from the more shadowy reports about the activities of this family, it is to be recalled that both the Duke and Duchess of Windsor were in contact with Mr. James Mooney of General Motors, who attempted to act as mediator of a negotiated peace in the early winter of 1940; that they have maintained correspondence with Charles Bedaux, now in prison in North Africa and under charges of trading with the enemy, and possibly of treasonable correspondence with the enemy; that they have been in constant contact with Axel Wenner-Gren, presently on our Blacklist for suspicious activity; etc. The Duke of Windsor has been finding many excuses to attend to "private business" in the United States, which he is doing at present.

While the memorandum further confirms that James Mooney and the Duke of Windsor were in communication during Sir

William Wiseman's abortive peace attempt, the absurdity of this position was exposed just a couple of months later in September 1943, when J. Edgar Hoover—the very man who was monitoring the duchess—proudly showed the ducal couple around FBI headquarters in Washington. As the duchess noted sardonically: "I begin to think I'm Mata Hari!"

Of course the continued hostility of the royal court never ceased to amaze the duke. Even though the Colonial Office, Churchill, and Roosevelt admitted that he had performed well in his role as governor, there was no lessening in the chill wind from Buckingham Palace. (Ironically, no matter what his achievements as governor, his tenure would be and has always been associated with the lurid circumstances surrounding the unsolved murder on July 8, 1943, of Sir Harry Oakes, the Canadian gold millionaire who was the second most famous man on the islands.) When he discussed with Churchill a bigger job, he was offered the governorship of Bermuda, a small island staging post seven hundred miles off the American coast. There had been some talk at the Colonial Office of offering him the governorship of the federation of the British West Indies but that came to nought, as did Churchill's suggestion that he become governor of Madras. In the United States there was even a society called "Friends of the Duke of Windsor in America," whose members hoped to see him given an ambassadorial post of some kind in their country.

The duke set up a loose-knit cabal of supporters in the Cabinet, civil service, and media, known as the Second Front, to lobby those with influence—such as Lord Beaverbrook—for a meaningful job after the war. Somewhat improbably, the duke, one of the most famous men in the world, even offered to undertake undercover work for the Foreign Office in liberated France. It all came to nothing, every new suggestion vetoed by Buckingham Palace.

As the Duchess confided to her friend Rosita Forbes:

They only murdered Sir Harry Oakes once. They will never stop murdering the Duke of Windsor.... It is his own family who are against him.

It was all the more galling when in November 1944 his brother—the dull and utterly uncharismatic Prince Henry, Duke of Gloucester—was made governor-general of Australia. As far as the king's private secretary, Alan Lascelles, was concerned there was no room for another rival royal wheel in the delicate timepiece of empire. After consultation with constitutional experts he concluded that, even though the duke was a "competent" governor, it was out of the question to make him governor-general or ambassador anywhere in the empire. Furthermore, he warned the prime minister that the constant harping on this issue might have a serious effect on the king's health. His proposed solution was for the duke and duchess to make their home in America and use their name and influence for charities or other non-governmental work.

Certainly, as Churchill informed the duke, the royal family would not countenance him settling in England. Nor would Queen Mary or the queen ever meet his wife. They were "inflexibly opposed." However, they were prepared to meet the duke on his own. The prime minister agreed to let the duke relinquish his governorship in September 1944, though tying up the remaining constitutional and economic loose ends took up the best part of a year, during which time the duchess underwent an operation for stomach cancer in a New York hospital. They finally left the islands on May 3, 1945, and headed for the Waldorf Towers in New York, where they were advised to remain until the turmoil in France, where they intended to settle, had calmed.

As they awaited developments in France, a cache of German Foreign Office documents further complicated their unique situation. The top-secret papers, which concerned their time marooned in Spain and Portugal during the war, made uncomfortable reading. The words "unpatriotic," "disloyal," even "treasonous" hung in the air.

As the king's counsellor Sir Alan Lascelles noted portentously in his diary:

> If the Windsors' reactions were as implied in this correspondence the result is to say the least highly damaging to themselves.

It was the beginning of a fresh saga, with the duke and duchess at its beating heart, a story that lasted twice as long as the war, straining and snapping friendships, political allegiances, and diplomatic alliances.

CHAPTER THIRTEEN

———— ⟨❧⟩ ————

The Hunt for Pirate Gold

He wasn't much of a soldier. Nor did he look like one, even though his bearing was erect and his manner tended towards formality. In the khaki uniform of a British lieutenant colonel, Robert Currie Thomson looked stiff and uncomfortable, a man who would rather be elsewhere. It was a curious chain of circumstances which placed the taciturn Scotsman at the heart of a discovery that would eventually involve British war leader Winston Churchill, the Duke and Duchess of Windsor, and a clutch of American presidents.

The son of an impoverished market gardener from Corstorphine on the outskirts of Edinburgh, Thomson was an exceptionally bright boy who was educated at a local high school thanks to the generosity of his uncle. In 1906, at a time when only the sons of the privately educated joined the civil service, Thomson, then eighteen, won a civil service scholarship and took up an appointment at the prison service in Edinburgh before being transferred shortly afterwards to the Foreign Office in London. In those leisurely days, work did not begin until eleven in the morning, and

Thomson discovered that members of staff who took the trouble to learn foreign languages earned a salary increment. Over the next few years he became proficient in German, French, Spanish, Russian, Polish, and Italian, his skills as a translator earning him a place on the diplomatic staff of two major international treaties, at Rapallo in 1922 and at the milestone Locarno treaty conference, which secured a postwar territorial settlement for Western Europe, signed in London in 1925.

As well as achieving the rank of chief translator, he was a king's messenger, carrying diplomatic communications to foreign embassies and accompanying the diplomatic bag to and from British embassies abroad. This gave him diplomatic immunity at border crossings, Thomson using this privilege to extend his trips and undertake undercover work as a missionary, carrying Bibles and other Christian literature in the diplomatic pouch. During the 1920s and '30s he travelled far and wide, focusing on Eastern Europe and Russia, where he preached in remote villages. As he had been raised in poverty and adversity, the primitive conditions—travel was often by horse and cart—were hardships he bore with fortitude. He would frequently ask his travelling companions: "Are you ready to sleep in a haystack? Can you eat stale bread? Can you shave in cold water?"

As both missionary and diplomat, he built up a network of contacts, often entertaining fellow believers at his home in Pinner, a well-to-do London suburb, where he lived with his Swedish-born wife, Anna, who worked as a nurse.

Yet his contacts and linguistic talents were consistently overlooked by his superiors. While he harboured dreams of joining the diplomatic corps, his primary career inside the Foreign Office was as an archivist and librarian. In this backwater, the Scotsman became increasingly embittered as he watched those with less ability but from the right families and class promoted over his head. By birth and geography, he would never be a member of the Old

Boys' Club. He never forgot—nor was allowed to forget—his modest Scottish roots, nor was he able to hide the resentment he felt towards the English Establishment. If, during his travels, he was mistaken for an Englishman, he would say: "I am nothing of the kind. Haven't you heard of Scotland?" As his friend Roger Weil recalls: "He had contempt for the English ruling class and indifference towards the royal family."

When he was later awarded the MBE for his Foreign Office service, he refused to go to Buckingham Palace to accept the honour from King George VI. Eventually, in a gesture of disdain and indifference towards the ruling classes, he gave his medals away to a youngster from his church.

As much as he may have bridled at the system, his Foreign Office work as a translator and librarian brought him into contact with the European elite, Thomson making lifelong friendships. One such individual was Wilhelm Achilles, a consul at the German embassy in London during the tenure of ambassador von Ribbentrop in the mid-1930s. Achilles refused to join the Nazi Party and, sensing the oncoming rush of war, sent his wife to Zurich in Switzerland to escape the imminent conflict. The couple saved what money they could and, shortly before he was transferred back to Berlin, he asked his trusted friend Robert Currie Thomson if he would forward funds from London to Switzerland to help his wife see out the war. Even though the two friends were now on opposite sides, Thomson was as good as his word, regularly transferring money to Achilles's wife.

In the closing months of the war, with Germany about to capitulate, Achilles managed to get a message through to Thomson via his wife in Switzerland. He told Thomson that because of the sustained Allied bombardment of Berlin and the approach of the Soviet armies, the entire records of the German Foreign Office, together with the coffins of Frederick the Great and Field Marshal von Hindenburg and his wife, had been removed from Potsdam and sent in secrecy to remote castles in the Harz Mountains in Thuringia, at one time the home of composer J. S. Bach.

When Thomson received this message, Thuringia was in the American zone of operations, though it was shortly to be handed over to the Russians. Once the Soviets arrived there was no telling what would happen to these vital documents. It was imperative that the German archives be found and moved to the permanent British or American zones of occupation.

Once he briefed his superiors, it was decided that Thomson was the best man for the job of finding the papers and spiriting them away from the Harz Mountains. In the late spring of 1945, as the war reached its bloody conclusion, Thomson, then fifty-seven, found himself fitted out in an officer's uniform, swapping his position as assistant librarian at the Foreign Office, albeit temporarily, for the exalted rank of lieutenant colonel. This would ensure that Thomson, now head of the Foreign Office field team, had sufficient seniority to deal with any American and British officers he may meet.

On May 1, just days before Germany's unconditional surrender on May 9, Thomson received a hasty briefing on the rudiments of military etiquette and flew to France on the first leg of an adventure that would change the course of history.

⁓

This was no haphazard mission. Under what was known as the Goldcup Plan, the Allies had been plotting the capture of key German documents for several years. Indeed, by December 1944, Thomson was in regular contact with Dr. E. Ralph Perkins of the State Department's research division, trying to work out a common policy on how to deal with these vital archives. The British in particular had learned a harsh lesson from the First World War; Germany may have lost the war but it won the subsequent propaganda battle. "The records will play a vital part in the ideological battles of the future," noted E. Wilder Spaulding in a State

Department memo of January 1944. In a later note, sent in August, Spaulding, who was head of the research and publication division, underlined the hunger for the Nazi archive: "The Germans have doubtless raped half of the diplomatic archives of Europe and it would be most unfortunate should we not seize this opportunity to obtain some of their most important records."

During the First World War, the German empire seized archives in occupied areas and used them—for instance, through the publication of seized documents from occupied Belgium—as weapons of propaganda. The practice of publishing enemy documents, forged or authentic, for one's own advantage was brought to perfection by the Nazi regime. As the Allied armies advanced, they discovered whole Nazi technical units dedicated to the forgery of documents relating to nations the Germans had conquered.

German officials had long realized the essential value of records, and as the Allied bombing of Berlin and other cities intensified, orders went out to move the files to safe places in rural areas. At first the relocation of records was carried out under the greatest secrecy, as any action of this kind would have been seen as pure defeatism. In November 1944 orders were given to relocate the records officially to the Riesen Mountains near the Czech border. Just three months later, further Soviet advances forced the German High Command to move them once more, to Meisdorf and Falkenstein in the Harz Mountains. In the final days of the war, German librarians were ordered to destroy the secret records, SS units sent to ensure the task was completed. These instructions were largely circumvented by German civil servants who hid the files or burned only inconsequential or duplicate documents, hoping that this service would help them save their own skins when the Allies arrived. The destruction of archives was treated very seriously by the Allies. Civilians faced severe criminal penalties if they wilfully destroyed or concealed official German government records. One German woman who lived near Aachen, for instance, was jailed for six years in October 1944 for destroying records of her local Nazi women's organization.

During this elaborate game of hide-and-seek, the Allies had drawn up a so-called Black List of high-value targets, focusing essentially on the records of Hitler, Foreign Minister von Ribbentrop, the German Foreign Office, and the Japanese embassy. Allied teams of document hunters known as Target Forces or simply T-Forces stood ready to sniff out hidden or missing documents. The identification and protection of German archives became a top priority, so that by January 1945 some 287 officers and nearly 900 soldiers awaited deployment for this task. As document hunter E. Ralph Perkins asked of his boss, E. Wilder Spaulding: "Wish me good hunting."

While the Allies were eager to snag high-worth German documents, in the confusion of war no one was quite sure where they were hidden—hence the value of Thomson's private intelligence. It was a haphazard process of discovery, which seemingly relied as much on dumb luck as smart planning. In January 1945 Robert Murphy, political advisor to the State Department—essentially the department's czar in Europe—was given a list of eleven locations where the archives of the *Auswärtiges Amt*, the German Foreign Ministry, were stored. Only four turned out to be accurate.

For all the discussion and planning, the two most important discoveries of German documents took place thanks to Lady Luck and personal altruism. On April 12, Captain David Silverberg, a young Jew who fled Germany in 1936, was part of the American First Army advancing through the Harz Mountains and still meeting stiff resistance. As Silverberg and his men reached the town of Meisdorf he noticed a German army vehicle lying in a ditch with a confetti of papers strewn around. When he investigated further he was astonished to discover a document signed by Nazi foreign minister von Ribbentrop. As he later told documentary filmmaker Denys Blakeway: "Quite frankly, when you come right down to it, it was a simple piece of paper, wet and wrinkled, the signature smeared, but I recognized that one signature and it was the most important piece of paper I think that I have ever had in my hands."

Clutching his booty, Silverberg and his unit drove into town to find out more about this mystery. After questioning several locals, he discovered that since 1943 the quiet little town of Meisdorf had been regularly disturbed by heavy trucks carrying bundles of documents to the local schloss that villagers had helped unload. Silverberg followed the trail to the castle. After cautiously walking down a few steps at the entrance, he heard a trembling voice cry out: "Please don't shoot. Please don't shoot."

Emerging from the shadows was a middle-aged German, smartly dressed in a suit and tie. Once he calmed down he explained that Meisdorf was one of four locations where German Foreign Office documents had been stored. He went on to explain that the guards were under orders to destroy the archives rather than allow them to get into the hands of the Allies. They secured the archive at Meisdorf and then, armed with this fresh intelligence, Silverberg and his men sped off to the nearby schloss at Degenershausen, where they were assured more documents were stored. "We were absolutely stunned," recalled Silverberg when he described entering a room and discovering an archival treasure trove. There were documents going back to the nineteenth century, some bearing the signatures of Kaiser Wilhelm I and Bismarck. Others were signed by Hitler and von Hindenburg. There was also a copy of the Ribbentrop-Molotov pact, the partly secret 1939 agreement between Germany and Russia pledging non-aggression, as well as maps, some bearing the writing of the two foreign ministers. One room was filled to the rafters with documents, wrapped in brown waxed paper and secured with twine. One word was prominently displayed: *Geheim*, or Secret.

These documents, together with others discovered at three other locations in the region, formed the overwhelming bulk of target P-67, the Allied identification for German Foreign Office documents.

The immediate problem facing the Allies was the fact that the region containing these vital records had been assigned to the Soviet zone of influence. As there was no appetite to share this booty with the Russians, the British and American authorities decided to transport the four hundred tons of documents west into the American zone. With the Russians gathering at the River Elbe there was little time to waste. After consultation with the British, US political advisor Robert Murphy decided to have the German records transported 150 miles by road to the castle of Marburg, north of Frankfurt. It took 237 trucks travelling in shuttle convoys several days to move the precious booty.

Once safely stored—ironically, the Americans used Russian labour for the heavy lifting—the documents were catalogued, microfilmed, and finally analysed by a team of experts. This slow and painstaking procedure was overseen by American intelligence representative Gardner C. Carpenter and Lieutenant Colonel Thomson. It was the hope of Thomson—and the Foreign Office— that the documents would provide proof that Germany had been planning the war for the past twenty years. Not everyone was convinced. As one official noted: "Do not believe that Thomson's optimism in finding what he wants is especially justified, since the most interesting information is probably not on record."

Besides analysing the bundles of papers, senior officers were busily questioning German archivists, diplomats, and other officials about the trove of documents. With his excellent German, Thomson took a leading role. He left Carpenter supervising the evacuation of documents and headed to Thuringia to interview Foreign Office staff. While there, he was reunited with his old friend Wilhelm Achilles, the former chancellor of the German embassy in London who had first contacted him about the archives. With his help, Thomson secured another fifteen truckloads of Foreign Office archives, which were duly dispatched to Marburg. Achilles was part of that convoy, Thomson anxious for his old friend to find safe passage into the American zone. Achilles subsequently supervised the German clerical staff who helped organize and catalogue the mountain of paper files.

With Achilles safely out of harm's way, Thomson was returning alone from Mühlhausen, Thuringia, after interviewing a key German Foreign Ministry official, when he was approached by a German, aged about thirty-six, who spoke to him in faultless English.

According to Thomson's report about the extraordinary episode, the smartly dressed gentleman had an extraordinary request. He asked him to take a letter to Duncan Sandys, Churchill's son-in-law and the then British minister for housing. Thomson was taken aback and told him that he could take the letter only if he had some idea of the contents.

The mysterious German then revealed himself as Carl von Loesch, the understudy to Hitler's personal interpreter Dr. Paul Otto Schmidt. Both men had been present during virtually all of the Führer's meetings, both official and private, with world leaders and Axis politicians. Loesch explained that he was at Oxford University at the same time as Sandys, hence the letter to the Conservative member of Parliament.

Loesch had an offer that he hoped the Allies would be unable to refuse. He explained that in February 1945, when von Ribbentrop's office was evacuated, he was sent to Thuringia with the most secret German archives from the years 1933 onwards. The haul included the original files and microfilm copies. As the Allies advanced he was ordered to destroy these highly sensitive documents. He obeyed orders, burning the original archive and the cardboard cartons in which the microfilm had been packed. He had repacked the film in a metal container and buried the container, wrapped in an old plastic raincoat, in the grounds of a country estate in the vicinity of Mühlhausen.

In return for revealing the whereabouts of this hidden treasure, von Loesch wanted to be flown to Britain. As his mother was English and he himself had been born in London, he thought this would be possible. It was a calculated gamble, as an unforgiving conqueror could have tried him for treason. Loesch reckoned that the cards he held in his hand were worth the gamble. "I would stress the fact," he wrote to Sandys, "that this lot contains only the essential but also all the essential documents. There has never existed a similar collection in Germany."

Furthermore, he offered to help in the evaluation and examination of the trove, placing the documents in historical context. "I honestly believe them to be the clue to the true history of our times when used as a complement to those in possession of the British Government," von Loesch wrote to Sandys.

On the surface it seemed a remarkable fluke for Thomson, the only British officer in the area, to have met von Loesch. In fact the German had already been identified as a person of interest to the Allies. As early as April 30, 1945, a top secret CIOS (Combined Intelligence Objectives Subcommittee) memorandum was already in circulation describing von Loesch as living on a farm after having hidden thirty cases of Foreign Office documents. The memo recommended that the man be found "if possible."

This intelligence, however, was not acted on. As Thomson wrote in his subsequent report: "It transpired later that the man had no idea that I was searching for the very things which he was willing to reveal but merely spoke to me because I was a British officer, a somewhat rare specimen in Thuringia."

Given the fact that both he and von Loesch were experienced Foreign Office interpreters who may have met before the war and that Thomson had travelled to Thuringia in part to secure the safe passage of his diplomat friend Wilhelm Achilles, who had alerted him to the whereabouts of German Foreign Office files in the first place, it seems that more planning and forethought had gone into this "chance encounter" than Thomson subsequently revealed. Over the next few months Thomson's solicitous attitude towards von Loesch aroused the suspicion of his American opposite number, Gardner Carpenter, who wrote a long memo of complaint to Robert Murphy.

Following his initial encounter with von Loesch, Thomson fortuitously teamed up with Dr. Ralph Collins of the State Department, who was on a similar mission. Together they tried to find military intelligence officers to advise on the next step. After taking soundings from several senior officers the duo decided to trust von Loesch and allow him to lead them to the hidden microfilm. On Monday, May 14, just five days after the unconditional German surrender, Thomson and Collins found themselves motoring to a large country house twenty-five miles from Mühlhausen. This was the place where the alleged treasure was buried. It was also the temporary quarters of a detachment of the Fifth Armored Division. Once the duo arrived and met up with von Loesch, as a precaution they requested the services of an armed American officer. Following von Loesch's lead, the unlikely quartet, which now included Captain Albert Folkard, who volunteered to be their bodyguard, made their way along a private track to a steep valley where, the German official assured them, the microfilm was buried.

In his report Thomson described the moment of discovery:

We had to descend, rather uncomfortably, a steep ravine banked with pine trees. Our guide halted at a certain spot where he and Captain Folkard with iron bars soon scraped the soil from a waterproof cape covering a large battered metal can. This Captain Folkard brought to the top of the declivity and placed under guard at the mansion.

Such store was placed on this archival treasure that Colonel Douglas Page, of the Fifth Armored Division, provided an M40 armoured carrier to transport the find back to Marburg. Certainly von Loesch was not exaggerating about the value of the film. On the journey Thomson met with an RAF microfilming unit at Dentine Camp and was able to use their magnifying apparatus to take a first look. It didn't take long for Thomson to realize that the contents of the microfilm went to the very heart of German foreign policy. As he noted: "They fully correspond to the informant's description and will undoubtedly supply information of immense value which may not be obtainable elsewhere."

Even though von Loesch was as helpful as he could be, he was treated with suspicion by his new masters. "The man may be an opportunist but he quite accepts the situation that he is in our power and to my mind seems quite prepared to be useful to us in the interests of his own future," noted Thomson. "His Germany is gone forever and he is quite willing to adjust himself to a new state of affairs. I am seeing that he is treated with courtesy and consideration but without tenderness."

He proved to be a willing ally as well as a wily negotiator. Less than a month later, on June 12, 1945, he revealed the whereabouts of a large wooden box containing the private films of Dr. Paul Otto Schmidt, official interpreter at the German Foreign Ministry. These films, which were recovered from the grounds of the same country estate near Mühlhausen, showed the records up to late 1944 of meetings between Hitler, von Ribbentrop, and other Nazi leaders as well as politicians from collaborating nations.

Of immediate interest to the British were the files relating to the English comic writer P. G. Wodehouse, who had been detained as an enemy alien following the invasion of France, allowed to see his wife only after taping five light-hearted broadcasts for the Germans. His controversial actions caused some, including the writer A. A. Milne, to accuse him of being a collaborator. For a time his books were banned by a number of British libraries.

The Schmidt box and the von Loesch microfilms were easily

the most valuable of the many tons of documents now possessed by the Allies. By the time the Schmidt box was uncovered, the von Loesch microfilm was in London and the 9,725 pages in the slow process of being translated and examined. At first the find was treated with a degree of scepticism, officials concerned that it was an elaborate "plant" to embarrass the Allies. So joy was unconfined when Oxford historian Ernest Llewellyn Woodward, who was attached to the Foreign Office, reported at the end of May that the documents were indeed genuine.

Dr. E. Ralph Perkins of the State Department, who was one of the first to review the content, spoke of a "tale of pirate gold hunting." Other Foreign Office officials immediately recognized the sensational nature of the contents. "I saw enough to convince me that they are dynamite," wrote one. "It is obvious that there is redhot propaganda material in this can of films," concluded another. This was even before the reports relating to the Duke and Duchess of Windsor made their provocative appearance, throwing all Allied thinking into turmoil.

The publicity value of the existing documents was obvious enough. "I have seen a red hot letter from Franco to Hitler...and there is a lot of dirt on Molotov," noted Foreign Office official Geoffrey W. Harrison. In the first few heady weeks of discovery, the Allies were eager to exploit the find to convince the world—especially neutral countries—of the justice of the Allied cause and the perfidy of the Nazi regime.

A note for a Foreign Office meeting on June 19, 1945, to discuss the "finds" of German and Italian documents confirmed both the size of the discovery and the propaganda potential. "We are left with an embarrassingly large quantity of documents (far more than we expected) which throw light on every major aspect of German and Italian policy." While the author acknowledged the scale of the task, he identified five key foreign policy interests where immediate publication would be of benefit. Besides German-Italian and

German-Russian exchanges, and evidence of Vichy collaboration, German, Italian, and Spanish negotiations were singled out for special attention. "We might decide to publish without asking Franco and in order to discredit him."

The author even recommended that Britain take the initiative and announce that they held a cache of German and Italian documents and that, together with the Americans, they planned to publish the highlights.

This conclusion was based on the assumption that the Americans would want to exploit the German records, a surmise that proved to be right on the money. The eager Americans wanted to convince not just neutral countries but their fellow countrymen that America had fought a just war, that the sacrifice in blood and treasure was not in vain. Decades before WikiLeaks had ever been heard of, State Department officials were anxious to use official German Foreign Office documents for American advantage. One unsigned memo that circulated around the State Department about this time summarized the mood:

> The documents are rich in information which, if made public, might exercise considerable influence on the thinking of American citizens on the subject of German occupation policy.
>
> It is obvious that some of this material must for the time being remain unpublished. This includes material the release of which might embarrass present negotiations with foreign governments, but there is documentary background material available here for an almost limitless number of general topics bound to prove of extreme interest to newspaper and magazine writers, radio commentators, and so forth.

While the Allies may have differed on the extent of publication for propaganda purposes, where they were united was in using the files to underpin their fundamental war aim—namely, to stop Germany from ever starting another war. This point was stressed in the Talisman plan for the occupation of Germany, which was drafted in August 1944.

By July the State Department alone had accumulated 750,000 documents and microfilms; a month later that figure had risen enormously to 1,200 tons of files held under joint Anglo-American control inside the American zone. Most documents lay unopened and untranslated. Not so the material supplied by Carl von Loesch.

This was pirate gold indeed, the investigated documents seen as the archival equivalent of the crown jewels. Among the gems were comparatively full reports of conversations between Hitler and von Ribbentrop and Japanese foreign minister Yosuke Matsuoka during his visit to Berlin in 1941, at which time the Germans strongly urged that Japan attack British-held Singapore. Also in the archive was ample proof of the close collaboration between Germany and the Spanish dictator, General Franco. For example, one letter from Franco to Hitler dated February 26, 1941, included a pledge of his friendship and the urgent recommendation for the closing of the Strait of Gibraltar.

However, the most incendiary material—and the most politically controversial—were the records concerning the relationship between the Nazis and their one-time ally, the Soviets. There were notes of conversations between Hitler, von Ribbentrop, and Soviet foreign minister Molotov, as well as documents containing the text of the non-aggression agreements made between Germany and the Soviet Union in September 1939. The most contentious information related to the secret supplementary protocol to the Ribbentrop-Molotov pact regarding the division of Poland and other territories by these two powers. It was, observed historian Astrid Eckert, "a find perhaps second only to the protocol of the Wannsee Conference [the meeting of Nazi officials that put 'the final solution' of the Jewish question into effect] in impact on international politics." An early indication, too, that the von Loesch files were a Pandora's box of treasure. With Russia still an ally and part of the four-power division of Germany, the release of these documents would have far-reaching diplomatic consequences.

It was not until January 1948, when the cooling of relations between the Soviets and the Allies had transitioned to the Cold War, that the State Department published *Nazi-Soviet Relations, 1939–1941*, a book that became an international bestseller and was the first effective blow in an ideological propaganda war. The publication of the secret protocol provoked fury in Russia, where Soviet historians and politicians described the documents as forgeries. This bitter controversy was not resolved until December 24, 1989, when the Soviet Congress of People's Deputies passed a resolution that finally admitted to the existence of the supplementary protocol.

At the time, though, the discovery of the supplementary protocol came as a profound inconvenience to both the British and American governments. As Thomson, Perkins, and others perused the find, the overriding concern of the Allies was to keep the Russians out of the information loop for as long as possible. However, it was not long before rumours of the "pirate gold" reached British newspapers, in May several reporting that three planeloads of files of the German Foreign Office had been flown to London. At the time, the physical files were still at Marburg Castle, which gave British officials the opportunity to brush aside demands from the Russians, notably the Soviet ambassador Feodor T. Gusev, to see these materials. When the *Sunday Chronicle* reported on June 24, 1945, that the von Loesch files had been flown to Britain, the cat really was out of the bag. "Germany's Most Secret Documents Are Safe in Allied Hands" shouted the headline, causing the Foreign Office to launch an inquiry to find the source of the leak.

Their sensitivity was understandable. Publicity and propaganda purposes aside, the documents were vital for the intelligence service but also as evidence in the forthcoming International Military Tribunal in Nuremberg. In June 1945, Supreme Court Justice Robert H. Jackson, who was the chief prosecutor, announced that captured German documents would be used as evidence. At the time, the British thought it appropriate to offer documents to the French and the Norwegian governments in their prosecutions of Philippe Pétain and Pierre Laval and the political collaborator Vidkun Quisling. Officials soon realized that this would set off a chain reaction: The courts would ask for the originals, the story of the find would emerge, and the Russians would ask how documents discovered in their zone were in the hands of the British and Americans.

Just weeks after the discovery of the German Foreign Office files, the British came to the horrifying realization that not just Stalin, Franco, and others would be embarrassed by the documents—but themselves. It was not long before they were limiting their co-operation with the war crimes tribunal, compromising their relations with the Americans and attempting to destroy incriminating files—a criminal action that had put a number of Germans behind bars.

The first sign of this volte-face came in correspondence relating to the man once considered a possible British prime minister, Sir Oswald Mosley. As leader of the British Union of Fascists, he was interned at the beginning of the war. Captured Italian archives showed that Mosley, who was a leading advocate of a negotiated peace, had been funded by Mussolini's government. How to deal with Britain's own Quislings, particularly those from the ruling classes, was the question that now exercised official minds. A top secret note, dated July 21, 1945, from George Middleton of the British embassy in Washington to W. C. Dowling in the State Department, gave a sign of British thinking:

The question of the publication of these papers naturally raises important issues which will require consideration by the cabinet. It is therefore of great importance to us that there should be no premature leakage. While it is our understanding that there should be no publication of these Italian or German archives pending agreement between the two Governments, we should nevertheless be grateful if particular care could be taken to ensure that there is no possibility of the contents of the documents relating to Sir Oswald Mosley becoming public knowledge.

Dowling was able to reassure him that the papers had been classified as "secret" and would not be published.

However, if the activities of high-born Fascists—when Mosley, the son of a baronet, married Diana Mitford in Germany, the 1936 nuptials were attended by Hitler—provoked official demands for concealment and secrecy, what of other, more reputable Establishment figures?

On July 17, 1945, the brilliant young historian Rohan Butler, an acolyte of Llewellyn Woodward, was spending a hot afternoon at the Foreign Office leafing through translated documents from the German Foreign Office files. On his desk was a slim manila folder containing the translated contents of film B15, the negatives ranging from B002527 to B003018. It was part of the contents of the fabled von Loesch hoard, which had been first photographed on June 13.

What he read left him shocked, surprised, and somewhat at a loss as to what to do next. The file contained details of the Duke and Duchess of Windsor's stay in Spain and Portugal following the collapse of France in 1940. It was not just the fact that the ducal couple were at the centre of an elaborately hare-brained Nazi kidnap plot, but that the former king showed such disloyalty to his country and his family. With laconic understatement the

Oxford-educated don's memo simply stated that Edward's comments placed him "in a somewhat curious light."

As Butler recalled several decades later: "I reacted with surprise. I had no idea of that particular episode. I wrote a short and flat minute rather deliberately. I thought it was perhaps a judicious way of describing what was distinctly unusual material."

The jaw-dropping contents of the file concerned the wartime activities of the Duke of Windsor, the German diplomatic documents painting an astonishing portrait of a man who was disaffected with his position, disloyal to his family, and unpatriotic towards his country. Such was his disaffection that his lifelong friend and staunch supporter, war leader Winston Churchill, had threatened him with court-martial if he failed to obey orders and take up his post as the wartime governor of the Bahamas.

Edward uttered distinctly treacherous sentiments during the brief stay in Madrid and Lisbon in 1940, after he and his wife were forced to leave their home in the south of France following the invasion of France. During that sojourn many of his unguarded utterances were recorded by German diplomats, Spanish aristocrats, politicians, and others. Then they were duly sent to Berlin and pored over by Hitler and von Ribbentrop.

Not only did he express himself strongly against Churchill and the war; he was also convinced that if he had stayed on the throne, conflict would have been avoided. Only the continued heavy bombing of British cities, he believed, would bring the United Kingdom to the negotiating table.

Taken at face value the duke was speaking high treason, giving succour to the enemy when Britain faced its darkest hour of the war. If the German files were to be believed, here was a man who had little faith in his country's leaders or his own family but fully approved of Hitler and his spurious plans for peace. As John Costello noted: "Such subversive statements would have been unforgivable for any British citizen. When they were promulgated from the lips of a former King who made no secret of his pro-German sympathies, it was tantamount to treason."

Even his official biographer, Philip Ziegler, considers him "indiscreet," talking to the wrong people at the wrong time in the wrong place about the wrong things. "There has been a lot of embroidery and exaggeration along the way but there is no doubt that the Germans genuinely believed that he could be set up as a potential puppet ruler," Ziegler told Denys Blakeway. "They believed that he was to some extent on their side."

Such was the dangerous import of these unguarded private utterances that it gave the Nazi High Command utter faith in a bizarre plot to entice the duke to stay in Spain, where he would wait for the Germans to invade his homeland. Then the man who spent his honeymoon in Austria before the war and visited Germany in October 1937 as Hitler's honoured guest would return to Britain as the Führer's puppet king. The Germans even had a code name for the plot—Operation Willi.

Just three days before Butler began reading about the frenetic merry-go-round of diplomatic telegrams between Lisbon, Madrid, and Berlin linked to the duke, the Norwegian government had asked the Foreign Office for access to captured German Foreign Office documents in order to bolster their prosecution of politician Vidkun Quisling, whose collaboration with the Nazis at the expense of his own country had made his name a byword for treachery. His fervent belief that Germany was a bulwark against Bolshevism and his attempts to broker a peace between the Nazis, Britain, and France in 1939 bore remarkable similarities to the Duke of Windsor's own sentiments and behaviour. The difference was Norway was conquered and occupied, Quisling doing the political bidding of the nation's new Nazi masters. Found guilty of war crimes, Quisling was executed by firing squad in October 1945.

Once the implications of the duke's utterances had leap-frogged up the chain of command—first to the Foreign Office, then Downing Street, and finally Buckingham Palace—it pro-voked a radical rethink about how to use the captured German Foreign Office documents. From being gung-ho about using these documents to discredit Allied enemies, the British rapidly put on the policy brakes.

This policy rethink had consequences not just for the propa-ganda uses of the German Foreign Office records themselves but also for the use of documents for the International Military Tribu-nal and the historical record itself. Powerful voices in Britain and some in America now urged the complete destruction of German Foreign Office documents as they related to the duke.

The man who came close to destroying the sacred compact between the palace and the people as a result of his abdication in 1936 now stained and strained the so-called special relation-ship between Britain and America, pitting civil servant against civil servant, politician against politician, and historian against historian.

It could be argued that two events firmly rooted in Britain's class system, namely the tug-of-war over the Windsor file and the belated discovery of the Cambridge spy ring, radically corroded the hitherto close working relationship between the two Allies.

Not only did the contents of that slim manila folder provoke one of the biggest attempted cover-ups in history, involving King George VI, Winston Churchill, Prime Minister Clement Attlee, and General Dwight Eisenhower, but it also exposed the essen-tial cultural and political divide between the two countries. It was soon apparent that while a belief in openness was in the American DNA, the British instinctively reached for the blue marker pen to censor and delete. Secrecy was their default position, and when mixed with reflex deference towards the House of Windsor it cre-ated a potent and on occasion explosive cocktail.

During this time, the Duke of Windsor was a man effectively exiled from his homeland and consistently denied any official position. He had resigned in March 1945 from his post as governor of the Bahamas and was currently staying at a suite in the Waldorf Towers in New York, the duke and duchess blithely unaware of the consternation they were causing on both sides of the Atlantic. Their focus was on cultivating New York society, in particular the friendship of their next-door neighbours, songwriter Cole Porter and his wife, Linda.

It is little wonder, then, that the Americans were nonplussed by the British behaviour, baffled that their allies would expend so much diplomatic and political capital on a man with no discernible official future. For the next twelve years—more than twice the length of World War Two—the British fought a tenacious and highly effective diplomatic and political rearguard action to prevent the Duke of Windsor's unguarded and embarrassing words from reaching the wider world. "No other group of documents was pursued with so much determination and energy by the Foreign Office," observes Astrid Eckert. "The British obsession with the Windsor file and the demand that it be destroyed undermined the trust of the Americans directly involved with the *Auswärtiges Amt* records. The conduct of the British in this matter was another impediment to co-operation."

By a curious paradox of history, the most resolute opponent of publication was wartime leader Winston Churchill, who was ousted from power following the Labour Party's election landslide in July 1945. He firmly and consistently urged that the Windsor file be consigned to the dustbin of history. Churchill was no stranger to the suppression of publications of record: In 1943 he had been able to successfully persuade President Roosevelt to stop the ongoing publication of the special series on the Paris Peace Conference of 1919, the *Papers Relating to the Foreign Relations of the United States*.

Yet throughout the period, not only was he granted privileged access to secret official documents for his majestic series of books on the Second World War (he was awarded the Nobel Prize for literature for the work in 1953) but his personal relationship with the Duke of Windsor, whom he had known and supported for most of his life, was at a low ebb precisely because of the Duke's behaviour during the conflict.

Such was his instinctive loyalty to the institution of monarchy that just a day after being shown details of the file by Prime Minister Clement Attlee on August 25, 1945, he wrote back: "I earnestly trust it may be possible to destroy all traces of these German intrigues."

The new prime minister was equally anxious that the documents never see light of day. He considered they had "little or no credence" and "might do the greatest possible harm." After consultations with his Cabinet colleagues, the consensus was for destruction. While technically the duke may not legally have committed treason, at the court of public opinion he may well have been found guilty—with dire consequences for the Crown.

Attlee's opinion was doubtless reinforced by his first visit to Balmoral in the late summer of 1945. There he spent the traditional "prime minister's weekend" as a guest of George VI and Queen Elizabeth. During strolls across the heather, the Duke of Windsor was the central topic of conversation. The king was pleased with Attlee's attitude towards his brother. He told Queen Mary that the prime minister "agrees with me that he cannot live here permanently owing to his wife and he is not prepared to offer D [David] a job here or anywhere."

The king immediately appreciated the potential for the Windsor file to compromise not just his elder brother but the family as a whole. At the time, no one knew for certain either at the State Department, the Foreign Office, or for that matter Buckingham Palace what further embarrassments concerning the duke, his American wife, or other members of the royal family would be revealed in the German or Italian Foreign Office records. After all, the duke had visited Germany in 1937 and famously spent nearly an hour in private conversation with Hitler at his mountain retreat at Berchtesgaden. Where was the official record of that interchange now lurking? There was much more. Before the war, Edward had spent time with his German cousin Prince Philipp of Hessen, now on trial for his life over his intimate association with Hitler and the Nazi Party. It had not escaped the palace's notice that there were high-grade rumours swirling around suggesting that in the early months of the war the Duke of Windsor had secretly met the now disgraced Prince Philipp in an effort to secure a negotiated settlement.

Much closer to home, George VI himself was also party to the informal but palace-sanctioned diplomatic activities of his younger brother George, Duke of Kent, who had also met with his now toxic cousin, Prince Philipp. If those documents were found, they, too, could prove an embarrassment.

With appeasement a wholly discredited policy and the horrific contours of the Nazi regime daily becoming clearer, it was not just the Duke of Windsor who would be embarrassed by the release of German and Italian Foreign Office documents but the entire royal family. As Sarah Bradford, George VI's biographer, observes: "From the king's point of view, the first sifting of the documents seems to have been highly embarrassing and necessitated urgent action."

———— ◈◈◈ ————

CHAPTER FOURTEEN

Sovereigns, Secrets, and Spies

The summer of 1945 saw a concerted British blitzkrieg to obliterate the Windsor file. Downing Street, the Foreign Office, and Buckingham Palace strained every sinew, pulled every string, called every old boy in the network to wipe the toxic file from the face of history. Moreover, King George VI set in train a series of secret missions to remove diaries, documents, jewelry, and other important royal artefacts from the castles, châteaux, and *Schlösser* of recently liberated mainland Europe. Many historians and commentators believe that this operation was put in place to ensure no incriminating evidence regarding the duke, his American-born wife, and other members of the royal family could ever be viewed by prying eyes. It was not just the antics of the Duke and Duchess of Windsor that worried the king. There were other royals, too, whose private behaviour the House of Windsor was anxious to stop becoming a public embarrassment. As Sarah Bradford explains: "The king was very concerned about the image of the monarchy. He took several steps to ensure that the crown would not encounter hostility or be unnecessarily damaged."

On August 3, 1945, the king sent two courtiers on a highly sensitive mission onboard a military plane to Germany. One was Sir Owen Morshead, a much decorated war hero who served the king and his father, George V, with distinction as royal librarian. The other was Anthony Blunt, a homosexual intellectual and art historian who once shocked the queen when he told her that he was an atheist. Blunt, who had only recently accepted the position of Surveyor of the King's Pictures, was a major in British counterintelligence, MI5, as well as a Soviet spy who had been feeding secrets to the Soviets since 1937.

Their stated task was to recover the historic and lengthy correspondence between Queen Victoria and her eldest daughter, the Princess Royal who married Frederick III of Prussia in 1858, became the mother of Kaiser Wilhelm II and, in 1888, Empress Frederick of Germany. The four thousand or so missives, known as the "Vicky letters," were currently housed in Schloss Friedrichshof, a few miles outside Frankfurt, which was the main residence of the king's cousins, the von Hessen family. Given the widespread looting of property by Allied troops and the fact that the castle was now an American officers' mess, it was felt prudent to recover the letters, which were the property of the Hessen family, and bring them to Windsor Castle for safekeeping. Several weeks before the duo set off, the king's private secretary, Alan Lascelles, had written to "My Dear Jacob," presumably Lieutenant General Sir Ian Jacob, military assistant to the Cabinet, on July 25, requesting that General Eisenhower provide Blunt and Morshead every facility, including transport and accommodation, to complete the assignment.

The King understands that there are in the Schloss a number of the private papers, diaries etc. of the Empress Frederick which, besides being of considerable historical importance are naturally of great interest to the Royal

Family; it is essential that these papers should not fall in to the wrong hands.

The task required some delicacy, as the current head of the house of Hessen—the landgrave—was Prince Philipp, then ranked number 53 among the most-wanted Nazis and under guard at an American-run interrogation centre. Even as Blunt and Morshead boarded their plane, he was being vigorously questioned about his role in bringing Hitler to power as well as his personal relations with Mussolini.

The two men were an unlikely double act; Morshead, some fourteen years older than his colleague, had trained to be an engineer before the First World War intervened. During his service on the French and Italian fronts he was awarded a Distinguished Service Order and a Military Cross and was mentioned in dispatches five times. After the war he took a degree in modern languages at Cambridge before switching to a career as a librarian, becoming the royal librarian in 1926, the same year that he married his wife, Pacquita. Friendly, outgoing, and a noted conversationalist with a fund of anecdotes, he became a genuine friend of George V and Queen Mary.

Such was his position of trust inside the Royal Household that when the Tower of London, home to the crown jewels, suffered a bombing attack in 1940, George VI consulted him about how best to safeguard the priceless gems. The jewels were moved from the Tower to Windsor Castle, where the king and his most trusted courtier borrowed pliers and other workmen's tools and set to work wrenching diamonds, rubies, and other precious gems, including the fabled Koh-i-noor diamond, from their settings. They placed the gems in hatboxes and hid them in the basement of the castle, the two men vowing that, if the Germans landed, they would hide the jewelry in a tin box and sink it in one of the ponds surrounding the castle. As Sir Owen recalled: "In the event of one of us disappearing, a record of these facts was to be kept in a safe place. During the entire war I kept this secret."

Morshead had first encountered Blunt as a young art historian in 1932, but it wasn't until midway through the war that they became friends, after he asked Blunt to catalogue the Old Master drawings held by the palace. The tall, aquiline, rather patrician Blunt visited Morshead's Berkshire home where, to the surprise of his circle, he enjoyed playing surrogate uncle to Morshead's three children. Most surprising, though, was his acceptance of the position of surveyor of the king's pictures in April 1945 after the resignation of the incumbent, Kenneth Clark. "We all thought it was a joke for a communist to become a courtier," recalled his friend, librarian Lillian Gurry.

Not only was he compromising his political principles to work in the world's largest privately held art collection, but the haughty young aesthete and connoisseur was entering a world where the middlebrow and middle-of-the-road were the norm. George V thought J. M. W. Turner, one of the finest English artists, was "mad," and the king once attacked a Cézanne with his cane. His son George VI was little better. When artist John Piper was commissioned by the queen to paint a series of watercolours of Windsor Castle in 1942 during the darkest days of the war, the king's comment on the paintings, which showed a delicately tinted stone castle drawn against a brooding, forbidding sky, was revealing: "You have been unfortunate with the weather, haven't you, Mr. Piper." He later confessed to Blunt that he never knew if the name on the bottom of a portrait was that of the artist or the sitter.

While there has been much speculation about Blunt and his role inside the palace, what seems clear is that his decision to accept the unpaid post was not suggested by his Soviet handlers. Former Soviet ambassador to Britain Viktor Popov, who wrote a profile of Blunt that was published in Russian in 2005 and was based on his exclusive access to the Russian Foreign Intelligence Service (SVR) and to one of Blunt's Soviet "minders," confirms that the first the

KGB knew about the appointment was an announcement in the *Daily Telegraph*.

Blunt's complex life as a Soviet agent, an art expert, and a royal knight has inevitably added considerable spice not only to his work inside Buckingham Palace but also to the 1945 mission to Friedrichshof Castle in the town of Kronberg. In his biography of Blunt, Popov suggests that Blunt did relay to the Russians the contents of conversations he had had with the king and his courtiers as well as with Cabinet ministers. While he was working at the palace, Blunt, according to Popov, even recruited two more "influential" Soviet informers. Tantalizingly, they are not named, nor does he say if they worked inside or outside the palace. Blunt's British biographer Miranda Carter thinks it "unlikely" that he would have exerted himself to recruit fresh agents, as he left MI5 shortly after taking up the palace post and was generally exhausted by his efforts during the war.

However, according to Popov's account, translated for the first time for this book, Blunt's minder is certain that Blunt was still passing on secrets. He stated:

> Blunt's minder not only confirmed my idea that Blunt continued his active work [for Soviet intelligence] while in the palace but added: "Blunt was getting a lot of information from his conversations with Cabinet ministers and the queen's personal secretary. I suspect that when he had to quit British counter-intelligence, 'our people' agreed, thinking that getting into the king's retinue would give him access to new sources of information."

The minder also stressed that in his new position Blunt managed to recruit two very influential informers.

Like Blunt's career, the continuing ambiguity and suspicion surrounding the true purpose of the royal mission to Germany in 1945 came into sharp relief in 1964 when the urbane courtier was exposed by fellow traveller Michael Straight as a member of the Cambridge spy ring. It was not until 1979 that his double life as traitor and royal knight was publicly revealed by the then prime minister, Margaret Thatcher, in a statement in the House of Commons.

Even after he was unmasked, Sir Anthony remained tight-lipped about revealing any details of his mission to Schloss Friedrichshof. Author Peter Wright, who wrote the dramatic exposé *Spycatcher*, was the MI5 officer tasked with questioning and debriefing Blunt. At one stage he asked him about his visit to Germany. "At this point Blunt immediately became very aggressive, and said nastily: 'Now this isn't on. You know you're not supposed to ask me that!'" His comment implied that a deal had been made beforehand, shielding the spy from inquiries related to his royal duties. This was underlined, according to Wright, by the queen's private secretary, Sir Michael Adeane, who told him before he began questioning the traitor: "You may find Blunt referring to an assignment he undertook on behalf of the Palace—a visit to Germany at the end of the war. Please do not pursue this matter. Strictly speaking, it is not relevant to national security." Reflecting on his many weeks spent interrogating Blunt, Wright admitted that he never did learn the secret of Blunt's mission to Germany.

This intriguing and unresolved episode, particularly Adeane's dour warning, has focused historians on the ulterior motive that may have underpinned the mission to collect the Vicky letters, namely that Blunt and Morshead were sent by the king to recover damning correspondence between the Duke of Windsor and Prince Philipp and other Nazi leaders, including Hitler himself.

Roland Perry, Michael Straight's biographer, reflects this perspective:

> The real assignment was to find letters and memoranda of conversations by the monarch's brother, the Duke of Windsor, with Hitler and top Nazis. Blunt and Morshead were to

search for transcripts of telephone calls made by the Duke of Windsor during his visit to Germany in October 1937. Of particular concern was the October 22, 1937, meeting... with Hitler....Better that they did not end up in American hands, especially the press.

As for the details of the mission itself, these are wreathed in drama and deceit. First there is the jaunty account written by one of the protagonists, Sir Owen Morshead, which is lodged in the Royal Archives at Windsor Castle.

In his version, he explains that he was sent on the mission because he was known to the Hessen family. Blunt came along for his "agreeable companionship," his excellent German, and because, as an intelligence officer, he had to undertake military business in the Frankfurt region. As they needed the permission of the seventy-three-year-old Landgravine Margarethe to remove the papers, it was felt that, as she had lost three sons in two world wars and felt a "rancorous hatred" towards Britain, the presence of an English officer might scupper the deal. Blunt kept a low profile, helping Morshead locate the letters and various signed books in the castle library while he made a cursory inventory of the important paintings.

When it came to winning the agreement of Princess Margarethe, Morshead was in his element, showering the family with the vital components of postwar German life—toilet paper, soap, tea, coffee, and matches. As the Landgravine had been given the statutory four-hours' notice by the American army to quit the hundred-room castle and was now living in the estate manager's cottage, these supplies were very welcome. In order to assist with the transaction, Morshead decided to bring along the widowed Princess Christoph of Hesse, Princess Sophia of Greece and Denmark and sister of the current Duke of Edinburgh. A favourite of the Landgravine, she was in favour of the transfer of family archives to Windsor Castle.

The princess, together with her children, their pet dog, and a tame wild boar called Bambi, clambered into Morshead's loaned Rolls-Royce and motored to see the Landgravine. The reunion with her family, the legendary charm of a pair of palace courtiers, and a few bars of chocolate seemed to do the trick, and Landgravine Margarethe signed an agreement for the duo to remove the letters from the castle.

Here it becomes complicated. In an interview with journalist Colin Simpson in 1979, Blunt described how they had gone to the castle to retrieve the papers but were refused access by an American woman officer, Captain Kathleen Nash. She was in nominal control of the castle, which was now a rest-and-recreation club for senior American officers. Now biographer Roland Perry takes up the narrative. In the increasingly terse exchange between the British intelligence officer and the American, Nash felt a frisson of doubt about her initial decision, especially after Blunt, according to Perry, told her that Winston Churchill supported the mission. He insisted that Nash call her headquarters. The female officer, who hailed from Saint Paul, Minnesota, had never met a man like Blunt. As Perry described it: "He was polite yet remote. He behaved as if he had real, if obscure authority." In the end she phoned headquarters, and while she was otherwise occupied, Morshead and two British privates manhandled packing cases containing the royal letters down the steps from the library, loaded them onto an army truck, and drove off into the night. A similar version is described by authors Martin Allen and John Costello, who add for good measure that the crates of letters removed from the upper floor of the castle (the library is in fact on the ground floor) contained documents chronicling the Duke of Windsor's treasonous activities.

Espionage expert Chapman Pincher gave the yarn a further twist. When the Americans refused Blunt and Morshead access to the letters, they returned to Princess Margarethe of Hesse, who directed them to a back entrance where, in the dead of night, they were able to break in and make off with their booty. Once back in Britain, Blunt, who had, according to Perry, made a secret micro-film of the incriminating documents about the Duke of Wind-sor, met his Soviet minder in a seedy East End public house and handed it over for safekeeping. The microfilm dishing the dirt on the duke was his security in case he was ever unmasked.

Author Kenneth D. Alford asserts that the Americans, far from being uncooperative, did all they could to facilitate the visit of the two British VIPs from Buckingham Palace. It was a trip long in the preparation. After the castle was liberated by the Ameri-cans on April 19, 1945, Eisenhower received a letter from British general Hastings Ismay—presumably after Lascelles sent his initial request for assistance in July—asking that Queen Victoria's letters be handed over to Sir Owen Morshead.

Responsibility for working with the British fell on the shoulders of Captain Julius Buchman. He and his men travelled to Kronberg to prepare the royal correspondence and to tidy up the library, which had suffered extensive looting, with visiting GIs stealing family silver, porcelain, and other heirlooms. It was this advance party who, according to Alford, were barred from entering the library by Captain Nash. After speaking with Buchman's superior officer, Colonel Mason Hammond, the matter was resolved, and Buchman was later issued with an official citation "for tact and industry" in dealing with the chaotic organization in the library. He jokingly told Blunt that he had headed off an international inci-dent, as the Americans were fearful that the British would com-plain about the state of the castle and its contents. Buchman and Colonel Hammond comprised the greeting party for Blunt and Morshead at Rhein-Main air base, the American duo escorting them to the castle.

On August 6, according to Alford, George VI's emissaries removed sixty-two volumes of letters between Queen Victoria and the empress dating between 1858 and 1901, together with five further volumes of telegrams between mother and daughter. A year later, American colonel John Allen acknowledged the transfer of documents to Windsor Castle in a memo.

There was no mention of any irregularities. Their visit was so brief that Blunt and Morshead missed other related items, notably Queen Victoria's gilt-edged Bible and prayer book, a photograph of Queen Victoria and her consort, Prince Albert, and nine volumes of correspondence between Empress Frederick and her daughter Princess Viktoria. These were subsequently stolen by American army thieves. In any case, they were on such a tight schedule that they had little opportunity to forage for other material, including the Windsor letters, while annotating the Vicky correspondence. Shortly after they left the rambling castle, for instance, three valuable letters written by Florence Nightingale, the Victorian nurse and philanthropist, were discovered in an unlocked desk drawer by souvenir-hunting American officers.

Shortly after Anthony Blunt—his Soviet code name was variously Tony, Tomson, or Yan—went on his secret military assignment, and Morshead went back to London with the trove of Vicky letters in the hold of the plane, there was a further bizarre chapter in this extraordinary story. Captain Nash, her lover Colonel Jack Durant, and their friend Major David Watson stole the Hessen family's fabled collection of jewelry, which had been carefully hidden in a special container in the castle basement. They sent it back to America in sealed wooden boxes but were caught a year later. Only two-thirds of the multimillion-dollar booty—as well as more letters from Empress Frederick to her daughter—were ever recovered. Members of the Hesse family, particularly Prince Wolfgang, blamed what the *New York Times* called "the greatest gem theft in modern times" on the Blunt and Morshead visit, believing that their arrival had excited interest in the castle and its contents.

This is a truly remarkable episode in the chronicles of the

House of Windsor, the Blunt-Morshead mission all the more intriguing because they flew to Germany only days after George VI had been told about the existence of the secret German Foreign Office files relating to the duke's behaviour in the Iberian peninsula. It would have been uppermost in his mind, along with his awareness that the late Duke of Kent had also met with Prince Philipp von Hessen just before the war in the hope of sparking backdoor peace talks. The potential for embarrassment was enormous. Years later, the *Sunday Times* of London interviewed Prince Wolfgang von Hessen, who confirmed that Prince Philipp was indeed a peace intermediary, via the Duke of Kent, between Hitler and the Duke of Windsor. As the 1979 article stated: "George VI had every reason to believe that the Hessen archives might contain a 'Windsor file.'"

As Professor Jonathan Petropoulos, the biographer of the von Hessen family, observes: "I not only think there was a concern on the part of George VI and others in and close to the British royal family that damaging letters existed, but I think that such letters existed in 1945." He points to the continued paucity of papers and correspondence relating to the widely travelled Duke of Kent as further circumstantial evidence that records may well have been destroyed or hidden.

At the very least it would seem that the two trusted courtiers were given a nod and a wink by the king to keep a weather eye out for any other incriminating royal correspondence besides the Vicky letters that might need "safekeeping" at Windsor Castle. The king's biographer Sarah Bradford believes that to be the case. "He got into such a frightful flap about the Marburg papers and he was really nervous about documentary evidence emerging that Windsor was a traitor." Certainly the timing and the subsequent reaction of Sir Michael Adeane, the queen's private secretary, regarding the limits on the questioning of Blunt suggest an ulterior motive.

As Professor Petropoulos argues: "In all likelihood, Blunt was instructed to keep a lookout for any incriminating documents involving the Duke of Windsor or the royal family. Certain retainers around the royals expressed the belief that there were files in Germany that needed to be secured."

In short to the age-old question of what did he know and when did he know it, it seems that King George VI did not know of the discovery of the Windsor file before plans were set in motion to send Blunt and Morshead off to Germany to secure the Vicky letters. Historian Rohan Butler discovered the embarrassing file only on July 17, 1945, and a week later Lascelles was organizing transport to Germany for the two courtiers. Even the most ardent conspiracy theorist would have difficulty in arguing that the Palace knew about the file *before* they began planning the Vicky operation. That said, it is likely that by August 3, when the two men set off, the king had been alerted by the prime minister to the existence of the file. At the very most, however, the king's men can only have been told to keep a weather eye out for anything that may be of further interest to the British Crown—their visit was too brief to assume that their purpose was anything other than securing the Vicky letters.

This was not the only mission undertaken on behalf of the king. Later in 1945 Blunt and Morshead made trips to Schloss Marienburg, the German family seat of the Hanoverians, and the Kaiser's home in Doorn, Holland.

While all the evidence points to there being correspondence between the two royal houses before and possibly during the war, there is little to suggest, then or now, that Blunt or Morshead found it. In fact, when Blunt reported for duty back in London his boss, Guy Liddell, the director of counter-intelligence, briefly noted in his diary: "Anthony has returned from Germany and has brought with him Queen Victoria's letters to Empress Frederick. They are only on loan."

The Soviet spy even told his colleague, historian Hugh Trevor-Roper, that he had found a letter from a Victorian court official who had called on Karl Marx.

What is indisputable is that the mission to Germany was just one of many undertaken by courtiers on a royal operation staged after the war to mop up correspondence relating to potentially embarrassing episodes. In short, the royal family knew where the bodies were buried and sent their courtiers off to dig them up.

On May 14, just days after the celebration of VE day, Queen Mary summoned the king's private secretary, Alan Lascelles, to discuss the vexatious matter of letters belonging to her uncle Prince George, Duke of Cambridge. Once considered a possible suitor for Queen Victoria, he led a potentially scandalous life, not for the fact that he was commander in chief of the British army for thirty-nine years but because of his colourful love life.

Unlike Queen Victoria, he was opposed to arranged marriages, believing that they were doomed to failure. Instead he followed his heart, in 1847 marrying actress and servant's daughter Sarah Fairbrother. During their marriage he followed his heart again, living with a certain Louisa Beauclerk, who was his mistress for more than thirty years. She was the love of his life, Prince George choosing to be buried in the mausoleum in Kensal Green cemetery about sixty feet from Mrs. Beauclerk's grave. His wife, Sarah Fairbrother, though, is buried with him. It was his boxes of love letters, then deposited in Coutts bank, that greatly concerned Queen Mary. She was worried that these billets-doux could be put to "undesirable" use by the Duke of Cambridge's descendants. Lascelles was dispatched to make sure the letters never saw light of day.

This was not the only family black sheep to be herded into safer pastures, namely the Royal Archive at Windsor Castle. King George VI was equally vexed about incriminating love letters between Queen Victoria's third son, Prince Arthur, Duke of

Connaught, and his long-time mistress, Lady Leonie Leslie, aunt to Winston Churchill and a member of one of the largest land-owning families in Northern Ireland. For more than thirty years she "ruled the Duchess and ran the Duke," the vivacious sister of Jennie, Lady Randolph Churchill, and her husband, Sir John Leslie, accompanying the Connaughts on various official overseas visits. The duke even rented Blayney Castle near to her family seat of Castle Leslie so he could be close to his mistress.

Understandably, the king did not want any more royal dirty linen washed in public. Owen Morshead was asked to approach Lady Leslie's son, the noted author and poet Shane Leslie, with a view to disposing of the incriminating correspondence. A similar exercise had been undertaken by Lady Patricia Ramsay, the young-est daughter of the Duke and Duchess of Connaught, who had destroyed Lady Leslie's letters to her late father. As Alan Lascelles recorded in his diary entry, made on the day he saw Queen Mary at Windsor Castle: "Perhaps he will gallantly retaliate in kind and set royal minds to rest."

In fact it was his brother Seymour Leslie who, according to the Public Record Office of Northern Ireland, presented "several hundred" letters from the duke to Lady Leslie to the Royal Archive at Windsor, where they "remained closed to inspection." In the papers of Lady Leonie Leslie, which are held by the University of Chicago, there is not one letter between herself and her royal lover, Prince Arthur.

These episodes help explain why authors, journalists, and aca-demics see conspiracies and cover-ups in relation to matters royal. It is often, as with the case of the destruction of the Leslie corre-spondence, simply because there are.

Not only are relevant archives often inaccessible but, as Las-celles recorded, the royal family, bred with dynastic history in their bones, are instinctively adept at covering their tracks. It is a prac-tice that continues to the present day. Princess Margaret burned several plastic bags of letters written by the late Diana, Princess of Wales, to Queen Elizabeth the Queen Mother. Even the queen mother's official biographer, William Shawcross, was moved to comment: "No doubt Princess Margaret felt that she was protecting her mother and other members of the family. It was understandable, although regrettable from a historical viewpoint."

The House of Windsor are not the only culprits: Numerous German royal houses, for obvious reasons, do not allow historians access to family correspondence lest any probings disturb Nazi skeletons that have been hidden in the most secure cupboard in the schloss.

Whatever trove Morshead and Blunt brought back from their visits to Germany, the existence of the Windsor file, which was now in the hands of the Allies, was undeniable. It was a very tricky situation, forcing the king and his senior courtiers to wrestle with the question of how to react and what to do with, in Lascelles's phrase, a "highly damaging" series of cables and telegrams.

As was often the case in this cosy postwar milieu, palace courtiers instinctively turned to the security services for counsel. After all, the headquarters of MI5 was in St. James's, only a short walk from Buckingham Palace and the private clubs of Pall Mall. Lascelles was known to consult his friend Guy Liddell on a variety of issues, ranging from discreet background checks on possible palace appointments to informed if unofficial advice on which way the wind was blowing inside Downing Street and other government departments.

On August 24 Lascelles arranged to meet Liddell at his private members' club in central London in mid-August to chew over the problem. After a convivial dinner, Liddell and Lascelles went to his office in the palace, where Liddell reviewed the embarrassing German Foreign Office telegrams. After reading the incriminating ciphers, Liddell suggested that the guiding hand behind the plot was none other than Charles Bedaux and made the point that the Windsors' Portuguese host, Dr. Santo Silva, owned a bank well known for transmitting funds to German agents.

"Various statements are attributed to the Duke by these agents which are not of a very savoury kind," noted Liddell. "Although it seems doubtful whether the Duke was scheming for his own restoration, it is fairly clear that he expressed the view... that the whole war was a mistake and that if he had been king it never would have happened."

Aware of palace concerns, he promised to have German intelligence chief Walter Schellenberg, then under British control, questioned about the affair and have the telegrams to and from the Silva bank, which were intercepted during the war, investigated. From memory he recalled a "singularly compromising" telegram from Madame Fern Bedaux to the Duchess of Windsor.

He soothed a clearly agitated Lascelles by telling him that in his experience most agents in Spain and Portugal had a tendency to report what they thought their masters wanted to hear and that much may have been lost or changed in the translation.

This may have calmed Lascelles but the king remained concerned about the worrying turn of events. After a meeting with the king at Buckingham Palace, Lord Cadogan noted in his diary of October 25: "King fussed about the Duke of Windsor File and Captured German Documents."

CHAPTER FIFTEEN

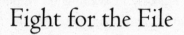

Fight for the File

As the king, prime minister, and foreign secretary wrestled with how to deal with the embarrassing Windsor file, the man at the centre of the drama decided to make an appearance. The Duke of Windsor wrote to the king, whom he had not seen since before the war, and requested an audience at Buckingham Palace in early October. It was not a reunion the king relished, especially knowing the contents of the Windsor file, a subject he did not raise during their meeting.

He anticipated that this encounter would probably involve another acrimonious conversation about the duchess, her title, and her reception at court, as well as the duke's demands for a prestigious diplomatic position, preferably in America. All of his requests would be met in the negative, with the resulting unpleasant emotional contretemps. It was enough to set the king off on one of his "gnashes," the queen's name for his outbursts of anger.

Actually the dreaded reunion with his brother went rather well, Lascelles describing the feeling after the duke had left the palace as akin to that when the all-clear sounded after a bombing raid. Even though he "persisted" in raising the issue of his mother Queen Mary and the king receiving Wallis—a non-starter—the conversation was amicable and civilized. Once again the king patiently explained that he could neither live in Britain nor work for the Crown—a position the duke refused to accept.

Afterwards he lobbied Winston Churchill, now the leader of the Opposition, about his desire to be given some honorary post with the British embassy in Washington. While Churchill dutifully championed his cause, he somewhat mournfully admitted failure in this regard while musing, too, on his own problems. "The difficulties of leading the Opposition are very great and I increasingly wonder whether the game is worth the candle."

The duke remained undaunted, a year later personally making his case to Prime Minister Attlee about a diplomatic position in Washington. He was given short shrift, as Churchill's wartime minister of information, Brendan Bracken, wrote to Lord Beaverbrook: "The Windsor lady must have been sadly disillusioned by her husband's interview with Attlee. Nothing could have been more stark than his declaration that no Governmental employment will be given to the Ducal democrats. I am sorry for them."

As much as the duke set his cap at some kind of ambassadorial position based in America, the royal couple decided to settle in France where, Lascelles noted, he had developed the bad habit of telling the French how to run their country. "A hearth rug bore" was how Lascelles described him.

Yet never in the annals of British government has so much diplomatic effort and bureaucratic energy been expended on a hearth-rug bore, and a seemingly unemployable bore at that. Ironically it was the leaders of the most radical and Socialist government in Britain's history, an administration that introduced free health care for all, who worked diligently to quarantine the lethal Windsor file.

When Prime Minister Attlee first discussed the matter with the king that summer, there were three Windsor files in existence—the original and two copies. The original microfilm of the von Loesch file, which had been brought to London in triumph by Thomson, was now back at Marburg Castle under joint Anglo-American control. Two copies of the incriminating file, which contained the Windsor revelations, were made. One was sent to the Foreign Office, the other to the American embassy in London for onward courier to the State Department in Washington.

It was now imperative to ensure that the files were brought under sole British control. This meant consulting their American cousins and obtaining the files from Marburg and the State Department.

With regard to the files held at Marburg, it seems that Brigadier Sir James "Jimmy" Gault, the British military attaché to General Dwight Eisenhower, Supreme Allied Commander Europe (SACEUR), became involved.

Brigadier Gault—Eton, Cambridge, the Scots Guards, and a close friend of Ike—then approached Eisenhower and explained the importance of extracting the file from Marburg and returning it to the British in London. Eisenhower, a great Anglophile himself, needed little persuasion, especially as there was already a precedent: The State Department's political czar Robert Murphy had returned the file on comedy writer P. G. Wodehouse, which was discovered in the Schmidt papers. He considered it of interest only to the British.

After listening to the arguments, Eisenhower concluded of the Windsor file "that there was no possible value in them, that they were obviously concocted with some idea of promoting German propaganda and weakening Western resistance, and that they were totally unfair to the Duke."

Eisenhower spoke to his friend General Lucius Clay, military governor of Germany, and ordered him to obtain the file. Even though Clay was furious about the decision, feeling that Ike was kowtowing to the British, he obeyed the command. Recalling the incident some twenty-five years later, he was still angered by that order. "It rubbed him up the wrong way," recalled his official biographer, Jean Edward Smith, who interviewed Clay in January 1971 about the early days of the occupation. "He felt it wasn't right. He felt that the British had got to him [Ike] and he did not think that this was appropriate behaviour. It was certainly not something President Truman would have ever ordered. Ike was very explicit. The purpose of the order was to remove anything pertaining to the Duke's activities before he went to the Bahamas in 1940."

While there remains some ambiguity about whether the palace or Downing Street or both initiated the process, Clay carried out Eisenhower's decision, deputing Brigadier General Edward C. Betts, then the deputy director for war crimes, to make the arrangements to bring the file to Eisenhower's headquarters. Military courier Lieutenant Hans F. Scheufele was dispatched to Marburg and duly signed out the 490-page dossier on September 5, 1945.

Shortly after reading a one-page summary of the folder, Eisenhower ordered the file be sent to John Winant, the American ambassador in London, who eventually passed it on to the Foreign Office.

Such was the secrecy surrounding the handover that even Sir William Strang, Britain's political advisor in Germany, was unaware of Eisenhower's decision. On September 11, 1945—a week after the file had been transferred to Eisenhower's keeping—he wrote a memo to his American counterpart, Robert Murphy, opposing his decision to move the German Foreign Office files from Marburg Castle to Kassel, where their other partners in the European Advisory Commission—the Russians and French—could gain easier access to the files.

Access to German documents, especially by the Soviets, was a consistent concern of the British, and inevitably the Windsor file, which Strang did not even name, formed the cornerstone of his argument. As mentioned previously, it seems, from the undated files held at the Sonder Archiv in Moscow, that the Russians already had a sketchy outline of the Nazi plot to encourage the duke and duchess to stay in Spain and to collaborate with the Axis powers.

Clearly unaware of recent developments, Strang wrote:

> A further argument which occurs to me is derived from the case which I discussed with you the other day, and which I need not mention directly, in which we were anxious to secure the withdrawal from the German archives of a certain dossier. It seems to me, given the German talent for getting hold of the wrong end of the stick, that certain documents may well turn up which would be embarrassing to both or either of us, although representing a complete distortion of the facts. If these were accessible to our colleagues on the Commission, which sooner or later seems inevitable at Kassel, we might find them given to the world in a way that suggested that they represented true statements.

By then, the Windsor file was under lock and key in the office of Brigadier Betts, pending its secret transfer to London. The microfilm copy held on the other side of the Atlantic proved rather more difficult to capture. At first, British efforts to quietly extract the microfilm copy from the State Department in Washington seemed to go smoothly. During a meeting to discuss the inauguration of the United Nations in San Francisco, Lord Halifax took Secretary of State Edward R. Stettinius to one side and persuaded him of the necessity of keeping the number of copies of the von Loesch file to an absolute minimum. It was later agreed between the two diplomats "that neither government would make additional copies or otherwise reveal information on activities in Spain of a member of the Royal family."

This verbal agreement was followed by a top secret aide-mémoire sent to the State Department by British embassy chargé d'affaires John Balfour. His note was sent on August 6, 1945, only a few days after historian Rohan Butler had first identified the duke's "curious" statements and while Blunt and Morshead were in Germany. This rapid response by the normally dilatory Foreign Office was a sign of how seriously the matter was being taken.

These documents have no bearing on the general history of the war or on war crimes, which His Majesty's Government take to be the subjects for which German archives should be primarily used. On the other hand owing to the personalities concerned and the type of German and Spanish intrigues involved the documents would clearly have the highest publicity value.

Given the enthusiasm inside the Foreign Office that first greeted incriminating statements made by, among others, Franco and Molotov, Balfour's note was somewhat disingenuous. He further asked that the State Department place special restrictions on the file.

Just two weeks later, on August 20, 1945, the British sent a further aide-mémoire, formally asking the State Department to destroy the Windsor file or hand it over to the British government for "safekeeping." Once again they emphasized: "It will be appreciated that the documents in question have no bearing on war crimes or on the general history of the war."

In a matter of weeks, the British had performed a policy flip-flop, switching from cheerfully exploiting the German Foreign Office files for publicity and propaganda—even the official unit was named Exploitation German Archives—to destroying those documents that were embarrassing to the government and its high-ranking subjects. Their volte-face immediately impacted on their co-operation with the war crimes tribunal, the British realizing that granting other powers complete access to the files would make it likely that the Windsor file would be uncovered.

In the same August memorandum, the British finessed their official position. In order to avoid a snub to the French or Russians, the British were willing to allow the right of inspection but on condition that each of the four governments should reserve the right to withhold documents that they had found themselves from the other allies. For instance—here the consequences of the Windsor embarrassment are clearly visible—in connection with the handling of their own quislings.

The memo ended with a sentence that neatly swept the awkward Windsor file—and any other undiscovered royal ordnance—beneath the carpet of history. "His Majesty's government have also considered the question of publishing German political documents but they take the view that the formulation of a policy should await more complete knowledge of the contents of all documents in possession of the Allies."

Given the fact that there were approximately 1,200 tons of German documents held in the American zone alone, most of which were unexamined and untranslated, the Windsor issue seemed to have been well and truly buried under a mountain of Nazi paperwork.

There the matter might have ended, and the world would have been none the wiser, but for a maverick Texan. At the war's end David Harris, a feisty and somewhat loquacious Stanford University history professor, was working in Berlin for the State Department as assistant chief in the Division of Central European Affairs.

A distinguished expert on modern European history, he was asked to review the secret British aides-mémoire relating to the Windsor file. It was made clear to him that the State Department had accepted the British position and that Harris's job was simply to draft a reply rubber-stamping the agreement. Harris, slightly built and bespectacled, was the David who took on the government Goliath. Described by colleagues as a man of "quiet, genuine courage," Harris, then forty-five, would have none of it, profoundly disagreeing with the destruction of historical documents on moral and legal grounds. Later he recalled that one of his first duties was to speak to the legal advisor and "put a stop" to the transaction over the file.

On August 27, he sent a robust memo to his immediate department boss, John Hickerson, taking issue with much of the British government's position. Not only did he contest the assertion that the Windsor file had no historical value, it was his assessment, as an expert on modern European history, that the episode was a "significant chapter in German and Spanish maneuvers toward a negotiated peace with the United Kingdom in 1940."

He continued:

> It is undoubtedly disagreeable to the British Government that the Duke of Windsor should have been the object of German and Spanish intrigue and that the Duke's not entirely unknown imprudence asserts itself in the papers, but nonetheless, in my judgement the documents are an essential part of the diplomatic record of 1940. There is I believe a moral responsibility resting on this government to preserve all the records in its possession, an obligation which takes precedence over a tender feeling for the ultimate reputation of the Duke of Windsor.

Perhaps his most telling argument was legal, referring to the United States statute that prevents government representatives from destroying official documents without a congressional hearing held in public. It was this legal fig leaf that the State Department ultimately used in their considered response to their allies.

A week later, on September 4, he indignantly wrote to his

superior, H. Freeman Matthews, director of European affairs, about the impropriety of destroying official historical files.

> *Further, if you will permit the professional historian to assert himself for the moment, I consider it a moral obligation of this Government, or of any Government, to preserve all the records in its possession for the use, at the appropriate time, of responsible students. I remain perennially angry that the British government in the days of Queen Victoria destroyed precious records of the sixteenth century because they contained certain allegedly unpalatable references to the private life of Queen Elizabeth.*

It seems that the force of Harris's argument, particularly the legal pitfalls and penalties for destroying records, held sway inside the State Department. When Under-Secretary of State Dean Acheson met with John Balfour in September, the legal and moral difficulties were explained. Even after Balfour reported the bad news, the British foreign secretary Ernest Bevin doggedly strived for the file's destruction. In early October, Bevin asked "if it would meet your difficulties if the passages in question were destroyed by the State Department instead of communicated to us."

Once again the law remained an unbridgeable obstacle, State Department counsel Herbert S. Marks formally advising Acheson as to the "drastic" penalties facing government officials who tamper with official documents.

This led to a further request from Bevin a month later that the Americans at the very least destroy all *duplicates* of the file.

In October, following three months of internal debate inside the State Department, the new secretary of state, James F. Byrnes, formally informed British ambassador Lord Halifax that, for legal and historical reasons, they were not prepared to destroy the file.

Byrnes was, though, able to sugar the pill. "The British Government is assured, however, that the Department of State will take all possible precautions to prevent any publicity with respect to the documents in its possession relative to the Duke of Windsor without prior consultation with the British Government."

This was simply wishful thinking. There was now a certain cachet among the higher military, diplomatic, and political echelons to having first-hand knowledge of the "secret" Windsor file, the royal dossier rapidly gaining mythic status. There were various requests by high-ranking officers who had no direct interest in the case, either to have a summary of the file disclosed to them or to read a copy of the original.

When, for example, Colonel W. D. Hohenthal, director of political affairs in Germany, asked for a "gist of the Duke of Windsor Papers," he was sent a top secret summary from the State Department in Washington. This State Department summary focused on the Nazi-inspired plot to lure the duke back from Lisbon to Madrid rather than the duke's critical stance about the war.

> The bait used was seemingly that the Duke would be set up as a peace mediator between England and Germany and that thereafter he would be set up as a regent for England. As justification for such a crude approach, reference appears more than once to the Duke's alleged statements that, had he been on the throne, the War would never have been allowed to start.
>
> They appear to have tried to play on his pride, and on his desire for his own and his wife's prestige, by belittling the Bahamas assignment as unworthy of his background and abilities. They must have thought they were succeeding for the Madrid-Lisbon-Berlin dispatches for two or three weeks reflected a touch-and-go excitement....What spoiled their scheme might have been a timely message to the

Duke from his Prime Minister, threatening military arrest unless he carried out his orders.

Hohenthal's colleague Robert Murphy, who had strongly objected to the fact that his political department was not sent copies of the general German Foreign Office file in the first place, was reduced to reading a three-page handwritten summary of the Windsor file. While the duke's behaviour was at the heart of the three-page report, the duchess also got a look in. "The Duke's wife entered the conversations at many points. She showed considerable animosity towards the royal family, especially the Queen."

This inside knowledge in London, Washington, and Berlin became all the spicier when conflated with Blunt's continued secret missions on behalf of the king. In the eighteen months after his visit to Kronberg with Morshead, the Soviet agent made three further trips to Germany and Holland. These top secret excursions excited much comment, especially on his own side. In December 1945, even his gossipy fellow spy Guy Burgess described Blunt's "looting" on the king's behalf when he flew to Westphalia to meet the Duke of Brunswick or Braunschweig, heir to the kings of Hanover, whose family have close blood ties to the Windsors.

Blunt merely added to the mystery, telling his old source Leo Long, whom he met "by chance" at the airfield where he landed, that the work he was doing on behalf of the king was very "hush-hush." Of course this merely served to stir the pot of speculation, two of Blunt's former pupils, now in the military and based in Germany, believing that the art historian had come "on behalf of Queen Mary to recover some documents of a private nature which she had sent her relatives, the Brunswicks."

Actually, as Guy Liddell noted in his diary of December 1945, Blunt returned with a diplomatic sack full of Christmas presents for the king, goodies that included the diamond crown of Queen Charlotte, the wife of George III.

"Anthony has brought back on behalf of the King some very valuable miniatures and other antiques worth about £100,000 [approx. £3 million or $4.75 million today] but it has been made quite clear that these are only on loan from the Duke of Brunswick." He went on to describe his haul of gold and silver plate as well as a unique twelfth-century illuminated manuscript of the Four Gospels, which had once belonged to Henry the Lion, Duke of Saxony.

Blunt and Morshead subsequently flew to Doorn in Holland, where they visited the estate of the deceased ex-Kaiser in order to secure various regal possessions, including those of Queen Victoria, Empress Friedrich, and other European royals. Their brief was to examine objects that once belonged to Queen Victoria and, as Morshead coyly noted in a letter to Tommy Lascelles, to find anything relevant "to relations between the Courts of England and Germany during the past hundred years."

While portraits, several Garter badges, and gifts from Queen Victoria to the Kaiser were "quietly secured" by the British ambassador to Holland, no documentary material was discovered.

These freelance trips, which yielded priceless bounty—though not the incriminating letters between British and German royals—did concern the Foreign Office. At a time when thousands of troops, particularly American GIs, were taking home souvenirs of war, the Foreign Office were extremely concerned about how it would look if the king was seen to be "liberating"—or, as Guy Burgess pithily noted, "looting"—archives and objects, especially when Britain was lecturing the other Allies about their own corrupt behaviour.

The British were not the only ones who believed they occupied the moral high ground, their American allies increasingly believing that it was the Brits who were playing fast and loose with the truth, especially with regard to their stewardship of the German Foreign Office archives. "It is imperative," declared one American officer, "that we have at Marburg an administration by American forces so as to 'free'...the American elements from British rule, I dare say, tyranny."

The lightning rod for the growing disenchantment among the allies was the Windsor file. In the months following Allied victory, it changed the day-to-day working relationship between the Americans and their British counterparts. Trust and co-operation were replaced by suspicion and resentment, the Americans now believing that every objection the British made, be it to the American decision to move the German Foreign Office records from Marburg Castle first to Kassel and then to Berlin—as suggested by US general Lucius Clay—or giving Russia, France, and neutral countries access to the files for the International Military Tribunal, was motivated by a deferential impulse to protect the Duke of Windsor or other high-ranking members of the British Establishment who were guilty of appeasement or collaboration. "All sorts of unsavoury stories are getting into circulation," noted American attaché John T. Krumpelmann at a conference to explain the mysterious gaps in the German Foreign Office files.

The Americans had a point. The fear of disclosing the contents of the Windsor file to others, particularly the Russians, coloured every British decision. A note from Robert Currie Thomson in October concerning American plans to move the German Foreign Office archive from Marburg reflected official British thinking: "silly to flit [move] lest certain documents be seen by some parties we have in mind."

The tone of the correspondence between the two sides, while always polite, grew chillier as winter closed in. In November 1945 the State Department explicitly refused to allow documents to be taken to the British zone of occupation. Quite simply, they no longer trusted the British, noting that "on previous occasion documents taken to England from the custody of U.S. forces in Germany had not been made available for exploitation by U.S. representatives."

This cynicism about the duplicitous Brits was articulated in an angry memo to Secretary of State Byrnes from his director of European affairs, H. Freeman Matthews, on January 31, 1946. While he was responding to complaints from British ambassador Lord Halifax about the transfer of the files from Marburg to Berlin—a subject that also vexed the foreign secretary—his note focused on the underhand behaviour of their partner in peace.

After lamenting the illegality of destroying official records he continued:

> I personally do not believe in efforts to alter historical records by the destruction or permanent withholding of official documents. Quite frankly, conditions at Marburg are such that the British are, in the opinion of some of our people, enabled thereby to play fast and loose with the documents there. I feel sure they would not hesitate to remove any which showed appeasement policies of high British personalities in an unfavourable light. We have on occasion had difficulty obtaining microfilm copies of certain documents.
>
> The British, on one occasion, formally requested us to sanction the destruction of certain documents dealing with the Duke of Windsor's passage through Spain and Portugal in the summer of 1940. I think that we should protect legitimate British rights and interests with respect to the German Foreign Office archives, in particular in the matter of releasing them to representatives of other powers, but that we should have in mind our large responsibility towards the security and safeguarding of these irreplaceable historical archives.

The scene was set for a conflict as the tapestry of shared beliefs began to unravel. The view of the State Department's director of

European affairs, John Hickerson, reflected the bewildered attitude of many American officials towards their British allies.

In a top secret memo he wrote:

> I am convinced that the British government will adamantly resist any suggestion on our part that any of the documents relating to the Duke of Windsor be made public. There is throughout the United Kingdom an unreasoning devotion to the monarchial principle and an almost fanatical disposition to do everything possible to protect the good name of the institution of the monarchy.

He went on:

> I think the British Government is wrong about this whole matter and that all of these documents, including agents' reports, should be made public in the ordinary course of events. But I am not a British subject and I do not view the institution of the monarchy through their eyes.

It would be many years before Hickerson had his wish.

CHAPTER SIXTEEN

———— ✦ ————

Burying the "Hot Potato"

It began, as many things have, with an eloquent letter to the *Times* of London. Long before the war was over, two of Britain's most distinguished historians, Sir Lewis Namier and E. Llewellyn Woodward, called for the publication of German and British documents on events leading up to Germany's invasion of Poland in September 1939 and the beginning of World War Two. In their letter of September 23, 1943, they argued that never again should the interpretation of the recent past be left to the Germans, as was the case with the previous conflagration.

It was an argument that fell on fertile ground in both London and Washington, the Allies acutely aware that the German people had to understand and appreciate their collective responsibility for the conflict. The eventual re-education of the German nation was a central war aim, Woodward repeating his arguments at a gathering of diplomats and historians six months before the war ended, suggesting a joint enterprise to publish an authoritative collection of documents on German foreign policy. The impact of material related to the German Foreign Office and other German ministries' official material was amply demonstrated at the International Military Tribunal, which began at Nuremberg in November 1945, where top Nazi leaders were convicted on the evidence of their own documents. Of the forty-two published volumes of the proceedings of the court, some seventeen were devoted to the documents.

As historian John Wheeler-Bennett put it: "It had been a fundamental principle of policy among the allied powers that the German people should be convinced irrefutably of the cause, the magnitude, and the consequences of their defeat. There must be no danger of the repetition of the mistakes made at the conclusion of the First World War, when this impression was never fully brought home to Germany."

By January 1946 the proposal was discussed by the Foreign Office, who in turn sounded out the State Department in Washington. A central question was whether the department was "prepared to support a policy of complete disclosure" even if some documents may prove embarrassing to the government.

Both Dean Acheson and John Hickerson, the under-secretary and director of European affairs, answered in the affirmative, Hickerson commenting: "It seems to me that this Government should not consider publishing in any way under its name a collection of German official documents if it is not prepared to let the whole story be told honestly in accordance with the best criteria of historical research." It seemed that Hickerson, who was baffled by the British deference to the monarchy, was about to have his wish of seeing incriminating German documents made public.

These noble ideals were codified in the agreement signed between Britain and the United States—Russia declined to take part—on June 19, 1946. The selection and editing, the agreement stated, was to be "performed on the basis of the highest scholarly objectivity" and the project entrusted to "outside scholars of the highest reputation."

To doubly underline the academics' freedom to roam, readers were informed at the introduction of the first four volumes that: "The editors wish to state at the outset that they have not only been permitted, but enjoined, to make the selection on this basis [scholarly objectivity] alone." It was envisioned that twenty volumes of between eight hundred and a thousand pages would be published in both German and English, dealing with the period 1918 to 1945.

For historians and other academics who were hobbled by Britain's fifty-year rule before the release of official documents—it was reduced to thirty years in 1968—the chance to investigate essentially contemporary documents, albeit of another country, was a glorious opportunity. As Dr. George Kent, a member of the American historical team, recalled: "It was a goldmine. We were able to look into the innermost secrets of German foreign policy." Without the Nuremberg trials and the political decision to demonstrate to the German people the causes of the war, this would never have occurred. The Harvard historian William L. Langer noted: "The historian could not ordinarily expect to have access to such records in less than fifty or a hundred years, and only the fortunes of war have brought this mine of information to our shores."

For the British, John Wheeler-Bennett, a well-connected Establishment figure and gentleman historian, accepted, somewhat reluctantly, the position of editor in chief, and Raymond Sontag, of the University of California at Berkeley, whose Irish ancestry made him deeply sceptical towards the British, was appointed the American chief. In April 1947 Sorbonne professor Maurice Baumont joined the group as the French chief editor. So began an uneasy relationship, shot through with distrust and suspicion. For example, when a vital file from 1937—the apogee of British appeasement and the Duke of Windsor's private conversation with Hitler during his visit to Germany—went missing, Sontag suspected that

Lieutenant Colonel Robert Currie Thomson had purloined it on behalf of the British government. It was later discovered that the file had been mislabelled.

In fact the historians had barely begun work when the explosive Windsor file, variously referred to as "the Marburg file," "the special file," or "the particular difficulty," hove into view, this time thanks to an article in *Newsweek* in autumn 1946. It reported, in part erroneously, that the publication of German Foreign Office documents was being delayed by the State Department in deference to British wishes not only about the suppression of documents related to "the Duke of Windsor's pre-war ideas on European politics and the Third Reich" but other subjects, too. This may have been a reference to the earlier concern over Sir Oswald Mosley.

The *Newsweek* publication elicited a sharp protest from the new British ambassador, Lord Inverchapel, a friend of the queen, who was concerned about the fact that the reference to the Duke of Windsor indicated a breach of the secret agreement between the two governments.

In a "Top Secret and Personal" letter to Dean Acheson, he wrote:

> *I am at a loss to know what explanation I can give to the Foreign Office with regard to this leakage in view of the special precautions which your Department agreed to undertake.*

In his reply on November 18, 1946, Acheson expressed his regret and promised an investigation to find the source of the leak. The existence of the "unmentionable file" was naturally a source of concern for the British and American editors in chief, who were eager to track down this almost mythical document. When Wheeler-Bennett made inquiries, he was informed that the file had been extracted from Marburg on the orders of Eisenhower himself. He and Sontag agreed that their positions as independent editors would be "rendered ludicrous" if they allowed documents to be withheld. Furthermore, the resignation of distinguished historians because of perceived government interference would defeat the object of the entire exercise, as its fundamental principles were impartiality and editorial freedom.

As Wheeler-Bennett appreciated, the Americans would want to publish this material, more so given media interest and speculation, and to resist would only make the British look "very foolish."

His friend Robert Bruce Lockhart recorded in his diary of November 23, 1946, that Wheeler-Bennett did not intend to "accept interference unless it came direct from King George." A week later, Bruce Lockhart was told by Foreign Office mandarin Orme Sargent that "Jack Wheeler-Bennett has not a free hand on the documents. That is a matter for HMG [His Majesty's Government] to decide."

In Wheeler-Bennett's narrative he contacted Under-Secretary Orme Sargent at the Foreign Office, who was aware of the file's existence but "horrified at its disappearance." He said they must speak to the foreign secretary, Ernest Bevin, who, as has been described, had tried manfully to have the file destroyed from the moment it had been discovered at the end of the war. After listening silently as Wheeler-Bennett explained the ramifications of the file's disappearance, Bevin said: "This is a 'ot potato. We've got to get the file back, and you must 'ave a look at it and decide with your American friend what to do with it." He added that they would have to tell the palace about this matter. The next day Orme Sargent and Wheeler-Bennett went to Buckingham Palace to meet with Sir Alan Lascelles, who assured them that the king would share the position of the foreign secretary.

As Wheeler-Bennett recalled: "The important consequence of this curious incident was that the Marburg File was speedily returned to our custody and we duly included the bulk of its contents in the *Series D, Vol X*."

In fact the file, with the approval of George VI, was returned to Berlin, where the initial sifting of the documents was undertaken, in July 1947. Before the king agreed to this measure, he warned the man at the centre of this secret wrangle, his brother the Duke of Windsor. According to Godfrey Thomas, the duke's private secretary when he was Prince of Wales, he made light of the whole affair, "suggesting that the German Ambassador was making up a good story on the lines that he thought would please his chief, von Ribbentrop."

Yet the infamous file was not dispatched to Berlin without a last-minute attempt by the royal family's unlikely champion, man of the people Ernest Bevin, to have it destroyed. The foreign secretary, with his bluff speech, ill-fitting suit, and hand firmly stuck in his pocket even when greeting the sovereign, became a familiar figure shambling along the red-carpeted corridors of Buckingham Palace. His "call a spade a spade" way of speaking was easily mocked, as in Wheeler-Bennett's "'ot potato" but it hid a degree of guile and cunning.

In March 1947, according to George VI's biographer Sarah Bradford, Bevin quixotically tilted at this diplomatic windmill once again. In Moscow for the foreign ministers' meeting, he sent an urgent request to his opposite number, American secretary of state General George Marshall, about the Windsor file.

In turn, Marshall sent a top secret "Personal, For Your Eyes Only" telegram to Dean Acheson in the State Department. Dated March 15, midnight, it read:

Bevin informs me that Department or White House has on file
a microfilm copy of a paper concerning the Duke of Windsor.
Bevin says only other copy was destroyed by Foreign Office, and

asks that we destroy ours to avoid possibility of a leak to great
embarrassment of Windsor's brother [George VI]. Please attend
to this for me and reply for my eyes only.

A search has so far failed to locate the reply, though it is known
that Acheson did send a telegram two days later.

As Bevin had already been formally informed that neither the
State Department nor any government official could destroy official documents without a vote of Congress, it seems like the last
vain throw of the dice, an instinctive act of deference from a loyal
British subject to his sovereign.

For the time being, British policy shifted from destroying the
Windsor file to delaying or obstructing publication. This was a
perfectly legitimate position to take. When Wheeler-Bennett had
accepted the position of editor in chief, he had breezily told the
Oxford Mail in early 1947: "We shall begin somewhere about the
year 1937 and then come forward to the end of the Nazi regime. I
think we shall then work backwards from 1937 to the Bismarck era."

Given the prodigious amount of material the historians needed
to wade through for every volume, it would be several years before
the Allied academics arrived at the summer of 1940, when the
German ambassadors to Spain and Portugal sent von Ribbentrop
potentially embarrassing reports about the duke and duchess and
their defeatist views on the war.

Meanwhile the duke's relationship with the rest of the royal
family continued to deteriorate. His hopes of landing a position
as a roving envoy at the British embassy in Washington had lan-
guished, the duke told by Bevin that he was unable to recommend
any kind of formal attachment. Even his scheme to encourage
greater educational links between the two nations, an idea supported by the then Opposition leader Churchill, had fallen on
stony ground. While the king encouraged him to live in America
and undertake work in a strictly unofficial capacity, the duke and

duchess, who had come to loathe the American press and were concerned that they would lose their tax exemptions, preferred to live at La Croë, their rented home in the South of France. The palace turned a deaf ear, too, to pleas from the duke and duchess that they should be allowed to return to England for several months of the year.

Everything English seemed to be cursed. In the autumn of 1946 they stayed for a month at Ednam Lodge, the country house near Windsor Great Park owned by Eric, Earl of Dudley. It was the Duchess's first visit to England since the outbreak of the war and is remembered solely for the spectacular theft of the Duchess's jewels, worth £13 million ($20 million) at today's prices. The audacious heist from Ednam Lodge gave rise to popular rumours that, as the duke was believed to have given family baubles to Wallis Simpson during their courtship, the robbery was an inside job instigated by the royal family to recover for the king and his daughters, Princesses Elizabeth and Margaret, family property that was rightfully theirs.

While this was so much nonsensical supposition—a local housebreaker was the prime but unconvicted suspect—it does demonstrate that the public were instinctively aware of the complete rift inside the royal family, a rupture that no amount of smooth evasions by courtiers could cover up.

When the duke's niece Princess Elizabeth married Prince Philip of Greece and Denmark at Westminster Abbey in November 1947, the duke and duchess, as well as Philip's Nazi relations, were not on the guest list. Two years later, in December 1949, the duke made a final angry entreaty to his brother to give the duchess the title of Her Royal Highness. The king was immovable, as he was in their wrangling about his allowance. As the queen wrote to her daughter just before Christmas:

Uncle David came and had one of his violent yelling conversations, stamping up and down the room, and very

unfairly saying that because Papa wouldn't (and couldn't)
do a certain thing, that Papa must hate him. So unfair,
because Papa is so scrupulously fair and thoughtful and
honest about all that has happened. It's so much easier to
yell and pull down and criticize, than to restrain, and build,
and think right—isn't it.

The duke's decision to write his memoirs up to the date of the abdication further served to anger his brother and mother as well as senior royal courtiers. The king was "very distressed" according to Harold Nicolson, appalled that his brother would sell the most traumatic period of his life to the highest bidder.

The court refused to co-operate at all, even denying the request by his ghost writer, American journalist Charles Murphy, to visit his childhood home at York Cottage, Sandringham. When the book, entitled *A King's Story*, was published in April 1951 it created an international sensation, though the duke's delight was marred by the discovery that his wife was suffering from cancer of the womb, which forced her to undergo a hysterectomy.

It might be thought that the deaths of George VI on February 6, 1952, and his mother, Queen Mary, a year later, would have healed the family split, with a new younger generation taking control of the Crown. Not a bit of it. The duke's "jaunty" behaviour at his brother's funeral attracted unfavourable comment. It was clear he could not wait to get away from his family—"these ice-veined bitches" as he ungraciously described the royal ladies in a letter to his wife.

He wrote to the duchess in a similar tone a year later at the funeral of his "hard as nails" mother, Queen Mary, on March 31, 1953: "What a smug stinking lot my relations are and you've never seen such a seedy worn out bunch of old hags most of them have become."

The new Elizabethan age kept the duke and duchess outside

the palace gates, neither the duke nor the duchess being invited to the Coronation of Queen Elizabeth II on June 2, 1953. This changing of the guard coincided, somewhat ironically, with a renewed campaign led by Churchill, who was back in government as prime minister, to have the Windsor file wiped from history. Not only did he enrol his wartime friend, President Eisenhower, in this enterprise but he also encouraged the Cabinet and several eminent British historians to finally consign the file to the dustbin of history. Churchill, whose romantic and misty-eyed view of monarchy often clouded his judgement, felt passionately that the duke, his late brother George VI, and a "certain lady," namely the queen mother, should not be embarrassed by the release of these documents.

As Sarah Bradford observes: "The Queen Mother regarded herself as the guardian of the image of the monarchy which she had done a great deal to create and prop up. She regarded it as a sacred trust and did not want these disagreeable facts emerging."

It was almost too late. While the Windsor file had been kicked into the long grass, by now that grass had been duly mown by historians, who had reached the critical period of June 1940 and the Nazi machinations surrounding the Duke and Duchess of Windsor.

The Windsor file itself first appeared on the editorial agenda on June 15, 1949, at a conference of historians presided over by E. J. Passant, librarian of the Foreign Office. Professor E. Malcolm Carroll of Duke University argued that "the essential documents should be published," while his English colleague Mr. Passant confirmed that the Windsor file was indeed available if selected. Given the slow pace of the project, that process, even without political interference, would take another five years.

The Windsor documents were incorporated in Volume X Series D of the *Documents on German Foreign Policy*, which had been edited and translated by the American team of historians based in Washington. The "'ot potato" was ready to be digested by the waiting world.

With an ever widening circle of those with knowledge of the Windsor file, it was becoming a matter of national pride that it be published. The former German diplomat Erich Kordt, the father of modern German diplomacy, had discussed the existence of the documents and "defied the Allies to publish them." An American historian, countering the challenge via the columns of an historical review, pledged that they would be.

Not if Eisenhower and Churchill could help it. A month after the Coronation, on July 3, 1953, General Bedell Smith, undersecretary of state and formerly chief of staff to Eisenhower at Supreme Headquarters Allied Expeditionary Force (SHAEF), arranged to see Bernard Noble, head of the historical division at the State Department, at his offices in Washington. The only item on the agenda was the contents of Volume X Series D. Noble later recounted the conversation to the American editor in chief, Dr. Paul Sweet.

He recalled that the general began very formally, almost like one government speaking to the representative of another. Smith said: "I have instructions to tell you that the British government is going to communicate a list of the documents on the Duke of Windsor which it wishes to have left out of Volume X. You are to inform the editor of the German documents that when he receives the list he will agree to the elimination of these documents."

When Noble informed the general that the fundamental underpinning of the entire project was editorial independence, Smith told him that the Eisenhower administration did not feel bound by undertakings entered into by the administration of President Truman.

As the contentious documents were not due to be published for some time, Professor Sweet was puzzled by this crude political interference. He wondered aloud if Churchill, who ironically had just been awarded the Nobel Prize for literature, was behind the renewed attempt to suppress the Windsor file. Noble indicated in the affirmative, noting that General Smith was acting on instructions from Eisenhower, who in turn had been contacted by Churchill.

If the Eisenhower administration continued with this new line of censorship, the only weapon in the historian's armoury was resignation. That night, Sweet told his wife that he might be leaving his job before long.

Sweet's instincts proved correct. Just days after suffering a minor stroke, Churchill had written a three-page letter to Eisenhower on June 27, 1953, asking him to use his influence to prevent the publication of the Windsor file.

> *The historical importance of the episode is negligible,*
> *and the allegations rest only on the assertions of German*
> *and pro-German officials in making the most of anything*
> *they could pick up. I feel sure your sense of justice and*
> *chivalry will make you wish to prevent the United States,*
> *by an official publication, from inflicting distress and*
> *injury upon one who has so long enjoyed their kindness and*
> *hospitality.*

He added that he was approaching the French authorities for their agreement in "refusing to allow the official publication . . . to anybody outside the secret circles."

The president's reply was swift, on July 2 writing that he was "completely astonished" that a microfilm record existed. He recalled that when he was first informed of the documents' existence in 1945 he had them "thoroughly examined" by Ambassador Winant and a member of his own intelligence staff.

"They completely agreed that there was no possible value to them, that they were obviously concocted with some idea of promoting German propaganda and weakening Western resistance, and that they were totally unfair to the Duke." In a subsequent note he was hopeful that the matter would be settled with "decency, justice, and finality."

With the Cold War at its height, the Korean War in its death throes, and Senator McCarthy beginning his witch hunt against perceived Communists, gays, and others, this unanimous decision by the two Allied leaders should have sealed the fate of the Windsor file for good. Even though the climate in the 1950s favoured suppression and repression, the historians did not prove so malleable. Bedell Smith reported that the "American editor in chief evidently did not like the idea of doing what he was told about this matter."

In a sarcastic note to President Eisenhower, Bedell Smith wrote: "Since all historians (including our own engaged in this project) think that history is more important than anything else, some of them will probably leak." His assumption proved correct; the historians seemed horrified at this change of policy.

In a letter to Bernard Noble, Pulitzer Prize–winning historian Bernadotte E. Schmitt laid out the "disastrous" consequences for the British, American, and French governments if they went down the road of censorship and expurgation:

> I am reluctant to believe that the United States
> government would be guilty of going back on the undertaking
> given to the successive American editors-in-chief.... If Volume
> X appears without the documents in question the editors will
> not be able to say that they have enjoyed a free hand....
> Questions will be asked and I fancy the Governments will be
> hard put to give satisfactory answers.

As for the British, the current editor in chief, the Honourable Margaret Lambert, indicated that she had an obligation to resign if she was forbidden to publish the documents. Even though the historian came from a Conservative political family—her father, Viscount George Lambert, had served as a member of Parliament under Gladstone and often hosted the Churchills at his Devon home—initially she stoutly resisted political interference.

They were helped in this rearguard action by the behaviour of the French. After two months waiting for a reply to his letter regarding the Windsor file, Churchill sent Sir Walter Monckton to Paris to speak personally with the French foreign minister, Georges Bidault.

In his "Top Secret and Personal" report of September 1, 1953, Monckton returned with unhappy tidings. "Throughout the conversation," reported Monckton, "M. Bidault showed an obvious disposition to help, though he could not, he felt, order the historians to omit the documents." As a historian himself, Bidault had taken the trouble to consult with the academics working on the papers. The French were of the same mind as their American counterparts:

> Historians are not to be commanded. If this were attempted in the present instance the French historians would resign. In these circumstances he said that the suppression of the documents was impossible but agreed that it would be possible to postpone publication by taking the documents of a different period first.

Churchill, who had taken responsibility for foreign affairs in April when Anthony Eden took six months' medical leave, was still for censorship. He took soundings from Lord Beaverbrook, who read the Windsor file on July 18 at his country home of Cherkley Court. Unfortunately there is no note about his response, though it did not change the mind of the prime minister who, as John Colville reported, was "still set on suppression."

At a Cabinet meeting on August 25, a few days before Monckton reported the French position, Churchill passionately argued
that the publication of the documents would "give pain to the
Duke of Windsor" and was of slight historical value. "I propose to
interview the British editor in chief and to propose that publication be postponed for at least ten or twenty years, and preferably
the Duke's lifetime." Lord Salisbury, lord president of the council,
argued for publication, saying that the documents' suppression
would "only give the impression that they were more damaging
than they in fact were."

During the Cabinet discussion Lord Salisbury revealed that he
had spoken with the British editor in chief, Miss Lambert, and he
believed that she might be more accommodating than had been
previously suggested. While she would not welcome any government attempt to limit the historians' editorial discretion, she herself suggested that publication of this vexed correspondence might
be delayed if the documents of an earlier period, notably the Weimar Republic, were published in advance of Volume X Series D.
Effectively the Windsor file would be kicked back into the long
grass.

With delay rather than complete suppression the emerging
British position, the prime minister, in the company of Minister of
Labour Sir Walter Monckton—who had had a ringside seat at the
unfolding events in Lisbon in 1940—and Lord Salisbury met with
Margaret Lambert on September 16, 1953. Immediately after the
Downing Street meeting she informed the American and French
editors, Paul Sweet and Maurice Baumont, of the radical change
of plan, focusing on the Weimar Republic and suspending work on
the virtually complete Volume X Series D.

In a four-page letter to Sweet on October 8, 1953, Lambert
outlined the real reasons why she, other noted British historians, and the prime minister—a historian of international note
himself—wished to delay the publication of the Windsor papers.

The argument bore all the imprint of Churchill's romanticized dalliance with the monarchy.

Lambert explained that she had initially agreed with the publication of the Windsor documents even though the whole affair was reported in a way that was "grotesque and mendacious." She continued:

> But at the same time it was put to me that the appearance of these papers in an official publication in the near future would cause much pain to a certain recently bereaved lady, who with her late husband is referred to in them. Such references were bound to be pounced on and sensationally exploited in a peculiarly unpleasant way. We could not prevent this happening. It was felt better that time should be allowed to do its work first.

Other historians, notably John Wheeler-Bennett, who was now working on an official biography of King George VI from an office at Buckingham Palace, "whole heartedly agreed" with the change of policy, namely to leave Series D and concentrate on the Weimar Republic. It was a course of action endorsed by Churchill, who felt it was "very valuable and important" to see what went wrong after the 1925 Locarno treaty. As for Series D, it should now finish with the fall of France in June 1940, thus keeping the Windsor file in suspension—but not censored.

A week later, on October 15, Lambert's advisory committee of historians, a formidable array of esteemed academics, agreed unanimously with this change of emphasis. The elephant in the room, the Windsor file, was never mentioned. Neither was a "certain recently bereaved lady." It is perhaps the ultimate irony in this whole episode that the queen mother, who loathed the duke and duchess as much as they despised her, was used as the reason to shield the Windsors from unfavourable publicity.

This lachrymose royal entreaty to focus anywhere but the House of Windsor cut little ice with the American editor in chief. Dr. Sweet recalled: "They [the Windsor documents] were part of the historical record even if they were objectionable to the royal family. It offended my sensibilities. The whole thing was cooked up."

There followed an increasingly tart exchange of correspondence between Sweet and Lambert, all the years of American suspicion about British duplicity and obscurification rising to the surface. Sweet described the decision to switch direction and focus away from 1940 and 1941 as "shattering," telling Lambert: "If publication of volume X is too long delayed, awkward questions are certain to be raised which will put in question the integrity of the project."

A month later his tone was even more accusatory: "It seems to me...that certain decisions have been made on political grounds which I am now being requested to justify retroactively 'as a historian.' Thus for example a political decision would seem to have been made on your side with respect to suspending publication of Series D beyond volume VIII. It does not seem to me that I ought to be asked to give reasons 'as a historian' for such a decision."

As Dr. Sweet later admitted, his letter reflected his "considerable exasperation" with the British. His reference to a "British decision on political grounds" rankled. Miss Lambert tartly informed him that rather than "political," the appropriate phrase was "non historical." With Sweet's colleague Bernard Noble about to depart to London in November for further discussions with the British, Sweet handed him a memorandum stating that the American team was "deeply resentful" of the tone of the correspondence and that the British had adopted an "intolerable" strategy. Ominously he wrote: "We have no intention of continuing our participation in the project if this is to be henceforth the spirit in which business is conducted."

The principled disagreement went right to the top, with Sweet summoned to see Joseph Phillips, deputy assistant secretary of state for public affairs, who told him that the British ambassador, Sir Roger Makins, had said that unless agreement was reached quickly between himself and Miss Lambert, the prime minister intended to raise the matter during a forthcoming summit with President Eisenhower in Bermuda.

In a more placatory vein, Miss Lambert addressed the issue of resignation, arguing that for an official historian to resign implied loss of confidence in the host government. "Actually," she wrote, "I was decidedly impressed by the scrupulous care with which my views were treated by the Prime Minister downwards." She felt that the use of resignation because of a change of emphasis, rather than suppression, was inappropriate.

At first Lambert succeeded in obtaining a degree of American agreement for the revised plan, Bernard Noble telling Sweet that he had little option but to approve stoppage of the work on Series D. Nonetheless Sweet, hopeful of a change in political climate with the eventual retirement of the British prime minister, continued to work on the virtually complete series.

Churchill, though, was still on the warpath. He was so obsessed with the issue that he had taken to telephoning Miss Lambert late at night to harangue her about the cursed file.

——— ✧ ———

CHAPTER SEVENTEEN

Traitor King or Duped Duke?

Churchill's determined rearguard action to stop the publication of the Windsor file was looking increasingly shaky. Not only was he facing stubborn resistance from the Americans and French, in 1953 the Germans entered the fray, catching him in a deadly pincer movement.

As part of the process of restoring democracy and economic stability to West Germany, Chancellor Adenauer was insistent that the Allies return the mountain of official German documents that they still held under their control. It was a matter of national pride to recover what was considered to be the archival soul—"the bare bones of history"—of the new nation rising from the ruins of war. Germany wanted her history back. The Americans were sympathetic but once again the British were concerned to keep the vexatious Windsor file away from prying foreign eyes. It was the Russians who raised the stakes even further, returning the official German records they had captured to Communist East Germany in 1955, thus enabling the German Democratic Republic to dismiss West Germany as a "puppet state" of the Allies.

It was not just the events of 1940 that threatened to embarrass the duke and the royal family. In January 1954 *another* unwelcome file, this time concerning the duke's "unfavourable" constitutional behaviour during his brief reign as King Edward VIII in 1936, was discovered. It could not have happened at a more inconvenient moment. As the Germans were pressing hard for the return of their files, it placed the British government in a predicament. As a negotiating gambit, they might have been able to withhold the existing Windsor file from the Germans in exchange for handing over the bulk of archival material. What, though, of these new royal embarrassments emerging like unexploded bombs among the tons of official papers the archivists were slowly sifting through? Once again British foreign policy was compromised, the existence of the Windsor file staining and straining relations with another nation, this time the newly democratic West Germany.

The communal head-scratching by ministers and senior civil servants was almost palpable. In a memo of March 4, 1954, Minister of State Anthony Nutting pondered how to deal with the added complication of "another document which I understand records certain very unfortunate and unconstitutional sayings to the Germans by King Edward VIII during his reign about the attitude of Mr. Baldwin and the government of the day to the reoccupation of the Rhineland. The difficulty here is that whatever we do we cannot be absolutely certain that these documents will not fall into the wrong hands."

The episode itself relates to the reports by the king's friend, German ambassador von Hoesch, who made clear to Berlin that the king was taking an active part in diplomacy surrounding the Rhineland crisis. Apparently he had summoned his senior ministers, including Baldwin and Chamberlain, to the palace and insisted that Britain should resist an attack on Germany over their territorial incursion.

As von Hoesch reported: "The directive given to the Government from there [Buckingham Palace] is to the effect that, no matter how the details of the affair are dealt with, complications of a serious nature are in no circumstances to be allowed to develop."

That same month Frank Roberts, deputy under-secretary at the Foreign Office, was tasked with producing a Cabinet paper to the effect that the Germans could have their records returned—they had chosen Schloss Gymnich in Westphalia as the centre for storage and research—if the British could retain the Windsor file. The Cabinet agreed with the proposal, Churchill urging: "All steps should be taken to extract these [Windsor] papers from any which are handed back to Germany."

The one consolation from this added complication was that the controversial material, which related to events in 1936, was not scheduled to be published by the official historians for many years hence. In fact the material was finally released in 1966, thirty years after the king's reign, in series C, volume V.

Not so the main Windsor file. At an editors meeting in July 1954, Sweet and the French editor Baumont returned to the attack, even though they faced fierce opposition from Wheeler-Bennett, E. Llewellyn Woodward—who first suggested the project—and five other distinguished historians, including Miss Lambert, the editor in chief.

As E. James Passant later minuted: "It is very clear that, if such a programme [continuation of Series D] is now adopted, the documents in dispute will be published in 1956, unless the whole project collapses before then." Effectively the only way to prevent publication of the Windsor file was to go nuclear and explode the entire exercise, thus compromising a primary war aim, namely to educate the German people about their folly.

In a memorandum to justify the continuation of Series D and the subsequent publication of the Windsor file, Dr. Sweet argued that the decision to suspend work was "made at governmental direction" rather than for any historical considerations. As a result, the current position was uncomfortable bordering on the "intoler-able." Lambert was furious, complaining to Passant that Sweet's attitude was "deplorable." She made it clear that she could proceed with the publication of Volume X Series D only if Churchill and the Cabinet waived any objections.

Shortly after this transatlantic clash of the historians, Church-ill got an early reaction to the likely impact of the publication of German diplomatic reports regarding the Duke of Windsor. In November 1954, the Duke of Windsor's wartime activities came to light in an entirely different official volume, this time Volume VIII Series D, where the German ambassador in The Hague reported in January and February 1940 on the duke's behaviour.

Count Julius von Zech-Burkersroda, German minister to The Hague, had, in two dispatches dated January 27 and February 19, 1940, reported that the duke was "not entirely satisfied with his position" and sought a field of activity in which he would have an active rather than a merely representative role (all of which was true and seemingly non-contentious). Zech-Burkersroda went on to say: "He has expressed himself in especially uncomplimentary terms about Chamberlain, whom he particularly dislikes and who, as he thinks, is responsible for his being frozen out."

During a brief visit to London that month the duke shrugged off the matter when asked by reporters, saying that the documents were false. His long-time defender Winston Churchill, speaking in the House of Commons, also made light of the matter, dismissing the veracity and source of the allegations.

In May last, after these three documents had been selected for inclusion in the Eighth Volume of this work, they were brought to my attention. I naturally thought it proper to show them to the Duke of Windsor, and on 25 May I told him that they were to be published in the United States and in this country later this year. His Royal Highness did not raise any objection. He thought, and I agreed with him, that they could be treated with contempt.... They are of course quite untrue.

Then he paused and, to guffaws of laughter, added: "They may rest in the peculiar domain which this formula describes as 'the highest scholarly objectivity.'"

It seems that Churchill's witty spearing of the international body of historians, the subdued reaction, and the paucity of headlines may have convinced the prime minister to slacken the reins of resistance regarding publication. Just six weeks later, on December 23, 1954, Britain's ambassador to Washington visited Douglas MacArthur II, counsellor of the State Department. He told him that the British would no longer press their objections to the publication of the documents in Volume X Series D and that the documents could be published in due course. He requested that the British have at least two months' advance warning before publication so that they could consider how to answer any questions about the duke's behaviour.

Shortly afterwards, in January 1955, the same month that the duke visited President Eisenhower at the White House, the ex-king was working out his public position on the imminent publication of the "unmentionable" file. It was, observed his biographer Frances Donaldson, no secret to the duke's advisors and those closest to him that, during the period that elapsed between his receiving this information and the publication of the documents, he was an "exceedingly unhappy and worried" man.

He asked his old friend and lawyer Sir Walter Monckton to draft a suitable statement.

I regard it as essential... that the Foreign Office 'dementi' [official denial] should be entirely general in character and should ignore all specifically alleged anti-British statements attributed to me, as a pack of lies....And with regard...to your persuasive powers...it would be only fair to emphasise that I needed no persuasion, whatsoever, firstly, not to return to Spain, nor secondly, to sail for the Bahamas on August 1st, the date stipulated by Winston and to which I agreed.

If the duke was contemplating the inevitable, the royal family were not finished yet, launching their secret nuclear weapon in the shape of King George VI's biographer, John Wheeler-Bennett. Since 1953 he had been working from the Pine Room at Buckingham Palace and had become part of the wider royal family, on excellent terms with Sir Alan Lascelles, a small army of courtiers, and influential politicians like Anthony Eden and Harold Macmillan.

He was flattered to be asked to be the official royal biographer and made no attempt to hide the adoration he felt for the queen mother, describing with much affection the "gracious kindness" she displayed at their first meeting at Buckingham Palace.

"Queen Elizabeth, beautiful in her mourning, greeted me with a warmth and charm which I have never forgotten and which has remained unvarying throughout the succeeding years during which she has been so wonderful a friend to Ruth [his wife] and me." Such was their friendship that he dedicated the last volume of his memoirs to the queen mother.

He was sensitive to the demands of court, particularly the bitter relationship with the Duke and Duchess of Windsor, skirting around the issue in his royal biography. As Dr. Sweet pithily observed: "In the end, for the years after his abdication, the Duke of Windsor received a single sentence and one perfunctory mention in a volume of 891 pages."

Even that modest inclusion illustrated the rift at the heart of the House of Windsor. When the duke asked Wheeler-Bennett, whom he had helped with childhood reminiscences about his brother, to review passages of the manuscript referring to himself, royal officials prevaricated about sending him the relevant pages. They relented only after a threat of legal action. In July 1956 he wrote to his lawyer, Sir George Allen:

> *I am incensed by this latest display of rudeness towards me from the Palace and am determined that, unless my niece has the common courtesy to give me an opportunity of reading all references to myself in Wheeler-Bennett's official biography of my late brother, then no mention of me whatsoever shall appear therein.*

Little wonder that Wheeler-Bennett's biography has failed to pass the test of time. Dismissed by historian David Cannadine as "courtly and obsequious," the book portrays the late king as an icon on a pedestal rather than a flesh-and-blood human being. While it is biography as if written from the bended knee, it had the effect of making the historian thoroughly acceptable to the royal family and their courtiers.

Uniquely placed as a historian and a courtier *manqué*, he used his influence to try and end the tripartite historical project in order to protect his friends at court. If the French and Americans were adamant that Volume X Series D be published, placing the Windsor file before the public, then the only option, as Passant had perceptively minuted, was to deliberately collapse the entire enterprise, thus ensuring that the House of Windsor escaped any public unpleasantness.

Wheeler-Bennett was not the only one who believed the project was doomed but was probably the only one motivated purely by a desire to safeguard the reputation of the royal family.

The other primary argument for ending the project was the pressure from the German government, somewhat tardily supported by the British Foreign Office, to move the archival venture back to Germany. The cabal of British historians believed it would compromise the objectivity of the operation. Such was the rancour felt towards the British historians that a British diplomat, who complained bitterly about their obstructive behaviour, said "the British historians are a stink in our nostrils."

Wheeler-Bennett was lobbying for the project to be ended without the knowledge of the British editor in chief, Margaret Lambert, a friend of twenty years' standing. Ironically, his underhand behaviour led to a reconciliation between Dr. Sweet and the British editor in chief. They now recognized a common enemy in the avuncular historian. As Miss Lambert wrote on January 31, 1956:

> Wheeler-Bennett on his own and without a word to me decided to recommend that we be closed down forthwith, went to various high-ups and said so. I can hardly tell you what a jolt this gave me; at first I could not believe it.
>
> As to the prime mover in all this, our guess is that his motives are only indirectly connected with us but are personal. We know he is much gratified by his new role as biographer and it may well be that the old love gets a bit in the way of the new. There was publicity here for one aspect of the last volume [the reports on the Duke of Windsor in volume VIII] and presently there will be a lot more.

With help from Sir Lewis Namier, she was able to avert an imminent shutdown, the project not winding up until March 1959.

Publication of the much anticipated, much feared volume was further delayed by the Swiss government, who were concerned that certain documents chosen for publication in Volume X Series D would reveal that it had breached its much vaunted neutrality during the war. They were worried that any publication would affect the way the Swiss were treated by foreign governments in the future.

With the publication of Walter Schellenberg's racy but post-humous memoirs in July 1956 by André Deutsch, the wrangling about the Windsor file was all becoming a little, well, academic. The German spymaster's story, ghosted by Louis Hagen, an Allied glider pilot who had written a bestseller about the Arnhem landings, made headlines around the world with its lurid claims that the duke was offered fifty million Swiss francs to go over to the Germans. The story, which was published in magazines in Sweden and West Germany and reprinted in the London *Sunday Dispatch*, was quickly and comprehensively denied by the duke.

> I have not read the newspaper reports of Nazi intrigue which are supposed to concern me. No doubt the Schellenbergs of Hitler's regime had all kinds of devious schemes in the back of their minds. I had no communication or contacts whatsoever with Schellenberg and nor for that matter did I ever hear of him until this alleged matter developed. As for Ribbentrop I met him only in his official capacity and never saw him after 1937.

Posthumously, Schellenberg had dug the duke out of a hole, the public gaze firmly focused on Nazi conspiracies rather than ducal perfidy. Even so, Schellenberg's revelations were soon overshadowed by the duke's wife, who published her own ghost-written autobiography, *The Heart Has Its Reasons*, in the same year. As it concentrated on the human side of the romance of the century, it gave the watching world, especially women, a vivid insight into her life and times.

In the end, the main event, the long-awaited publication of Volume X Series D on 1 August 1957, was something of an anti-climax. The Foreign Office worked hard to corral Fleet Street editors and correspondents, briefing them on the angle that the duke was an innocent party caught in a web of Nazi intrigue, a royal dupe rather than a traitor king.

The resulting editorials reflected Establishment thinking: "Plot Against the Duke" was the *Manchester Guardian* headline, reflecting the consensus that he was a victim rather than an ersatz Quisling. "Nazi Efforts to Bring the Duke of Windsor under German Influence" was the rather more long-winded effort on the front page of the *New York Times*. The story was merely a passing storm; the next day the same newspapers announced that the duke had signed a deal with publishers Houghton Mifflin to write on the other great passion of his life, gardening. As Sarah Bradford noted: "The Foreign Office mounted quite a campaign in Fleet Street at the time. The press were quite naïve."

Just to emphasize the point, an official Foreign Office notice, inserted in the volumes issued by HM Stationery Office, contained the following passage:

> The Duke was subjected to heavy pressure from many quarters to stay in Europe, where the Germans hoped that he would exert influence against the policy of His Majesty's government. His Royal Highness never wavered in his loyalty to the British cause or in his determination to take up his official post as Governor of the Bahamas on the date agreed. The German records are necessarily a much tainted source. The only firm evidence is of what the Germans were trying to do in the matter, and of how completely they failed to do it.

Of course that begged the question that if the German records were such a "much tainted source," why were they used so successfully in the Nuremberg trials? And why had historians from France, Britain, and America laboured over them for more than a decade? Why indeed had Churchill, Eisenhower, and others invested so much political and diplomatic capital in trying to censor them?

For good measure, the duke's lawyer also issued a statement roundly dismissing the reports of the German ambassadors to Spain and Portugal as "part complete fabrications, and in part gross distortions of the truth."

The duke stated:

> While I was in Lisbon certain people, whom I discovered to be Nazi sympathizers, did make definite efforts to persuade me to return to Spain and not to take up my appointment as Governor of the Bahamas. It was even suggested to me that there would be a personal risk to the Duchess and myself if we were to proceed to the Bahamas.
>
> At no time did I ever entertain any thought of complying with such a suggestion, which I treated with the contempt it deserved. At the earliest practicable opportunity the Duchess and I proceeded to the Bahamas, where I took up my appointment as Governor, in which I served for five years.

That he and his wife visited Germany in 1937 and made cosy with Hitler, that he blurted out sensitive intelligence regarding the transportation of German naval shells to an Axis diplomat, that he made discreet overtures to the German enemy with regard to his rented properties in Paris and the Riviera, that he carefully considered the offer made by his long-time friends to sit the war out in a castle in Spain, that he suspected the British of a plot to murder him and his wife, and that he asked Churchill to let him stay on in Portugal and delay sailing to the Bahamas was rather lost in the shuffle.

If anything, the German cables were much less damning than the splenetic exchanges between Churchill and the Duke of

Windsor, the prime minister spending precious hours dealing with a petulant princely prima donna who refused to obey orders. If the press and public had been aware that the duke made hysterical demands at this perilous moment, with the Nazi jackboot poised over Britain's throat, it is doubtful the verdict about his behaviour would have been so benign.

There was, however, a smoking gun concealed in the documents, identified, according to Frances Donaldson, only by the *Daily Telegraph* newspaper. This was the revelation about the telegram the duke apparently sent from Bermuda to his Portuguese host, Dr. Ricardo Espirito Santo, on August 15, 1940. In a communiqué to Berlin, the German ambassador to Portugal, Hoyningen-Huene, passed on the following information:

> The confidant has just received a telegram from the Duke from Bermuda, asking him to send a communication as soon as action was advisable. Should any answer be made?

While it has been suggested that the confidant, Dr. Santo, fabricated the communication, most historians believe that the duke did indeed send the incriminating telegram. It therefore suggests that far from being an innocent victim of Nazi conspiracies, the duke was reopening lines of communication with the enemy.

His biographer Frances Donaldson believes that he should be assigned "comparative" rather than "actual" guilt for this disloyal behaviour, while the duke's one-time associate and ghost writer Charles Murphy points out that although the couple laughed off the idea of a plot they were "highly interested parties" if not "active accomplices":

> Although there is little doubt that Windsor's mood was mutinous, and that he said things that no loyal Englishman should, it must be borne in mind that the Nazi

sympathizers who listened to him were eager to ingratiate themselves with their masters, whether German or Spanish.

His official biographer, Philip Ziegler, is more benevolent, arguing that he had always remained a patriot and "could not have allowed himself to rule by favour of the Germans over a sullen and resentful people." While he was indiscreet, defeatist, and irresponsible, as well as "childish and naïve," he could not, according to Ziegler, be described as hoping for the downfall of his country. In short, he could be condemned for his behaviour, but not convicted.

Historian Michael Bloch, author of the masterly *Operation Willi*, opts for a more prosaically domestic explanation: The duke was indeed in contact with Dr. Santo, but about the whereabouts of the ducal trunks—particularly the royal linen—which were en route from Paris and the Riviera. His precious possessions rather than peace in Europe were his primary concerns.

His behaviour was part of a pattern, the duke dancing around the fringes of disloyalty and duplicity but never quite committing. Like a flirt in a nightclub, the duke suggested much but delivered very little. In Lisbon and Madrid he teased the Nazis, giving them the come-on signs, but then peeled away once he had them excited, leaving them confused and empty-handed. In London at the beginning of the war he toyed with Beaverbrook's treasonous notion of becoming a peace candidate and suing for a truce with Germany.

That idea collapsed when the royal exile realized he would have to pay tax if he returned to Britain. Within months of landing in the Bahamas, the royal governor coquettishly suggested that he would support Roosevelt if he advanced a peace proposal and was suspected of teasingly becoming involved, probably by telephone and telegraph, with James Mooney in Sir William Wiseman's freelance peace plans. His behaviour was totally at variance with the government he then represented.

That said, his pursuit of peace deals by back channels made

him little different from half the aristocrats of Europe—including his brother the king and the Duke of Kent. They all uniformly subscribed to the view that another European conflagration so soon after the horrors of World War One was to be avoided at all costs. The duke was, though, more of a passive rather than active conspirator, always looking for others to do the heavy lifting. He was always an ideal figurehead, a rallying point, the charisma of royalty his primary contribution. It is clear from the trajectory of his life that he had little if any political guile or cunning nor the energy or drive to pursue what ambitions, apart from pleasing his wife, he truly had. He made mistakes, he said things he shouldn't, and met people he should have shunned. The duke was the ultimate loose cannon; cut free from the ties of monarchy but not from the ship of state, he careened around Europe and America causing some alarms but little damage. Ultimately he was a garrulous nuisance rather than a calculating traitor.

During and after the war his opinions remained constant, and he stayed in contact with those viewed with suspicion by the Allies. In August 1941, for example, Ambassador Huene sent a telegram to Berlin regarding a letter sent by the duke to his one-time host Dr. Santo Silva about his interview with American journalist Fulton Oursler:

> The intermediary familiar to us from the reports at the time has received a letter from the Duke of Windsor confirming his opinion as recently stated in a published interview that Britain has virtually lost the war already and the USA would be better advised to promote peace, not war.

After the end of World War Two his political views were essentially those of a right-wing aristocrat, lamenting the lost order, sniffy about the very Socialists who were trying, without his knowledge, to save his ducal hide, and terrified of the spread of Communism. He was a man of the people only in the popular imagination. Given his subsequent behaviour, his "something must be done" phrase rings somewhat hollowly down the decades. Gardening, gossip, golf, and pleasing his wife were the mainstays of his life.

When conversation turned to the war, he remained firm in his conviction that Britain should have remained neutral, that a negotiated peace should have been made with Hitler in 1940, thus allowing the Axis powers to take on and destroy the Soviets. Communism rather than National Socialism was always his greatest fear. He never forgot that the Bolsheviks killed his godfather Czar Nicholas II and his family.

When British diplomat Sir John Balfour dined with the duke and his friend, American railroad tycoon Robert R. Young, in Washington shortly after the war, Balfour was struck by their right-wing attitudes. He noted:

> Both of them seemed oblivious to Nazi misdeeds and were at one in thinking that, had Hitler been differently handled, war with Germany might have been avoided in 1939.

Eventually the couple settled permanently in France, where they enjoyed tax exemptions and, as in the Bahamas, duty-free alcohol, tobacco, and other goods thanks to the British embassy. It meant that he was able to entertain in the grand manner, employing at La Croë some twenty-two staff, the equivalent of a mid-size embassy. If something was to be done about the world, it was not going to be by him, especially if it endangered his tax status. Money was his mantra and his motivation, his meanness legendary. The suggestion by the king, Alan Lascelles, Churchill, and others that he settle in America and turn his private home into a centre for the betterment of Anglo-American relations collapsed the moment he realized he would have to pay income tax.

In Paris his regular guests included his near neighbours, Sir Oswald and Lady Diana Mosley, who were interned by the British during the war, and other members of the "tarnished nobility" of Germany and elsewhere. His cousin, former Nazi Prince Philipp of Hessen, who was effectively cleared of war crimes after several appeals, as well as members of the Bismarck family, including Countess Mona Bismarck, were all welcome. Lady Mosley told author Charles Higham that the duchess concurred with her views on Nazi Germany, arguing that there would have been no need for a Holocaust had Hitler been allowed to deport Jews to Britain and America. The war, she argued, was the result of the clashing egos of Hitler and Churchill. "If the right people had been in power in England, particularly Lloyd George, there could have been a negotiated peace."

To that end the duke approved the repressive policies of Cuban dictator President Batista and heartily supported Arizona senator Barry Goldwater, who campaigned for president in 1964 on a platform that included the use of tactical nuclear missiles in Vietnam to stop the spread of Communism. He was pleased when United Nations secretary general Dag Hammarskjöld died in a plane crash, believing that it would hasten the end of an organization that gave such influence to the Soviet Union.

Of course he was entirely sympathetic to Prime Minister Eden's decision to join with the French and invade the Suez Canal Zone in 1956 following the provocative decision by Egypt's President Nasser to nationalize the vital passageway.

Before the war he was unemployed, an outcast from his own land. During the war he was treated with much suspicion, a Quisling or Laval in the making, watched warily by both Washington and London. His close friends were arrested or blacklisted for their pro-German views, his wife's mail was censored, their movements monitored by Hoover's FBI. After Pearl Harbor, staff on the Combined Chiefs of Staff committee in Washington were warned that the Duke of Windsor was under no circumstances to be allowed to enter the basement room in which the strategic maps and plans were kept.

His wife, thanks to her perceived relationship with von Ribbentrop, was, according to official thinking, only a hair's breadth away from being a spy. At the palace "that woman" always remained a witch, a sorceress who had cast a malign spell on the king who was never crowned. After the war the duke was officially unemployable, living for the rest of his life in genteel exile, the triangle of New York, Palm Beach, and Paris forming the contours of the couple's annual round from their home in the French Riviera. By his early fifties, the duke was becoming a somewhat pathetic, disjointed figure. Their long-time friend, Lady Diana Cooper, dined with them in May 1949 and afterwards noted in her diary: "Wallis herself in fine repair.... The Duke looked his withered self and never made head or tail of anything I said."

Everywhere they went, their trio of cairn terriers—later pugs— went with them. They were more than just companions, they were family. "You see we can't leave the dogs behind; they're all we have," Wallis told Lady Halifax.

While it is not conclusively proven that this ultimately isolated and forlorn figure flirted with treason or collaboration, what is undeniable is that the casual remarks of a man without place or position in British society, as reported by the German ambassadors to Portugal and Spain, led to remarkable efforts by the British and even some powerful Americans to have the potentially damning Windsor file destroyed, sequestered, or suppressed.

It was an attempted cover-up that lasted from the moment the file was discovered in a wooded valley in May 1945 to its contentious publication in August 1957. The fact that it was ever published at all was, to misquote Wellington, a "damned close-run thing." If not for the actions of a couple of cussed American historians, notably Professor David Harris and Dr. Paul Sweet, the world would have heard of Operation Willi only in the unreliable memoirs of easily discredited German diplomats and agents.

As Dr. Sweet observes, the episode displays "remarkable deference to the perceived interests of the royal family. From first to last the political leadership exercised a protecting hand, never allowing itself to be seen as under pressure from Buckingham Palace. Far from being an anachronism in the modern secular society of Great Britain today, the institution fulfils a vital, unique and intuitively recognized function."

Nor was that deference confined to the romantic love of monarchy as expressed by Winston Churchill. Among the most stalwart defenders of the Crown were the Socialist prime minister Clement Attlee and his working-class foreign secretary, Ernest Bevin.

Historian John Wheeler-Bennett exemplifies this contradiction. At the time of Edward VIII's accession he was gossiping with the best, passing on his considered and well-informed view that Wallis Simpson was being used by von Ribbentrop to gain access to the new king. Yet when the institution of monarchy was threatened, he was prepared to destroy a historical project of vital national importance in order to protect the royal family. As lyricist W. S. Gilbert wrote in *The Pirates of Penzance*:

We yield at once with humbled mien,
Because, with all our faults, we love our queen.

Nor was this episode simply a British Establishment cover-up. They were supported in the endeavour by America's most powerful man, Dwight Eisenhower, both as president and as Supreme Allied Commander Europe. His view may have displeased his generals, historians, and civil servants—as well as being illegal—but this was the way royalty was seen on both sides of the Atlantic. Royalty, even a royal outcast, was treated as a special case. In those halcyon days, misdemeanours by Hollywood stars and White House incumbents never appeared in the popular prints.

There was, though, a high political and diplomatic price to be paid. It was a special case that chipped away at the special relationship, the Americans coming to view the British as untrustworthy, shifty, and unreliable, the existence of the Windsor file corroding the bonds that had united the two countries through six years of war. A special case that shaped and reshaped British foreign policy, altering the way the government approached central war aims, namely the prosecution of war criminals and the re-education of the German people so that they fully appreciated the causes of the war and why they had lost it.

Would, for example, more war criminals have faced trial at Nuremberg had not the British, because of the discovery of the Windsor file, tightened the rules of access to German Foreign Office files? Certainly Britain's postwar relations with Germany would have begun on a surer footing had there not been so much prevarication around the return of the German government documents, a decision tainted, once again, by the existence of the Windsor file.

Given the effort expended by the British and the Americans in trying to destroy a vital piece of historical evidence, it is easy to understand why the Blunt-Morshead missions to Germany and Holland were treated by historians and journalists with such suspicion. It is an avenue of history where conspiracy theories are de rigueur. While there is no direct evidence that either man was tasked with specifically locating correspondence between the Duke of Windsor and his German cousins, it is highly likely that the king suggested that they keep their eyes and ears peeled.

Meanwhile, other courtiers were busily squirrelling away other correspondence relating to other royal black sheep that could damage the good name and image of the House of Windsor.

Illusion and reality, a balancing act that goes to the heart of monarchy, the king and all his courtiers instinctively working to ensure that the audience never pays attention to the man behind the curtain. The sentiments of Prime Minister Baldwin's advisor Thomas Jones about Edward VIII during the abdication had the same resonance and relevance in the years after the war: "What a problem the king has been. We invest our rulers with qualities which they do not possess and we connive at the illusion—those of us who know better—because monarchy is an illusion which works. It has 'pragmatic sanction.'"

The Windsor file exposed that man, his faults, his frailties, and his petty indulgences. He may have been blackballed from the club but he was once a member of a very exclusive guild of kings and sovereigns without a throne. To expose him would, by association, have exposed the monarchy, that national crucible of duty, honour, and stability, to possible shame and contumely. The monarchy is the beating heart of the nation, its patriotic soul. Anything other than complete fealty to the flag is a sign of dishonour, a stain on the institution, especially by one of the blood royal. The Duke of Windsor was deemed to have tainted the monarchy by his perceived treachery and disloyalty. At least that was the thinking.

The Windsor file, though, was published and the sky did not fall in, the world continued on its axis, Queen Elizabeth's reign remained untroubled, and the duke and duchess continued their social round. It was only in death that the duke and duchess were finally readmitted to the royal club, lying side by side in the royal burial ground at Frogmore in the grounds of Windsor Castle. A family feud that cost the country so much in compromised democratic principles finally laid to rest.

Source Notes

Chapter One: The Peter Pan Prince

to dance with him: Hugo Vickers, *The Private World of the Duke and Duchess of Windsor* (London: Michael Joseph, 1995), 133.

innate decency of mankind: Duke of Windsor, *A King's Story: The Memoirs of H. R. H. The Duke of Windsor* (London: Cassell, 1951), 131.

Senators' daughters than by talking to Senators: Frank Prochaska, "Edward VIII: A Prince in the Promised Land," *History Today* 58, no. 12 (2008).

tremendous curtain call: Duke of Windsor, *A King's Story*, 151.

pleasing point about him: Frank Prochaska, "Edward VIII," *History Today*.

They murdered him with kindness: J. Bryan III and John Murphy, *The Windsor Story* (London: Granada, 1979), 46.

things they most believe: Philip Ziegler, *King Edward VIII* (New York: Knopf, 1991).

their press-made national hero: Ibid., 143.

boring people and conventions: Ibid., 163.

long and long to die: Ibid., 107.

lonely person, lonely and sad: Bryan and Murphy, *The Windsor Story*, 47.

never wanted to become King: Philip Ziegler, *King Edward VIII*, 17.

miserableness I had to keep to myself: Bryan and Murphy, *The Windsor Story*, xvi.

like any other boy of my age: John Parker, *King of Fools* (New York: St. Martin's Press, 1988), 15.

a lost lamb: Neil Balfour and Sally Mackay, *Paul of Yugoslavia: Britain's Maligned Friend* (London: Hamish Hamilton, 1980), 28.

what does it matter if I am killed?: Hugo Vickers, *The Private World of the Duke and Duchess of Windsor* (London: Harrods Publishing, 1995), 68.

impressed me most enormously: Duke of Windsor, *A King's Story*, 117–18.

drowned in shell holes: Ibid., 128.

he could keep him out of it: R. G. Casey to Stanley Bruce, February 23, 1928, www.dfat.gov.au/publications/historical/volume-18/historical-document-18-105.html.

go to church on Sunday mornings: Frank Prochaska, "Edward VIII," *History Today*; also papers of Sir Esme Howard, Cumbria Archive Centre, Carlisle, Cumbria.

you are a cad: John Parker, *King of Fools*, 23.

I have often thought the same: Duff Hart-Davis, ed., *King's Counsellor: Abdication and War; The Diaries of "Tommy" Lascelles* (London: Weidenfeld & Nicolson, 2006), 104.

wrong sort of person to be Prince of Wales: Ibid., 105.

Chapter Two: Adolf Hitler, Royal Matchmaker

Very nice but terribly young: Alan Palmer, *Crowned Cousins: The Anglo-German Royal Connection* (London: Weidenfeld and Nicolson, 1985), 201.

far from being a pacifist: Philip Ziegler, *King Edward VIII*, 38.

it would have been brought off: Ibid., 39.

'cos it'll destroy me: Ibid., 151.

fundamentally afraid of women: Christopher Wilson, "The Night that Edward Confronted Wallis over Her Gay Lover," *Mail on Sunday*, September 20, 2014.

never out of a woman's legs: Hugo Vickers, *Behind Closed Doors: The Tragic, Untold Story of the Duchess of Windsor* (London: Hutchinson, 2011), 276.

every mother's heart beats high: Philip Ziegler, *King Edward VIII*, 83.

bad blood: "The Earl of Dudley" (obituary), *Daily Telegraph*, November 26, 2013.

the prince might have been his father: Ibid.

his love is so obvious and undisguisable: Philip Ziegler, *King Edward VIII*, 89.

to what the world is saying: John Parker, *King of Fools*, 24.

just DIPPY to die with YOU: Anne Sebba, *That Woman: The Life of Wallis Simpson, Duchess of Windsor* (New York: St. Martin's Press, 2012), 78.

no party was complete without us: William Shawcross, *Queen Elizabeth the Queen Mother: The Official Biography* (London: Macmillan, 2009), 114.

maintenance of the Empire: R. G. Casey to Stanley Bruce, February 16, 1928, http://www.dfat.gov.au/publications/historical/volume-18/historical-document-18-100.html.

we were not prepared to put pressure on our daughter: Jonathan Petropoulos, *Royals and the Reich: The Princes von Hessen in Nazi Germany* (New York: Oxford University Press, 2006), 162.

doubtful whether World War II could have occurred: Charles Higham, *The Duchess of Windsor, The Secret Life* (New York: John Wiley, 2004), 77.

heedless of where the voyage would end: John Parker, *King of Fools*, 47–48.

I can see nothing but disaster ahead: Hugo Vickers, *The Private World of the Duke and Duchess of Windsor*, 109.

more original from the Prince of Wales: Duke of Windsor, *A King's Story*, 257.

most attractive personalities I have ever met: Bryan and Murphy, *The Windsor Story*, 67.

Chapter 3: Sex, Drugs, and Royal Blackmail

career than Edward VIII had: Bryan and Murphy, *The Windsor Story*, 20.

stole my husband while I was ill: Charles Higham, *The Duchess of Windsor*, 44.

wardrobes in Paris for the visit: George S. Messersmith papers, MSS 109 2017-00, Special Collections, University of Delaware Library, Newark, DE.

I thought you said we all looked ghastly: Anne Sebba, *That Woman*, 88.

her conversation deft and amusing: Duke of Windsor, *A King's Story*, 257.

I was unaware of his interest: Anne Sebba, *That Woman*, 94.

too much of a bad thing: William Shawcross, *Counting One's Blessings: The Selected Letters of Queen Elizabeth the Queen Mother* (London: Macmillan, 2012), 198–99.

looked after him exceedingly well: Philip Ziegler, *King Edward VIII*, 198.

No letter, no nothing. Just silence: Paul Vallely, "Royal Albums: The King's Favourite: Mrs Simpson; Moves to the Heart of Edward's Life," *Independent*, February 14, 1998.

religious, almost holy: Bryan and Murphy, *The Windsor Story*, 59.

good sense of fashion. Nothing more: Hugo Vickers, *Gladys, Duchess of Marlborough* (London: Hamish Hamilton, 1979), 220.

decrease as one sees them more often: Anne Sebba, *That Woman*, 100.

Business foul: Michael Bloch, ed., *Wallis and Edward: Letters, 1931–1937* (New York: Summit Books, 1986), 59.

I can see no happy outcome to such a situation: Ibid., 126.

boundary between friendship and love: Anne Sebba, *That Woman*, 101.

the day the clocks stopped: Ibid., 97.

charming, cultivated woman: Philip Ziegler, *King Edward VIII*, 202.

hypnotized by the American adventuress: Ibid., 205.

intimate relations take place: Anne Sebba, *That Woman*, cited June 25, 1935, marked "Secret," MEPO 10/35 NA PRO.

getting all they could out of HRH: Philip Ziegler, *King Edward VIII*, 207.

blackmail upon an extravagant basis: Anne Sebba, *That Woman*, 126.

the only woman who can exercise any influence on him: Jim Wilson, *Nazi Princess: Hitler, Lord Rothermere and Princess Stephanie von Hohenlohe* (Stroud, Gloucs.: History Press, 2011), 34.

a huge portrait of Hitler: Ibid., 97.

Chapter Four: Seduced by von Ribbentrop's Dimple

I don't want to be mixed up with Asiatics: David Cannadine, *The Decline and Fall of the British Aristocracy* (New Haven, CT: Yale University Press, 1990), 354.

Mrs Simpson and gave parties for her: Anne Sebba, *That Woman*, 121.

she speaks favourably of the present regime in Germany: Jim Wilson, *Nazi Princess*, 96.

Charlie Chaplin's moustache: Christopher Sykes, *Nancy: The Life of Lady Astor* (New York: Harper & Row, 1972), 377.

why does Herr Hitler dislike the Jews?: Bryan and Murphy, *The Windsor Story*, 105.

Herr Ribbentrop through Mrs Simpson: Jim Wilson, *Nazi Princess*, 97.

Gratify the duke's sexual desires: Rob Evans and David Hencke, "Wallis Simpson, the Nazi Minister, the Telltale Monk and an FBI Plot," *Guardian*, June 29, 2002, http://www.theguardian.com/uk/2002/jun/29/research.monarchy.

often tragically misleading: Martha Schad, *Hitler's Spy Princess: The Extraordinary Life of Princess Stephanie von Hohenlohe* (Stroud, Gloucs.: Sutton, 2004), 51.

echoes with work and song: Duke of Windsor, *A King's Story*, 103.

the winning side, and that will be German, not the French: Philip Ziegler, *King Edward VIII*, 179.

victors of the contest will be the Soviets: Edward VIII to Herman Rogers, from the estate of Lucy Livingston Rogers.

the savour of high diplomacy: HRH the Duke of Windsor, *The Crown and the People 1902–1953* (London: Cassell, 1953), 41.

Dictator of the Empire: Jim Wilson, *Nazi Princess*, 96.

difficult enough task for an English King: Ibid.

we might want one in England before long: Charles Higham, *The Duchess of Windsor*, 64.

Ferdinand would no doubt have agreed: Ibid., 65.

the German people grasp most eagerly the hand: Ibid., 100.

peace-loving conciliatory Britain: Dr. Paul Schwarz, *This Man Ribbentrop: His Life and Times* (New York: Julian Messner, 1943), 134.

that's a good sport: Philip Ziegler, *King Edward VIII*, 182.

where foreign affairs are concerned: Duke of Windsor, *A King's Story*, 254.

the German protagonist: Philip Ziegler, *King Edward VIII*, 181.

British foreign policy seemed paralyzed: Duke of Windsor, *A King's Story*, 254.

goose stepping around the living room: Bryan and Murphy, *The Windsor Story*, 112.

wave a red flag myself: William Shawcross, *Queen Elizabeth the Queen Mother*, 364.

at loggerheads with his eldest son: Alan Palmer, *Crowned Cousins*, 217.

the Führer was insane: Jonathan Petropoulos, *Royals and the Reich*, 173.

no differences to my feelings for you: Ibid., 199.

My sympathies for your people: Martha Schad, *Hitler's Spy Princess*, Appendix III.

to discuss drawing closer to the English royal house: Jonathan Petropoulos, *Royals and the Reich*, 160.

His wife is equally anti-French: Ibid., 201.

fascination of London society for aristocratic Fascism: John Costello, *Mask of Treachery: The Dossier on Blunt, Buckingham Palace, MI5 and Soviet Subversion* (London: Pan Books, 1989), 283.

family relations in Germany have been used to spy: Jonathan Petropoulos, *Royals and the Reich*, 190–91.

Chapter Five: Courting the New King

much joy and relaxation: Ben Urwand, "Hitlerwood: Yes, Hitler was Obsessed by Movies—But Did He *Really* Persuade Hollywood to Collaborate with the Nazis?" *Daily Mail*, November 16, 2013.

American's figure was "not bad": Charles Higham, *The Duchess of Windsor*, 229.

encourage pro-German feeling: Author interview.

might well help to bring about an understanding: Greg King, *The Duchess of Windsor: The Uncommon Life of Wallis Simpson* (New York: Citadel, 2003), 147.

I myself wish to talk to Hitler: Philip Ziegler, *King Edward VIII*, 231.

good relations established between Germany and Britain: Ibid., 231.

personal influence did much to retard British policy: George S. Messersmith papers, MSS 109 0809-00.

in the pocket of Ribbentrop: William Shawcross, *Queen Elizabeth the Queen Mother*, 366.

undesirable reflection upon their king: Paul Schwarz, *This Man Ribbentrop*, 132.

any question of marriage: Keith Middlemas and John Barnes, *Baldwin: A Biography* (London: Weidenfeld and Nicolson, 1969).

Ribbentrop used Mrs. Simpson: N. A. Rose, ed., *Baffy: The Diaries of Blanche Dugdale 1936–1947* (Edgware, Middlesex: Vallentine Mitchell, 1973), 34.

German pay. I think this is unlikely: William E. Ellis, *Robert Worth Bingham and the Southern Mystique: From the Old South to the New South and Beyond* (Kent, Ohio: Kent State University Press, 1997), 183.

in no circumstances to be allowed to develop: Greg King, *The Duchess of Windsor*, 149.

He is keeping his promise: Albert Speer, *Inside the Third Reich: Memoirs* (New York: Simon & Schuster, 1970).

I must inform Berlin immediately: Philip Ziegler, *King Edward VIII*, 234.

natural and unaffected good manners: Diana Mitford, *The Duchess of Windsor: A Memoir* (London: Gibson Square, 2011), 77.

less spectacular role by Edward VIII: Author interview.

a nice way to start my reign: Charles Higham, *The Duchess of Windsor*, 120.

a new trick pulled out of the hat: Ronald Tree to Nancy Tree, April 1, 1936, Langhorne Papers, MSS 1 L2653 B281-362.

under orders to let the Germans win: Christopher Sykes, *Nancy*, 241.

regimentation of opinion: Jacques Poitras, *Beaverbrook: A Shattered Legacy* (Fredericton, NB: Goose Lane, 2007), 41.

Lord Rothermere... "a traitor": John Vincent, ed., *The Crawford Papers: The Journals of David Lindsay, the Twenty-Seventh Earl of Crawford and Tenth Earl of Balcarres, 1871–1940, during the Years 1892 to 1940* (Manchester, UK: Manchester University Press, 1984), 557.

It has never entered our head: N. J. Crowson, ed., *Fleet Street, Press Barons and Politics: The Journals of Collin Brooks, 1932–1940* (London: Cambridge University Press, 1998), 113.

Adolf the Great: Jim Wilson, *Nazi Princess*, 85.

George Washington of Germany: Jonathan Petropoulos, *Royals and the Reich*, 202.

War with Britain at any time: Martha Schad, *Hitler's Spy Princess*, 52.

hated Wallis for it: Charles Higham, *The Duchess of Windsor*, 120.

glorious flowers: Anne Sebba, *That Woman*, 126.

archives that might shed more light on them remain closed: Chris Hastings and Stephanie Plentl, "Mrs Simpson Not Worthy of Blue Plaque," *Daily Telegraph*, June 7, 2008.

Chapter Six: Edward on a Knife Edge

his hat, which was discovered by the maid: Bryan and Murphy, *The Windsor Story*, 136.

Are you sincere? Do you intend to marry her?: Ibid., 136.

she hadn't any intention of divorcing Simpson: Greg King, *The Duchess of Windsor*, 153.

access to all Secret and Cabinet papers: Anne Sebba, *That Woman*, 125.

infatuations usually wear off: Mabell, Countess of Airlie, *Thatched with Gold: The Memoirs of Mabell, Countess of Airlie* (London: Hutchinson, 1962), 198.

supplanted by some younger rival: John Vincent, ed., *The Crawford Papers*, diary entry, February 2, 1936.

robustly maintained for nearly twenty years: Duff Hart-Davis, ed., *King's Counsellor*, 113.

my prime minister must meet my future wife: Anne Sebba, *That Woman*, 130.

charm or a kind of beauty: Anne Morrow Lindbergh, *The Flower and the Nettle: Diaries and Letters of Anne Morrow Lindbergh* (San Diego: Harcourt Brace Jovanovich, 1976), 51, 62–63.

Very convenient: "The Earl of Dudley" (obituary), *Daily Telegraph*, November 26, 2013.

the flatterers, the sycophants, and the malice: Michael Bloch, *The Duchess of Windsor* (London: Weidenfeld & Nicolson, 1996), 82.

no wish of hers: Sarah Bradford, *King George VI* (London: Weidenfeld & Nicolson, 1989), 176.

Aird…"despised" him as a king: Philip Ziegler, *King Edward VIII*, 247.

I honestly don't think you can me: Michael Bloch, *The Duchess of Windsor*, 88.

I came to dine with the king: Sarah Bradford, *King George VI*, 172.

immediately to expunge his memory: Nigel Nicolson, ed., *Leave the Letters Till We're Dead: The Letters of Virginia Woolf, 1936–41* (London: Chatto & Windus, 1980), 10–11.

hurt your popularity in the country: Michael Bloch, *The Duchess of Windsor*, 89.

silence all this weird conspiracy: Ian Kershaw, *Making Friends with Hitler: Lord Londonderry and Britain's Road to War* (London: Penguin, 2005), 188.

I doubt if he will ever regret it: Herman Rogers to Endicott Peabody, October 23, 1937, from the estate of Lucy Livingston Rogers.

damaging scandal would erupt: Sara Delano Roosevelt to Herman Rogers, from the estate of Lucy Livingston Rogers.

tragedy for him and catastrophe for me: Michael Bloch, *The Duchess of Windsor*, 99.

horrible position for us naturally: William Shawcross, *Counting One's Blessings*, 225.

battle against the plotters: Christopher Andrew, *Defend The Realm: The Authorized History of MI5* (New York: Alfred Knopf, 2009), 199.

recipient of endless pin pricks: Diana Mitford, *The Duchess of Windsor*, 107.

ambassador of that foreign government: Jonathan Petropoulos, *Royals and the Reich*, 210; Martha Schad, *Hitler's Spy Princess*, 65.

then terrible things began to happen: John Colville, *Footprints in Time: Memories* (Norwich, Norfolk: Michael Russell, 1984), 203.

every possible rumour, however absurd: John Vincent, ed., *The Crawford Papers*, 573.

signed two abdications and torn them up: Miranda Seymour, *Ottoline Morrell: Life on the Grand Scale* (New York: Farrar, Straus and Giroux, 1993), 365.

Did you hear what he has said?: Hugo Vickers, *The Private World of the Duke and Duchess of Windsor*, 36.

The drawbridges were going up behind me: Duke of Windsor, *A King's Story*, 413.

Chapter Seven: Love in a Cold Climate

dangerous adventuress: Philip Ziegler, *King Edward VIII*, 203.

she believed had hypnotized him: Hugo Vickers, *The Private World of the Duke and Duchess of Windsor*, 160.

painting Wallis's toenails: Paul Vallely, "Royal Albums: The King's Favourite," *Independent*, February 14, 1988.

arch adventuress of the worst type: Adrian Fort, *Nancy: The Story of Lady Astor* (London: Jonathan Cape, 2012), 248.

ambitious, scheming and dangerous: Stephen Bates and Owen Bowcott, "Papers Bring Deeper Insight, but No Change," *Guardian*, January 30, 2003.

a respectable whore: Philip Ziegler, *King Edward VIII*, 215.

I am here today: George S. Messersmith papers, MSS 109 2017-00.

Mrs. Simpson "intended to flit": Owen Bowcott and Stephen Bates, "Fear that Windsors Would 'Flit' to Germany," *Guardian*, January 30, 2003.

I must remain hidden: Michael Bloch, *The Secret File of the Duke of Windsor: The Private Papers 1937–1972* (New York: Harper & Row, 1988), 18.

Make no mistake he can't live without her: Mabell, Countess of Airlie, *Thatched with Gold*, 201.

in defence of Mrs. S.: Herman Rogers to Sara Delano Roosevelt, from the estate of Lucy Livingston Rogers.

could not possibly get away with it: Adrian Fort, *Nancy*, 248.

must make even Judas queasy: William Shawcross, *Queen Elizabeth the Queen Mother*, 393.

Absolutely brilliant: Ibid.

study of her and her friends: William Shawcross, *Counting One's Blessings*, 285–86.

the battle could have been won: Colin Cross, *The Fascists in Britain* (New York: St. Martin's Press, 1963), 165.

wanted Edward to stay on the throne: Martha Schad, *Hitler's Spy Princess*, 64.

Especially if one is king: Ibid., 63.

details orally to my Führer: Christopher Andrew, *Defend The Realm*, 199.

in the face of this nonsense: Ibid., 199.

tenuous connection with his official post: Gerhard L. Weinberg, *Hitler and England, 1933–1945: Pretense and Reality*, German Studies Review 8, no. 2 (May 1985): 299–309.

important details miscarried: Ian Kershaw, *Making Friends with Hitler*, 190.

unalloyed gain for Britain: Ibid., 189.

most prescient statesman then living: Patrick J. Buchanan, *Churchill, Hitler, and the Unnecessary War* (New York: Crown, 2008), 357.

forbade Prince Lu to attend: Jonathan Petropoulos, *Royals and the Reich*, 160.

lovely to look forward to: Letter from Duke of Windsor to Herman Rogers, December 22, 1936, from the estate of Lucy Livingston Rogers.

a monarch's service: "Sir Dudley Forwood, Bt" (obituary), *Daily Telegraph*, January 27, 2001.

They were always made for me: George S. Messersmith papers, MSS 109 2017-00.

a constant anxiety to me: H. Montgomery Hyde, *Walter Monckton* (London: Sinclair-Stevenson, 1991), 93.

kings don't take tricks, they only abdicate: Alan Truscott, "Bridge; No Tricks for a King," *New York Times*, July 18, 1982.

impediment in his speech: H. Montgomery Hyde, *Walter Monckton*, 80.

hanging about doing nothing: William Shawcross, *Queen Elizabeth the Queen Mother*, 388.

arts and graces that please: H. Montgomery Hyde, *Walter Monckton*, 94.

definite ideas as to dictatorship: Charles Higham, *The Duchess of Windsor*, 180.

right to return to it—for all time: Stephen Bates, "Edward Forced to Stay in Exile or Risk Income," *Guardian*, January 30, 2003.

without my approval: Paul Reynolds, "Royals Kept Windsors in Exile," BBC News, January 30, 2003.

an extremely difficult situation: President Roosevelt to Edmund Rogers, from the estate of Lucy Livingston Rogers.

proper backing would mean so much: Michael Bloch, *The Duchess of Windsor*, 111.

the wife—who hates us both: Ibid.

one of the most dangerous of Nazi spies: Charles Higham, *The Duchess of Windsor*, 102.

"So degrading," noted the queen: William Shawcross, *Queen Elizabeth the Queen Mother*, 424.

many German business contacts: Jonathan Petropoulos, *Royals and the Reich*, 211.

those who still believe in this ideal: *Kingston Daily Freeman* (Kingston, NY), October 27, 1937.

we could meet it side by side: Michael Bloch, *The Duchess of Windsor*, 117.

the 'other one' wouldn't have done: Mary Soames, *Clementine Churchill: The Biography of a Marriage* (New York: Houghton Mifflin, 1979), 274.

a fine wedding present: Philip Ziegler, *King Edward VIII*, 311.

automatically on marriage: William Shawcross, *Queen Elizabeth the Queen Mother*, 422.

your own future happiness: National Archives, file NA PRO HO 144/22945. Released January 2003.

alienating us from my family: H. Montgomery Hyde, *Walter Monckton*, 83.

none of the family is going to the wedding: William Shawcross, *Queen Elizabeth the Queen Mother*, 422.

nail in the coffin of monarchy: Ibid., 421.

he was deeply, deeply hurt: Charles Higham, *The Duchess of Windsor*, 206.

no interest at all in politics: Helena Normanton, "Intrigue Is Denied by Mrs. Warfield," *New York Times*, June 1, 1937.

I think I can make him happy: H. Montgomery Hyde, *Walter Monckton*, 86.

I did step into the breach: William Shawcross, *Queen Elizabeth the Queen Mother*, 423.

increasingly suspicious of the duke's behavior: Conversation with Edward after his abdication, George S. Messersmith papers, MSS 109 2017-00.

Chapter Eight: Hitler's Good Queen Wallis

dominated by his fine, dark eyes: Janet Flanner, "Annals of Collaboration," *New Yorker*, September 22, 1945.

make the arrangements with Hitler: "Sir Dudley Forwood, Bt" (obituary), *Daily Telegraph*, January 27, 2001.

value to any universal—not political—world cause: Herman Rogers to Dr, Peabody, October 23, 1937, from the estate of Lucy Livingston Rogers.

more than anything else is peace: Michael Bloch, *The Secret File of the Duke of Windsor*, 109.

a "more sinister" figure: Jonathan Petropoulos, *Royals and the Reich*, 212.

the Windsors, Bedaux, Solbert, and Watson reveals this thinking: Author interview.

bombshell and a bad one: William Shawcross, *Queen Elizabeth the Queen Mother*, 425.

private stunts for publicity purposes: Michael Bloch, *The Secret File of the Duke of Windsor*, 115.

a bite of luncheon: Ibid.

bombshell after bombshell: Ibid., 116.

respect felt for an equal: Gerwin Strobl, *The Germanic Isle: Nazi Perceptions of Britain* (Cambridge: Cambridge University Press, 2000), 109.

so-called guests of the Third Reich: Jonathan Petropoulos, *Royals and the Reich*, 209.

where they store the cold meat: "Sir Dudley Forwood, Bt" (obituary), *Daily Telegraph*, January 27, 2001.

trophies at an exhibition: Bryan and Murphy, *The Windsor Story*, 362.

quarrelsome, a four flusher: Ibid.

What a shame! What a terrible shame: Gerwin Strobl, *The Germanic Isle*, 109.

could have saved Europe from her doom: Charles Higham, *The Duchess of Windsor*, 225.

I did salute Hitler: Bryan and Murphy, *The Windsor Story*, 364.

He was frank and friendly with Hitler, and displayed the social charm: R .H. C. Steed, ed., *Hitler's Interpreter* (London: Heinemann, 1951), 75.

peculiar fire: Bryan and Murphy, *The Windsor Story*, 362.

Nazi salute that the Duke returned: Jonathan Petropoulos, *Royals and the Reich*, 209.

would have made a good queen: Ibid.

she was most ladylike: Martha Schad, *Hitler's Spy Princess*, 67.

a devoted admirer, on the British throne: Jonathan Petropoulos, *Royals and the Reich*, 206.

distinction and success: Philip Ziegler, *King Edward VIII*, 339.

strong pro-Fascist sympathies: Ibid., 209–210.

royalty's warm feelings for the Nazis: William Stevenson, *Spymistress: The Life of Vera Atkins, the Greatest Female Secret Agent of World War II* (New York: Arcade, 2007), 57.

the Weimar Republic, which had been extremely socialist: "Sir Dudley Forwood, Bt" (obituary), *Daily Telegraph*, January 27, 2001.

popular appeal which the Duke of Windsor possesses: Charles Higham, *The Duchess of Windsor*, 235.

semi-fascist comeback in England: Ibid., 221–22.

movement could be found than in the Duke of Windsor: Sarah Bradford, *King George VI*, 255.

recalled to the throne as a dictator: Sol Bloomenkranz, *Charles Bedaux: Deciphering an Enigma* (Bloomington, IN; iUniverse, 2012), 50–53.

"delayed" so...they would miss the sombre ceremony: Charles Higham, *The Duchess of Windsor*, 238.

diplomatic complications: Cornelius Vanderbilt to Herman Rogers, June 18, 1937, from the estate of Lucy Livingston Rogers.

the problems of labour or the poor and needy: Charles Higham, *The Duchess of Windsor*, 237.

regime's hold on the working classes: Michael Bloch, *The Secret File of the Duke of Windsor*, 117.

quit public life: Charles Higham, *The Duchess of Windsor*, 269.

a sharp and salutary lesson: John Vincent, ed., *The Crawford Papers*, 585.

lovely innocent trip: Michael Bloch, *The Secret File of the Duke of Windsor*, 119.

accept the presidency of the English Republic: Philip Ziegler, *King Edward VIII*, 342.

like a small boy at Christmas: Bryan and Murphy, *The Windsor Story*, 378–79.

delivered from the fears that beset us: Michael Bloch, *The Secret File of the Duke of Windsor*, 137.

to choose such a moment: William Shawcross, *Queen Elizabeth the Queen Mother*, 453.

discreet political missions: Jonathan Petropoulos, *Royals and the Reich*, 192.

betterment of Anglo-German relations: Ibid., 201.

private domain of royal cousins: Tom MacDonnell, *Daylight upon Magic: The Royal Tour of Canada, 1939* (Toronto, ON: Macmillan of Canada, 1989), 43.

not the purview of the royals: Jonathan Petropoulos, *Royals and the Reich*, 193–94.

if war came: Philip Ziegler, *King Edward VIII*, 345.

Complete strangers embraced in the streets: Gerwin Strobl, *The Germanic Isle*, 130.

Chapter Nine: The Game of Thrones

YOU talk of your PRIDE: Anne Sebba, *That Woman*, 227.

He might not even exist: Michael Bloch, *The Secret File of the Duke of Windsor*, 144.

Admit that man has charm: Diana Mitford, *The Duchess of Windsor*, 155.

they HATE her: William Shawcross, *Counting One's Blessings*, 279–80.

she should not be here in wartime: William Shawcross, *Queen Elizabeth the Queen Mother*, 494.

babble out state secrets without realizing: Charles Higham, *The Duchess of Windsor*, 300.

victors of the contest will be the Soviet: Duke of Windsor to Herman Rogers, October 16, 1939, from the estate of Lucy Livingston Rogers.

visiting the French front: Michael Bloch, *The Secret File of the Duke of Windsor*, 147.

Go ahead sir, I will back you: Philip Ziegler, *King Edward VIII*, 357.

source of any intelligence: Jonathan Petropoulos, *Royals and the Reich*, 212.

He knows too much: John Costello, *Mask of Treachery*, 413–14; Bryan and Murphy, *The Windsor Story*, 418.

peace with the Nazis on any terms they could: Author interview with Gerhard Weinberg.

favourable circumstances might acquire a certain significance: Charles Higham, *The Duchess of Windsor*, 308.

source of military intelligence: John Costello, *Mask of Treachery*, 415; Sarah Bradford, *King George VI*, 434–35.

Did the duke know what this person was doing?: Author interview with Gerhard Weinberg.

information made its way into German hands: Charles Higham, *The Duchess of Windsor*, 302–6.

a whole nation against one lone woman: Bryan and Murphy, *The Windsor Story*, 418.

betrayed military secrets to Hitler: Ben Fenton, "Lies and Secrets," *Financial Times*, May 3, 2008.

marry her and maintain the throne: FOIA, FBI file of the Duke and Duchess of Windsor, Edward Tamm to J. Edgar Hoover, September 13, 1940.

not just to his fellow countrymen: Philip Ziegler, *King Edward VIII*, 375.

wasn't completely out of character: Neill Lochery, *Lisbon: War in the Shadows of the City of Light 1939–1945* (New York: Public Affairs, 2011), 61.

arriving in Barcelona on June 20: Michael Bloch, *Operation Willi: The Nazi Plot to Kidnap the Duke of Windsor, July 1940* (New York: Weidenfeld & Nicolson, 1984), 23.

please confirm that I am acting correctly: Ibid., 48.

establishing contact with him: German Foreign Ministry (Auswärtiges Amt) document AA-B15/B002531, Stohrer to Ribbentrop, June 23, 1940, *Documents on German Foreign Policy, 1918–1945*, Series D, 1937–1945 (London: H.M.S.O., 1949–; Washington: US Government Printing Office, 1949–), cited in Michael Bloch, *Operation Willi*.

suggestion came from Germany: German Foreign Ministry document AA-B15/B002532, Ribbentrop to Stohrer, June 24, 1940, *Documents on German Foreign Policy*.

appealed directly for peace: Frances Donaldson, *Edward VIII* (London: Weidenfeld & Nicolson), 385–86.

if reasonable conditions could be obtained: Donald C. Watt, ed., *Contemporary History in Europe: Problems and Perspectives* (London: Allen & Unwin, 1969), 197.

nebulous peace overtures were made: Jonathan Petropoulos, *Royals and the Reich*, 189.

England's destiny after the war: Rob Evans and David Hencke, "Hitler Saw Duke of Windsor as 'No Enemy' US File Reveals," *Guardian*, January 24, 2003.

no quarter was given: Michael Bloch, *The Duchess of Windsor*, 149.

ensure that such an error never occur again: Michael Bloch, *The Duke of Windsor's War* (London: Weidenfeld & Nicolson, 1982), 75.

using the duke and duchess: Alan Palmer, *Crowned Cousins*, 221–22.

military uprising. Nothing came of it: John Colville, *The Fringes of Power: Downing Street Diaries 1939–1955* (London: Weidenfeld & Nicolson, 2004), 57.

Good God, no: Neill Lochery, *Lisbon*, notes, 28.

give the duke a naval command: Philip Ziegler, *King Edward VIII*, 364.

when everything can be considered: Michael Bloch, *Operation Willi*, 62.

no conditions, about the Duchess or otherwise: John Colville, *Fringes of Power*, 176.

only fitted to be a café society royal: Kenneth de Courcy papers, Hoover Institution Archives, Stanford University.

brinkmanship of an appalling kind: Bryan and Murphy, *The Windsor Story*, 434.

any need for a prompt return: Michael Bloch, *Operation Willi*, 57–58.

following developments from afar: Ibid., 58–59.

governments after the war: German Foreign Ministry document AA-490/232262, Memorandum by the State Secretary Ernst von Weizsäcker, June 30, 1940, doc. 65: 68, *Documents on German Foreign Policy*.

prolonged destruction and suffering: Michael Bloch, *Operation Willi*, 59.

very pleasant, very genial, and very witty: MSS 1W4126cFA2, Weddell, A.W., Box 4, Elizabeth W. Weddell, Weddell Collection, Virginia Historical Society.

any peace party that may emerge: Michael Bloch, *Operation Willi*, 60–61.

a cowardly and rapacious vulture: Paul Preston, *The Politics of Revenge: Fascism and the Military in 20th Century Spain* (London: Routledge, 1995), 57.

against Churchill and against the war: German Foreign Ministry document AA-B15/B002538, Stohrer to Ribbentrop, July 2, 1940, *Documents on German Foreign Policy*.

Chapter Ten: Plot to Kidnap a King

wishes of the government: Martin Gilbert, *Winston S. Churchill Vol. 6, Finest Hour, 1939–1941* (London: Heinemann, 1983), 698.

as he had been in December 1936: Roy Jenkins, *Churchill: A Biography* (London: Macmillan, 2001), 561.

before arranging the day and time: Lord Moran, *Churchill: The Struggle for Survival, 1940–1965* (London: Constable, 1966), 97.

forestall flight out of the country: Bryan and Murphy, *The Windsor Story*, 431.

Not as much as his brother will: John Colville, *Fringes of Power*, 184.

embarrassing both to HM and the Government: Martin Gilbert, *Finest Hour*, 700.

pretty freely criticized: John Barnes and David Nicholson, eds., *The Empire at Bay: The Leo Amery Diaries 1929–1945* (London: Hutchinson, 1988), 631.

lowest of the low: William Shawcross, *Queen Elizabeth the Queen Mother*, 520.

my brother has behaved disgracefully: Jonathan Petropoulos, *Royals and the Reich*, 217.

arch beachcombers of the world: Sybil Eccles and David Eccles, *By Safe Hand: Letters of Sybil and David Eccles 1939–42* (London: Bodley Head, 1983), 128, 133.

done your best for me in difficult circumstances: Michael Bloch, *Operation Willi*, 79.

exile to St. Helena: Michael Thornton, "The Queen Mother? That Spiteful Old Soak Dedicated Herself to Making Our Lives Hell," *Daily Mail*, September 19, 2009.

European ally to be kidnapped: Author interview with Douglas Wheeler.

until four in the morning: Jimmy Burns, *Papa Spy: Love, Faith, and Betrayal in Wartime Spain* (New York: Walker, 2009), 124.

heavy bombing will make England ready for peace: German Foreign Ministry document AA-B15/B002549 (GD D/X/152), Hoyningen-Huene to Ribbentrop, July 10, 1940, *Documents on German Foreign Policy*.

President of the Great British Republic: Michael Bloch, *Operation Willi*, 95.

Operation Cleopatra Whim: Bryan and Murphy, *The Windsor Story*, 435.

A prince does not ask favours: Michael Bloch, *Operation Willi*, 133.

suitable for a king: German Foreign Ministry document AA-B15/B002549–51 (GD D/X/152), Ribbentrop to Stohrer, July 11, 1940, *Documents on German Foreign Policy*.

planned a public declaration: German Foreign Office document AA-B15/B002582-3, Stohrer to Ribbentrop, July 23, 1940, *Documents on German Foreign Policy*.

the duchess in particular became very thoughtful: German Foreign Office Document AA-B15/B002588 (GD D/X/290), Stohrer to Ribbentrop, July 25, 1940, *Documents on German Foreign Policy*.

cantankerous and maddening: Philip Ziegler, *King Edward VIII*, 369.

messed about quite long enough: Ibid., 370.

we shall be alright: Ibid., 369.

Cordell Hull, in Washington: National Archives, Diplomatic Branch 841.0011.102 1/2, Herbert Claiborne Pell to Secretary of State, 4:00 p.m., July 20, cited in Philip Ziegler, *King Edward VIII*, 366.

Frenchmen in his company: Philip Ziegler, *King Edward VIII*, 366.

She has great influence over the duke: Michael Bloch, *Operation Willi*, 144.

every step has to be watched with care: Ibid., 174.

how can we be of any use to them?: H. Montgomery Hyde, *Walter Monckton*, 104.

you should not be too far away: Neill Lochery, *Lisbon*, 82.

disregarded or allowed to be destroyed: Michael Bloch, *Operation Willi*, 206.

the expected invasion of Britain: Martin Gilbert, *Finest Hour*, 709.

Germans could keep in contact: German Foreign Office document AA-B15/B002617-18 (GD D/X/265), Ribbentrop to Hoyningen-Huene, July 31, 1940, *Documents on German Foreign Policy*.

almost able to touch it: Michael Bloch, *Operation Willi*, 201.

admiration and sympathy for the Führer: German Foreign Office document AA-B15/B002632-3 (GD D/X/276), Hoyningen-Huene to Ribbentrop, August 2, 1940, *Documents on German Foreign Policy*.

German intrigues with the duke: John H. Waller, *The Unseen War in Europe: Espionage and Conspiracy in the Second World War* (New York: I. B. Tauris, 1996), 172.

cousins did not try to work for a negotiated peace: Jonathan Petropoulos, *Royals and the Reich*, 218.

this theory seems implausible: Waller, *The Unseen War in Europe*, 171.

maid situation desperate: Michael Bloch, *Operation Willi*, 228.

their pink sheets: "Royal Feud," *Royalty* 5, no. 3, https://www.royalty -magazine.com/archive/feud.html.

strange suspicions: H. Montgomery Hyde, *Walter Monckton*, 107.

banishment a wise move: Sarah Bradford, *King George VI*, 436.

Chapter Eleven: A Shady Royal in a Sunny Place

show of loyalty to friends: Helen Worden, "The Duchess of Windsor," *American Mercury* (June 1944), 675–81.

However...c'est la guerre: Author archive.

petty humiliations: Michael Bloch, *The Secret File of the Duke of Windsor*, 178.

there would have been no war: Charles Higham, *The Duchess of Windsor*, 337.

prepared to say yes or no: Diary of Guy Liddell, Deputy Director General of the Security Service, June to November 1945, KV 4/466, National Archives, Kew, UK.

conviction on it: Philip Ziegler, *King Edward VIII*, 395.

belief that they can do it: David Reynolds, *Lord Lothian and Anglo-American Relations, 1939-40*. Transactions of the American Philosophical Society 73, Part 2 (Philadelphia: American Philosophical Society, 1983).

initiating an effective peace move: Notes on Meetings with Sir William Wiseman, 09/02/1940–01/08/1941, GTM.GAMMS98, James D. Mooney papers, Box 1, Folder 22, Georgetown University Library Special Collections Research Center; also David Hayward, *Mr. James D. Mooney: A Man of Missions*, www. gmhistory.chevytalk.org/James_D_Mooney_by_David_ Hayward.html.

in order to bring England down: George S. Messersmith (Havana) to Cordell Hull (Secretary of State, Washington), George S. Messersmith papers, MSS 109, Box 12 F90.

Windsor linked to Mooney separate peace: Jonathan Pile, *Churchill's Secret Enemy* (Lulu.com, 2012), Appendix 2.

continuing his fight with Britain: Jim Wilson, *Nazi Princess*, 156–59; Scott Newton, *Profits of Peace: The Political Economy of Anglo-German Appeasement*. (London: Oxford University Press, 1996), 179–84.

she was a go-between: Robert Houghwout Jackson, *That Man: An Insider's Portrait of Franklin D. Roosevelt* (New York: Oxford University Press, 2003), 70.

as importantly as he might: *Palm Beach Post*, November 18, 1940.

a success from every point of view: Michael Bloch, *The Secret File of the Duke of Windsor*, 183.

Bahamian islands for navy ships: Box 7, Grace Tully Collection, Franklin D. Roosevelt Presidential Library and Museum, Hyde Park, NY.

partisanship of the Windsors: John Colville, *Fringes of Power*, 332.

betrayal of Allied secrets: Fulton Oursler Jr., "Secret Treason," *American Heritage* 42, no. 8 (December 1991), 61.

Edward, Duke of Windsor: Boake Carter, "But-Says," *Milwaukee Sentinel*, December 31, 1940.

there isn't a chance: Michael Pye, *The King over the Water: The Scandalous Truth about the Windsors' War Years* (London: Hutchinson, 1981), 77–78.

Chapter Twelve: Tropic of Rancour

paying US Customs duties: Andrew Roberts, *The Holy Fox: The Life of Lord Halifax* (London, Head of Zeus, 2014), 394.

their primary concern: Sarah Bradford, *King George VI*, 442.

a revolution they don't want: Philip Ziegler, *King Edward VIII*, 393–94.

avoid discrediting him: Fred Taylor, ed., *The Goebbels Diaries, 1939–41* (London: Hamish Hamilton, 1982), 344–45.

grow up and behave: Andrew Roberts, *The Holy Fox*, 393.

I used to in the past: Michael Bloch, *The Secret File of the Duke of Windsor*, 186.

always tried to play my part: Ibid., 188.

America for herself: Philip Ziegler, *King Edward VIII*, 394.

supplant our democratic government: *New York Times*, October 8, 1937.

king of England: Charles Higham, *The Duchess of Windsor*, 364.

English defeat were to be achieved: FBI files: 65-31113-19.

gave the Nazi salute: Martin Allen, *Hidden Agenda: How the Duke of Windsor Betrayed the Allies* (London: Macmillan, 2000), 275.

holding himself in readiness: Michael Bloch, *Operation Willi*, 223.

cruelty to animals: Andrew Roberts, *The Holy Fox*, 392.

this side of the Atlantic: Michael Bloch, *The Secret File of the Duke of Windsor*, 189.

harm and not good: Philip Ziegler, *King Edward VIII*, 401.

his hotel was picketed: Michael Bloch, *The Duke of Windsor's War*, 221.

he met him in the Bahamas: Philip Ziegler, *King Edward VIII*, 396.

the Nipponese hordes: Michael Bloch, *The Duke of Windsor's War*, 225.

better than being on the outside: Ibid., 226.

replaced by one more conciliatory: John Colville, *Fringes of Power*, 516.

by which we were surprised: Lord Moran, *Churchill: The Struggle for Survival, 1940–1965* (London: Constable, 1966), 97.

which he is doing at present: Charles Higham, *The Duchess of Windsor*, 383.

I'm Mata Hari: Michael Bloch, *The Duke of Windsor's War*, 289.

It is his own family who are against him: Ibid., 335.

highly damaging to themselves: Duff Hart-Davis, ed., *King's Counsellor*, 351.

Chapter Thirteen: The Hunt for Pirate Gold

Can you shave in cold water?: Roger Weil, "The Unique Ambassador," *Sword & Trowel*, no. 1 (2001).

a youngster from his church: Author interview with Roger Weil.

State Department memo of January 1944: Astrid M. Eckert, *The Struggle for the Files: The Western Allies and the Return of German Archives after the Second World War* (New York: Cambridge University Press, 2012), 35.

their most important records: Historical Office Records relating to the German Documents Project, 1944–1983, Box 6, German War Documents 1944–1945, no. 2 of 2, Record Group 59, National Archives and Records Administration, College Park, Maryland.

local Nazi women's organization: Astrid Eckert, *Struggle for the Files*, 30.

Wish me good hunting: Letter from E. Ralph Perkins to E. Wilder Spaulding (London), April 2, 1945, Historical Office Records relating to the German Documents Project, 1944–1983, Box 9, GWD—for George O. Kent, no. 1 of 2, Record Group 59, National Archives and Records Administration, College Park, Maryland.

***Geheim*, or Secret**: *The Marburg File*. BBC Radio 4, August 31, 1995, Tape 128/44.1.

probably not on record: Sacha Zala, *Geschichte unter der Schere politischer Zensur: Amtliche Aktensammlungen im internationalen Vergleich*, trans. Nathan Ernst (Munich: Oldenbourg, 2001), 165.

report about the extraordinary episode: Robert C. Thomson, *Discovery of Secret Archives of German Foreign Ministry*, report of May 22, 1945, PRO FO 371/46712C2548/G, National Archives, Kew, UK.

found "if possible": Combined Intelligence Objectives Subcommittee memorandum, April 20, 1945, CF 1945–1949, Box 4130, FW 840.414/5-145, Record Group 59, National Archives and Records Administration, College Park, Maryland.

the documents were indeed genuine: Astrid Eckert, *Struggle for the Files*, 67.

red-hot propaganda material: Ibid., 64.

German and Italian policy: Note of Foreign Office meeting, June 19, 1945, FO 371/46713 C3209/G, National Archives, Kew, UK.

writers, radio commentators: Sacha Zala, *Geschichte*, 169.

inside the American zone: Ibid., 183.

impact on international politics: Astrid Eckert, *Struggle for the Files*, 64.

find the source of the leak: Ibid., 76.

Mosley becoming public knowledge: Note from George Middleton (Brit Emb Washington) to W. C. Dowling, July 21, 1945, Box 5702, 840.414/7-2145, RG 59, National Archives and Records Administration, College Park, Maryland.

distinctly unusual material: *The Marburg File*, BBC Radio 4.

tantamount to treason: John Costello, *Ten Days to Destiny: The Secret Story of the Hess Peace Initiative and British Efforts to Strike a Deal with Hitler* (New York: William Morrow, 1991).

to some extent on their side: *The Marburg File*, BBC Radio 4.

impediment to co-operation: Astrid Eckert, *Struggle for the Files*, 70.

Paris peace conference of 1919: Sacha Zala, *Geschichte*, 291.

these German intrigues: John Costello, *Mask of Treachery*, 419.

greatest possible harm: Ibid.

a job here or anywhere: William Shawcross, *Queen Elizabeth the Queen Mother*, 599.

secure a negotiated settlement: Jonathan Petropoulos, *Royals and the Reich*, 218.

necessitated urgent action: Sarah Bradford, *King George VI*, 427.

Chapter Fourteen: Sovereigns, Secrets, and Spies

fall in to the wrong hands: Alan Lascelles to Sir Ian Jacob, July 25, 1945, NA RA 802 775057, National Archives, Kew, UK.

I kept this secret: Associated Press, June 10, 1990.

haven't you, Mr Piper: Andrew Morton, *Theirs Is the Kingdom: Wealth of the Windsors* (London: Michael O'Mara, 1989), 78.

the artist or the sitter: Miranda Carter, *Anthony Blunt: His Lives* (New York: Farrar, Straus and Giroux, 2001), 305.

his efforts during the war: Author interview.

two very influential informers: Viktor Popov, *The Queen's advisor who was a super agent of the Kremlin* [in Russian] (Moscow: Mezhdunarodnye Otnosheniya, 2005), 131–41.

the royal mission to Germany in 1945: Jonathan Petropoulos, *Royals and the Reich* (New York: Oxford University Press, 2006), 340–41.

especially the press: Roland Perry, *Last of the Cold War Spies: The Life of Michael Straight* (Boston: Da Capo, 2005), 163.

he had real, if obscure authority: Ibid., 165–69.

make off with their booty: Jonathan Petropoulos, *Royals and the Reich*, 337–38; Miranda Carter, *Anthony Blunt: His Lives*, 312.

handed over to Sir Owen Morshead: Kenneth Alford, *The Spoils of World War II: The American Military's Role in Stealing Europe's Treasures* (New York: Birch Lane, 1994), 116.

souvenir-hunting American officers: Ibid., 118, 165.

a 'Windsor file': Jonathan Petropoulos, *Royals and the Reich*, 342.

such letters existed in 1945: Author interview.

Windsor was a traitor: Author interview.

files in Germany that needed to be secured: Jonathan Petropoulos, *Royals and the Reich*, 341.

They are only on loan: Diary of Guy Liddell, KV 4/466, National Archives, Kew, UK.

called on Karl Marx: John Costello, *Mask of Treachery*, 406.

set royal minds to rest: Duff Hart-Davis, ed., *King's Counsellor*, 324–25.

regrettable from a historical viewpoint: William Shawcross, *Queen Elizabeth the Queen Mother*, 899.

it never would have happened: Diary of Guy Liddell, KV 4/466, National Archives, Kew, UK.

Captured German Documents: Miranda Carter, *Anthony Blunt: His Lives*, 313.

Chapter Fifteen: Fight for the File

worth the candle: Martin Gilbert, *Winston S. Churchill. Vol. 8, Never Despair, 1945–1965* (London: Heinemann, 1983), 174.

I am sorry for them: Brendan Bracken, Max Aitken Beaverbrook, and Richard Cockett, *My Dear Max: The Letters of Brendan Bracken to Lord Beaverbrook, 1925–1958* (London: Historians' Press, 1990), 65.

hearth rug bore: Duff Hart-Davis, ed., *King's Counsellor*, 367.

of interest only to the British: Paul Robinson Sweet papers, PRO notes, 20, Hoover Institution Archives, Stanford, California.

unfair to the duke: John Costello, *Mask of Treachery*, 419.

to the Bahamas in 1940: Author interview.

dossier on September 5, 1945: J. D. Beam to Murphy, October 2, 1945, Record Group 84, POLAD, entry 2531B, Box 37, National Archives.

passed it on to the Foreign Office: Astrid Eckert, *Struggle for the Files*, 72.

represented true statements: POLAD, Classified General Correspondence, 1945–49, Record Group 84, entry 2531B, Box 37, [Archives] Location 350/57/18/02, US National Archives and Records Administration.

member of the royal family: Memorandum [no author], May 20, 1946, Record Group 59, Lot File 78D441, Historical Office, Box 13, National Archives.

special restrictions on the file: Record Group 59, CDF, 1945–49, 862.414/8–645, National Archives.

history of the war: Record Group 59, CDF, 1945–49, 862.4016–862.42, Box 6836, National Archives.

transaction over the file: David Harris papers, Box 22, Hoover Institution Archives, Stanford.

peace with the United Kingdom in 1940: Record Group 59, Lot File 78D441, Historical Office Records relating to the German Documents Project, 1944–83, Box 6, Historical Office, National Archives.

private life of Queen Elizabeth: Record Group 59, Lot File 78D441, Historical Office, National Archives.

communicated to us: John Balfour to Dean Acheson, October 7, 1945, Record Group 59, Lot File 78D441, Box 6, Historical Office, National Archives.

tamper with official documents: Herbert S. Marks to Dean G. Acheson, October 10, 1945, Record Group 59, Lot File 78D441, Box 13, Historical Office, National Archives.

consultation with the British government: Record Group 59, Lot File 78D441, Box 13, Historical Office, National Archives.

unless he carried out his orders: Record Group 59, Lot File 78D441, Box 24, Folder C103, Historical Office, National Archives.

especially the Queen: Robert D. Murphy papers, Box 163, Folder 5, Hoover Institution Archives, Stanford.

her relatives, the Brunswicks: Miranda Carter, *Anthony Blunt: His Lives*, 315.

Henry the Lion: Diary of Guy Liddell, KV 4/467, National Archives.

past hundred years: Miranda Carter, *Anthony Blunt: His Lives*, 318.

their own corrupt behaviour: Ibid., 315.

I dare say, tyranny: Astrid Eckert, *Struggle for the Files*, 74.

gaps in the German Foreign Office files: Record Group 59, Lot File 78D441, Historical Office, National Archives.

parties we have in mind: Paul Robinson Sweet papers, PRO notes, 7, Hoover Institution Archives, Stanford.

exploitation by U.S. representatives: Sacha Zala, *Geschichte*, 188.

irreplaceable historical archives: H. Freeman Mathews (EUR) to Secretary of State James F. Byrnes (Washington), January 31, 1946, Record Group 59, CF 1945–49 (Conf.), Box 5703, FW 840.414/1–2946, National Archives.

monarchy through their eyes: Record Group 59, Lot File 78D441, Historical Office, National Archives.

Chapter Sixteen: Burying the "Hot Potato"

brought home to Germany: Sir John Wheeler-Bennett, *Friends, Enemies and Sovereigns* (London: Macmillan, 1976), 66–67.

information to our shores: Astrid Eckert, *Struggle for the Files*, 294.

file had been mislabelled: Letter from Otto Pflanze to Paul Sweet, September 22, 1991, Paul Robinson Sweet papers, Hoover Institution Archives, Stanford.

Department agreed to undertake: Sarah Bradford, *King George VI*, 428.

for HMG to decide: Sir Robert Bruce Lockhart, *The Diaries of Sir Robert Bruce Lockhart, Vol II, 1939–1965*, ed. Kenneth Young (London: Macmillan, 1980), 572.

bulk of its contents: Sir John Wheeler-Bennett, *Friends, Enemies and Sovereigns*, 81–82.

please his chief, Ribbentrop: Philip Ziegler, *King Edward VIII*, 473.

telegram two days later: Sarah Bradford, *King George VI*, 427.

the Bismarck era: Victoria Schofield, *Witness to History: The Life of John Wheeler-Bennett* (New Haven, CT: Yale University Press, 2012), 185.

think right—isn't it: William Shawcross, *Counting One's Blessings*, 421.

to the highest bidder: Sarah Bradford, *King George VI*, 447.

undergo a hysterectomy: Michael Bloch, *The Secret File of the Duke of Windsor*, 244.

ice-veined bitches: Sarah Bradford, *King George VI*, 448.

bunch of old hags: Michael Bloch, *The Secret File of the Duke of Windsor*, 279.

disagreeable facts emerging: Author interview.

take another five years: Security Information, July 28, 1953, Paul Robinson Sweet papers, Hoover Institution Archives, Stanford.

they would be published: Paul R. Sweet, "The Problem of Official Intervention in the Publication of Documents on German Foreign Policy, 1933–1941," Sweet papers, Hoover Institution Archives, Stanford, p. 17, edited version in *Historian* 59, no. 2 (December 1997).

leaving his job before long: Ibid.

outside the secret circles: Winston Churchill to Dwight D. Eisenhower, June 27, 1953, President–Churchill (vol. 11) May 28, 1953 to October 14, 1953 (3), Box 18, Eisenhower, Dwight D.: Papers as President of the United States, 1953–61 (Ann Whitman File), Dwight D. Eisenhower Presidential Library, Abilene, Kansas.

decency, justice and finality: Dwight D. Eisenhower to Winston Churchill, July 2, 1953, President–Churchill (vol. 11) May 28, 1953 to Oct 14, 1953 (5), Box 18, Eisenhower, Dwight D.: Papers as President (Ann Whitman File).

told about this matter: Beaverbrook papers, BBK/G/25/xx40L, House of Lords Record Office, London.

will probably leak: Memo, personal and confidential, from General W. Bedell Smith to Dwight Eisenhower (Washington), July 6, 1953, Record Group 59 CF 1950–1954, Box 967, 023.1/7–653, National Archives.

satisfactory answers: Bernadotte E. Schmitt to Bernard Noble, July 30, 1953, Paul Robinson Sweet papers, Hoover Institution Archives, Stanford.

different period first: Beaverbrook papers, BBK/G/25/xxi 40L, House of Lords Record Office, London.

still set on suppression: John Colville, *Fringes of Power*, 675.

into the long grass: Astrid Eckert, *Struggle for the Files*, 251, 254, cited Confidential Record of Cabinet Discussion on August 25, 1953. C. C. (53) 50th Conclusion, Top Secret, No Circulation Record.

do its work first: Margaret Lambert to Paul Sweet, October 8, 1953, Paul Robinson Sweet papers, Hoover Institution Archives, Stanford.

cooked up: *The Marburg File*, BBC Radio 4.

integrity of the project: Paul Sweet to Margaret Lambert, October 4, 1953, Paul Robinson Sweet papers, Hoover Institution Archives, Stanford.

for such a decision: Ibid., November 4, 1953.

Eisenhower in Bermuda: Paul Sweet, "The Problem of Official Intervention in the Publication of Documents on German Foreign Policy, 1933–1941," Sweet papers, Hoover Institution Archives, Stanford, 28.

Prime Minister downwards: Margaret Lambert to Paul Sweet, November 13, 1953, Paul Robinson Sweet papers, Hoover Institution Archives, Stanford.

Chapter Seventeen: Traitor King or Duped Duke?

democratic West Germany: Captured German Documents, FO 370/2371, 29 January 54, National Archives, Kew, UK.

fall into wrong hands: Captured German Documents, FO 370/2371, Top Secret 38a, National Archives, Kew, UK.

allowed to develop: Philip Ziegler, *King Edward VIII*, 234.

handed back to Germany: PRO, FO 2371, Top Secret 38 Green, 46 Green; CAB 128: Records of Cabinet, cited by Paul R. Sweet in "The Problem of Intervention in the Publication of Documents on German Foreign Policy, 1933–1941," Sweet papers, Hoover Institution, Stanford, 29.

educate the German people: Astrid Eckert, *Struggle for the Files*, 254.

waived any objections: PRO, FO 2374, 129, 143, cited by Paul R. Sweet in "The Windsor File."

highest scholarly objectivity: *Times* (London), November 17, 1954.

the duke's behaviour: Paul Sweet, "The Problem of Intervention in the Publication of Documents on German Foreign Policy, 1933–1941," Sweet papers, Hoover Institution, Stanford, 29.

exceedingly unhappy and worried: Frances Donaldson, *Edward VIII*, 428.

to which I agreed: Astrid Eckert, *Struggle for the Files*, 254, cited letter from Duke of Windsor to Sir Walter Monckton, January 18, 1955, PRO CAB 21/3776.

so wonderful a friend: Sir John Wheeler-Bennett, *Friends, Enemies and Sovereigns*, 139.

no mention of me shall appear therein: Michael Bloch, *The Secret File of the Duke of Windsor*, 296.

family and their courtiers: David Cannadine, *History in Our Time* (New Haven, CT: Yale University Press, 1998), 60.

stink in our nostrils: Astrid Eckert, *Struggle for the Files*, 258.

will be a lot more: Margaret Lambert to Paul Sweet, January 31, 1956, Paul Robinson Sweet papers, Hoover Institution Archives, Stanford.

never saw him after 1937: Associated Press, July 23, 1956.

press were quite naïve: Author interview.

they failed to do it: *Times* (London), August 1, 1957.

"actual" guilt: Frances Donaldson, *Edward VIII*, 428–29.

German or Spanish: Bryan and Murphy, *The Windsor Story*, 429.

not convicted: Philip Ziegler, *King Edward VIII*, 375.

his primary concerns: Michael Bloch, *The Secret File of the Duke of Windsor*, 227–28.

promote peace, not war: *Documents on German Foreign Policy*, no. 1862, vol. V, 8, 108869.

avoided in 1939: John Parker, *King of Fools*, 236–37.

a negotiated peace: Charles Higham, *The Duchess of Windsor*, 441.

maps and plans were kept: Sarah Bradford, *King George VI*, 435.

anything I said: Lady Diana Cooper, *Darling Monster: The Letters of Lady Diana Cooper to Her Son John Julius Norwich, 1939–1952* (London: Chatto & Windus, 2013), 379.

they're all we have: Andrew Roberts, *The Holy Fox*, 393.

pragmatic sanction: Peter Viereck, *Conservative Thinkers: From John Adams to Winston Churchill* (New Brunswick, NJ: Transaction Publishers, 2005), 50.

Select Bibliography

Airlie, Mabell, Countess of. *Thatched with Gold: The Memoirs of Mabell, Countess of Airlie.* London: Hutchinson, 1962.

Alford, Kenneth D. *The Spoils of World War II: The American Military's Role in Stealing Europe's Treasures.* New York: Birch Lane Press, 1994.

Allen, Martin. *Hidden Agenda: How the Duke of Windsor Betrayed the Allies.* London: Macmillan, 2000.

Allen, Peter. *The Crown and the Swastika: Hitler, Hess and the Duke of Windsor.* London: Robert Hale, 1983.

Andrew, Christopher. *Defend The Realm: The Authorized History of MI5.* New York: Alfred Knopf, 2009.

Balfour, Neil, and Sally Mackay. *Paul of Yugoslavia: Britain's Maligned Friend.* London: Hamish Hamilton, 1980.

Barnes, John, and David Nicholson, eds. *The Empire at Bay: The Leo Amery Diaries 1929–1945.* London: Hutchinson, 1988.

Birkenhead, Frederick Winston Furneaux Smith. *Walter Monckton: The Life of Viscount Monckton of Brenchley.* London: Weidenfeld & Nicolson, 1969.

Bloch, Michael. *The Duchess of Windsor.* London: Weidenfeld & Nicolson, 1996.

———. *The Duke of Windsor's War.* London: Weidenfeld & Nicolson, 1982.

———. *Operation Willi: The Nazi Plot to Kidnap the Duke of Windsor, July 1940.* New York: Weidenfeld & Nicolson, 1984.

———. *Ribbentrop.* New York: Crown, 1992.

———. *The Secret File of the Duke of Windsor: The Private Papers 1937–1972.* New York: Harper & Row, 1988.

———. ed. *Wallis and Edward: Letters, 1931–1937.* New York: Summit Books, 1986.

Bloomenkranz, Sol. *Charles Bedaux: Deciphering an Enigma.* Bloomington, IN: iUniverse, 2012.

Boyd, William. *Any Human Heart*. London: Hamish Hamilton, 2002.

Boyle, Peter G., ed. *The Churchill-Eisenhower Correspondence 1953–1955*. Chapel Hill: University of North Carolina Press, 1990.

Bradford, Sarah. *King George VI*. London: Weidenfeld & Nicolson, 1989.

Bryan, J., III, and Charles J. V. Murphy. *The Windsor Story*. London: Granada, 1979.

Buchanan, Patrick J. *Churchill, Hitler, and the Unnecessary War: How Britain Lost Its Empire and the West Lost the World*. New York: Crown, 2008.

Burns, Jimmy. *Papa Spy: Love, Faith, and Betrayal in Wartime Spain*. New York: Walker, 2009.

Cannadine, David. *The Decline and Fall of the British Aristocracy*. New Haven, CT: Yale University Press, 1990.

———. *History in Our Time*. New Haven, CT: Yale University Press, 1998.

Carter, Miranda. *Anthony Blunt, His Lives*. New York: Farrar, Straus and Giroux, 2001.

Colville, John. *Footprints in Time: Memories*. Norwich, Norfolk: Michael Russell, 1984.

———. *The Fringes of Power: Downing Street Diaries 1939–1955*. London: Weidenfeld & Nicolson, 2004.

Costello, John. *Mask of Treachery: The Dossier on Blunt, Buckingham Palace, MI5 and Soviet Subversion*. London: Pan Books, 1989.

———. *Ten Days to Destiny: The Secret Story of the Hess Peace Initiative and British Efforts to Strike a Deal with Hitler*. New York: William Morrow, 1991.

Cross, Colin. *The Fascists in Britain*. New York: St. Martin's Press, 1963.

Dilks, David, ed. *The Diaries of Sir Alexander Cadogan, 1938–1945*. London: Cassell, 1971.

Donaldson, Frances. *Edward VIII*. London: Weidenfeld & Nicolson, 1974.

Eccles, Sybil, and David Eccles. *By Safe Hand: Letters of Sybil and David Eccles 1939–42*. London: Bodley Head, 1983.

Eckert, Astrid M. *The Struggle for the Files: The Western Allies and the Return of German Archives after the Second World War*. New York: Cambridge University Press, 2012.

Fort, Adrian. *Nancy: The Story of Lady Astor*. London: Jonathan Cape, 2012.

Gilbert, Martin. *Winston S. Churchill. Vol. 6, Finest Hour, 1939–1941*. London: Heinemann, 1983.

———. *Winston S. Churchill. Vol. 8, Never Despair, 1945–1965*. London: Heinemann, 1983.

Hart-Davis, Duff, ed. *In Royal Service: The Letters and Journals of Sir Alan Lascelles 1920–1936*. London: Hamish Hamilton, 1989.

———. *King's Counsellor: Abdication and War; The Diaries of "Tommy" Lascelles*. London: Weidenfeld & Nicolson, 2006.

Higham, Charles. *The Duchess of Windsor: The Secret Life*. New York: John Wiley, 2004.

Hyde, H. Montgomery. *Walter Monckton*. London: Sinclair-Stevenson, 1991.

Jackson, Robert H. *That Man: An Insider's Portrait of Franklin D. Roosevelt*. New York: Oxford University Press, 2003.

James, Robert Rhodes, ed. *"Chips": The Diaries of Sir Henry Channon*. London: Phoenix, 1993.

Jenkins, Roy. *Churchill: A Biography*. London: Macmillan, 2001.

Kershaw, Ian. *Making Friends with Hitler: Lord Londonderry and Britain's Road to War*. London: Penguin, 2005.

King, Greg. *The Duchess of Windsor: The Uncommon Life of Wallis Simpson*. New York: Citadel, 2003.

Lindbergh, Anne Morrow. *The Flower and the Nettle: Diaries and Letters of Anne Morrow Lindbergh*. San Diego: Harcourt Brace Jovanovich, 1976.

Lochery, Neill. *Lisbon: War in the Shadows of the City of Light, 1939–1945*. New York: PublicAffairs, 2011.

Middlemas, Keith, and John Barnes. *Baldwin: A Biography*. London: Weidenfeld and Nicolson, 1969.

Mitford, Diana. *The Duchess of Windsor: A Memoir*. London: Gibson Square, 2011.

Montague Browne, Anthony. *Long Sunset: Memoirs of Winston Churchill's Last Private Secretary*. Ashford, Kent: Podkin Press, 2009.

Moran, Lord. *Churchill: The Struggle for Survival, 1940–1965*. London: Constable, 1966.

Newton, Scott. *Profits of Peace: The Political Economy of Anglo-German Appeasement*. London: Oxford University Press, 1996.

Niblo, Stephen R. *Mexico in the 1940s: Modernity, Politics, and Corruption*. New York: Rowman and Littlefield, 2000.

Nicolson, Nigel, ed. *Leave the Letters Till We're Dead: The Letters of Virginia Woolf, 1936–41*. London: Chatto & Windus, 1980.

O'Sullivan, Donal. *Dealing with the Devil: Anglo-Soviet Intelligence Cooperation during the Second World War*. New York: Peter Lang, 2010.

Palmer, Alan. *Crowned Cousins: The Anglo-German Royal Connection*. London: Weidenfeld and Nicolson, 1985.

Parker, John. *King of Fools*. New York: St. Martin's Press, 1988.

Perry, Roland. *Last of the Cold War Spies: The Life of Michael Straight*. Boston: Da Capo, 2005.

Petropoulos, Jonathan. *Royals and the Reich: The Princes von Hessen in Nazi Germany*. New York: Oxford University Press, 2006.

Picknett, Lynn, Clive Prince, and Stephen Prior. *Double Standards: The Rudolf Hess Cover-Up*. London: Time Warner Books, 2001.

———. *War of the Windsors: A Century of Unconstitutional Monarchy*. Edinburgh: Mainstream Publishing, 2002.

Pile, Jonathan. *Churchill's Secret Enemy*. Lulu.com, 2012.

Pincher, Chapman. *The Spycatcher Affair: A Revealing Account of the Trial That Tried to Suppress a Book but Made It a Bestseller*. New York: St. Martin's Press, 1988.

———. *Their Trade Is Treachery: The Full, Unexpurgated Truth about the Russian Penetration of the Free World's Secret Defences*. London: Sidgwick & Jackson, 1981.

Poitras, Jacques. *Beaverbrook: A Shattered Legacy*. Fredericton, NB: Goose Lane, 2007.

Popov, Viktor. *The Queen's Advisor Who Was a Super-Agent of the Kremlin*. Moscow: Mezhdunarodnye Otnosheniya, 2005.

Preston, Paul. *The Politics of Revenge: Fascism and the Military in 20th Century Spain*. London: Routledge, 1995.

Pye, Michael. *The King over the Water: The Windsors in the Bahamas 1940–45*. London: Hutchinson, 1981.

Roberts, Andrew. *The Holy Fox: The Life of Lord Halifax*. London: Head of Zeus, 2014.

Rose, N. A., ed. *Baffy: The Diaries of Blanche Dugdale 1936–1947*. Edgware, Middlesex: Vallentine Mitchell, 1973.

Schad, Martha. *Hitler's Spy Princess: The Extraordinary Life of Princess Stephanie von Hohenlohe*. Stroud, Gloucs.: Sutton, 2004.

Schofield, Victoria. *Witness to History: The Life of John Wheeler-Bennett*. New Haven, CT: Yale University Press, 2012.

Schwarz, Dr. Paul. *This Man Ribbentrop: His Life and Times*. New York: Julian Messner, 1943.

Sebba, Anne. *That Woman: The Life of Wallis Simpson, Duchess of Windsor*. New York: St. Martin's Press, 2012.

Seymour, Miranda. *Ottoline Morrell: Life on the Grand Scale*. New York: Farrar, Straus and Giroux, 1993.

Shawcross, William. *Queen Elizabeth the Queen Mother: The Official Biography*. London: Macmillan, 2009.

———. *Counting One's Blessings: The Selected Letters of Queen Elizabeth the Queen Mother*. London: Macmillan, 2012.

Soames, Mary. *Clementine Churchill: The Biography of a Marriage*. New York: Houghton Mifflin, 1979.

Steed, R. H. C., ed. *Hitler's Interpreter*. London: Heinemann, 1951.

Strobl, Gerwin. *The Germanic Isle: Nazi Perceptions of Britain*. Cambridge: Cambridge University Press, 2000.

Sykes, Christopher. *Nancy: The Life of Lady Astor*. New York: Harper & Row, 1972.

Taylor, A. J. P. *Beaverbrook*. London: Hamish Hamilton, 1972.

Taylor, Fred, ed. and trans. *The Goebbels Diaries 1939–1941*. London: Hamish Hamilton, 1982.

Thomas, Gwynne. *King Pawn or Black Knight?* Edinburgh: Mainstream Publishing, 1995.

Thornton, Michael. *Royal Feud: The Queen Mother and the Duchess of Windsor*. London: Michael Joseph, 1985.

Vickers, Hugo. *Gladys, Duchess of Marlborough*. London: Hamish Hamilton, 1979.

———. *The Private World of the Duke and Duchess of Windsor*. London: Harrods Publishing, 1995.

Waller, John H. *The Unseen War in Europe: Espionage and Conspiracy in the Second World War*. New York: I. B. Tauris, 1996.

Weinberg, Gerhard L. *A World at Arms: A Global History of World War II*. New York: Cambridge University Press, 2005.

Wheeler-Bennett, Sir John. *Friends, Enemies and Sovereigns*. London: Macmillan, 1976.

Wilson, Jim. *Nazi Princess: Hitler, Lord Rothermere and Princess Stephanie von Hohenlohe*. Stroud, Gloucs.: History Press, 2011.

Windsor, Duke of. *A King's Story: The Memoirs of H. R. H. The Duke of Windsor*. London: Cassell, 1951.

Windsor, HRH the Duke of. *The Crown and the People, 1902–1953*. London: Cassell, 1953.

Windsor, Wallis. *The Heart Has Its Reasons*. London: Michael Joseph, 1956.

Young, Kenneth, ed. *The Diaries of Sir Robert Bruce Lockhart 1915–1938*. London: Macmillan, 1973.

———. *The Diaries of Sir Robert Bruce Lockhart 1939–1965*. London: Macmillan, 1980.

Zala, Sacha. *Geschichte unter der Schere politischer Zensur*. Translated by Nathan Ernst. Munich: Oldenbourg, 2001.

Ziegler, Philip. *King Edward VIII*. New York: Alfred A. Knopf, 1991.

Unpublished Sources

Georgetown University Library
WASHINGTON, D.C.
Papers of James D. Mooney.

Hoover Institution, Stanford University
STANFORD, CA
Papers of Kenneth Hugh De Courcy.
Papers of David Harris.
Papers of Prinzessin Stephanie zu Hohenlohe-Waldenburg-Schillingsfürst.
Papers of Robert Daniel Murphy, 1913–1977.
Papers of Paul Robinson Sweet.

University of Delaware Library Special Collections
NEWARK, DE
George S. Messersmith papers.

Virginia Historical Society
RICHMOND, VA
Correspondence of Ronald Tree. Langhorne Papers MSS 1L2653 B281–362.
Correspondence of Alexander Weddell. Weddell Papers MSS 1W4126
    CFA2 Box 4.
Correspondence of Charles Murphy. MSS 5.9 B 8405:97–160.

Franklin D. Roosevelt Presidential Library
HYDE PARK, NY
Correspondence of Herman Rogers. Private papers held by estate of Lucy
    Livingstone Rogers.

Sonder Archiv
MOSCOW
Material in Special Catalogue, 1525-1-69.

Cumbria Archive Centre
CARLISLE, CUMBRIA
Papers of Sir Esme Howard.

Index